The Perennial Philosophy
Series

World Wisdom
The Library of Perennial Philosophy

The Library of Perennial Philosophy is dedicated to the exposition of the timeless Truth underlying the diverse religions. This Truth, often referred to as the *Sophia Perennis*—or Perennial Wisdom—finds its expression in the revealed Scriptures as well as the writings of the great sages and the artistic creations of the traditional worlds.

The Underlying Religion: An Introduction to the Perennial Philosophy appears as one of our selections in the Perennial Philosophy series.

The Perennial Philosophy Series

In the beginning of the twentieth century, a school of thought arose which has focused on the enunciation and explanation of the Perennial Philosophy. Deeply rooted in the sense of the sacred, the writings of its leading exponents establish an indispensable foundation for understanding the timeless Truth and spiritual practices which live in the heart of all religions. Some of these titles are companion volumes to the Treasures of the World's Religions series, which allows a comparison of the writings of the great sages of the past with the perennialist authors of our time.

THE
UNDERLYING RELIGION

An Introduction to
the Perennial Philosophy

Edited by

Martin Lings
&
Clinton Minnaar

World Wisdom

The Underlying Religion: An Introduction to the Perennial Philosophy
© 2007 World Wisdom, Inc.

Library of Congress Cataloging-in-Publication Data

The underlying religion : an introduction to the perennial philosophy / edited by
Martin Lings & Clinton Minnaar.
    p. cm. -- (The library of perennial philosophy) (The perennial philosophy
series)
  Includes bibliographical references and index.
  ISBN 978-1-933316-43-7 (pbk. : alk. paper) 1. Religion--Philosophy. 2.
Philosophy and religion. 3. Tradition (Philosophy) I. Lings, Martin. II. Minnaar,
Clinton, 1972-
  BL51.U64 2007
  200--dc22

                                                              2007015535

Printed on acid-free paper in Canada.

For information address World Wisdom, Inc.
P.O. Box 2682, Bloomington, Indiana 47402-2682

www.worldwisdom.com

Dedicated to the memory of

FRITHJOF SCHUON (1907-1998)

on the occasion of the

centenary of his birth

CONTENTS

VI. BEAUTY

VII. VIRTUE AND PRAYER

PREFACE

It was suggested to me that I should write a preface to this collection of essays, but in fact an ideal preface already exists in the form of a poem, namely *The Wine-Song* (*Al-Khamriyyah*) of 'Umar ibn al-Fārid, which opens with these words:

> Rememb'ring the Belovèd, Wine we drink
> Which drunk had made us ere the vine's creation.[1]

We are given the wonderful privilege of drinking an altogether transcendent Wine to the Glory of God, and becoming thereby drunk, a Wine that is far beyond the level of the created universe to which the vine itself belongs. But by way of preface let us simply quote the poet's closing lines which speak for themselves. On analogy with what has been said about the transcendence of the Wine, our readers will be able to exalt other words also to a correspondingly higher level. I have written "Tavern" with a capital because it signifies here the secluded place where the Sufis assemble to perform their rites. The words "bid It unveil" are suggestive of a flagon that has been kept so long in treasured storage that it is covered with cobwebs.

> Go seek It in the Tavern; bid It unveil
> To strains of music. They offset Its worth,
> For Wine and care dwelt never in one place,
> Even as woe with music cannot dwell.
> Be drunk one hour with It, and thou shalt see
> Time's whole age as thy slave, at thy command.
> He hath not lived here, who hath sober lived,
> And he that dieth not drunk hath missed the mark.
> With tears then let him mourn himself, whose life
> Hath passed, and he no share of It hath had.

My being asked for a preface has also been ideally anticipated, but in a very different way, by the late Frithjof Schuon in a hitherto unpublished text which forms part of a series of messages or instruc-

---

[1] For the original Arabic with my English translation on the opposite page, see *Sufi Poems: A Mediaeval Anthology* (Cambridge, UK: The Islamic Texts Society, 2004), pp. 68-74.

tions concerning the spiritual path and which had been set down on behalf of his disciples. The text in question, number 717, is entitled "Two Unequal Heredities." In it he reminds us that despite whatever we may have inherited from recent and not very gifted ancestors, each one of us has in the depths of his or her soul man's primordial heredity which is precisely *Religio Perennis*, the Perennial Philosophy. He begins by pointing out that this deep-seated "absolute" heredity "can erupt in the soul by a kind of providential atavism." In these words he is clearly thinking of the very rarely granted Divine Grace of becoming suddenly a "throwback" to the far past. But quite apart from such miracles, there could clearly be no such thing as esoterism in the ordinary sense, that is, humanly organized esoterism under Divine Guidance, if it were not for the hidden reality of man's higher heredity.

Every esoteric order is itself a chain of spiritual heredity going back to the Divine Messenger whose function it was to found the religion in question and who himself, as such, is necessarily a personification of the Primordial Heredity. The rite of initiation into the Mysteries, often referred to as a second birth, is nothing other than the grafting of this chain of spiritual succession onto the psychic substance of the new initiate, thereby replacing the profane natal heredity which must not be allowed to reassert itself. It may attempt to do so, but normally any such attempts dwindle to nothing. There is no power at the psychic level that can resist the power of the Spirit to which the new initiate now has access thanks to his initiation.

Martin Lings
April 14, 2005*

---

* Editor's Note: A special debt of gratitude is owed to Dr. Martin Lings (1909-2005) for having generously agreed to co-edit *The Underlying Religion* when he was already in his early 90s and at a time when he was preparing several other manuscripts for publication; then, for having taken such considered efforts (over a period of some two years) to select a balanced collection of articles suitable for serving as an introduction to the perennial philosophy; and finally, for having written the valuable Preface to this anthology, which he completed less than a month before his death at age 96. (In fact, work on the anthology was concluded less than two days before his passing away.)

INTRODUCTION

The essays compiled in this anthology are intended to provide an accessible introduction to the "traditionalist" or "perennialist" school of comparative religious thought. This current of thought, which saw the light of day in the early twentieth century in the pioneering writings of the French metaphysician and symbologist René Guénon (1886-1951), and which was amplified by the prodigious scholarship of the Anglo-Ceylonese orientalist and art historian Ananda K. Coomaraswamy (1877-1947), received its fullest exposition in the writings of the German-Swiss metaphysician, painter, and poet, Frithjof Schuon (1907-1998).[1] In the pages that follow, the reader will encounter the penetrating writings of these major authors, as well as many other prominent "perennialist" writers such as Titus Burckhardt,[2] Lord Northbourne, Marco Pallis, Martin Lings (co-editor of this volume), Whitall Perry, William Stoddart, and Seyyed Hossein Nasr. What we intend to offer now is a broad outline of the essential features of the perennial philosophy in the hope of providing the reader with a clear compass and sure orientation in approaching both the arrangement and the content of the essays here included.

The perspective of the "traditionalist" or "perennialist" school of thought has variously been called the *philosophia perennis* (perennial philosophy), *sophia perennis* (perennial wisdom), or *religio perennis* (perennial religion). These terms, which are essentially identical, each

---

[1] See Kenneth Oldmeadow, *Traditionalism: Religion in the Light of the Perennial Philosophy* (Colombo: Sri Lanka Institute of Traditional Studies, 2000) for an excellent introduction to the "perennialist" perspective.

[2] Frithjof Schuon also acknowledged the importance of the writings of the German-Swiss art historian and orientalist Titus Burckhardt (1908-1984) in saying that the "traditionalist" or "perennialist" school had two "originators" (Guénon and Schuon) and two "continuators" (Coomaraswamy and Burckhardt). If this view ostensibly clashes with chronology it should be recalled that Coomaraswamy's mature and properly "perennialist" writings only began at around 1935, whereas Guénon's works began to appear in 1921 and Schuon's in 1933 (William Stoddart, "Four Spokesman of the Perennialist or Traditionalist Current of Intellectuality and Spirituality," unpublished). The "originality" of Schuon is especially evident—apart from his masterful exposition of integral metaphysics—in his treatment of art, beauty, prayer, and virtue, subjects on which Guénon did not touch. The works of Schuon are drawn on extensively in this introduction.

contain a distinctive nuance or accentuation. For instance, the term *sophia* is to be preferred to *philosophia* when "philosophy" is understood in its purely modern sense of "rationalist or skeptical thought" and not, as its etymology and ancient practice suggests, the "love of wisdom." Similarly, the term *religio* is to be preferred to *sophia* or *philosophia* when it is necessary to emphasize that it is not only intellectual doctrine or belief that constitutes "wisdom" or the "love of wisdom," but, in addition, the methodical or ritual practices that religion provides in order to effectively realize that wisdom. It must be acknowledged, however, that "perennial philosophy" has proved the most popular of the three terms, and it will therefore be employed most frequently in what follows.

What then is the perennial philosophy? It is both absolute Truth and infinite Presence. As absolute Truth it is the perennial wisdom (*sophia perennis*) that stands as the transcendent source of all the intrinsically orthodox religions of humankind. In the words of St. Augustine, it is that "uncreated Wisdom, the same now, as before, and the same to be for evermore" (*Confessions*, 9:10). As infinite Presence it is the perennial religion (*religio perennis*) that lives within the heart of all intrinsically orthodox religions. In the words of Cardinal Nicholas of Cusa: "There is . . . one sole religion and one sole worship for all beings endowed with understanding, and this is presupposed through a variety of rites" (*De Pace Fidei*, 6).

Now it is precisely this "sole religion" that Frithjof Schuon has called the "underlying religion"[3] or "religion of the heart" (*religio cordis*), which is the heart of all religion.[4] It should be clearly understood, however, that the "underlying religion" is of an essentially supra-formal, universal, or spiritual nature. Although it resides as an immanent and underlying presence within the religions, it is not itself a formal or particular religion (as are the various religions of humankind, e.g. Judaism, Christianity, Islam, Hinduism, Buddhism, Confucianism, Taoism, and the Native American religion of the Sun Dance and the Sacred Pipe). In other words, the "underlying religion" remains tran-

---

[3] See Frithjof Schuon, *Light on the Ancient Worlds* (London: Perennial Books, 1965), p. 143 and *Christianity/Islam: Essays on Esoteric Ecumenism* (Bloomington, IN: World Wisdom Books, 1985), p. 138. Schuon was also the author of a private, unpublished text called "The Underlying Religion."

[4] This is an adaptation of William Stoddart's saying, "Mysticism is the heart of religion and the religion of the heart" ("Quotations: A Personal Collection," unpublished), itself a paraphrase from Goethe.

scendent vis-à-vis the religions, even while being a vivifying presence within them. It is in no way a "new religion."

The perennial philosophy thus has a transcendent dimension, and this is absolute Truth or Wisdom, and an immanent dimension, and this is infinite Presence or Union, the first aspect referring to the intelligence and the second to the will. As Frithjof Schuon notes:

> The essential function of human intelligence is discernment between the Real and the illusory or between the Permanent and the impermanent, and the essential function of the will is attachment to the Permanent or the Real. This discernment and this attachment are the quintessence of all spirituality; carried to their highest level or reduced to their purest substance, they constitute the underlying universality in every great spiritual patrimony of humanity, or what may be called the *religio perennis.*[5]

These specifications allow for an initial definition of the perennial philosophy as: (1) metaphysical discernment between the Real and the unreal, or the Absolute and the relative (i.e. the aspect of Truth or metaphysics); and (2) mystical concentration on the Real (i.e. the aspect of Presence or unitive prayer).[6] This twofold definition also contains "the criteria of intrinsic orthodoxy for every religion and all spirituality":

> In order to be orthodox a religion must possess a mythological or doctrinal symbolism establishing the essential distinction in question, and it must provide a path that guarantees both the perfection of concentration and its continuity; in other words a religion is orthodox if it provides a sufficient, if not always exhaustive, idea of the Absolute and the relative, and thus of their reciprocal relationships, and a spiritual activity that is contemplative in its nature and effectual with regard to our ultimate destiny.[7]

It might be wondered, though, if the heart of religion can indeed be reduced to the simple polarity "discernment-concentration." Are

---

[5] Frithjof Schuon, *Light on the Ancient Worlds* (Bloomington, IN: World Wisdom, 2005), pp. 119-120.

[6] See Patrick Laude (ed.), *Pray without Ceasing: The Way of the Invocation in World Religions* (Bloomington, IN: World Wisdom, 2006) for a wide selection of writings dealing with prayer, particularly of the quintessential or invocatory kind.

[7] Frithjof Schuon, *Light on the Ancient Worlds*, p. 121.

there not a multitude of differences between the religions and is it not contrary to truth to overlook these same differences? Or again, are the religions not being placed in a strait-jacket—one that takes no account of their unique spiritual contours—in order to make them conform to a putative definition of the heart of religion? Let us quote at length a passage from Frithjof Schuon dealing with the perennial philosophy— in this case speaking on Christianity, Islam, and Buddhism—keeping in mind the twofold definition of the perennial philosophy mentioned above:

> In Christianity—according to Saint Irenaeus and others—God "became man" that man might "become God"; in Hindu terms one would say: *Ātmā* became *Māyā* that *Māyā* might become *Ātmā*. In Christianity, contemplative and unifying concentration is to dwell in the manifested Real—the "Word made flesh"—in order that this Real might dwell in us, who are illusory, according to what Christ said in a vision granted to Saint Catherine of Siena: "I am He who is; thou art she who is not." The soul dwells in the Real—in the kingdom of God that is "within us"—by means of permanent prayer of the heart, as is taught by the parable of the unjust judge and the injunction of Saint Paul.[8]
>
> In Islam . . . discernment between the Real and the non-real is affirmed by the Testimony of Unity (the *Shahādah*):[9] the correlative concentration on the Symbol or permanent consciousness of the Real is effected by this same Testimony or by the divine Name [*Allāh*] which synthesizes it and which is thus the quintessential crystallization of the Koranic Revelation. . . . The Real "descended" (*nazzala, unzila*); it entered into the non-real or illusory, the "perishable" (*fānin*), in becoming the Koran—or the *Shahādah* that summarizes it, or the *Ism* (the "Name") that is its sonorous and graphic essence, or the *Dhikr* (the "Mention") that is its operative synthesis—in order that upon this divine barque the illusory might return to the Real. . . . In this reciprocity lies all the mystery of the "Night of Destiny" (*Laylat al-Qadr*), which is a "descent," and of

---

[8] Editor's Note: The parable of the unjust judge (Luke, 18:1-8) begins: "And he [Christ] spake a parable unto them to this end, that men ought always to pray, and not to faint." The well-known injunction of St. Paul is: "Pray without ceasing" (I Thessalonians, 5:17). These verses form the basis of the method of ejaculatory prayer in Eastern Christianity, also known as the Jesus Prayer.

[9] Editor's Note: The Islamic Testimony of Unity is: "There is no god but God" (*Lā ilāha illa' Llāh*), which enunciates the fundamental discernment between the Absolute and the relative, or (less rigorously) between God and the world.

the "Night of Ascension" (*Laylat al-Mi'rāj*), which is the complementary phase. . . .

In Buddhism the two terms of the alternative or of discernment are *Nirvāna*, the Real, and *Samsāra*, the illusory; in the last analysis the path is the permanent consciousness of *Nirvāna* as *Shūnya*, the "Void," or else it is concentration on the saving manifestation of *Nirvāna*, the Buddha, who is *Shūnyamūrti*, "Manifestation of the Void." In the Buddha—notably in his form Amitabha—*Nirvāna* became *Samsāra* that *Samsāra* might become *Nirvāna*; and if *Nirvāna* is the Real and *Samsāra* is illusion, the Buddha is the Real in the illusory. . . . The passage from the illusory to the Real is described in the *Prajnāpāramitā-hridaya-sūtra* in these terms: "Gone, gone—gone for the other shore, attained the other shore, O Enlightenment, be blessed!"[10]

For those with "eyes to see" the reading of this passage will unveil a very satisfying dimension of "transcendent unity."[11] Moreover, it will be understood that this unity transcends the differences between the religions without in any way denying those same differences on their own level. Unity is not uniformity just as synthesis is not syncretism. Thus, Christianity is very clearly different from Islam or Buddhism *qua* form; but it is one with them *qua* essence (or *qua* perennial philosophy). Readers should consult Section V ("The Perennial Philosophy") for a more detailed exposition of the "transcendent unity of the religions." This crucial section provides both a synthesis and a summation of the whole book. Doctrine (metaphysical discernment) and method (unitive concentration) are dealt with more fully in Section III ("Metaphysics") and Section VII ("Prayer and Virtue") respectively. Readers should also note that Section II ("Traditional Cosmology and Modern Science") carries the dimension of discernment into the cosmological realm where a thorough critique of modern scientism—and particularly transformist evolution—is presented, while in Section IV

---

[10] Frithjof Schuon, *Light on the Ancient Worlds*, pp. 122-124. In Hinduism, this twofold definition of the perennial philosophy is most succinctly expressed in the Vedantic maxim: "Brahman is Reality; the world is appearance; the soul is not other than Brahman."

[11] See Frithjof Schuon, *The Transcendent Unity of Religions* (Wheaton, Ill: Quest, 1993) for a foundational elucidation of this key "perennialist" idea. See also Whitall Perry's monumental *A Treasury of Traditional Wisdom* (Louisville: Fons Vitae, 2000), which presents a vast array of sayings from the world's religions to illustrate the idea of "transcendent unity."

("Symbolism") the age-old science of symbolism and the doctrine of the multiple degrees of Reality is reaffirmed.

If metaphysical discernment refers to the Truth, and unitive concentration to the Way, what then of virtue, which pertains to the spiritual Life? Do not doctrine and method, discernment and union, suffice unto themselves? Assuredly not, for as Frithjof Schuon says,

> Spiritual realization [i.e. method] imposes on the soul an immense disproportion owing to the fact that it introduces the presence of the sacred into the darkness of human imperfection; this inevitably provokes disequilibrium-producing reactions which in principle carry with them the risk of an irremediable fall, reactions which moral beauty, together with the graces which by its very nature it attracts, can largely prevent or attenuate. It is precisely this beauty that ambitious dilettantes without imagination believe they can disdain.[12]

Without conformity of the soul to the Real—through virtue—the spiritual life risks becoming merely a mental play of the mind or a technical effort of the will. For the integral human being is comprised of an intelligence, a will, *and* a soul (or sentiment):[13] while the Truth requires the deployment of the intelligence ("with all thy mind"), and the Way (or Prayer) requires the activity of the will ("with all thy strength"), the Life (or Virtue) requires conformity of the sentiment ("with all thy soul").[14] In the spiritual life the fundamental virtues are: humility, or the effacement of the ego; charity, or the giving of oneself to others; and veracity, or pure objectivity. These correspond respectively to the fundamental spiritual stages of purification, perfection, and union. The above twofold definition of the perennial philosophy (i.e. discernment-concentration) can thus be expanded to include three pillars: Truth, Way (or Prayer), and Virtue (or Life). The first part of Section VII ("Prayer and Virtue") deals with this subject in more detail, making a clear distinction between intrinsic virtue and social morality.

---

[12] Frithjof Schuon, *Esoterism as Principle and as Way* (Pates Manor, Bedfont: Perennial Books, 1981), p. 111.

[13] See Frithjof Schuon, *Esoterism as Principle and as Way*, pp. 93-100.

[14] "Thou shalt love the Lord thy God . . . with all thy soul, and with all thy mind, and with all thy strength" (Mark, 12:30).

Beauty—which will now be considered as the fourth pillar of the perennial philosophy—is a support of incalculable value in the spiritual life; far from being a mere "sensible consolation" or an expendable luxury, it has on the contrary the fundamental role of being, in the words of Frithjof Schuon, an "exteriorization with a view to an interiorization." Now this message of interiorization "is both intellectual and moral: intellectual because it communicates to us, in the world of accidentality, aspects of [divine] Substance, without for all that having to address itself to abstract thought; and moral, because it reminds us of what we must love, and consequently be."[15] As the "splendor of the truth," Beauty provides the intellective soul with the occasional cause for a Platonic "recollection"—i.e. an objective "vision"—of the heavenly archetypes; and as "external goodness," Beauty provides the contemplative soul with an existential—and not merely mental or conceptual—reminder of its original nature of primordial perfection (i.e. its pure state of virtue before the fall).[16] Among the most direct manifestations of Beauty and its message of interiorization are firstly virgin nature,[17] then sacred art,[18] and lastly holy company; as "'exteriorizations of the Inward' they encourage the 'interiorization of the outward.'"[19] But Beauty must also reverberate in our immediate environment: in dress, comportment, and the ambience of the home, all of which should echo or evoke our heavenly homeland. Readers

---

[15] Frithjof Schuon, *Esoterism as Principle and as Way*, p. 179.

[16] It is said that the exceptional outward beauty of the Virgin Mary—she who personifies the pure and immaculate soul—was a cause, not of concupiscence, but of profound interiorization.

[17] "There is a concordance between the *religio perennis* and virgin nature and by the same token between it and primordial nudity, that of creation, birth, resurrection, or the high priest in the Holy of Holies, a hermit in the desert, a Hindu *sādhu* or *sannyāsin*, a Red Indian in silent prayer on a mountain. Nature inviolate is at once a vestige of the earthly Paradise and a prefiguration of the heavenly Paradise; sanctuaries and garments differ, but virgin nature and the human body remain faithful to the initial unity" (Frithjof Schuon, *Light on the Ancient Worlds*, pp. 25-26). For primordial peoples such as the Native American Indians, virgin nature is the primordial "book" of revelation; it is also the Divine art.

[18] See especially Frithjof Schuon, *Art from the Sacred to the Profane: East and West*, edited by Catherine Schuon (Bloomington, IN: World Wisdom, 2007) and Titus Burckhardt, *Sacred Art of East and West* (Bloomington, IN: World Wisdom, 2002) for remarkable insights into the meaning of sacred art.

[19] Frithjof Schuon, *Logic and Transcendence* (Bedfont: Perennial Books, 1975), p. 190.

will find a fuller elucidation of the spiritual role of Beauty in Section VI ("Beauty").

Truth, Prayer, Virtue, Beauty: these four constituent elements of the perennial philosophy must, however, be inaugurated upon the basis of a traditional Religion. Why? Because the truths conferred by the Intellect—that supra-rational faculty of transcendent knowledge within man—have been occluded since the time of the fall. And it is precisely the role of divine Revelation to remind us of these truths from the "outside," namely to "'crystallize' and 'actualize' . . . [the] nucleus of certitudes that not only abides forever in the Divine Omniscience, but also sleeps by refraction in the 'naturally supernatural' kernel of the individual [i.e. the Intellect]."[20] The religious traditions are thus the providential vehicles—because instituted by Heaven and not at the initiative of fallen man—for Truth, Prayer, Virtue, and Beauty, though of necessity they are presented in a mode suited to the particular cultural, ethnic, or linguistic community to which they are addressed. The religious traditions are thus the vehicle of a heavenly Grace which man could not possibly draw from himself. Traditional Religion thus stands as an indispensable fifth pillar of the perennial philosophy. Section I ("Tradition and Modernity") provides the reader with a detailed explanation of the necessity of traditional Religion, the role of revelation and "tradition" (which should not be confused with mere custom or habit), and the requirements of orthodox belief and practice.

A question that imposes itself at this point is: why are there multiple revelations? Does not one revelation suffice for all? Humanly speaking, it can be said that a multiplicity of revelations is necessitated by the diversity of racial, ethnic, cultural, and linguistic communities, as well as by the gradual degeneration of these communities over time. Metaphysically speaking, it can be said that it is the "overflowing" divine Infinitude (and *a fortiori* the divine Mercy) which calls forth multiple revelations.[21] For although Truth is one and absolute, it is "situated beyond forms, whereas Revelation, or the Tradition derived from it, belongs to the formal order . . . [and] to speak of form is to

---

[20] Frithjof Schuon, *Light on the Ancient Worlds*, p. 119.

[21] "When righteousness is weak and faints," says Krishna, "and unrighteousness exults in pride, then my Spirit arises again on earth. For the salvation of those who are good, for the destruction of evil in men, for the fulfillment of the kingdom of righteousness, I come to this world" (*Bhagavad Gītā*, 4:7-8).

speak of diversity, and thus plurality."[22] But does not the diversity of revelations also imply their relativity? In respect of their form "yes," though not in respect of their supra-formal and universal content (or essence). For by their transcendent essence religions enunciate the absolute Truth, but not in respect of their particular forms, which, *qua* forms, inevitably partake of limitation and diversity, and hence of relativity.

Nevertheless, the religious forms are providential vehicles of the transcendent essence; they are, so to speak, finite receptacles that "contain" the Infinite. They thus perform the fundamental role of communicating the Truth to man (doctrine), and of providing him with the means to assimilate its sacramental and sanctifying Presence (method). For fallen man identifies primarily with his formal nature (his body and his soul) and not with his supra-formal or transcendent nature (his spirit); he has thus to approach the Real through the hallowed forms willed by Heaven and not otherwise. In consequence, these same forms cannot simply be repudiated or dismissed in the name of a pretentious and wholly unrealistic desire to realize the "pure spirit."

In this regard it is important to distinguish the "traditionalist" or "perennialist" understanding of religious forms—which acknowledges both their relativity and their necessity—from the views of the so-called "religious pluralists" and "new age" cults. The "religious pluralists," who are much given to dialogue and are susceptible to fragmentary notions of universality, seem ever willing to compromise the forms of religion in order to further their pointedly postmodern political and sentimental agendas. They forget that the religious forms—as inalienable symbols of the essence—are dispensed with at great spiritual peril. In fact, so-called "religious pluralism" is nothing more than a "horizontal" and worldly caricature of the "vertical" and spiritual perspective of the "transcendent unity of the religions."

Even worse are the modern syncretistic cults, who, in the name of a vague ideal of "universal truth"—and influenced by anti-traditional progressivist and evolutionist ideas—proclaim a so-called "new age" of the spirit.[23] In their blind presumption they would seek to dispense

---

[22] Frithjof Schuon, *Gnosis: Divine Wisdom* (Bloomington, IN: World Wisdom, 2006), p. 17.

[23] Anti-traditional exponents of a new so-called "universal truth" include: Anthroposophy, Baha'i, Aurobindo Ghose, G.I. Gurdjieff, Jiddu Krishnamurti, Rajneesh (Osho), Subud, the Theosophical Society, Vivekananda (disciple of Ramakrishna, the great Hindu saint),

with the age-old religious forms and establish a new universal "religion" (or "society"), henceforth free from all "divisive dogma" and "exclusivist formalism."[24] With an ego-flattering "self-realization" as their goal they invariably seek to develop "latent powers," which, needless to say, are of a decidedly psychic and not spiritual nature. In order to see how dangerously heterodox are the subjectivist beliefs and improvised practices of these groups, it suffices to expose the central flaw of their counterfeit spirituality: the claim—common to all false mysticisms—that would equate the fallen and unregenerate soul with the Divine.[25] To the contrary, all genuine spirituality insists on the purification and perfection of the soul, along with the grace of God, as indispensable prerequisites for union with the Divine.

Let us now leave these aberrant groups and return to the authentic perennial philosophy. An important final question remains: what is the relationship of the perennial philosopher—whose nature is irresistibly drawn to the "underlying religion" or the "religion of the heart"—to the various formal elements of the religion to which he belongs by birth? The perennial philosopher will seek to esoterize and universalize these religious forms from within, rather than bemoan their "restrictiveness" from without; for "Truth does not deny forms from the outside, but transcends them from within."[26] Thus, when Jesus proclaims in the Gospel that "no man cometh unto the Father but by Me" (John, 14:6), or when the Prophet of Islam says that "no man shall meet God who has not first met the Prophet," the perennial philosopher will understand these sayings to mean (in addition to their all-too-evident exoteric and exclusivist meanings): access to the Real is to be attained through the universal Logos, one particular manifes-

---

Alan Watts, and Mahesh Yogi. See Whitall Perry, *Challenges to a Secular Society* (Oakton, VA: The Foundation for Traditional Studies, 1996), pp. 7-16, 65-79 for a thorough critique of these authors. Among this group must also be placed the author Aldous Huxley, well known for his anthology *The Perennial Philosophy* (1945). This work, despite its many excellent selections, is flawed through its individualistic commentary, wherein the author "picks and chooses" whatever in religion is to his liking, and on the contrary dismisses all that is not in keeping with his idiosyncratic tastes.

[24] "A vine has been planted without the Father and, as it is not established, it will be pulled up by its roots and be destroyed" (*The Gospel According to Thomas*, Logion 40).

[25] William Stoddart, *Outline of Buddhism* (Oakton, VA: The Foundation for Traditional Studies, 1998), p. 33.

[26] Frithjof Schuon, *Spiritual Perspectives and Human Facts* (London: Perennial Books, 1987), p. 118.

tation of which is Jesus Christ and another of which is the Prophet of Islam; but others of which include: Abraham, Moses, Zoroaster, Krishna, Rama, the Buddha, Confucius, Lao Tzu, and Pte San Win (the "White Buffalo Cow Woman," celestial revealer of the Sacred Pipe to the Native American Lakota Indians). By proceeding in such a manner—both universalist and esoterist—the perennial philosopher discerns the "underlying religion" within the religious tradition to which he is called by divine Providence; he sees with the eye of his heart that Truth, Prayer, Virtue, and Beauty are the heart of religion and thus the "religion of the heart."

Clinton Minnaar

I

TRADITION AND MODERNITY

Thus saith the Lord:
"Stand ye in the ways, and see,
and ask for the old paths, where is the good way,
and walk therein, and ye shall find rest
for your souls."
But they said,
"We will not walk therein."

JEREMIAH 6:16

1 RELIGION AND TRADITION

Lord Northbourne

The word "religion" is often used today simply to mean whatever an individual or a group regards as being true, or that whereby conduct is regulated. Even Communism is sometimes loosely called a religion, regardless of its origin and its tendencies, and regardless of the fact that it is no more than a construction of the human mind. Such things as Communism may be substitutes for religion, but to call them religions is an abuse of the word which can give rise to a very pernicious kind of confusion.

In its original and only valid sense the word "religion" applies only to something which is, above all, not a construction of the human mind, but is, on the contrary, of divine origin, so that it can be said to be supernatural, revealed, or mysterious. Its purpose is to provide an effective link between the world and God. The word "Religion" is always used hereafter in this strict sense, and to emphasize this it is spelt with a capital R.*

All that follows is applicable to the Christian Religion. In the main it is also applicable to what are sometimes called the great Religions of the world. It is assumed here that each has its validity for a particular group of peoples, despite outward differences and even apparent contradictions. What matters for each person is adherence to one Religion, normally that of the country of one's birth, rather than attempts to reconcile it with others, or purely academic excursions into the field of comparative religion.

The completeness and uniqueness of a Religion implies that from the point of view of its followers it is preferable to any other. It really is so for them, but not necessarily for other people. There may often be good reason for defending it against other Religions in order to preserve its purity and the coherence of its symbolism. That does not alter the fact that all "orthodox" Religions—that is to say those that are linked by an unbroken chain of tradition to an authentic Revelation—are paths that lead to the same summit. If that were not so, God

---

* Editors' Note: A usage confined to the first two chapters of the present anthology.

would have denied the possibility of salvation to a vast majority of the earth's inhabitants, past and present. It is surprising how cheerfully many of the followers of a Religion based on love and charity accept this conclusion.

Paths that lead to a summit are widely separated near the base of the mountain, but they get nearer together as they rise. The wise climber takes the path on which he finds himself and does not worry too much about people on other paths. He can see his path but cannot see theirs properly. He will waste an enormous amount of his own time if he keeps on trying to find another and better path. He will waste other people's time if he tries to persuade them to abandon theirs, however sure he is that his is the best.

Religion is founded on the belief—or rather on the certainty—that God has shown His love, as well as His justice and His wisdom, to the world in the first place and most directly in His Revelation of Himself through the founder (or founders) of the Religion in question. This implies that the founder did not invent that Religion, his part being entirely receptive, insofar as a distinction can be made between his divine and human nature.

Revelation is therefore by definition something greater than anything purely human, including reason. Its validity is beyond rational or observational proof or disproof; nevertheless it would not be what it is if it did not contain internally the evidence of its own truth. That evidence will be acceptable or discernible or self-evident to the eye of faith or of wisdom, although it may not be accessible to analytical investigation.

Revelation enters into the definition of Religion because it is the foundation of everything in the world that has hitherto been called Religion—and not least of the Christian Religion. Revealed Religion does not deny the possibility of individual inspiration—far from it; but it offers itself as the one universal and accessible means of grace available to all both collectively and individually, and as a framework within which individual inspiration can thrive unimpeded and can exercise its influence freely.

In His infinite Mercy, God has given us both freedom and a means of grace. Can we expect to be able to claim the one and refuse the other with impunity? Religion therefore implies not only an abstract belief in God, but also a concrete belief in His Revelation of Himself, His "descent into form." The imitation of that form then becomes the concrete or practical aspect of Religion, the means whereby it is made real and effective in the world rather than being merely notional or theoretical.

From this point of view, man is much more than a mere thinking animal. He is privileged above all other creatures in being given dominion over them as well as by the gifts of reason and of free will. Those privileges are accorded to him in his capacity as responsible guardian of revealed Religion, and for no other reason.

If, like all other creatures, man could not help following the commandments of God, as the plant cannot help turning towards the sun, then his situation would be neutral with respect to good and evil as theirs is. There would then be open to him no possibility better than this world—no heaven; and correlatively no possibility worse than this world—no hell.

The whole duty of man, and his whole advantage, reside in the preservation intact of the chain of tradition that connects him with Revelation. This applies with particular force in these days to the more specifically religious aspect of tradition.[1]

The word "Tradition" will hereafter be spelt with a capital T* because it suffers from the same kind of vague usage as the word "Religion." It is often used as if it were equivalent to "custom" or "style." Properly speaking, Tradition comprises all the distinctive characteristics that are derived from the past, and make a civilization what it is, including those that can be more specifically described as religious. Religion could be said to be the way whereby man serves God most directly. The other aspects of Tradition comprise all the less direct, but scarcely less essential ways, such as service to a hierarchical superior, obedience to the appropriate laws, defending Tradition against assaults from without, and so on.

The notion of Tradition is no mere arbitrary or invented one. Its foundations lie at the very root of our being. It can be accounted for in a way that is exceedingly simple and impregnably logical—for anyone who understands it. The Beginning and the End are the same;[2] therefore to be effectively linked to the Beginning is already to have found the End.

* * *

---

[1] There have been others that have been largely forgotten, or that survive unnoticed.

* Editors' Note: A usage confined to the first two chapters of the present anthology.

[2] "I am Alpha and Omega" (Revelation 1:8).

If these notions of Revelation and Tradition are accepted, it becomes evident that a Revelation must be accepted as a whole and not in part. The doctrinal, ritual, and ethical prescriptions of Religion are inseparable. A belief in God which rejects any of them is not Religion; indeed it is precisely one of those compromises by which people try to salve their consciences without too much trouble. Such a belief in God may perhaps be better than nothing, but it is something purely individual, whereas Religion is supra-individual. This is a very vital point.

The three elements mentioned—*doctrinal, ritual,* and *ethical*—can be discerned in every Religion. There is a correspondence between them and the three main divisions of the human faculties—intellectual, active, and volitive—so that Religion neglects nothing human. These three elements will now be considered in order.

Doctrine is fundamental. It is the intellectual element concerned with the comprehension and formulation of truth and the combating of falsehood. As such it is necessarily the province of a relatively small intellectual elect which stands at the head of a hierarchy through which the truth is interpreted to the multitude in a form which they can accept.

However simple the primary formulation of a truth may appear to be (for example, "God is Love"), its interpretation in terms of common experience is anything but simple. Insofar as the more elevated aspects of truth are concerned it must inevitably be dogmatic. Dogma and dogmatism are almost terms of abuse in these days. It is true enough that dogmatism applied to human affairs which are matters of opinion or of taste cannot be justified, but the case is very different when Religion is concerned. Dogma is a necessary feature of a Religion which is intended for everyone, since a large majority are not capable of grasping the more profound doctrinal truths in any other form. A doctrine fully comprehensible to the average intelligence would not be very profound. It would be intellectually insignificant and so would have no defense against perversion.

For example, every Religion either insists on the reality of heaven and hell, or expresses the same fundamental truth in a different way. This insistence is dogmatic, in the sense that heaven and hell represent something that is by definition beyond the limits of life on earth. They cannot be proved or disproved by means that appertain to that life on earth alone. Nevertheless if there is something greater than man there must also be a life greater than human life. That life is not subject to the same limitations as human life and so not imaginable or ascertainable by the individual as such. Some would accept this insofar as it relates to heaven, but not to hell. This is pure sentimentalism. Either man is not free to choose, a mere machine without responsibility, or he is free to choose and must take the consequences of his choice. No question of arbitrary reward or punishment is involved; it is merely a question of cause and effect.[3]

Ritual is the second essential element in Religion. It is derived directly from the original Revelation, which it recapitulates in a certain sense. This is particularly evident in the case of the Eucharist. God must be worshipped not only in thought and word but also in deed. No act proceeding from the human will alone could adequately meet this need; God has therefore told us what we must do. However simple a ritual based on revelation may appear to be, we can be sure that its significance is inexhaustible and that its mysterious power extends beyond the confines of this world. It is effective simply by virtue of what it is and independently of the degree to which we may think we understand it. All this of course applies only to ritual that can be said to be strictly "orthodox," in the sense that it is an integral part of a revealed Religion. Without ritual there is no Religion.

Closely associated with the specific acts appertaining to an orthodox ritual, and not independent of it, is the reading or recitation of the Sacred Scriptures and the recitation of a revealed or canonical form of prayer (e.g., The Lord's Prayer). Such reading and recitation are not effective outside the framework of the Religion to which they belong. Within that framework they are indispensable. This is particularly true in these days when the psychic environment, instead of being traditional and thereby providing an ever-present corrective to error, is so actively hostile and subversive. The effectiveness of this reading and recitation is not conditional on a purely mental comprehension. In the absence of its corrective influence the soul has no point

---

[3] The perspective of reward and punishment is nevertheless legitimate and useful, otherwise it would not be characteristic of several Religions. Essentially it is simply an application of the law of compensation. As in so many other cases, a symbolical presentation in terms of familiar human situations brings the truth much nearer for most people than could any presentation in less familiar terms. This generation, with its literalism, has lost the habit of thinking in symbols: hence, among other things, its difficulty in understanding the Holy Scriptures. Symbolism, however, is not only every bit as precise as literalism, but also much less limitative. Literalism narrows the truth, symbolism broadens and enlivens it without in any way departing from it. A symbol in this sense is a reflection on the terrestrial plane of a truth subsisting on a higher plane. The symbol, whether it be dogmatic in form or not, is therefore the necessary vehicle of doctrine.

of reference, no anchorage, no refuge, nothing to which it can—and must—return again and again in its inevitable wanderings. There can be no substitute for these indispensable graces.

There is one other grace, closely related to those last mentioned, whose benefit is strictly contingent on a traditional attachment. It takes many different forms in different Traditions: a divine Name or Names, a formula, or a visible symbol. It is as it were incorporated in the gift of the original Revelation. It is an essential element in the formulae or prayers used in the methods of spiritual training associated with many Religions. No gift of God is more precious than this.

The third element is the ethical or moral. Without virtue the soul cannot become fit to be a receptacle of grace. That is what virtue is for; it is by no means mere social convenience.

The two other elements of Religion are concerned with man's relation to God, and therefore with the first ("and great") of the two New Testament commandments.* Virtue is concerned with man's relation to his "neighbor," that is, with everything that is not himself, but most immediately with his human neighbor. The neighbor exists by the will of God, so that to serve him is to serve God, and to offend him is to offend God. That is why the second commandment is "like unto" the first; it also explains why in giving offence the soul harms itself more than its victim.

As to what constitutes offence, the best guidance is that afforded by the code of conduct or legislation that forms part of every Tradition. This may not be the same everywhere because of differences in conditions. Virtue is indispensable, but it is not an end in itself. Its efficacy reaches beyond the confines of the social field in which its operation is usually considered, and indeed beyond the confines of this world.

The first of the two commandments is greater than the second, but neither can be dispensed with. They are not essentially different, but only accidentally so. A single celestial truth is manifested terrestrially in two different modes.

---

* Editors' Note: "Thou shalt love the Lord thy God with all thy heart, and with all thy soul, and with all thy mind. This is the first and great commandment. And the second is like unto it, Thou shalt love thy neighbor as thyself" (Matthew 22:37-39; cf. Deuteronomy 6:5, Leviticus 19:18, Mark 12:30-31, and Luke 10:27). A detailed exposition of the greater and lesser Biblical commandments can be found in Frithjof Schuon, "The Supreme Commandment" (*Esoterism as Principle and as Way* [Bedfont: Perennial Books, 1981], pp. 151-157), and Martin Lings, "Why 'With All Thy Mind'?" (*A Return to the Spirit: Questions and Answers* [Louisville, KY: Fons Vitae, 2005], pp. 29-43).

Superimposed on the threefold division outlined above there is another division, much less easily defined. Every Religion has an exoteric, dogmatic, and moral aspect, and an esoteric, metaphysical, and mystical aspect. The two may not be rigidly separated, and the latter may be little more than an intensification of the former. Sometimes they are separated, and may have distinct names: for instance in the Far East they are called respectively Confucianism and Taoism; in Judaism the esoteric aspect is called the Kabbalah, and in Islam, Sufism, or Tasawwuf. In Christianity and Buddhism there is no real separation, though in practice the esoteric aspect is the province of specialized organizations, often of a monastic type.

Esoterism is necessarily the province, or the calling, of a specially qualified and trained minority. It takes so many forms that no attempt at description could be satisfactory. Esoterism is the "heart" of Religion, and exoterism the "body." Esoterism, broadly speaking, is the repository and guardian of the mystery or secret which is the mainspring of Religion. By its derivation (from the Greek "to keep the mouth shut") the word "mystery" does not mean something that is unknown, but something that cannot be absolutely or adequately expressed in words, but which is not for that reason unknowable. That is always its meaning when it is used in connection with Religion. The Greek mysteries were the esoteric aspect of their Religion and mythology.

The resemblance between the words "secret" and "sacred" is no accident. The modern hatred and suspicion of the secret, of everything that is not laid open to public inspection, is also a hatred of the sacred, and of the "mysterious" in the true sense of the word. The mystery is secret because it is inexpressible, and it is inexpressible because it concerns the Infinite, about which nothing exhaustive can be said, because speech and thought are always in some way limitative.

As we have seen, it is the specific function of humanity, occupying as it does a central position in the world, to keep that world in touch with the Infinite. Within humanity it is the specific function of those who follow an esoteric path to apprehend the mystery of the Infinite as directly as possible. The apprehension of those who follow an exoteric way is less direct, but none the less real. Its foundation is belief rather than vision, but there may not always in fact be a rigid line of demarcation.

From all this it is easy to see that the choice between adherence to Religion and its neglect or rejection has something absolute about it. If Religion is true, then there is nothing else that really counts, and the only practical thing to do is to follow it as best one can. If it is untrue, then the only thing to do is to "eat, drink, and be merry, for tomorrow we die." There can be no compromise. Religion cannot be an optional extra.

The choice between the acceptance or rejection of a particular form of Religion does not always seem to be as simple as the above would imply. The Religion we choose must be orthodox in the sense that in the first place it is derived from an authentic Revelation, and in the second place that it is connected to its origin by an unbroken chain of Tradition. This means that it must be neither heretical nor schismatic. The criterion of orthodoxy is conformity to a traditional law and symbolism, and to an intrinsic truth. However, the boundary between legitimate adaptation and deviation may sometimes be extremely difficult to define.

2 MODERNISM
The Profane Point of View

Lord Northbourne

The contemporary decay of Religion is not an isolated phenomenon. It is not confined to a restricted domain distinct from the secular domain. It is part of a fundamental change of point of view in relation to the nature of man and of the universe.

Whenever a people has lived in and by Religion—or more broadly Tradition—there may have been abuses and superstitions, incomprehension, opposition, and sin; but the reality of heaven and hell was unquestioned. God was not a mere hypothesis without which the world could not be adequately accounted for, nor the devil an outmoded *façon de parler* [manner of speaking]. The terrestrial hierarchy was a reflection of the celestial, from which it drew both its form and its justification. Whenever questions arose, the authority of Tradition rather than the ingenuity of man was looked to to supply the answer.

Only quite recently has a contrary point of view gained ascendancy; the simplest name for it is the profane point of view. It is anti-traditional, progressive, humanist, rationalist, materialist, experimental, individualist, egalitarian, free-thinking, and intensely sentimental. Such a point of view has always existed in one form or another. What is new is its dominance. Now practically worldwide, it dominates almost every domain of human life and thought.

To get a fully adequate picture of a very complex and comprehensive situation it would be necessary to take account of many other of its aspects; for instance, how the scientistic attitude persuades man that he is master of his own destiny; or how, as the mainspring of industry, it destroys the kind of work that is natural and necessary to man. It would be necessary to consider how profane philosophy, sharing the outlook of science, creates inextricable confusion by trying to find the answer to the most crucial of all questions, "What am I," where it is not to be found, namely in the human brain (for the eye cannot see itself). It would be necessary to consider how art is the mirror of its times, and from being purely symbolical becomes purely aesthetic; and the parts played by literature, entertainment, and advertising in changing human nature. All these things and many more are integral parts of the same picture. They are by no means unconnected with its religious aspect. But we are not for the moment concerned so much with things that oppose Religion with secularism or materialism of various kinds, nor with things that merely distract attention from Religion. We are concerned with things that attack it in the first place by doing all they can to sap the sources of its strength, and in the second place by setting up against it many kinds of more or less plausible counterfeits.

The profane point of view applied to Religion has caused everything not susceptible of direct proof based on the evidence of the senses to be called in question. Many things that are by their nature not accessible to the understanding of the masses have been set aside; yet these things tend to be the intellectual elements that are really fundamental. The result is the growing prevalence of a Religion that is reduced to its third element, the ethical or moral.

With the weakening of the directing influence of the more intellectual elements everything tends increasingly towards a mere sentimental humanism, confined in its outlook to the things of this world, and therefore defenseless against the assaults of its enemies. It becomes a Religion without mystery, denuded of most of its essentials. Nothing greater than man remains. Very soon happiness rather than salvation becomes the biggest good and the final goal, and pain rather than damnation becomes the greatest evil and the ultimate dread. It is scarcely too much to say that Religion has then virtually ceased to be Religion, although it still professes a belief in God.

It is not surprising that a Religion thus attenuated fails to satisfy either the instinctively felt needs of the masses, or the minds of many who are intelligent enough to perceive its weakness.

Human inadequacy in no way affects the truth, which remains what it was and always will be. Truth being what it is, it necessarily reaches us through the superhuman channel of Revelation, and not through the purely human one of discovery.

We are indeed a long way from the strength and purity of the original Revelation. The chain of Tradition which links us to it has been greatly strained, but until it is completely broken a renewal is always possible. Religion has been grossly sentimentalized and humanized, distorted and even perverted, and sometimes reduced to little more than a kind of idealism or ideology competing with profane ideologies for the same ends, an alternative way of promoting welfare. One can say without exaggeration that today the Kingdom of God frequently appears to be envisaged as little more than a full realization of the ideals of the welfare state.

It is a fact, however, that no such ideals can command for long the natural loyalty of men, which tends towards what is above themselves and not to what is on their own level. In practice that means towards whatever in their civilization most nearly, or most accessibly, represents the supernatural, to Tradition in general and to a hierarchical superior in particular. The secret longing of man—hidden sometimes even from himself—is to serve God. When no satisfactory opportunity to do so, even indirectly, comes to him from his environment, when nobody tells him how to seek it but on the contrary every influence urges him to seek something else, his secret longing remains unsatisfied and he loses his sense of loyalty and of purpose.

Communism and other subversive movements know very well that a Religion identified with ideals of welfare has lost its *raison d'être* and is at their mercy. Things have gone a long way in that direction when it becomes necessary to point out that the end of Religion is not welfare but salvation, and that "faith in human nature" or "faith in the future" have nothing whatever to do with faith in God. If the attainment of salvation is the true purpose of human life, in what way does a mere raising of the standard of living contribute to the attainment of that purpose, if meanwhile faith in God decays?

It is as if the world were the scene of the development of a gigantic plot to turn man away from God, in the first place by eliminating Tradition, which is the vehicle of Religion because it is a perpetuation of Revelation. The plot is in fact just as real as the devil is. In the achievement of the objective of this plot the propagation of the notion of progress, or progressive evolution, has hitherto occupied a central position. As applied to Religion it carries the implication that Religion itself progresses as it were automatically, so that it tends to get better or purer as time goes on, and therefore that a modernized Religion is likely to be an improvement on an ancient one. This notion contradicts all that is implicit in the notion of the completeness and sufficiency of the original Revelation, and of the main duty of man being to lose as little as possible of that completeness through the lapse of time.

The maintenance of a true Religion is not compatible with the profane point of view, or, to give it another name, the modernistic outlook. Whenever attempts are made to accommodate Religion to the modernistic outlook (in its scientific dress or otherwise) the result is inevitably a denaturing of Religion. This often includes a rejection or ignoring of everything in the Sacred Scriptures which does not fit in with the new outlook, and the substitution of the kind of "gospel of well-being" already mentioned, which situates heaven in a terrestrial future and abolishes hell.

But it is not necessary to adopt the modernistic outlook simply because one is alive today. Even though it be almost impossible to maintain a traditional outlook in all phases of life today, it is still possible and even vitally necessary to do so in Religion. It is for this reason that Religion must nowadays be kept in a distinct domain, more or less apart from the secular domain, despite the disadvantages of any such separation. These disadvantages spring from the fact that there is strictly speaking nothing, not even such things as are undiluted manifestations of the profane point of view, that has nothing to do with Religion, simply because there is nothing that has nothing to do with God. Everything is either affirmation or denial of Him. Therefore to think of anything as being entirely detached from Religion is to ignore its most essential relationships.[1]

The propagation of the notion of progressive evolution is one of the many lines of attack that can be broadly grouped under the heading of materialism. It is not sufficient however from the point of view of the enemies of God merely to undermine religious faith by the propagation of materialism in one form or another, in order to divert attention from faith to the attractions of the world. The attractiveness of earthly things is apt to fade; the devil knows well enough that they can never be satisfying for long, and that the bait has to be changed with growing frequency. When materialism has done most of its work and is beginning to be called in question as its results show themselves to be increasingly unsatisfactory, people's minds begin to turn back towards Religion. But by then many have forgotten what Religion is. They get no help from their environment. Many no doubt turn back towards orthodoxy, but many more turn towards one of the innumerable pseudo-religious movements, sects, and cults which are increasingly taking the place of orthodox Religion. In many of these movements some of the outward characteristics of Religion are preserved. In some cases those characteristics that would usually be regarded as interior or esoteric are more or less closely imitated. Some are "sects" in the sense that ostensibly they are not detached

---

[1] It then becomes impossible to situate it correctly in the scheme of things. Nevertheless this may be a lesser evil than that of falsifying the nature of Religion, in circumstances such as the present, when one or the other is inevitable.

from their parent Religion. Practically all of their adherents are well-meaning and guileless—that is the tragedy of the situation—but the same cannot always be said of their originators and leaders.

These pseudo-religious movements, sects, and cults are by far the most insidious enemies of Religion. They can fill the vacuum caused by its absence without fulfilling its essential purpose. Being inventions and not traditions, whatever claim to orthodoxy or to inspiration they may make, they can never be a means of grace. On the contrary, at best they are totally ineffectual, and at worst there is no limit to the harm they can do, not so much to body or mind, though that can be great, but to the immortal soul.

The neglect or denial of Religion is one thing; its distortion or perversion is another. The former is at least straightforward and unequivocal; it leaves the soul empty. The latter is subtle and confusing; it fills the soul with poison. There is no real defense against it other than an unswerving, wholehearted, and uncompromising attachment to an orthodox Religion. Therefore what matters most is to know at least in principle what orthodox Religion is. It then becomes unnecessary to try to sort out the conflicting claims of the pseudo-religions.

It is impossible to overstress the seriousness of the danger that pseudo-religions represent. The world is obsessed by fear, but it is a fear of things that can destroy only the body, and it takes little or no account of things that can first distort and then destroy the soul. There is no comparison between the two objects of fear, for heaven and hell are more real than this ephemeral world of appearances and illusions.

Religious people, and particularly those who practice some kind of austerity, are sometimes accused of being concerned only with saving their own souls instead of doing good to others, as if they were doing something selfish or contrary to Christian charity. Nothing could be more absurd. Does Christianity really place terrestrial welfare above salvation? No man can save any soul but his own. How could anyone who has no experience of the way towards salvation hope to show it to anyone else, or even to avoid obstructing him? One who is good cannot help doing good. One who is not good cannot hope to do good whatever he does. The effect of every act, whether charitable in intention or not, is dependent on the "intent" of the doer, that is, on the direction in which his soul is oriented. If the intent is right, even a natural and unimportant act (such as giving a cup of cold water) will do good. If the intent is not right, even an outwardly charitable act will be turned towards evil. So the most charitable of all acts, the act without which no other act can be charitable, is one which is directed towards the saving of the only soul for which the doer is responsible.

But there is something more important still. Every spiritual act is done on behalf of humanity. It contributes to the fulfillment of the purpose for which man was created—that of keeping the world in touch with God and bringing it back to Him. Only in the spiritual act is man fully human, and without it every act is undertaken in vain.

This life is not an end in itself. It is not justified by its pleasantness, nor by its length, but only insofar as it serves to purify and perfect the soul, and to make that soul ready to meet its God, as it must. The only certainty in life is death. It could even be said that the only reality in life is death, for the reality of the world of appearances is not its own, and death is the moment when the veil of the flesh is torn away and we see the reality that lies behind it. We see it then not as now "through a glass, darkly," but "face to face" (1 Corinthians 13:12).

The immense reality of death and its significance seem to be lost to this generation, which has forgotten that it is not the fact of death that is a cause for concern, nor the time of its occurrence, but the readiness of the soul to meet it.

Even if everything that has been said so far is accepted, doubt may still remain as to how to apply it to a particular case—one's own for instance.

The guidance offered from sources claiming orthodoxy is often conflicting or vague or unconvincing. The guidance offered from other sources is still more conflicting and inevitably lacks authority. How pleasant it would be if one could offer a simple prescription suitable for anyone, thus putting an end to doubts and hesitations! But applications to particular cases cannot be dealt with without taking into consideration the qualifications and situation of the individual concerned. For that reason anything that can be said here must be in very general terms.

The important thing about any statement is not whether it is general or particular, but whether it is true or untrue. Unless the truth can be grasped in its broad essentials it is unlikely that specific action will be soundly based. In the end, therefore, everyone must seek for himself the application appropriate to himself.

His search is much more likely to be fruitful if he has some idea what he is looking for. If he is looking for a new Religion there is one thing to make quite sure about first, and that is whether what he already has may not after all be what he is looking for. Even if he is sure that it is not exactly that, it may still be the nearest practicable approach to it, and therefore something not to be lightly thrown to the winds. He must be sure that what he is looking for may not after all be discoverable there where he is rather than elsewhere.

God will not refuse His guidance to one who seeks it with humility, perseverance, patience, and confidence. He often allows us to be led astray for a time so that we may understand what is wrong; or to be confused for a time so as to test our real intention. Victory may not come till the last moment; it may come when least expected and in the most unexpected form.

God knows well how difficult things are at this time. He "trieth not a soul beyond its capacity" (Koran 2:286).

3 LOOKING BACK ON PROGRESS*

Lord Northbourne

Any intelligible conception of progress must be directional; that is to say, it must imply the simultaneous conception of a goal. When the conception of progress is applied to humanity as a whole, or to any section of it, the way in which that goal is conceived depends on the answers given to certain questions that are as old as mankind: questions such as "What is the universe?" "What is life?" "What is man?"

The search for answers to such questions is nothing less than the unending search of humanity for a stable principle to which all experience can be referred. That search is being pursued in one way or another as intensively today as ever before. As always, the directions in which it is pursued are contingent on the tendencies of the prevailing mentality.

The purpose of this chapter is to draw attention to the contrast between two mentalities. One or the other is almost always predominant. They arrive at different answers to the kind of questions already mentioned, and they can conveniently be distinguished as "traditional" and "progressive."

The traditional mentality, in the sense in which the word is used here, is characteristic of societies in which a revealed Religion, together with the accompanying Tradition, exercises a predominant influence. The progressive mentality is one in which a science founded on observation, together with a humanistic philosophy based on that science, is the mainspring of thought and action. Only within the last few centuries has the latter mentality become predominant.

Almost everyone would agree that a profound change of outlook has taken place during that period, and that it first became predominant in Western Europe, from whence it has spread to the rest of the world.

This change is commonly regarded as being of the nature of an awakening to reality, or as an opening up of new horizons, or as a development of powers previously latent, and in any case as repre-

* Editors' Note: The Introductory from Lord Northbourne's book *Looking Back on Progress.*

senting a progress leading from a state of relative ignorance and sub-servience to one of relative awareness and freedom.

The present confused and unhappy state of the world proves that the hoped-for results of this change of outlook have not yet been real-ized. Nevertheless, the world seems to see no hope of their realization except by way of an intensification and acceleration of the intellectual, social, and economic developments consequent on this change. Is it not time to question the validity of the direction of our present aims, rather than thinking only about our efficiency in pursuing them?

The fact that the unending search of humanity is essentially a search for freedom from the constraints that seem to be inseparable from terrestrial life proves that we are conscious that our terrestrial situation is in a real sense a bondage. Less often are we fully conscious of the dual nature of that bondage. For we are bound in the first place by the constraints imposed on us by our environment, that is to say, by everyone and everything that is other than ourselves; this is our out-ward situation, the "destiny we meet." We are bound also to our own individual physical and mental heritage, which we did not choose for ourselves; this is our ego, our inward situation, the "destiny we are."

The fact that we can be aware of our subjection to this double bondage, and can see it as such, is proof (if proof were needed) that our whole being is more than its terrestrial manifestation. We are strangers here, and we know it, even when we behave as though the place belonged to us and as if we were answerable to nothing and nobody but ourselves.

We are always more or less consciously trying to escape from some aspect of our double bondage. Two main lines of action are possible, related respectively to the two sides of its dual nature. One is to try to free the ego from the constraints imposed on it by its environment, that is to say, to improve its outward situation. That is what most of us are trying to do for most of the time. The other is to try to escape from the limitations of the ego as such. In other words, we can aspire to freedom *for* our terrestrial nature, or we can aspire to freedom *from* our terrestrial nature.

The choice is not between two alternative and more or less equivalent options. If our main objective is to bring our environment into subjection so that it may not restrict the freedom of our ego, we are not even going half-way towards release from our double bondage. So long as we are not inwardly free, we cannot take advantage of whatever our environment may have to offer, even though it should be wholly under our command and at our disposal.

Progress achieved towards the satisfaction of terrestrial needs, desires, and fancies contributes nothing by itself towards inward freedom; on the contrary, when pursued beyond what is necessary, it tends more and more to supplant and to suppress the search for inward freedom, thereby defeating its own ends. Yet it is precisely such a progress that has become almost the sole aim of contemporary humanity. Its goal is to possess or to command everything in its environment. This last sentence describes very simply the way we have chosen. It is the way of those who give first place to the freeing of the ego from outward constraints, and it is the natural choice of the mentality that has been summarily called "progressive."

It is less easy to describe the other way. That way is associated with the traditional mentality. Its final goal is not to command things external to itself, but rather to surpass itself. The knowledge that it seeks above all is not a knowledge of the outer world but a knowledge that will enable it to command itself, and this implies a knowledge of itself. It does not deny the validity nor the necessity of some command over and some knowledge of the outer world, but this must not supplant or suppress self-knowledge.

Our inmost being is really the only thing we do know for sure, though our knowledge of it is non-distinctive and intuitive. It alone is our one absolute certainty. We can be in doubt and in dispute about outward things and their relationships, but not about our own existence, without which there would be no perception, no knowledge, no doubt, and no dispute. Yet, although our intuitive awareness of it is the very starting-point of all our awareness, we cannot say what constitutes our own reality. As soon as we try to distinguish it, we are mentally trying to situate it outside itself so that it may examine itself, which is absurd, and is made even more so by the fact that it is essentially single and not multiple. Consequently, anything that we succeed in distinguishing is not the object of our search.[1]

Thus we are faced with the apparent paradox of an inward reality and unity which we cannot observe, although we are aware of it more

---

[1] Self-knowledge cannot come by observation. Observation implies a duality between observer and observed, knower and known. Nothing that can be observed is identifiable with the observer. Therein resides the whole difficulty. Despite its overriding importance it is one which a science based wholly on observation can only ignore. If nothing that we can possibly know distinctively is that within us which knows (either in sensorial or in cognitive mode) then our bodies and our souls (to the extent that they can be objects of distinctive knowledge) are external or peripheral with respect to our inmost being, to the "self that knows."

surely than we are of anything. We know moreover that everyone else is in the same position, so we must have a word for it. It can only be a token word, a name and not a description; and no word is more applicable than the word "spirit." That word derives from the Latin *spiritus,* meaning "wind" or "breath." The ubiquitous and vivifying air, invisible in itself, but perceptible through its dynamic functions as wind or breath, is an adequate or natural symbol on the material plane of the unseizable principle of our being that we call "spirit."[2]

Human individuals differ one from another in the degrees of development of their faculties, but the existence of any one individual is not different in kind from the existence of any other; all are animated by the same principle of being. When we want to emphasize the transcendence of that principle with respect to ourselves or to the universe, or to emphasize its intrinsic uniqueness, we usually refer to it as "the Spirit" with a capital S; but we also use the word without a capital, and sometimes in the plural, to express all sorts of different and more limited ideas. Such usages can give rise to confusion; nevertheless they can also serve to remind the discerning of the immanence, the ubiquity, and (if the word be allowable) the "non-specificity" of the Spirit itself. Our passion for exact definition, when it is indulged to excess, hides from us much that is precious, and even that which is most precious of all.

The Spirit is that of which the world and we ourselves are manifestations. Manifestation is an exteriorization or a deployment, implying change and movement in an outward direction; correspondingly, the Spirit, the changeless and motionless Origin, is inward with respect to its manifestations, including ourselves. Although it is not strictly speaking localizable, we must look inward in order to find it.

We are often told that the objective of the "way" we have collectively chosen, the outward-looking way, is to free the human spirit from bondage. If that is true, we are certainly going the wrong way about it. Our main endeavors are directed to the feeding—one might say to the fattening—of the desiring soul; of that aspect of the soul which is indissolubly attached to the body during life, and is the

---

[2] The characteristics of an adequate or natural symbol are analogous on their own plane to those of a prototype on a higher plane, the symbol being necessarily on the plane of the observable and communicable. Our senses are adapted only to two planes of existence, the physical and psychic. To suggest that these two planes comprise all possibility is to make our senses the measure of all things which, in view of their obvious limitations, is childish.

tightest of all the bonds that constrain the spirit, and the most difficult to identify and to loosen.

The way which we have rejected, the inward-looking way, seeks to free the human spirit from all its bonds by freeing it from those that are internal in the sense that they are part of the ego. It is they that confine the spirit most closely. In its purest form, this way is the way of the saint, whose goal is the unseizable Spirit and whose inward state it is beyond the power of words to convey.[3]

The withdrawal of the saint from the world, in his search for that which is within himself, is sometimes criticized as being selfish, on the grounds that he does not appear to be doing what he might do for the good of other people. The truth is the exact opposite. He is seeking a truth that can only be found by inner experience and not by observation, and it is the very truth without which humanity is lost. He is not seeking to obtain anything to satisfy his selfish ego, on the contrary, he is seeking to give himself wholly to God in love, and thereby to learn what love really is. The repercussions of his intense activity, which is undertaken on behalf of humanity, are unpredictable, and they are independent of whether he is a public figure or totally unknown to his fellow men. The inward experience of the saint brings a supra-rational certitude, whereas observation brings no more than probability, which is not the same as certitude, even when it is of a very high order. The modern world is conscious of many of its own deficiencies; it does not appear to be at all troubled about its lack of saints, although that is the deficiency that matters most of all and cannot be compensated for by anything else.

But everyone cannot be a saint, so this same way is by extension the collective way of all communities whose traditions, laws, customs, and habitual outlook are predominantly directed towards the pursuit of sanctity, and therefore towards the support of the saint as its vehicle, either directly through religious rites and observances and the selection and training of individuals, or indirectly through the maintenance and defense of a political, economic, and social order so directed that the main aim can be effectively pursued within it.

---

[3] Therefore anyone who tries to convey the nature of that inward state in words necessarily fails. This may not matter when both speaker and hearer are aware of the inadequacy of words in this connection; but when the inevitable failure is hidden in a morass of psychological jargon, which convinces many people by its apparent profundity that it has penetrated to the depths, then it matters very much indeed.

This kind of indirect support is normally the principal function of a large majority. By its exercise the participation of everyone in the pursuit of sanctity is made possible, whatever his situation or capacity. Such, in principle, is the framework of a traditional civilization, although it is of course never perfectly realized. Such a society is never immune from degeneration and abuse, as we can see all too clearly today everywhere.

All civilizations were originally traditional in outlook; each one has attributed its own origin to an initial divine Revelation or inspiration, and has regarded itself as the appointed preserver and guardian of the content of that Revelation.

This generalization is valid despite great differences in the outward forms of traditional civilizations, despite their many and obvious imperfections, and despite their impermanence. Their differences manifest the fact that the Spirit cannot be confined by any specific form. It can however manifest itself fully in an indefinity of different forms, sometimes mutually incompatible, without betraying itself, and always revealing itself. Their impermanence is a simple consequence of the fact that no civilization has ever been perfect, since it is a human and a temporal phenomenon; it is a manifestation of the Spirit, but it is not the Spirit itself which alone is imperishable. Everything, save the Spirit itself, carries within itself the seeds of its own dissolution.

* * *

Anyone who is disposed to emphasize the defects of traditional civilizations would do well to look dispassionately at our modern progressive—and therefore anti-traditional—civilization, and to look at it as it is, and not at what he thinks it is meant to be, or could be if only we could overcome this or that problem, or if only so-and-so would see sense. He should look at what it has in fact produced in the way of contentment, peace, beauty, or freedom, and then at what it has in fact produced in the way of anxiety, war and rivalry, ugliness (in the despoiling of Nature and in the arts), and subjection to its own insatiable desires, and to the inexhaustible demands of the machine. Then he should consider, no less dispassionately, what its prospects of durability appear to be, bearing in mind that all its present tendencies are bound to be accentuated in the future, their accentuation being in fact its principal objective. More and more and faster and faster is the

cry, as if the end of a continuous quantitative expansion could be anything but dispersion and fragmentation, either gradual or explosive.

Some such questionings are at the back of many people's minds
in one form or another today. Yet it seldom seems to occur to anyone
to question the doctrine of progress in principle rather than merely
in some of its consequences, nor yet to wonder seriously whether
traditional civilizations may after all have possessed something we
have lost, something that made life worth living even under conditions of poverty and hardship. Do we so excel in wisdom and virtue
as to have the right to assume that they—our ancestors physically and
intellectually—clung to Tradition merely from stupidity, from a false
sense of where their true interests lay, or from a superstitious blindness to the realities underlying their lives on earth? We are prepared
to admit that they often produced sanctity and nobility in man and
incomparable beauty in art, but we look down upon them for their
submission to a traditional hierarchy, and for their acceptance of their
often humble situations in it, and for their relative contentment with
service to it. We think that they accepted these things because they
knew no better, since they lacked a vision of the possibilities open to
humanity. The question is, of course, whether it is the followers of
Tradition or the devotees of progress who are lacking in a vision of
those possibilities.

If, as most people assume today, this life comprises all the possibilities open to humanity individually or collectively, then the satisfaction of the ego, the mitigation of pain, and the postponement of
death are indeed the best objectives we can choose, and we rightly
accord first place to them. If, however, as the traditional view has it,
death is a passage to another state of being in which we shall be confronted with the truth and see ourselves as we really are, and if pain
is a reminder of the imperfection of our present state and as such not
only inevitable but at least potentially beneficent, and if the salvation
of the immortal soul takes precedence over the satisfaction of the ego,
then the objectives named appear in a very different light. They do not
become invalid, but to give them first place becomes both foolish and
wicked. It seems to most people today to be foolish and even wicked
to give them any other place. The attitudes and actions of traditional
peoples seem to us often to be marked by both incomprehension and
callousness. But what is the use of our achievements in mitigating
pain and in postponing death if they are accompanied by the loss of
the very thing that made life and death and pain both comprehensible
and purposeful?

* * *

Tradition and hierarchy are inseparable. Together they constitute a chain linking civilization with the Spirit in successional mode and in simultaneous mode respectively; in time to a spiritual origin and in space to a spiritual center. The origin inspires the center, and the center perpetuates the origin.[4] The whole structure is founded on the conception of the reality of divine Revelation. Revelation alone confers on the chain of Tradition its directional or centripetal force. Human beings are always to some extent mutually interdependent; they are always linked together by chains of various sorts, physical, economic, or ideological. But such chains are accidental; human desires may give them a direction, which is always centrifugal rather than centripetal. If the chain of Tradition is anything at all, it is inherently directional and centripetal. It links mankind to its divine origin, and not to human wants or imaginings.

Revealed Religion is therefore the heart of Tradition; without it Tradition would be an empty shell, a form without significance; it would be no more than mere social convention. Conversely, Tradition, with all its many manifestations that are not specifically religious in form, is the indispensable support of Religion. Without that support Religion cannot be integrated with life, it becomes a thing apart, a supplement rather than the principal directing force; it tends to degen-

---

[4] The use of the word "center" and cognate words in this connection is of course symbolical. The sphere is the type of all spatial forms and the most generalized. The center of a sphere is the point to which all its dimensions are referred; it defines the sphere regardless of its size or qualitative constitution. The center is dimensionless, but its influence pervades and coordinates the entire space; it is thus an adequate symbol of the dimensionless spiritual origin of all things, and that not only in a verbal sense, but also in the concrete form of a sacred locality, be it a temple, a holy city, a holy mountain, or the heart of man. For the spiritual center is in reality everywhere, and it is therefore unseizable; and for that reason limited and localized beings who aspire towards it have need of a symbolical location to which they can direct their attention. And who can doubt that the Holy Spirit does indeed dwell in such places?

The fact that mankind feels the need of a symbolical center to which he can direct his aspirations makes possible, in periods of spiritual decadence, the substitution for the sacred center of other centers which are anything but sacred, but are simply rallying points for the delusions and passions of a humanity that has lost touch with a traditional center. They give rise to their own orders or systems which are often misleadingly referred to as hierarchies. The word "hierarchy" comes from the Greek and means "sacred order" and nothing else; it ought therefore to be applied only to a strictly traditional order, wherein all authority, even in its social aspects, derives its legitimacy from the sacred center.

erate into a vague individual belief in God, or into a mere ideology competing with other ideologies on their own plane.

Religion and Tradition are inseparable, they are two closely related aspects of the same thing. They are however seldom met with in their pristine purity, since their temporal manifestations necessarily carry within themselves the seeds of their own dissolution, as has already been indicated. Those seeds germinate slowly but, like weeds in a crop, once well established can overwhelm the crop and even virtually replace it altogether. The process is gradual but accelerative. At most times there is a mixture of crop and weed in varying proportions. The assessment of the exact proportion of each present at any given time may be difficult; but it is always possible to discern and to describe the intrinsic nature of each.

The point of departure of the traditional approach to reality is everywhere and always the same. This is true despite great differences in the historical development of traditional civilizations. Existence is envisaged as proceeding from an origin or prime cause which is transcendent with respect to all its productions, and is symbolically the center from which all existence radiates without ever becoming detached from it, on pain of ceasing to be. It is the center not only of the universe, the macrocosm, but also of the individual being, the microcosm, since the latter reflects the wholeness of the former.

In any community, its own particular sacred center, and in the individual, the heart, represents or symbolizes the universal center.[5] Therefore the gaze of the intelligent individual in search of the source of existence, or, what amounts to the same thing, the source of truth, is directed inwards, towards the sacred center of his particular world, and at the same time towards the center of his own being. His outlook on all that he sees and knows is conditioned by the direction

---

[5] The psycho-physical complex that constitutes a human individual is a coherent unit, a little world on its own, a microcosm. All its organs are mutually interdependent, and each has a distinct function. Most people nowadays would regard the brain as performing the highest function of all, but the function of the brain, and the nervous system that is continuous with it, is mainly one of interpretation and coordination. It is the heart, and not the brain, that vivifies the whole, and is therefore the source of all its potentialities, including the potentiality of intelligence. The correspondence on their respective planes between the heart and the spiritual center is therefore far from being merely fanciful (see also footnote 4). When the heart is spiritually inert, the individual is not truly alive, but is a mere machine, however active the mind or the body may be. When the heart is spiritually active, the individual is truly alive, and is at peace whether he be outwardly active or not. "I sleep, but my heart waketh" (Song of Songs 5:2).

of his aspiration. In more familiar words, he "seeks the Kingdom of Heaven" where it is to be found, namely, "within you." It is worth noting that the word "you" (or *vos* in Latin) can equally well be taken to be addressed to the collectivity with its more or less localized sacred center, or to the individual with his heart. Wherever Tradition is the controlling principle of human activity, every man, whether he be intelligent or not, and whatever his function, is (consciously or otherwise) involved in this centripetal tendency.

The point of departure of the progressive outlook on reality, closely associated as it is with modern science, is observation. It looks exclusively outwards towards its environment, and not inwards towards the principle of its own being, which is at the same time the principle of all being. It does not consider existence as such, but only things that exist, and it regards their forms and qualities as products of their observable structure and their interaction with each other. It seeks to discern and to define the modes of operation of these interactions, hoping to discover some kind of fundamental law governing all relationships, and thus to arrive at something which, if not the absolutely prime cause of all things, represents at least as near an approach thereto as can be made by the human mind. Its point of departure precludes its taking into account anything which is not within the capacity of the human mind. God, therefore, must either be rejected or be rationalized and humanized, and the consequence is that Religion is eventually reduced to the status of an unproved hypothesis, "improbable" first in the etymological and then in the contemporary sense of the word. Thence it is but a step to the total rejection of Religion, or to its substitution by ideologies or fancies originating exclusively in the brain or the sentiments of men. Tradition dies. Man is in no doubt about his own reality, and thus becomes supreme in his own eyes. At this point it becomes possible to say that man is now god.[6]

Nothing then remains but to glorify as far as possible man's achievements in subordinating his environment to his desires, a difficult task, in view not only of the triviality of those achievements on a terrestrial, and still more on a cosmic, scale, but above all in view

---

[6] These very words constitute as it were the text of the Reith lectures on the B.B.C. for 1967, given by Prof. R. MacLean. But he is not the first to make a public statement to this effect. Some years ago a pronouncement stating that "the people are now god" came from Soviet Russia, certainly without official disapproval. In the Russian case it appeared that man was considered to be qualified for a divine status by his merits rather than by his capacities, whereas in Prof. MacLean's case the main qualification appears to be ingenuity.

of their conspicuous failure to satisfy. However, such talk is eagerly swallowed by a public acutely anxious about its own future, and all too ready to escape from facts into the realm of anticipations and to delude itself by considering, not what is, but what could be, if only science could have its way.

The outward look is separative. It emphasizes the duality between observer and observed, knower and known, man and Nature. Our environment becomes something to be exploited, albeit "sustainably." We become more conscious of it as an obstacle to the fulfillment of our desires than of our oneness with it. And since our human neighbor is, for each one of us, part of his environment, men become more and more separated one from another. The separativity of the outward look, when it is not balanced by its inward counterpart, divides man from his neighbor as well as from God, so that there is no longer a human family with God as its "Father" and Nature as its "Mother." Reality itself is departmentalized; it tends to disintegrate, and man becomes ever more lonely and puzzled.

By contrast, the inward look is unitive. The seeker who finds the center, the knower who knows himself, sees both himself and the outside world, Nature and his neighbor, as one through their connection with that center, not through their chance linkages with each other. Unity becomes the reality, separativity and relativity the illusion. Powerful though that illusion be, yet for him it is so to speak transparent. Yet he knows that he as an individual does not occupy a situation fundamentally different from that of his neighbor. Unity, which is indivisible, cannot therefore appertain to him alone. If he is sane, he knows that he as an individual is not God; or alternatively, that if he can in any legitimate sense be said to be one with God, the same can be said of his neighbor. He knows that his own separate existence is in the last analysis both illusory and paradoxical; but this knowledge is all a part of his overriding certitude that God is, and alone is wholly real, and that Nature, his neighbor, and himself, distinct though they be and even often in conflict, are one in God, and in God alone.

If the traditional view is the right one, the idea that progress, in the modern sense of the word, could ever fulfill the hopes and plans of its advocates must be deceptive, not primarily because men are weak, stupid, passionate, and sometimes vicious, nor yet because human desires are so often mutually incompatible, but primarily because the advocates of a scientific and progressive humanism are looking away from the luminous source of their being, which is reflected in the divine spark in their own hearts. They are looking towards a universe which, in the absence of a valid principle, appears to be made up of particles and blind forces in ceaseless conflict with the desires and delusions of the human ego. Accordingly, they inflate and even deify the human ego in order to convince it that victory is possible. The voice of a progressive humanism proclaims that man has at last found the means of satisfying his desires, thus opening up the possibility of his becoming the creator of an earthly paradise. He can at last see his way to getting all he wants from his environment, provided that he will work hard and be reasonable.

The voice of Tradition on the other hand, when it is not enfeebled or afraid to speak out, proclaims that the worth, the dignity, the whole justification of human life, lies in the preservation of the chain that binds man to God, who is his origin, preserver, and end, whose Paradise is the only Paradise; and further, that in order to find that Paradise man must seek it in the sacred center, and not in the periphery.

The measure of our bondage is the strength of our attachment to the world of our experience and the extent of our submission to the desires engendered by that attachment. We deceive ourselves if we seek to escape from our bondage by way of the satisfaction of those desires. The measure of our deception is the extent of our failure to realize that those desires, being fed to excess, will multiply and plague us the more. Instead, we can seek to forestall and counteract too strong an attachment to the world by giving priority to a conscious and active aspiration towards the eternal Principle of our being which, being changeless, is above and beyond all attachment and all desire.

We have the freedom to choose which of these two attitudes or tendencies shall predominate and which shall be subordinate in directing the course of our lives. Collectively we have chosen, and must accept the consequences, but the individual is always free to conform to that collective choice or to reject it. If he rejects it, he can act only within the limits of the possibilities of his individuality and his situation. God does not ask the impossible of anyone. Tradition and all it implies being virtually a dead letter, he will get little help from his environment and much hindrance. He will have to face not only open hostility, but also much more subtle and often tempting subversive influences, which are of many different kinds and have invaded every domain, even the very domain of Religion itself.

It may be thought that compromise of some kind must be possible, but the situation is such that compromise can never be anything but superficial and illusory. The opposition between the traditional and the progressive outlooks is strictly analogous to that between East and West, upward and downward, inward and outward, or any other two diametrically opposed directions. Since life is all movement and change, necessitating choice at every turn, an inward choice between the two directions is inescapable, even though it may seem to be involuntary or unconscious. That choice, and it alone, determines the orientation of the soul and therewith its fate. At the same time it determines the ultimate effect of every act.

In these days when circumstances seem to impose compromise, it is no small thing to assert the impossibility of an effective compromise between the two ways of approach to truth here designated as traditional and progressive. Individuals and societies frequently attempt compromises between things that are in reality incompatible, but when that is the case any apparent compromise is illusory and cannot endure. One or the other of the two factors involved is bound to win in the end. This generalization applies fully to the present case, and it is not difficult to see which of the two approaches in question appears now to be winning. The question is whether its final victory is possible. If it is impossible that the approach of modern science should penetrate to the foundations of the reality of existence, simply because that science is looking in the wrong direction, then the fact that Tradition is disappearing and Religion seems to be in eclipse does not affect in the slightest degree the certainty of the final victory of the approach that leads to truth, although the form that victory will take cannot be predicted.

*   *   *

Before concluding this chapter, three further points must be made. In the first place, it is often suggested that either modern psychology, or a philosophy that has developed in parallel with modern science, is working in the same direction as that pursued by traditional sages and philosophers and by the few who still seek to follow them, and that it is thus making an approach to the same goal. That is not so. The approach of modern psychology and philosophy coincides consciously and deliberately with that of modern science. It is a search for an outward and distinctive knowledge, either in order to gain more control over the environment or ourselves, or with no avowed objective other than that of increasing the sum of human knowledge. In either case, what is involved is the exteriorization and examination of phenomena with the greatest degree attainable of scientific detachment. This last word is very significant, because it implies the most complete separation possible between subject and object, knower and known. Such is the way of science. It has its own validity and produces its own kind of results; its dispassion is exemplary; nevertheless, the direction of its approach is diametrically opposed to that of what has, so far very briefly, been described as the traditional way. It therefore cannot lead to the same goal.[7]

The second point is more fundamental. There is an apparent illogicality in saying that the nature, or the end-point, of what one is talking about cannot be specified in words, and then going on talking about it. Might it not be better to retire within oneself and be silent? Well, it might. To do so would at least avoid the risk of leaving the reader puzzled or angry or, worse, bored. It is a serious risk. The reasons for taking that risk could be stated in many ways, among others as follows.

Words are primarily evocative; their descriptive use is conditional on their evocative power. They convey no meaning at all unless they fall into correspondence with some potentiality present or latent in the hearer. Only then do they evoke a response of any kind. The possibility of their descriptive use depends on their evocative power, but description is restricted to the plane of our terrestrial life. Words are in any case all derived from our common experience on that plane. If that plane alone comprises the whole of reality there is no further argument; but, if there are other planes of reality, they too are accessible to the purely evocative potentiality of words by virtue of the analogical relationship subsisting between all planes, and constituting the basis of all true symbolism.[8] Those who would limit the use and understanding of words to their purely descriptive function are, among other things, reducing to the commonplace all the Sacred Scriptures, and all the great poetry, writings and sayings that have ever pierced the veil of the terrestrial involvement of mankind. Let us admit once and

---

[7] If this is true in principle, nevertheless its application to particular cases is often difficult. In the case of psychology, the difficulty resides in the fact that, in its investigation of the "sub-conscious," it often fails to distinguish between the "supra-conscious," and the "infra-conscious," that is to say, between what is too exalted to descend into the distinctive consciousness and what is too debased to be raised to that level. It might be thought that such a distinction must be self-evident; but a right discrimination between the two is not within the power of the mind, because the "sub-conscious" is by definition excluded from the conscious mind; it can therefore only be accomplished by way of an interior or spiritual vision. Where that vision is lacking, either accidentally or because an approach that excludes it is adopted on principle, the result is a fatal confusion. The approach of much contemporary philosophy excludes that vision on principle; it is therefore liable to lead to error, however plausible its arguments may seem to be on the purely mental plane.

[8] See footnote 2.

for all that this world is no better than commonplace unless it is lifted out of itself towards a plane higher than its own. By the Grace of God it can be, provided that we do not insist on limiting our understanding of symbols, verbal symbols included, to that of their most outward or "literal" significance.

Finally: some people say that there is a conflict between Religion and science, others say that there is not. Who is right? The two incompatibles, which for the sake of brevity have been labeled "Tradition" and "progress," are not identifiable with Religion and with science respectively, in the first place because there is and always has been a sacred science. Sacred science is not restricted in its outlook as modern science is. It sees the temporal universe of phenomena as no more than an appearance, and it seeks a supra-phenomenal and intemporal reality, just as Religion does, but it follows a path which is parallel to, rather than coincident with, the path of Religion, at least until both attain to the summit.

In the second place, a Religion founded on Revelation remains now as always indissolubly linked with Tradition, and now as always it is centered on the supra-phenomenal and intemporal, even when, as a result of human weakness, it is not as evidently so as it might be. Meanwhile, science in its modern form has lost sight of the supra-phenomenal and intemporal, and has taken on the role of prophet, guide, and provider to an ideology of progress having as its goal a temporal and terrestrial utopia.

There is a conflict, but it is not between Religion and science as such, for they can be regarded as two normal, necessary, and parallel approaches to truth, provided always that the hierarchical superiority of the religious approach is recognized and acted upon. The conflict is between the two points of view here designated respectively as traditional and progressive. Religion and science come into conflict only insofar as they are associated with the one or with the other.

Attempts at compromise between the traditional and progressive points of view, as applied to the origin and destiny of man and of the universe, can only lead to confusion. Their mutual incompatibility is total and unequivocal. The ideology of progress envisages the perfectibility of man in terms of his terrestrial development, and relegates it to a hypothetical future, whereas Tradition envisages the perfectibility of man in terms of salvation or sanctification, and proclaims that it is realizable here and now.

II

TRADITIONAL COSMOLOGY AND MODERN SCIENCE

For men shall be . . . ever learning,
and never able to come
to the knowledge of the truth.

II Timothy 3:2, 7

4 THE PAST IN THE LIGHT OF THE PRESENT
&
THE RHYTHMS OF TIME

Martin Lings

Would the peoples of old have changed their attitude towards their earliest ancestors if they had known all that modern scientists now know? This is in some ways equivalent to another question: Is there any real incompatibility between religion and science?—for the opinions of our forefathers were largely based on religion.

Let us take one or two examples of "stumbling-blocks," considering them in the light of both religion and science, and not in the darkness of either. Does religion claim that pre-historic events can be dated on the basis of a literal interpretation of figures mentioned in the Old Testament, and that the approximate date of the Creation itself is 4,000 B.C.? It could hardly make such a claim, for "a thousand years in Thy Sight are but as yesterday" and it is by no means always clear, when days are mentioned in sacred texts, whether they are human days or whether they are Divine Days each consisting of "a thousand human years," that is, a period which bears no comparison with a human day.

Can science allow that the earth was created about 6,000 years ago? Clearly it cannot, for evidence of various kinds show beyond doubt that at that date the earth and man were already old. If science seems here to refute the letter of the Scriptures, it does not refute their spirit, for even apart from archaeological and geological evidence there are directly spiritual reasons for preferring not to insist on the letter of Genesis chronology. This does not mean that our mediaeval ancestors, many if not most of whom did accept a literal interpretation, were less spiritual or less intelligent than ourselves—far from it. But although, as we shall see later, they almost certainly had a more qualitative sense of time than we have, that is, a keener sense of its rhythms, they no doubt had less sense of time in a purely quantitative way; and it did not strike them, as it can scarcely fail to strike us, that there is something spiritually incongruous in the idea of an All-Powerful God's creation being so remarkably unsuccessful that *within a very short space of time* the Creator saw need to drown the whole human race, except for one family, in order to be able to start afresh. But even apart from questions of time, the men of the Middle Ages were too conscience-stricken to reason as we do, too overwhelmed by a sense of human responsibility—to their credit be it said. If what had happened was incongruous, not to say monstrous, all the more blame to man. This way of thinking certainly comes nearer to the truth than some more modern trends of thought do, but it does not correspond to the whole truth; and we who tend to look at the question more "detachedly" cannot help seeing that God has *His* responsibilities also. None the less it remains for each one of us to ask himself exactly how sublime his own detachment is, always remembering that a man who is standing idly down in the plain sometimes has a better view of certain aspects of a mountain than have those who are actually climbing it.

Whatever answers we may give to this question, the fact remains that our sense of what is to the Glory of God and what is not fits in less well, as regards bare chronology, with the perspective of mediaeval Christendom than it does with the perspective of the Ancient World, according to which it is only after having granted mankind many thousands of years of spiritual well-being that God has allowed it to pass through a relatively short period of decay, or in other words allowed it to "grow old." In any case this more ancient perspective cannot lightly be brushed aside. Its basis, the tradition of the four ages of the cycle of time which the Greeks and Romans named the Golden, Silver, Bronze, and Iron Ages, is not merely European but is also to be found in Asia, among the Hindus, and in America among the Red Indians. According to Hinduism, which has the most explicit doctrine on this subject, the Golden Age was by far the longest; the ages became increasingly shorter as they were less good, the shortest and worst being the Dark Age, which corresponds to the Iron Age. But even this last and shortest age, the age we live in, stretches back more than 6,000 years into the past. What modern archaeologists call "the Bronze Age" bears no relation to the third age of the four, and what they call "the Iron Age" merely happens to coincide with a fraction of the fourth age.

The ancient and world-wide tradition of the four ages does not contradict the Book of Genesis, but, like the evidence of science, it does suggest an allegorical rather than a literal interpretation. It suggests, for example, that certain names indicate not merely single individuals but whole eras of pre-history, and that the name Adam in particular may be taken as denoting not only the first man but also the whole of primordial humanity, spanning a period of many thousands of years.

*   *   *

But is it necessary for religion to maintain that at some time in the past man was created in a state of surpassing excellence, from which he has since fallen? Without any doubt yes, for if the story of the Garden of Eden cannot be taken literally, it cannot, on the other hand, be taken as meaning the opposite of what it says.[1] The purpose of allegory is, after all, to convey truth, not falsehood. Besides, it is not only Judaism, Christianity, and Islam which tell of the perfection of Primordial Man and his subsequent fall. The same truth, clothed in many different imageries, has come down to us out of the prehistoric past in all parts of the world. Religions are in fact unanimous in teaching not evolution but devolution.

Is this religious doctrine contrary to scientifically known facts? Must science, in order to be true to itself, maintain the theory of evolution? In answer to this last question let us quote the French geologist Paul Lemoine, editor of Volume V (on "Living Organisms") of the *Encyclopédie Française*, who went so far as to write in his summing up of the articles of the various contributors: "This exposition shows that the theory of evolution is impossible. In reality, despite appearances, no one any longer believes in it. . . . Evolution is a sort of dogma whose priests no longer believe in it, though they uphold it for the sake of their flock." Though undeniably exaggerated in its manner of expression—that is, as regards its sweeping implications of hypocrisy on the part of the "priests" in question—this judgment, coming where it does, is significant in more than one respect. There is no doubt that many scientists have transferred their religious instincts from religion to evolutionism, with the result that their attitude towards evolution is sectarian rather than scientific. The French biologist Professor Louis Bounoure quotes Yves Delage, a former Sorbonne Professor of Zoology: "I readily admit that no species has ever been known to engender another, and that there is no absolutely definite evidence that such a thing has ever taken place. None the less, I believe evolution to be just as certain as if it had been objectively proved." Bounoure comments:

---

[1] To this obvious fact Teilhard de Chardin turned a blind eye, and here lies one of the basic weaknesses of his standpoint.

"In short, what science asks of us here is an act of faith, and it is in fact under the guise of a sort of revealed truth that the idea of evolution is generally put forward."[2] He quotes, however, from a present day Sorbonne Professor of Palaeontology, Jean Piveteau, the admission that the science of facts as regards evolution "cannot accept any of the different theories which seek to explain evolution. It even finds itself in opposition with each one of these theories. There is something here which is both disappointing and disquieting."[3]

Darwin's theory owed its success mainly to a widespread conviction that the nineteenth-century European represented the highest human possibility yet reached. This conviction was like a special receptacle made in advance for the theory of man's sub-human ancestry, a theory which was hailed without question by humanists as a scientific corroboration of their belief in "progress." It was in vain that a staunch minority of scientists, during the last hundred years, persistently maintained that the theory of evolution has no scientific basis and that it runs contrary to many known facts, and it was in vain that they pleaded for a more rigorously scientific attitude towards the whole question. To criticize evolutionism, however soundly, was about as effective as trying to stem a tidal wave. But the wave now shows some signs of having spent itself, and more and more scientists are re-examining this theory objectively, with the result that not a few of those who were once evolutionists have now rejected it altogether. One of these is the already quoted Bounoure; another, Douglas Dewar, writes: "It is high time that biologists and geologists came into line with astronomers, physicists, and chemists and admitted that the world and the universe are utterly mysterious and all attempts to explain them [by scientific research] have been baffled";[4] and having divided evolutionists into ten main groups (with some subdivisions) according to their various opinions as to what animal formed the last link in the chain of man's supposedly "pre-human" ancestry, opinions which are all purely conjectural[5] and mutually contradictory, he says: "In 1921 Reinke wrote: 'The only statement, consistent with her dignity, that science can make [with regard to this question] is to say that

---

[2] *Le Monde et la Vie*, November 1963.

[3] *Le Monde et la Vie*, March 1964.

[4] *The Transformist Illusion*, preface (Ghent, NY: Sophia Perennis, 1995).

[5] Because "no evolutionist who values his reputation will name *any known fossil* and say that, while not human, it is an ancestor of *Homo sapiens*" (p. 114).

she knows nothing about the origin of man.' Today this statement is as true as it was when Reinke made it."[6]

If science knows nothing about the origins of man, she knows much about his prehistoric past. But this knowledge—to revert to our opening question—would have taught our ancestors little or nothing that they did not already know, except as regards chronology, nor would it have caused any general change in their attitude. For in looking back to the past, they did not look back to a complex civilization but to small village settlements with a minimum of social organization; and beyond these they looked back to men who lived without houses, in entirely natural surroundings, without books, without agriculture, and in the beginning even without clothes. It would be true then to say that the ancient conception of early man, based on sacred scriptures and on age-old traditional lore handed down by word of mouth from the remote past, was scarcely different, as regards the bare facts of material existence, from the modern scientific[7] conception, which differs from the traditional one chiefly because it weighs up the same set of facts differently. What has changed is not so much knowledge of facts as the sense of values.

Until recently men did not think any the worse of their earliest ancestors for having lived in caves and woods rather than houses. It is not so long ago that Shakespeare put into the mouth of the banished Duke, living in the forest of Arden "as they lived in the golden world":

> Here feel we but the penalty of Adam,
> The seasons' change. . . .
> And this our life, exempt from public haunt,

---

[6] p. 294.

[7] This word means what it says and is used here: (a) To exclude the bestial features which in the illustrations to so many school books are attributed to our remote ancestors. As the palaeontologist Professor E. A. Hooton remarks: "You can, with equal facility, model on a Neanderthaloid skull the features of a chimpanzee or the lineaments of a philosopher. These alleged restorations of ancient types of man have very little, if any, scientific value, and are likely only to mislead the public" (Quoted by Evan Shute, *Flaws in the Theory of Evolution* [London: Temside Press, 1966], p. 215); (b) To include evidence too often passed over in silence such as that of the Castenedolo and Calaveras skulls, which point to the existence of "men of modern type" at a period when, according to the evolutionists, *Homo sapiens* had not yet evolved (See Dewar, *The Transformist Illusion*, pp. 117-129, and Shute, *Flaws in the Theory of Evolution*, ch. XXI).

> Finds tongues in trees, books in the running brooks,
> Sermons in stones, and good in everything.
> I would not change it.

These words can still evoke in some souls an earnest echo, an assent that is considerably more than a mere aesthetic approval; and behind Shakespeare, throughout the Middle Ages and back into the furthest historical past, there was no time when the Western world did not have its hermits, and some of them were among the most venerated men of their generation. Nor can there be any doubt that these exceptional few who lived in natural surroundings felt a certain benevolent pity for their brethren's servile dependence upon "civilization." As to the East, it has never broken altogether with the ancient sense of values, according to which the best setting for man is his primordial setting. Among the Hindus, for example, it is still an ideal—and a privilege—for a man to end his days amid the solitudes of virgin nature.

For those who can readily grasp this point of view, it is not difficult to see that agriculture, after a certain degree of development had been reached, far from marking any "progress," became in fact "the thin end of the wedge" of the final phase of man's degeneration. In the Old Testament narrative, this "wedge," consisting no doubt of hundreds of human generations, is summed up in the person of Cain, who represents agriculture as distinct from hunting or herding, and who also built the first cities and committed the first crime. According to the Genesis commentaries, Cain "had a passion for agriculture"; and such an attachment, from the point of view of the nomadic hunter-herdsman and casual tiller of the ground, was a sharp downward step: professional agriculture means settling in one place, which leads to the construction of villages, which develop sooner or later into towns; and in the ancient world, just as the life of a shepherd was always associated with innocence, towns were always considered, relatively speaking, as places of corruption. Tacitus tells us that the Germans of his time had a horror of houses; and even today there are some nomadic or semi-nomadic peoples, like the Red Indians for example, who have a spontaneous contempt for anything which, like agriculture, would fix them in one place and thus curtail their liberty.

> The red man has no intention of "fixing" himself on this earth where everything, according to the law of stabilization and also of condensation—"petrification" one might say—is liable to become

"crystallized"; and this explains the Indian's aversion to houses, especially stone ones, and also the absence of a writing, which according to this perspective, would "fix" and "kill" the sacred flow of the Spirit.[8]

This quotation brings us from the question of agriculture to that of literacy; and in this connection we may remember that the Druids also, as Caesar tells us, held that to commit their sacred doctrines to writing would be to desecrate them. Many other examples could be brought forward to show that the absence of writing, like the absence of agriculture, can have a positive cause; and in any case, however accustomed we may be to thinking of linguistic prowess as inseparable from literacy, a moment's reflection is enough to show that there is no basic connection between the two, for linguistic culture is altogether independent of the written alphabet, which comes as a very late appendix to the history of language as a whole. As Ananda Coomaraswamy pointed out with reference to what he calls "that whole class of prophetic literature that includes the Bible, the Vedas, the Edda, the great epics, and in general the world's 'best books'": "Of these books many existed long before they were written down, many have never been written down, and others have been or will be lost."[9]

Countless altogether illiterate men have been masters of highly elaborate languages. "I am inclined to think that dialect the best which is spoken by the most illiterate in the islands . . . men with clear heads and wonderful memories, generally very poor and old, living in remote corners of remote islands, and speaking only Gaelic."[10] "The ability of oral tradition to transmit great masses of verse for hundreds of years is proved and admitted. . . . To this oral literature, as the French call it, education is no friend. Culture destroys it, sometimes with amazing rapidity. When a nation begins to read . . . what was once the possession of the folk as a whole becomes the heritage of the illiterate only, and soon, unless it is gathered up by the antiquary, vanishes altogether."[11] "If we have to single out the factor which

[8] Frithjof Schuon, *The Feathered Sun* (Bloomington, IN: World Wisdom, 1990), p. 67.

[9] A. K. Coomaraswamy, *The Bugbear of Literacy* (London: Perennial Books, 1979), p. 25.

[10] J. F. Campbell, *Popular Tales of the West Highlands* (Birlinn, 1994).

[11] G. L. Kittredge in his introduction to F. G. Childe's *English and Scottish Popular Ballads* (Hippocrene Books, 1989).

caused the decline of English village culture we should have to say it was literacy."[12] "In the New Hebrides the children are educated by listening and watching . . . without writing, memory is perfect, tradition exact. The growing child is taught all that is known. . . . Songs are a form of story-telling. . . . The lay-out and content in the thousand myths which every child learns (often word perfect, and one story may last for hours) are a whole library . . . the hearers are held in a web of spun words." They converse together "with that accuracy and pattern of beauty in words that we have lost. . . . The natives easily learn to write after white impact. They regard it as a curious and useless performance. They say: 'Cannot a man remember and speak?'"[13]

In addition to these quotations, all of which I have taken from Coomaraswamy, it may be remarked that among the pre-Islamic Arabs it was the custom of the nobles of Mecca to send their sons to be brought up among the Bedouins of the desert because these entirely illiterate nomads were known to speak a purer Arabic than their more "civilized" brethren of the town.

There is no doubt that, in general, "civilization" takes the edge off man's natural alertness and vigilance, qualities which are most necessary for the preservation of language. In particular, literacy lulls men into a sense of false security by giving them the impression that their everyday speech is no longer the sole treasury in which the treasure of language is safeguarded; and once the idea of two languages, one written and one spoken, has taken root, the spoken language is doomed to degenerate relatively fast and to drag down with it, eventually, also the written language—witness the new English translation of the Bible.

In the West of today, the degeneration of the spoken language has reached a point where, although a man will take more or less trouble to set down his thoughts in writing, pride of speech is something almost unknown. It is true that one is taught to avoid certain things in speaking, but this is for purely social reasons which have nothing to do with richness of sound or any other positive quality that language may have. And yet the way a man speaks remains a far more significant factor in his life than the way he writes, for it has an accumulative effect upon the soul which a little spasmodic penning can never have.

---

[12] W. G. Archer, *The Blue Grove*, preface (London: George Allen & Unwin, 1940).

[13] T. Harrison, *Savage Civilization* (1937), pp. 45, 344, 351, 353.

Needless to say, the purpose of these remarks is not to deny that the written alphabet has its uses. Language tends to degenerate in the natural course of events, even among the illiterate, and accidents such as exile or foreign domination can cause all sorts of things to be forgotten in a surprisingly short space of time. How much of the spiritual heritage of the Jews might have been lost, for example, but for written records? In any case, the manifest inspiration of some of the world's calligraphic arts suggests that when men began to record the spoken word in writing, they did so "by order of God," and not merely "by permission of God." It is not, after all, writing but printing that is responsible for having turned the world into the great rubbish-heap of books that it is today. None the less, writing cannot be said to confer any superiority on man, to say the very least, and it would no doubt even be true to say that it only became necessary, as the lesser of two evils, after a certain point of human degeneration had been reached.

Speech on the other hand was always considered to be one of the glories of man. In Judaism, as also in Islam, we find the doctrine that by Divine Revelation Adam was taught the true language, that is, the language in which the sound corresponded exactly to the sense. This conception of man's primordial speech as having been the most perfectly expressive or onomatopoeic of all languages is undoubtedly beyond the reach of any philological verification. None the less philology can give us a clear idea of the general linguistic tendencies of mankind, and in doing so it teaches us nothing which in any sense weighs against the traditional report. On the contrary, every language known to us is a debased form of some more ancient language, and the further we go back in time the more powerfully impressive language becomes. It also becomes more complex, so that the oldest known languages, those which are far older than history itself, are the most subtle and elaborate in their structure, calling for greater concentration and presence of mind in the speaker than do any of the later ones. The passage of time always tends to diminish the individual words both in form and in sonority, while grammar and syntax become more and more simplified.

It is true that although time tends to strip language of its quality, a language will always have, quantitatively speaking, the vocabulary that its people needs. A vast increase of material objects, for example, will mean a corresponding increase in the number of nouns. But whereas in modern languages the new words have to be artificially coined and added on from the outside, the most ancient known languages may be said to possess, in addition to the words in actual use, thousands of unused words which, if required, can be produced organically, as it were, in virtue of an almost unlimited capacity for word-forming which is inherent in the structure of the language. In this respect it is the modern languages which could be called "dead" or "moribund"; by comparison the more ancient languages, even if they be "dead" in the sense that they are no longer used, remain in themselves like intensely vital organisms.

This does not mean that the ancient languages—and those who spoke them—were lacking in the virtue of simplicity. True simplicity, far from being incompatible with complexity, even demands a certain complexity for its full realization. A distinction must be made between complexity, which implies a definite system or order, and complication which implies disorder and even confusion. A corresponding distinction must be made between simplicity and simplification.

The truly simple man is an intense unity: he is complete and whole-hearted, not divided against himself. To keep up this close-knit integration, the soul must readjust itself altogether to each new set of circumstances, which means that there must be a great flexibility in the different psychic elements: each must be prepared to fit perfectly with all the others, no matter what the mood. This closely woven synthesis, upon which the virtue of simplicity is based, is a complexity as distinct from a complication; and it has its counterpart in the complexity of the ancient languages to which the term "synthetic" is generally applied to distinguish them from modern "analytical" languages. It is only by an elaborate system of grammatical rules that the different parts of speech, analogous to the different elements in the soul, may be inflected so as to fit closely together, giving to each sentence something of the concentrated unity of a single word. The simplicity of the synthetic languages is in fact comparable to that of a great work of art—simplicity not necessarily of means but of total effect; and such no doubt, in an altogether superlative degree, was the simplicity of the primordial language and, we may add, of the men who spoke it. That at any rate is the conclusion to which all the available linguistic evidence points, and language is of such fundamental importance in the life of man, being so intimately bound up with the human soul of which it is the direct expression, that its testimony is of the highest psychological significance.

One of the legacies from the far past which has entered with exceptional fullness into the present, and which is therefore well qualified to serve as a "touchstone," is the Arabic language. Its destiny has been a strange one. When the Arabs first appear in history they are a race of poets, with a wide and varied range of metrical forms, almost their only prose being their everyday speech. They possessed a somewhat rudimentary script, which only a few of them could use, but in any case they preferred to pass down their poems by living word of mouth, and until the coming of Islam they were probably the most illiterate of all Semitic peoples. No doubt this explains, at least in part, why their language was so remarkably well preserved: although linguistic evidence shows it to be a falling away from an even more archaic, that is, an even more complex and more fully sonorous language, Arabic was still, in A.D. 600, more archaic in form and therefore nearer to "the language of Shem" than was the Hebrew spoken by Moses nearly two thousand years previously. It was Islam, or more particularly the need to record every syllable of the Koran with absolute precision, which imposed literacy on the seventh-century Arabs; but at the same time, the Koran imposed its own archaic language as a model, and since it was to be learned by heart and recited as much as possible, the detrimental effect of literacy was counteracted by the continual presence of Koranic Arabic upon men's tongues. A special science was quickly evolved for recording and preserving the exact pronunciation; and language-debasement was also checked by the sustained efforts of Moslems throughout the centuries to model their speech upon the speech of their Prophet. As a result, his language is still living today. Inevitably dialects have been formed from it in the course of time through leaving out syllables, merging two different sounds into one, and other simplifications, and these dialects, which vary from one Arab country to another, are normally used in conversation. But the slightest formality of occasion calls at once for a return to the undiminished majesty and sonority of classical Arabic, which is sometimes spontaneously reverted to in conversation also, when anyone feels he has something really important to say. On the other hand, those few who on principle refuse to speak the colloquial language at all are liable to find themselves in a dilemma: either they must abstain altogether from taking part in an "ordinary conversation" or else they must run the risk of producing an incongruous effect, like street urchins masquerading in royal robes. Idle chattering, that is, the quick expression of unweighed thoughts, must have been something comparatively unknown in the far past, for it is something that ancient languages do not lend themselves to; and if men thought less glibly, and took more trouble to compose the expression of their thoughts, they certainly took more trouble to utter them. Sanskrit tells the same story as Arabic: each, with its marvelous range and variety of consonantal sounds, leaves us no option but to conclude that in the far past man's organs of articulation and hearing were considerably finer and more delicate than they are today; and this is fully confirmed also by a study of ancient music, with all its rhythmic and melodic subtlety.[14]

If philology cannot reach the origins of language, it can none the less survey, in one unbroken sweep, thousands of years of linguistic history which means also, in a certain respect, thousands of years of the history of the human soul, a history that is one-sided, no doubt, but remarkably definite as far as it goes. In the light of this vista, which takes us far back into what is called "prehistory," we are forced to take note of a relentless trend; and this trend is itself simply one aspect of a more general tendency which, as Dewar remarks, most physicists, chemists, mathematicians, and astronomers are agreed upon, namely that "the universe is like a clock which is running down." So far religion and science stand together. But religion adds—as science cannot without going beyond the scope of its function—that there is a way of escape for individuals from the collective downstream drift, and that it is possible for some to resist it, and for some even to make upstream headway against it, and for a few to overcome it altogether by making their way, in this life even, back as far as the source itself.

* * *

It was easy for the ancients all over the world to believe in the sudden primordial establishment on earth of human perfection—a zenith from which there could be no rising but only falling away—because they saw that this first Divine intervention was continually repeated in lesser interventions. As regards our own forbears, the Old Testament is the story of a downward trend, as for example between the Fall and the Flood,[15] and then between the Flood and the Tower of

---

[14] See, for example, Alain Daniélou, *Introduction to the Study of Musical Scales* (Oriental Book Reprint Corporation, 1996).

[15] We might say also "between the Creation and the Fall," because this gradual deterioration is prefigured in the Earthly Paradise itself: there was a "time" when Eve was not yet distinct from Adam, another "time" when, although a separate being, she had not yet eaten of the forbidden fruit, and another "time" when she, but not yet Adam, had eaten of it.

Babel, a trend which is from time to time cut short, sometimes even by a re-establishment of relative perfection; and as soon as the grip of the Divine intervention relaxes its hold, the fatal trend reasserts itself once more, as if by a law of gravity.

It should be easier for us to see how the world goes than it was for our ancestors, for we have a wider view of history than they had, and history as a whole, in its fundamental aspects, tells the same story as that of the Old Testament and confirms its rhythm. The key events of the last three thousand years, the missions of Buddha,[16] Christ, and Muhammad, were sudden interventions: they did not follow smoothly in the wake of events which preceded them; they were in opposition to the general trend of events. In each case a small nucleus of humanity was snatched up and placed on a spiritual summit to act as an ideal and a guiding light for future generations. In view of such known historical events, it is not difficult to believe that the world should have received its first spirituality also—and in this particular case its first humanity—as something in the nature of a serene thunderbolt.

This "God-man" rhythm, a sudden rise followed by a gradual fall, the result of a combination of what is above time with what is subject to time, might be described in seasonal terms as a sudden spring racing into summer followed by a gradual autumn. How soon the autumn begins will depend on various factors. The great spring-summer of mankind as a whole, the Golden Age, is said to have lasted, according to some interpretations of the Hindu Purāṇas, for twenty-five thousand human years, and according to others for well over one and a half million. As regards the lesser cycles, such as those of the different religions, they are inevitably affected by their position in the great cycle. The initial spring-summer of one of the later religions, situated as it is in the autumn of the great cycle, is bound to be drawn relatively quickly towards its own autumn,[17] within which however there are the spring-summers of yet smaller cycles, for a great Saint sometimes

---

[16] Concerning the question of the differences between one religious perspective and another, for the moment let it be admitted that although there can be no true religion without the Divine Word, we cannot presume to limit the activities of the Word either in time or in space. Moreover we have been given a criterion for judging where and where not the seeds of religious truth have been sown, for "by their fruits ye shall know them."

[17] As regards England, for example, the spring-summer of Christianity began at the end of the sixth century, and perhaps it would not be far wrong to say—though clearly no one could presume to insist on this point—that the autumn had already set in by the time of the Norman Conquest.

has a mission of sudden redress which makes his appearance analogous, on a lesser scale, to that of the founder of the religion. To see this rhythm we must look at the backbone of history rather than at its surfaces, for although spirituality itself is by definition above time, the less direct effects of spirituality in time naturally tend to follow the temporal rhythm of gradual waxing and waning. It took Buddhism, Christianity, and Islam some time to spread out to their full extent over those portions of humanity for which Providence would seem to have intended them: the theocratic civilizations in question, with all their sciences and arts and crafts, clearly developed more gradually than the spirituality itself, though the "God-man" rhythm is always lying in ambush as it were, ready to rise to the surface at a moment's notice, for the more man is inspired in the true sense of the word, the more his activities will escape from the lower rhythm and the more they will conform to the higher one.

Art, for instance, in its highest aspects, is inextricably bound up with spirituality, though artistic inspiration by no means always comes at the very outset of a religion, for when spirituality in general is at its highest, men have less need of art than at any other time. In Christendom the decadent Greco-Roman style lingered on in some domains for three or four centuries before it was replaced by a genuinely Christian style; but the replacement was often more or less sudden.

To take a supreme example of art, the Jews had had no sacred architecture until Solomon built the Temple according to the plans which had been revealed to David. So sudden was the attainment of this architectural zenith that the builders had to be brought in from outside. Though this example is exceptional, being something more even than inspiration, namely direct revelation, inspiration none the less moves in a similar way. The earliest art that has come down to us is a striking example—sufficiently striking to force itself even upon those whose ideas it completely contradicts and who are "perplexed" by what would in fact be perplexing if it were otherwise.

> Undoubtedly the most perplexing aspect of the art phenomenon when it appears to us for the first time is the high degree of maturity shown in the earliest expressions. The sudden appearance of stylistically evolved works of art takes us completely by surprise, with a marvelous eruption of aesthetic values. . . . Even the examples which belong unquestionably to the earliest phase . . . are works of amazing artistic maturity.[18]

[18] Paolo Graziosi, *Palaeolithic Art* (London: Faber & Faber, 1960), pp. 23-24.

Many things are inexplicable unless we realize that there are two "currents" or "rhythms" at work in history instead of only one. Our ancestors were without any doubt aware of both, for everyone knows the surface current of gradual waxing and waning, and as to the sudden "up" and gradual "down" which are inevitable as regards all that is most qualitative in a civilization, did not Christians always look back to the early fathers with especial reverence[19] and above all, beyond these, to the Apostles themselves?

Similarly in Islam, whatever may have been achieved in lesser domains by later generations, Moslems have never had any difficulty—to say the least—in assenting with whole-hearted conviction to the saying of their Prophet: "The best of my people are my generation; then they that come immediately after them; then they that come immediately after those."

To take yet another example: "According to Buddhists there are three periods during which our capacity for understanding Buddhism grows less and less. These are counted from the death of Buddha: the first, which lasts for a thousand years, is called 'the period of true Buddhism'; the second, also of a thousand years, is called 'the period of imitation Buddhism'; the third, in which we are, we the men of the 'Last Days,' is the period of degeneration."[20]

The adherents of these three religions are not exceptional in their point of view. In fact, it would be true to say of all civilizations that history has record of, except the modern one, that they were pervaded by a general consciousness of imperfection, of falling far short of an ideal; and that ideal, which was kept fresh in men's intelligences by a chain of Saints across the centuries, had had its greatest profusion of flowering among the first representatives of the religion in question. Behind this summit, beyond the flats of intervening decadence—for of previous civilizations it was mostly no more than the decadent tail-ends that were known—there loomed the summit of the perfection of Primordial Man.

---

[19] St. Benedict spoke in advance with the voice of the whole of the Middle Ages when he said: "The conferences of the fathers and their institutes and their lives . . . what else are they but store-houses of the virtues of good-living and obedient monks? But to us, indolent, ill-living, and negligent, belong shame and confusion" (*The Rule of Saint Benedict* [London: S.P.C.K.], p. 106).

[20] Kanei Okamoto, Jodo bonze, quoted by E. Steinilder-Oberlin, *Les Sectes bouddhiques Japonaises* (Paris: G. Crès & Cie, 1930), p. 200.

According to the Jewish tradition, if Adam did not at first possess "the knowledge of good and evil," he surpassed even the angels in his knowledge of God; and although if we move to the Far East the manner of expression becomes very different, the truth that is expressed remains the same. Over two thousand years ago in China the Taoist sage Chuang Tzu said:

> The knowledge of the ancients was perfect. How perfect? At first they did not yet know that there were things (apart from Tao, the Way, which signifies the Eternal and Infinite). This is the most perfect knowledge; nothing can be added. Next, they knew that there were things, but did not yet make distinctions between them. Next they made distinctions between them but they did not yet pass judgments upon them. When judgments were passed, [the knowledge of] Tao was destroyed.[21]

Very different again outwardly, and yet essentially the same, is the message of an old Lithuanian song which has come down to us out of the shadows of prehistory. This song tells us how "the Moon married the Sun in the first spring," and then how the Moon "straying alone" caught sight of the Morning Star and fell in love with it, whereupon God, the Father of the Sun, cut the Moon in two.

The sun is universally the symbol of the Spirit, and sunlight symbolizes direct knowledge of spiritual truths, whereas the moon represents all that is human and in particular the mind, mental knowledge being, like moonlight, indirect and reflected. It is through the mind that "distinctions are made" and "judgments are passed."

"The Moon married to the Sun" is Primordial Man with his two natures, human and Divine; and just as the moon reflects the sun, so the human soul in all its faculties and virtues reflects the Divine Qualities. Thus the moon as a symbol of the human nature expresses the universal doctrine that man is "made in the image of God," and that he is "the representative of God on earth."

Creation means separation from God. The act of creating set in motion an outward, separative tendency to which all creatures as such are subject. But in the non-human creatures this tendency is arrested by lack of freedom. Being no more than remote and fragmentary reflections of the Creator they only reflect His Free Will in a very limited sense; and if they have less freedom than man for good, they

---

[21] Yu-Lan Fung's translation, p. 53.

have also less freedom to degenerate. For man the outward urge born of creation was perfectly balanced "in the first spring" by the inward magnetism of his higher nature.

The meeting point of the two natures, the summit of the soul which is also its center—for the Kingdom of Heaven is "within" as well as "above"—is what most religions name the Heart (written here with a capital to distinguish it from the center of the body); and the Heart is the throne of the Intellect in the sense in which *Intellectus* was used throughout the Middle Ages, that is, the "solar" faculty which perceives spiritual truths directly unlike the "lunar" faculties of reason, memory, and imagination, which are the differentiated reflections of the Intellect.

In virtue of "the marriage of the Moon and the Sun" the outbranching, separative "knowledge of good and evil" was completely subordinated to the inward-pointing, unitive Heart-knowledge which refers all creatures back to their Creator. "The cutting of the Moon in two" denotes the separation of Heart and mind, of Intellect and reason, and man's consequent loss of direct, unitive knowledge and his subjection to the dualism of indirect knowledge, the knowledge of good and evil.

It was mental independence, represented by "the Moon straying alone," which brought with it the possibility of purely profane impulses and actions. There was nothing spiritual in the Moon's forsaking the greater light for the lesser, just as there was nothing spiritual in the impulse which caused Pandora to open her box, or in that which caused the eating of the forbidden fruit; and the significance of this last act may be further understood in the light of the Zoroastrian religion according to which one stage in the corruption of man is marked by the enjoyment of food for its own sake and the failure to attribute its goodness to the Creator.

The Edenic state was in a sense above time, for there were no seasons and no death. Nor was there any religion, for the end to which religion is a means had not yet been lost, whereas the Golden Age, which begins immediately after the Fall, is by definition the age of religion, being named in Sanskrit *Krita-Yuga* because in it all men "performed perfectly" their religious duties. According to Hinduism the normal span of mortal life was then a thousand years, and this seems to be confirmed by Judaism. It is understandable however that Judaism and other still later religions do not dwell on the excellence of that age, for however good it may have been in itself, it none the less contained the seeds of ruin and had already been brought as it were into discredit by the Iron Age, the ultimate fruit of those seeds.

For the earlier religions the Golden Age stood for the supreme ideal of what was possible in earthly conditions after the Fall. But the nearer the cycle drew to its end, the more out of reach that ideal became. None the less, if we look at the extremely elliptical first chapters of Genesis, the Golden Age is there, not explicitly but in undeniable implication, personified by Adam after the Fall; and when we turn to the Genesis commentaries and to the Jewish apocryphal books we find Adam extolled not merely as being unique among men for having committed one sin only, but also as a great visionary: he is the Prophet who inaugurated religion upon earth; and at his death the Archangels descended from Heaven to bury him. We read moreover that in the times of Adam and Seth the corpses of the dead did not putrefy, and men were still born "in the image of God,"[22] whereas after Seth this was no longer the case, and the mountains, which had hitherto been fertile, became barren rock.

*   *   *

According to the Hindus, during the cycle of the four ages the downward trend is interrupted by eight sudden redresses, each brought about by the incarnation on earth of an aspect of the Divinity. The cycle is also inaugurated and closed by similar incarnations or "descents" (*Avatāras*) as they are called, which brings the number up to ten. The ninth was the Buddha who is called the *Mleccha Avatāra* (the Foreign Descent), for although he appeared as a Hindu, the destined scope of his mission lay outside the frontiers of Hinduism. The Brahmanic perspective could hardly fail to include this Divine

---

[22] See *Midrash Rabbah* on Genesis 4:26 (London: Soncino Press, 1939), Vol. 1, p. 196. In one sense—for a sacred text has always been held to be a synthesis of different meanings at different levels—the story of Adam, Cain, and Abel comprises the whole history of mankind: today the transgression of Cain is almost complete, the nomads having been almost altogether put out of existence by the town-dwellers (see René Guénon, *The Reign of Quantity and the Signs of the Times* [Ghent, NY: Sophia Perennis, 1995], chapter 21). From this point of view it may be said that a new allegory begins with the Adam-Seth narrative. But from another point of view, if Cain as it were recapitulates the Fall and personifies all the "worldly wisdom" which resulted from it, and if Abel stands for the loss of Eden, personifying the repentance of Adam and his expiation, Seth represents the relenting of God towards Adam and the establishment of the Golden Age.

intervention, though being naturally more or less limited to what concerns Hindus, it does not take into consideration the religions of the West; but the tenth descent, which has yet to take place, is for the whole world.

Kalki, the name of this last and tenth *Avatāra*, is represented as riding on a white horse, sword in hand, and some descriptions of him bear a marked resemblance to verses in the Apocalypse. The Kalki *Avatāra* is expected to put an end to the Dark Age, and to inaugurate a new cycle with a Golden Age.

This expectation, which all religions share, whatever name they may give to Kalki, has nothing in common with the modern belief in "progress." It is true that some of our contemporaries prefer to believe that it was human progress which eventually earned the first coming of Christ, and that still further progress will finally make the world fit for his second coming. But such ideas are altogether alien to mediaeval and ancient concepts. Far from holding that mankind had earned the Redemption, our ancestors believed that it was a pure Grace; and as to Christ's second coming, they believed that the signs of its imminence would be, not the virtues of an almost perfect world waiting for a final perfecting touch, but "wars," "rumors of wars," "earthquakes," "famines," and civil discords with "brother against brother," "father against son," "children against parents" and finally "the abomination of desolation." According to the sayings of Christ and the Prophets, which for our ancestors were fully confirmed by the rhythm of history, the Millennium was not something which would be led up to, but something which would be led down to, at least in so far as concerns the human collectivity taken as a whole. It was believed that a gradual decline, interrupted by certain redresses,[23] would lead to

---

[23] Is there anything in ancient belief from which we might conclude the probability or even the possibility of a redress between now and the end of the cycle? A part answer to this question may lie in the fact that when Christ said, in speaking of the signs which would precede his second coming, "And except those days should be shortened, there should be no flesh saved; but for the elect's sake those days shall be shortened" (Matthew 24:22), he was clearly not referring to the final "passing away" of "the first heaven and the first earth" in preparation for a "new heaven and a new earth" but to a preliminary partial destruction. The "days" in question would seem to be none other than what the Red Indians, in particular the Hopis, call Purification Day, which they consider to be imminent. As the word "purification" suggests, they expect the destruction to have also a positive aspect. Islam likewise has always looked forward to a short-lived spiritual regeneration with the coming of the Maḥdi, in the years immediately preceding the Antichrist; and in Christ's prophecy, the reason why

"great tribulation such as was not since the beginning of the world,"[24] and one may compare Christ's description of the signs which would mark the approach of his second coming with what other religions teach about the same event. The lowest ebb of humanity was to be marked by the reign of the Antichrist. Then the true Christ would appear, as suddenly "as the lightning cometh out of the East and shineth even unto the West."[25]

the days of destruction are to be shortened suggests that they will be followed by a kind of spiritual redress, if only a fleeting and a fragmentary one.

[24] Matthew 24:21.

[25] Matthew 24:27.

5 THE THEORY OF EVOLUTION

Titus Burckhardt

If the ancient cosmogonies seem childish when one takes their symbolism literally—and this means not understanding them—modern
theories about the origin of the world are frankly absurd. They are so,
not so much in their mathematical formulations, but because of the
total unawareness with which their authors set themselves up as sovereign witnesses of cosmic becoming, while at the same time claiming
that the human mind itself is a product of this becoming. What
connection is there between that primordial nebula—that vortex of
matter whence they wish to derive earth, life, and man—and this little
mental mirror that loses itself in conjectures (since for the scientists
intelligence amounts to no more than this) and yet feels so sure of
discovering the logic of things within itself? How can the effect make
judgments regarding its own cause? And if there exist constant laws of
nature—those of causality, number, space, and time—and something
which, within ourselves, has the right to say "this is true and this is
false," where is the guarantee of truth, either in the object or in the
subject? Is the nature of our mind merely a little foam on the waves
of the cosmic ocean, or is there to be found deep within it a timeless
witness of reality?

Some protagonists of the theories in question will perhaps say
that they are concerned only with the physical and objective domain,
without seeking to prejudge the domain of the subjective. They can
perhaps cite Descartes, who defined spirit and matter as two realities,
coordinated by Providence, but separated in fact. In point of fact, this
division of reality into watertight compartments served to prepare
people's minds to leave aside everything that is not of the physical
order, as if man were not himself proof of the complexity of the real.

The man of antiquity, who pictured the earth as an island surrounded by the primordial ocean and covered by the dome of heaven,
and the medieval man, who saw the heavens as concentric spheres
extending from the earth (viewed as the center) to the limitless
sphere of the Divine Spirit, were no doubt mistaken regarding the
true disposition and proportions of the sensible universe. On the
other hand, they were fully conscious of the fact—infinitely more
important—that this corporeal world is not the whole of reality, and

that it is as if surrounded and pervaded by a reality, both greater and more subtle, that in its turn is contained in the Spirit; and they knew, indirectly or directly, that the world in all its extension disappears in the face of the Infinite.

Modern man knows that the earth is only a ball suspended in a bottomless abyss and carried along in a dizzy and complex movement, and that this movement is governed by other celestial bodies incomparably larger than this earth and situated at immense distances from it. He knows that the earth on which he lives is but a grain in comparison with the sun, which itself is but a grain amidst other incandescent stars, and that all is in motion. An irregularity in this assemblage of sidereal movements, an interference from a star foreign to our planetary system, a deviation of the sun's trajectory, or any other cosmic accident, would suffice to make the earth unsteady in its rotation, to trouble the course of the seasons, to change the atmosphere, and to destroy mankind. Modern man also knows that the smallest atom contains forces which, if unleashed, could involve the earth in an almost instantaneous conflagration. All of this, from the "infinitely small" to the "infinitely great," presents itself, from the point of view of modern science, as a mechanism of unimaginable complexity, the functioning of which is only due to blind forces.

In spite of this, the man of our time lives and acts as if the normal and habitual operation of the rhythms of nature were something that was guaranteed to him. In actual practice, he thinks neither of the abysses of the stellar world nor of the terrible forces latent in every particle of matter. He sees the sky above him like any child sees it, with its sun and its stars, but the remembrance of the astronomical theories prevents him from recognizing divine signs in them. The sky for him is no longer the natural expression of the Spirit that enfolds and illuminates the world. Scientific knowledge has substituted itself for this "naïve" and yet profound vision, not as a new consciousness of a vaster cosmic order, an order of which man forms part, but as an estrangement, as an irremediable disarray before abysses that no longer have any common measure with him. For nothing now reminds him that in reality this whole universe is contained within himself, not of course in his individual being, but in the spirit or intellect that is within him and that is both greater than himself and the whole phenomenal universe.

*   *   *

The least phenomenon participates in several continuities or cosmic dimensions incommensurable in relation to each other; thus, ice is water as regards its substance—and in this respect it is indistinguishable from liquid water or water vapor—but as regards its state it belongs to the class of solid bodies. Similarly, when a thing is constituted by diverse elements, it participates in their natures while being different from them. Cinnabar, for example, is a synthesis of sulfur and mercury; it is thus in one sense the sum of these two elements, but at the same time it possesses qualities that are not to be found in either of these two substances. Quantities can be added to one another, but a quality is never merely the sum of other qualities. By mixing the colors blue and yellow, green is obtained; this third color is thus a synthesis of the other two, but it is not the product of a simple addition, for it represents at the same time a chromatic quality that is new and unique in itself.

There is here something like a "discontinuous continuity," which is even more marked in the biological order, where the qualitative unity of an organism is plainly distinguishable from its material composition. The bird that is born from the egg is made from the same elements as the egg, but it is not the egg. Likewise, the butterfly that emerges from a chrysalis is neither that chrysalis nor the caterpillar that produced it. A kinship exists between these various organisms, a genetic continuity, but they also display a qualitative discontinuity, since between the caterpillar and the butterfly there is something like a rupture of level.

At every point in the cosmic web there is thus a warp and a woof that intersect one another, and this is indicated by the traditional symbolism of weaving, according to which the threads of the warp, which hang vertically on the primitive loom, represent the permanent essences of things—and thus also the essential qualities and forms— while the woof, which binds horizontally the threads of the warp, and at the same time covers them with its alternating waves, corresponds to the substantial or "material" continuity of the world.[1]

The same law is expressed by classical hylomorphism, which distinguishes the "form" of a thing or being—the seal of its essential unity—from its "matter," namely the plastic substance which receives this seal and furnishes it with a concrete and limited existence. No modern theory has ever been able to replace this ancient theory, for

[1] René Guénon, *The Symbolism of the Cross* (Ghent, NY: Sophia Perennis, 1996), chapter 14, "The Symbolism of Weaving."

the fact of reducing the whole plenitude of the real to one or other of its "dimensions" hardly amounts to an explanation of it. Modern science is ignorant above all of what the Ancients designated by the term "form," precisely because it is here a question of a non-quantitative aspect of things, and this ignorance is not unconnected with the fact that modern science sees no criterion in the beauty or ugliness of a phenomenon: the beauty of a thing is the sign of its internal unity, its conformity with an indivisible essence, and thus with a reality that will not let itself be counted or measured.

It is necessary to point out here that the notion of "form" necessarily includes a twofold meaning: on the one hand it means the delimitation of a thing, and this is its most usual meaning; in this connection, form is situated on the side of matter or, in a more general sense, on the side of plastic substance, which limits and separates realities.[2] On the other hand, "form" understood in the sense given to it by the Greek philosophers and following them the Scholastics, is the aggregate of qualities pertaining to a being or a thing, and thus the expression or the trace of its immutable essence.

The individual world is the "formal" world because it is the domain of those realities that are constituted by the conjunction of a "form" and a "matter," whether subtle or corporeal. It is only in connection with a "matter," a plastic substance, that "form" plays the role of a principle of individuation; in itself, in its ontological basis, it is not an individual reality but an archetype, and as such beyond limitations and change. Thus a species is an archetype, and if it is only manifested by the individuals that belong to it, it is nevertheless just as real, and even incomparably more real, than they. As for the rationalist objection that tries to prove the absurdity of the doctrine of archetypes by arguing that a multiplication of mental notions would imply a corresponding multiplication of archetypes—leading to the idea of the idea of the idea, and so on—it quite misses the point, since multiplicity can in nowise be transposed onto the level of the archetypal roots. The latter are distinguished in a principial way, within Being and by virtue of Being; in this connection, Being can be envisaged as a unique and homogeneous crystal potentially containing all possible crystalline

---

[2] In Hindu parlance, the distinction *nāma-rupa*, "name and form," is related to this aspect of the notion under study, "name" here standing for the essence of a being or thing, and "form" for its limited and outward existence.

forms.[3] Multiplicity and quantity thus only exist at the level of the "material" reflections of the archetypes.

From what has just been said, it follows that a species is in itself an immutable "form"; it cannot evolve and be transformed into another species, although it may include variants, which are diverse "projections" of a unique essential form, from which they can never be detached, any more than the branches of a tree can be detached from the trunk.

It has been justly said[4] that the whole thesis of the evolution of species, inaugurated by Darwin, is founded on a confusion between species and simple variation. Its advocates put forward as the "bud" or the beginning of a new species what in reality is no more than a variant within the framework of a determinate specific type. This false assimilation is, however, not enough to fill the numberless gaps that occur in the paleontological succession of species; not only are related species separated by profound gaps, but there do not even exist any forms that would indicate any possible connection between different orders such as fish, reptiles, birds, and mammals. One can doubtless find some fishes that use their fins to crawl onto a bank, but one will seek in vain in these fins for the slightest beginning of that articulation which would render possible the formation of an arm or a paw. Likewise, if there are certain resemblances between reptiles and birds, their respective skeletons are nonetheless of a fundamentally different structure. Thus, for example, the very complex articulation in the jaws of a bird, and the related organization of its hearing apparatus, pertain to an entirely different plan from the one found in reptiles; it is difficult to conceive how one might have developed from the other.[5] As for the famous fossil bird *Archaeopteryx*, it is fairly and squarely a bird, despite the claws at the end of its wings, its teeth, and its long tail.[6]

In order to explain the absence of intermediate forms, the partisans of transformism have sometimes argued that these forms must have disappeared because of their very imperfection and precarious-

---

[3] It is self-evident that all the images that one can offer of the non-separative distinction of the possibilities contained in Being must remain imperfect and paradoxical.

[4] Douglas Dewar, *The Transformist Illusion* (Murfreesboro, Tennessee: Dehoff Publications, 1957) [Editors' Note: reprinted by Sophia Perennis, Ghent, NY, 1995]. See also Louis Bounoure, *Déterminisme et Finalité* (Collection Philosophie, Paris: Flammarion).

[5] Dewar, *The Transformist Illusion.*

[6] Ibid.

ness; but this argument is plainly in contradiction with the principle of selection that is supposed to be the operative factor in the evolution of species: the trial forms should be incomparably more numerous than the ancestors having already acquired a definitive form. Besides, if the evolution of species represents, as is declared, a gradual and continual process, all the real links in the chain—therefore all those that are destined to be followed—will be both endpoints and intermediaries, in which case it is difficult to see why the ones would be much more precarious than the others.[7]

The more conscientious among modern biologists either reject the transformist theory, or else maintain it as a "working hypothesis," being unable to conceive any genesis of species that would not be situated on the "horizontal line" of a purely physical and temporal becoming. For Jean Rostand,

> the world postulated by transformism is a fairy-like world, phantas-magoric, surrealistic. The chief point, to which one always returns, is that we have never been present, even in a small way, at *one* authentic phenomenon of evolution . . . we keep the impression that nature today has nothing to offer that might be capable of reducing our embarrassment before the veritably organic metamorphoses implied in the transformist thesis. We keep the impression that, in the matter of the genesis of species as in that of the genesis of life, the forces that constructed nature are now absent from nature.[8]

Even so, this biologist sticks to the transformist theory:

> I firmly believe—because I see no means of doing otherwise—that mammals have come from lizards, and lizards from fish; but when I declare and when I think such a thing, I try not to avoid seeing its indigestible enormity and I prefer to leave vague the origin of these

---

[7] Teilhard de Chardin (*The Human Phenomenon,* p. 129) writes on this subject: "Nothing is by nature so delicate and fugitive as a beginning. As long as a zoological group is young, its characteristics remain undecided. Its dimensions are weak. Relatively few individuals compose it, and these are rapidly changing. Both in space and duration, the peduncle (or the bud, which comes to the same thing) of a living branch corresponds to a minimum of differentiation, expansion, and resistance. How then is time going to act on this weak zone? Inevitably by destroying it in its vestiges." This reasoning, which abusively exploits the purely external and conventional analogy between a genealogical "tree" and a real plant, is an example of the "imaginative abstraction" that characterizes this author's thought.

[8] *Le Figaro Littéraire,* April 20, 1957.

scandalous metamorphoses rather than add to their improbability that of a ludicrous interpretation.[9]

All that paleontology proves to us is that the various animal forms, such as are shown by fossils preserved in successive earthly layers, made their appearance in a vaguely ascending order, going from relatively undifferentiated organisms—but not simple ones[10]—to ever more complex forms, without this ascension representing, however, an unequivocal and continuous line. It seems to move in jumps; in other words, whole categories of animals appear all at once, without real predecessors. What does this order mean? Simply that, on the material plane, the simple or relatively undifferentiated always precedes the complex and differentiated. All "matter" is like a mirror that reflects the activity of the essences, while also inverting it; this is why the seed comes before the tree and the bud before the flower, whereas in the principial order the perfect "forms" pre-exist. The successive appearance of animal forms according to an ascending hierarchy therefore in nowise proves their continual and cumulative genesis.[11]

On the contrary, what links the various animal forms to one another is something like a common model, which reveals itself more or less through their structures and which is more apparent in the case of animals endowed with superior consciousness such as birds and mammals. This model is expressed especially in the symmetrical disposition of the body, in the number of extremities and sensory organs, and also in the general form of the chief internal organs. It might be suggested that the design and number of certain organs, and especially those of sensation, simply correspond to the terrestrial surroundings; but this argument is reversible, because those surroundings

---

[9] Ibid.

[10] The electron microscope has revealed the surprising complexity of the functions at work within a unicellular being.

[11] The most commonly mentioned example in favor of the transformist thesis is the hypothetical genealogy of the *Equidae*. Charles Depéret criticizes it as follows: "Geological observation establishes in a formal manner that no gradual passage took place between these genera; the last *Palaeotherium* had for long been extinct, without having transformed itself, when the first *Architherium* made its appearance, and the latter disappeared in its turn, without modification, before being suddenly replaced by the invasion of the *Hipparion*" (*Les Transformations du Monde animal*, p. 107). To this it can be added that the supposed primitive forms of the horse are hardly to be observed in equine embryology, though the development of the embryo is commonly looked on as a recapitulation of the genesis of the species.

are precisely what the sensory organs grasp and delimit. In fact, the model underlying all animal forms establishes the analogy between the microcosm and the macrocosm. Against the background of this common cosmic pattern the differences between species and the gaps that separate them are all the more marked.

Instead of "missing links," which the partisans of transformism seek in vain, nature offers us, as if in irony, a large variety of animal forms which, without transgressing the pre-established framework of a species, imitate the appearance and habits of a species or order foreign to them. Thus, for example, whales are mammals, but they assume the appearance and behavior of fishes; hummingbirds have the appearance, iridescent colors, flight, and mode of feeding of butterflies; the armadillo is covered with scales like a reptile, although it is a mammal; and so on. Most of these animals with imitative forms are higher species that have taken on the forms of relatively lower species, a fact which *a priori* excludes an interpretation of them as intermediary links in an evolution. As for their interpretation as forms of adaptation to a given set of surroundings, this seems more than dubious, for what could be, for example, the intermediate forms between some land mammal or other and the dolphin?[12] Among these "imitative" forms, which constitute so many extreme cases, we must also include the fossil bird *Archaeopteryx* mentioned above.

Since each animal order represents an archetype that includes the archetypes of the corresponding species, one might well ask oneself whether the existence of "imitative" animal forms does not contradict the immutability of the essential forms; but this is not the case, for the existence of these forms demonstrates, on the contrary, that very immutability by a logical exhausting of all the possibilities inherent in a given type or essential form. It is as if nature, after bringing forth fishes, reptiles, birds, and mammals, with their distinctive characteristics, wished still to show that she was able to produce an animal like the dolphin which, while being a true mammal, at the same time possesses almost all the faculties of a fish, or a creature like the tortoise, which possesses a skeleton covered by flesh, yet at the same time is enclosed in an exterior carapace after the fashion of certain mol-

---

[12] On the subject of the hypothetical transformation of a land animal into the whale, Douglas Dewar writes: "I have often challenged transformists to describe plausible ancestors situated in the intermediate phases of this supposed transformation" (*What the Animal Fossils Tell us*, Trans. Vict. Instit, vol. LXXIV).

lusks.[13] Thus does nature manifest her protean power, her inexhaustible capacity for generation, while remaining faithful to the essential forms, which in fact are never blurred.

Each essential form—or each archetype—includes after its fashion all the others, but without confusion; it is like a mirror reflecting other mirrors, which reflect it in their turn.[14] In its deepest meaning the mutual reflection of types is an expression of the metaphysical homogeneity of Existence, or of the unity of Being.

Some biologists, when confronted with the discontinuity in the paleontological succession of species, postulate an evolution by leaps and, in order to make this theory plausible, refer to the sudden mutations observed in some living species. But these mutations never exceed the limits of an anomaly or a decadence, as for example the sudden appearance of albinos, or of dwarfs or giants; even when these characteristics become hereditary, they remain as anomalies and never constitute new specific forms.[15] For this to happen, it would be necessary for the vital substance of an existing species to serve as the "plastic material" for a newly manifested specific form; in practice, this means that one or several females of this existing species would suddenly bear offspring of a new species. Now, as the hermetist Richard the Englishman writes:

> Nothing can be produced from a thing that is not contained in it; for this reason, every species, every genus, and every natural order develops within the limits proper to it and bears fruits according to its own kind and not according to an essentially different order; everything that receives a seed must be of the same seed.[16]

Fundamentally, the evolutionist thesis is an attempt to replace, not simply the "miracle of creation," but the cosmogonic process—largely suprasensory—of which the Biblical narrative is a Scriptural symbol; evolutionism, by absurdly making the greater derive from the lesser, is the opposite of this process, or this "emanation." (This

---

[13] It is significant that the tortoise, whose skeleton seems to indicate an extravagant adaptation to an animal "armored" state, appears all at once among the fossils, without evolution. Similarly, the spider appears simultaneously with its prey and with its faculty of weaving already developed.

[14] This is the image used by the Sufi 'Abd al-Karīm al-Jīlī in his book *al-Insān al-Kāmil*, chapter on "Divine Unicity."

[15] Bounoure, *Déterminisme et Finalité.*

[16] Quoted in the *Golden Treatise, Museum Hermeticum* (Frankfurt, 1678).

term has nothing to do with the emanationist heresy, since the transcendence and immutability of the ontological principle are here in no wise called into question.) In a word, evolutionism results from an incapacity—peculiar to modern science—to conceive "dimensions" of reality other than purely physical ones; to understand the "vertical" genesis of species, it is worth recalling what René Guénon said about the progressive solidification of the corporeal state through the various terrestrial ages.[17] This solidification must obviously not be taken to imply that the stones of the earliest ages were soft, for this would be tantamount to saying that certain physical qualities—and in particular hardness and density—were then wanting; what has hardened and become fixed with time is the corporeal state taken as a whole, with the result that it no longer receives directly the imprint of subtle forms. Assuredly, it cannot become detached from the subtle state, which is its ontological root and which dominates it entirely, but the relationship between the two states of existence no longer has the creative character that it possessed at the origin; it is as when a fruit, having reached maturity, becomes surrounded by an ever harder husk and ceases to absorb the sap of the tree. In a cyclic phase in which corporeal existence had not yet reached this degree of solidification, a new specific form could manifest itself directly from the starting-point of its first "condensation" in the subtle or animic state;[18] this means that the different types of animals pre-existed at the level immediately superior to the corporeal world as non-spatial forms, but nevertheless clothed in a certain "matter," namely that of the subtle world. From there these forms "descended" into the corporeal state each time the latter was ready to receive them; this "descent" had the nature of a sudden coagulation and hence also the nature of a limitation and fragmentation of the original animic form. Indo-Tibetan cosmology describes this descent—which is also a fall—in the case of human beings under the form of the mythological combat of the *devas* and

---

[17] René Guénon, *The Reign of Quantity and the Signs of the Times* (Ghent, NY: Sophia Perennis, 1995).

[18] Concerning the creation of species in a subtle "proto-matter"—in which they still preserve an androgynous form, comparable to a sphere—and their subsequent exteriorization by "crystallization" in sensible matter (which is heavy, opaque, and mortal), see Frithjof Schuon, *Light on the Ancient Worlds* (Bloomington, IN: World Wisdom, 1984, 2005), chapter 2, "In the Wake of the Fall," and *Dimensions of Islam* (London: George Allen & Unwin, 1969), chapter 5, "The Five Divine Presences." [Editors' Note: this chapter also appears in Schuon's *Form and Substance in the Religions* (Bloomington, IN: World Wisdom, 2002).]

asūras: the *devas* having created man with a body that was fluid, protean, and diaphanous—in other words, in a subtle form—the *asūras* try to destroy it by a progressive petrification; it becomes opaque, gets fixed, and its skeleton, affected by the petrification, is immobilized. Thereupon the *devas*, turning evil into good, create joints, after having fractured the bones, and they also open the pathways of the senses, by piercing the skull, which threatens to imprison the seat of the mind. In this way the process of solidification stops before it reaches its extreme limit, and certain organs in man, such as the eye, still retain something of the nature of the non-corporeal states.[19]

In this story, the pictorial description of the subtle world must not be misunderstood. However, it is certain that the process of materialization, from the supra-sensory to the sensory, had to be reflected within the material or corporeal state itself, so that one can say without risk of error, that the first generations of a new species did not leave a mark in the great book of earthly layers; it is therefore vain to seek in sensible matter the ancestors of a species, and especially that of man.

Since the transformist theory is not founded on any real proof, its corollary and conclusion, namely the theory of the infra-human origin of man, remains suspended in the void. The facts adduced in favor of this thesis are restricted to a few groups of skeletons of disparate chronology: it happens that some skeletal types deemed to be more "evolved," such as "Steinheim man," precede others, of a seemingly more primitive character, such as "Neanderthal man," even though the latter was doubtless not so apelike as tendentious reconstructions would have us believe.[20]

If, instead of always putting the questions: at what point does humankind begin, and what is the degree of evolution of such and such a type regarded as being pre-human, we were to ask ourselves: how far does the monkey go, things might well appear in a very different light, for a fragment from a skeleton, even one related to that of man, is hardly enough to establish the presence of that which constitutes man, namely reason, whereas it is possible to conceive of a great variety of anthropoid apes whose anatomies are more or less close to that of man.

---

[19] See Krasinsky, *Tibetische Medizin-Philosophie.*

[20] In general, this domain of science has been almost smothered by tendentious theories, hoaxes, and imprudently popularized discoveries. See Dewar, *The Transformist Illusion.*

However paradoxical this may seem, the anatomical resemblance between man and the anthropoid apes is explainable precisely by the difference—not gradual, but essential—that separates man from all other animals. Since the anthropoid form is able to exist without that "central" element that characterizes man—this "central" element manifesting itself anatomically by his vertical position, amongst other things—the anthropoid form must exist; in other words, there cannot but be found, at the purely animal level, a form that realizes in its own way—that is to say, according to the laws of its own level—the very plan of the human anatomy; the ape is a prefiguration of man, not in the sense of an evolutive phase, but by virtue of the law that decrees that at every level of existence analogous possibilities will be found.

A further question arises in the case of the fossils attributed to primitive men: did some of these skeletons belong to men we can look upon as being ancestors of men presently alive, or do they bear witness to a few groups that survived the cataclysm at the end of a terrestrial age, only to disappear in their turn before the beginning of our present humanity? Instead of primitive men, it might well be a case of degenerate men, who may or may not have existed alongside our real ancestors. We know that the folklore of most peoples speaks of giants or dwarfs who lived long ago, in remote countries; now, among these skeletons, several cases of gigantism are to be found.[21]

Finally, let it be recalled once more that the bodies of the most ancient men did not necessarily leave solid traces, either because their bodies were not yet at that point materialized or "solidified," or because the spiritual state of these men, along with the cosmic conditions of their time, rendered possible a resorption of the physical body into the subtle "body" at the moment of death.[22]

We must now say a few words about a thesis, much in vogue today, which claims to be something like a spiritual integration of paleontology, but which in reality is nothing but a purely mental sublimation of the crudest materialism, with all the prejudices this includes, from belief in the indefinite progress of humanity to a leveling and totalitarian collectivism, without forgetting the cult of the machine that is at the center of all this; it will be apparent that we are here referring to Teilhardian evolutionism.[23] According to Teilhard

---

[21] Like the Meganthrope of Java and the *Gigantopithecus* of China.

[22] In some very exceptional cases—such as Enoch, Elijah, and the Virgin Mary— such a resorption took place even in the present terrestrial age.

[23] Teilhard's materialism is revealed in all its crudity, and all its perversity, when this

de Chardin, who is not given to worrying over the gaps inherent in the evolutionist system and largely relies on the climate created by the premature popularization of the transformist thesis, man himself represents only an intermediate state in an evolution that starts with unicellular organisms and ends in a sort of global cosmic entity, united to God. The craze for trying to bring everything back to a single unequivocal and uninterrupted genetic line here exceeds the material plane and launches out wildly into an irresponsible and avid "mentalization" characterized by an abstraction clothed in artificial images which their author ends up by taking literally, as if he were dealing with concrete realities. We have already mentioned the imaginary genealogical tree of species, whose supposed unity is no more than a snare, being composed of the hypothetical conjunction of many disjointed elements. Teilhard amplifies this notion to his heart's content, in a manner that is purely graphic, by completing its branches—or "scales," as he likes to call them—and by constructing a pinnacle in the direction of which humankind is supposed to be situated. By a similar sliding of thought from the abstract to the concrete, from the metaphorical to the supposedly real, he agglutinates, in one and the same pseudo-scientific outburst, the most diverse realities, such as mechanical laws, vital forces, psychic elements, and spiritual entities. Let us quote a characteristic passage:

> What explains the biological revolution caused by the appearance of Man, is an explosion of consciousness; and what, in its turn, explains this explosion of consciousness, is simply the passage of a privileged

---

philosopher advocates the use of surgical means to accelerate "collective cerebralization" in his *Man's Place in Nature* (Harper & Row, New York, 1966). Let us also quote the further highly revealing words of the same author: "It is finally on the dazzling notion of Progress and on faith in Progress that today's divided humanity can be reformed.... Act 1 is over! We have access to the heart of the atom! Now come the next steps, such as the vitalization of matter by the building of supermolecules, the modeling of the human organism by hormones, the control of heredity and of the sexes by the play of genes and chromosomes, the readjustment and liberation by direct action of the springs laid bare by psychoanalysis, the awakening and taking hold of the still dormant intellectual and emotional forces in the human mass!" (*Planète III*, 1944), p. 30. Quite naturally, Teilhard proposes the fashioning of mankind by a universal scientific government—in short, all that is needed for the reign of the Antichrist. [Editors' Note: For a traditional critique of the views of the controversial Catholic priest and paleontologist, readers are referred to *Teilhardism and the New Religion: A Thorough Analysis of the Teachings of Pierre Teilhard de Chardin* (Rockford: Tan Books, 1988), by Wolfgang Smith, a respected scientist and mathematician who is also fully conversant with the Christian scholastic tradition.]

radius of "corpusculization," in other words, of a zoological phylum, across the surface, hitherto impermeable, separating the zone of direct Psychism from that of reflective Psychism. Having reached, following this particular radius, a critical point of arrangement (or, as we say here, of enrolment), Life became hypercentered on itself, to the point of becoming capable of foresight and invention.[24]

Thus, "corpusculization" (which is a physical process) would have as its effect that a "zoological phylum" (which is no more than a figure) should pass across the surface (purely hypothetical) separating two psychic zones. . . . But we must not be surprised at the absence of *distinguos* in Teilhard's thinking since, according to his own theory, the mind is but a metamorphosis of matter!

Without stopping to discuss the strange theology of this author, for whom God himself evolves along with matter, and without daring to define what he thinks of the prophets and sages of antiquity and other "underdeveloped" beings of this kind, we will say the following: if man, in respect of both his physical nature and his spiritual nature, were really nothing but a phase of an evolution going from the amoeba to the superman, how could he know objectively where he stands in all this? Let us suppose that this alleged evolution forms a curve, or a spiral. The man who is but a fragment thereof—and let it not be forgotten that a "fragment" of a movement is no more than a phase of that movement—can that man step out of it and say to himself: I am a fragment of a spiral which is developing in such and such a way? Now it is certain—and moreover Teilhard de Chardin himself recognizes this—that man is able to judge of his own state. Indeed he knows his own rank amongst the other earthly creatures, and he is even the only one to know objectively both himself and the world. Far from being a mere phase in an indefinite evolution, man essentially represents a central possibility, and one that is thus unique, irreplaceable, and definitive. If the human species had to evolve towards another more perfect and more "spiritual" form, man would not already now be the "point of intersection" of the Divine Spirit with the earthly plane; he would neither be capable of salvation, nor able intellectually to surmount the flux of becoming. To express these thoughts according to the perspective of the Gospels: would God have become man if the form of man were not virtually "god on earth," in other words,

---

[24] *Man's Place in Nature*, pp. 62-63.

qualitatively central as well as definitive with regard to his own cosmic level?

As a symptom of our time, Teilhardism is comparable to one of those cracks that are due to the very solidification of the mental carapace,[25] and that do not open upward, toward the heaven of real and transcendent unity, but downward toward the realm of lower psychism. Weary of its own discontinuous vision of the world, the materialist mind lets itself slide toward a false continuity or unity, toward a pseudo-spiritual intoxication, of which this falsified and materialized faith—or this sublimated materialism—that we have just described marks a phase of particular significance.

[25] René Guénon, *The Reign of Quantity and the Signs of the Times*, chapter 15, "The Illusion of Ordinary Life."

6 MODERN SCIENCE AND THE DEHUMANIZATION OF MAN*

Philip Sherrard

The denial that man possesses a capacity for metaphysical or spiritual knowledge typifies much of what passes for philosophy in our times. Yet it is no new phenomenon. To go no further and, as we shall see, one can go considerably further—it is already fully explicit in the thought of empirico-rationalist philosophers like Sir William Hamilton in the first half of the nineteenth century. Hamilton taught that all metaphysics must be rejected as illegitimate because through its very structure the human mind can know only what belongs to the physical and finite world of time and space. Human knowledge can refer only to this world. It must be empirical. It cannot be metaphysical. Even if there are realities of an order that transcends the world of time and space, the human mind cannot know or experience them because it cannot reach beyond the world of time and space. Man has no faculty or organ of intelligence by means of which he can perceive the realities of such an order. Since Hamilton expounded it, this kind of argument has become commonplace. It forms the basis of what is known as scientific or rationalist humanism. What is not so often emphasized or even pointed out is that the type of outlook—of epistemological outlook—which it expresses not only contradicts the claims of the religious intelligence to the effect that metaphysical realities both exist and can be apprehended. It also directly fosters the dehumanization of man and of the forms of the society which he builds in its image. I will attempt to clarify.

By the time Hamilton was writing in the first half of the nineteenth century our society was already well enmeshed in that process by means of which the strenuous activity of hard-headed industrialists and bankers, possessed by a single-minded devotion to making money and to extending their power through the production and use of complicated machines and other devices, was turning England's green and pleasant land into the black country of Charles Dickens. These men were crude, unbred, self-assertive people, pushers to the top, greedy

---

*Editors' Note: A revised version of this article is to be found in Philip Sherrard's book *The Rape of Man and Nature* (Ipswich: Golgonooza Press, 1987), pp. 63-89.

and ambitious, excellent speculators and organizers, wizards of the factory and of the counting-house, with little or no time or patience for normal human needs or such old-fashioned pursuits as the chase, idleness, or the bed. Their great achievement in the nineteenth century was to standardize the factory slum as the normal type of urban dwelling and to extend the area of human and natural desolation at a rate never before reached. There is no need to dwell on the consequences of their success—on the mile after mile of workers' dwellings placed back to back where people dragged out their existence in conditions of foulness and filth never known in the serf's cottage of the Middle Ages; on the deprivation of the most elementary facilities of sunlight and fresh air, and the cutting of all links between the city and country surrounding it; on the systematic defacement of the countryside itself, the spread of disease, the spread of noise, the cultivation of a taste for ugliness of the most vulgar kind, the wholesale disparagement of life's most basic needs. We who live in the throes of what we call the ecological crisis—which is primarily a crisis about man and not about his environment—are only too familiar with these consequences; and in any case to lament this growing contamination has been a persistent and seemingly ineffective pursuit at least since the time of the Romantic poets. All that need be said here is that as a result of the activity of these people and of their twentieth-century successors a new type of world has come into existence, the world of the modern urban industrial state.

In this world—the world of the artificial environment, of the sophisticated manipulation of machines and techniques—the human element is gradually being eliminated. What this world represents is a new type of order, a new inorganic order, one not created by God but invented by man—one that is, in fact, precisely an externalization of man's desire to make his own world without God. Briefly, one can say that in terms of western civilization what this new order has replaced is the type of society of the mediaeval world. The society of the mediaeval world was an organic integrated society. It was a kind of sacred order established by God in which everything, not only man and man's artifacts, but every living form of plant, bird, or animal, the sun, moon, and stars, the waters and the mountains, were seen as signs of things sacred (*signa rei sacrae*), expressions of a divine cosmology, symbols linking the visible and the invisible, earth and heaven. It was a society dedicated to ends which were ultimately supra-terrestrial and non-temporal, beyond the limits of this world. Indeed, a great deal of effort in the mediaeval world went into preserving and fostering and nourishing the sense of realities which we now call supernatural. Throughout the length and breadth of this world, visible images of these realities were set up and venerated, in icons, crosses, churches, shrines, in the collective ritual. They were the endless pursuit of monasteries, as of the saints and holy men who moved among the populace as naturally as birds among the leaves. Even when these saints and holy men retreated into solitude, everyone living in the world was aware that the woods and hills, the wildernesses and caves surrounding his home were peopled with these men ready to give counsel and benediction. The highest type of activity in the mediaeval world had nothing to do with what is practical or productive or efficient as we understand these terms. The highest type of activity was that of contemplation; and although the summits of this contemplative activity may have been reached by but a few, yet the realities among which these few lived were an undisputed and central fact of common awareness. At the same time, this awareness did not eclipse man's sense of his status as a creature of earth, shaped out of the earth and returning to it, his whole inner being nourished and enriched by his organic contact with nature and with the breath of the Spirit that had fashioned him as nature's masterwork. The mediaeval world also of course had its injustices and cruelties, its deprivations and ugliness, its suffering and sickness. It is not a question of idealizing this world, still less of proposing a return to it. It is one simply of indicating its overriding spiritual orientation and pursuits.

It is this type of world along with its overriding orientation and pursuits which we have destroyed. Our society is man-made, not a divine order. It is one in fact which represents a projection of the human mind that has cut its links with the divine and with the earth; and in so far as it has any ideals these are purely temporal and finite and concern only the terrestrial welfare of its members. A Dr. Caird, later to be Master of Balliol, writing in the 80s of the last century [i.e., the 1880s], depicts, in a language well suited to them, the situation and attitude of mind that characterize our world as compared with the mediaeval world which it has replaced. "It is the peculiar strength of modern times," wrote Dr. Caird, "that it has reached a clear perception of the finite world as finite; that in science it is positive, i.e. that it takes particular facts for no more than they are; and that in practice it is unembarrassed by superstition, i.e. by the tendency to treat things and persons as mysteriously sacred. The first immediate awe and reverence which arose out of a confusion of the absolute and universal with the relative and particular, or, in simpler language, of the divine and the human, the ideal and the real, has passed away from the world."[1]

It could hardly have been expressed more succinctly, or more crushingly. And it is of this type of mentality that our modern technological world is the social embodiment. Modern technology is this conception harnessed and put to work for us. It is this which has licensed the technical mind to desecrate the whole social context, the entire planet, and to send out squads of scientific-technical experts to chart, dissect, ransack, and ravage dispassionately, on the basis of empirical evidence and experiment, and if possible by the intervention of mathematics or other specialist methodology, the total fabric of human and cosmic life—outer space and inner conflict, art and history, public opinion and private guilt, education and health—one has only to look at the hundreds of magazines and journals in the science departments of universities and polytechnics to get an idea of the vast proliferation of this specialized interference and scrutiny. Everything is drawn into this vortex of specialization and submitted to its processes. Nothing is sacrosanct. Nothing belongs any longer to the sphere of the gods or to the sphere of the supernatural. There is nothing and nowhere which must not be investigated and if possible exploited. Neither the ocean bed nor the stars can escape. Nor—so long as they can be shown to be efficient in the sense of being the best and most effective means for achieving a certain measurable purpose—can these systematic invasions be stopped or repudiated. If efficient technical means for achieving something exists or can be produced, then these means must be put into action irrespective of what this thing is or of what the cost may be in human terms. Even those who were at first the victims of these processes—the industrial proletariat—have been seduced by their glamour and regard them as the magical talisman which will bring them all they need in life. As for the élite of our technocracy—those who manipulate its inexhaustible gadgetry of machines, devices, techniques, the computers and cybernated systems, the simulation and gaming processes, the market and motivational research, the immense codifications necessary to sustain and enlarge their empire of sterilized artificiality—their prestige is virtually unassailable because on them the whole edifice depends for its survival and prosperity. Moreover, if they are readers of Teilhard de Chardin they can add ideological grist to their pragmatic mill, for he will have

[1] E. Caird, *Hegel* (Edinburgh and London, 1883), p. 112.

taught them that it is through the consolidation of the "noosphere," that level of existence permanently dominated by the mind of man and its planning, that our species will execute its God-given task and fulfill its destiny.

There is, however, a price to be paid for fabricating around us a society which is as artificial and as mechanized as our own, and this is that we can exist in it only on condition that we adapt ourselves to it. This is our punishment. The social form which we have adopted cuts our consciousness to fit its needs, its imperatives tailor our experience. The inorganic technological world that we have invented lays hold on our interior being and seeks to reduce that to a blind inorganic mechanical thing. It seeks to eliminate whole emotional areas of our life, demanding that we be a new type of being, a type that is not human as this has been understood in both the religious and the humanist ages—one that has no heart, no affections, no spontaneity, and is as impersonal as the metals and processes of calculation in which it is involved. And it is not only our emotional world that is deadened. The world of our creative imagination and intelligence is also impoverished. The most average characterless type of mind is quite sufficient to master and apply the various skills, scientific and other, needed to run our society. At the same time, the objects which we now make or manufacture require little or no imaginative effort on our part; they are all the result of rational planning and design, of technical skill and efficiency, and we produce them—are forced to produce them—with the least possible personal struggle or commitment, entering into and becoming through producing them part of their objective, impersonal, and pitiless nature. For these products—machines, commodities, organizations, programs—are themselves totally lacking any imaginative quality: they mirror nothing which is not material, they are symbols of nothing, they are entirely consumed by their own lifeless and inorganic indifference; and man who must spend his days among them is reduced to a similar state.

Indeed, what goes by the name of work for the vast majority of the members of our society rots the very soul and body. It is work which takes no account whatsoever of the personal qualities of the individuals engaged in it; it has no direct connection with what a particular person really is or with that by virtue of which he is himself and not someone else; it is purely external to him and he can change it—if there is anything available—for an alternative which is equally impersonal and exterior. In relation to our work, the vast majority of us in our society are equivalent to mere "units" or objects or commodities, interchangeable, and are condemned for all our working lives to purely mechanical activities in which nothing properly human exists and whose performance is not in any way consistent with our inner and personal aptitudes and identities. When it is remembered that if an individual does not fulfill the function for which he is destined by nature and which is his vocation, but is forced to perform some other function not essentially connected with him, then he will produce in himself a dislocation and disharmony which affects the whole society to which he belongs, something of the sickness of our state may be grasped. For in our society, this is not the exception; it is the rule; and in these circumstances the dislocation affects not merely society, but the whole cosmic realm itself. It is superfluous to stress that this cosmic disorder, reflecting the radical dehumanization of our society, and incurable apart from a total re-personalization of the conditions of work in our society, is already well advanced. As the conditions of work in our society cannot be re-personalized or re-humanized without a dismantling of the whole present scientific industrial structure, we have something of the measure of the task that lies ahead.

The dismantling of the present scientific industrial structure, even if it can be envisaged, involves of course a great deal more than the mere destruction of its external features, and it will not be achieved either simply by a return to nature or by the cultivation of one's own garden. One of the things we have to recognize—are being forced to recognize—is that the form of society we build around us is the mirror of our own inner world; it is the extraversion of our inner world. In it the state of our consciousness and our attitude to the fundamental realities of human existence take shape and are given an external form. A society can be an image of integration and beauty and significance. It can also be an image of disintegration and ugliness and fatuity. Which it is will depend on ourselves. If we have fabricated a society whose forms now dehumanize us, this is because prior to such a fabrication on the external plane we have already given assent to thought-forms which deny and cripple the growth of our humanity. Correspondingly, if we are to remake our society in the image of an integrated humanity, we must first be clear in our minds what it means to be human. The first step in the task before us is one of clarification. And a preliminary aspect of it consists in conducting a kind of inquest or post-mortem examination or autopsy to discover what has gone wrong, what has happened in the sphere of our consciousness that has made us construct around ourselves the frightful dereliction in which most of us are now compelled to live. We must trace something of the stages through which the mental and material ground has been prepared for the emergence and growth of our fractured, inhuman society.

I said that our type of society, which has replaced that of the mediaeval world, is one whose ideals, if they can be called that, are purely temporal and finite and concern but the material welfare of its members. The form it is thought that this society should take is not the consequence of any supernatural revelation, but is simply the result of empirical and inductive methods of reasoning based primarily upon the observation of individual needs and characteristics. These needs and characteristics are regarded as ultimately mortal: the ends of life are seen as contained within its mortal span and as measurable in terms of the purely temporal and finite standards of this world. By the end of the eighteenth century the change in outlook between mediaeval times and modern times was virtually consummated: for all practical purposes this world was by now regarded as the only reality, the be all and end all, the one place where, as Wordsworth put it, man can find his happiness if he is ever to find it. There was a feeling of optimism in the air, a sense of moving forward into the future under the aegis of a new divinity, the Reason, which by now was extending its empire over the whole western consciousness. Man was naturally good. The world was a good place to live in. It could be a much better place if only its natural resources and man's ability to put them to his use could be exploited more fully and efficiently. And this could be done if you knew how to do it. It could be done if you could develop techniques, the technical means.

Here I would like to make a digression to dispel a common mis-understanding. It is often said that the mediaeval world also had its techniques and that these were not developed because no one knew how to develop them. It is not quite so simple as this. It is true that the mediaeval world had its techniques. But these techniques deliber-ately were not employed or developed beyond a certain point—the point at which they would begin to impede or prevent what was far more important: the realization of an over-riding imaginative view of life. Here the primary concern was religious, not technical, and technical processes that upset the over-riding conceptions of harmony and beauty and balance were, quite simply, rejected. This may seem strange to us today. We have become so used to the technical mastery of the West that we often go so far as to characterize the western mentality in general as active and practical, and to contrast it with the contemplative spirit of the East. In fact we go even further and see a direct lineal connection between the spirit of Christianity with its emphasis on the Incarnation and hence, it is supposed, on the reality of matter, and the emergence of the modern scientific mentality and its concomitants, the exploration and exploitation of nature; and we contrast this materializing spirit of Christianity with the more transcendentally-minded spirit of Hinduism or Buddhism or even of Islam, for which matter tends to be regarded as a kind of illusion, lacking all subsistent reality.

This view is of course a gross over-simplification and in many ways is the reverse of the truth. Until the modern age, it was the East which had the concrete "experimental" mind, not the West, and it was the East and not the West which possessed the mastery of techniques and technical processes, whether these had material or magical purposes, or purposes directly connected with the realization of the spiritual life. The idea of "method," whether applied to material or spiritual techniques, is above all an Eastern idea. It was from the East that ancient Greece, in the years of her decline from the second century onwards, borrowed her various technical devices: before this, although possessing considerable scientific knowledge—including, moreover, a knowledge of machines and their utilization—there had been persistent refusal to deduce or exploit the possible technical consequences. The Roman spirit, it may be said, was different from that of the Greeks, and sought to take advantage of concrete situations by the most effective practical means available but even here the main technical processes—the refining of gold and silver, glass-making, the tempering of weapons, pottery, ship construction, and so on—were of Eastern origin.[2]

This lack of technical concern in the West or, rather, this refusal to admit technical exploitation except in a very limited sphere, was emphasized, not undermined, by the spirit of Christianity. The period from the second century A.D. to the fifth century A.D. which saw the rise of Christianity, and which in Buddhist India was marked by astonishing developments in the artistic, political, and military fields, was marked in the West by a technical decline so great that the Emperor Julian the Apostate could accuse the Christians of ruining the Empire's industry. One of the architects of St. Sophia at Constantinople was quite capable of making a steam-engine (some one thousand two hundred years before James Watt "invented" it), but he used his skill only to make the house he was living in shake as though there was an earthquake in order to get rid of an unpleasant neighbor

---

[2] See Jacques Ellul, *The Technological Society* (New York, 1964), pp. 27ff.

living on the top floor. Except indeed for architecture—and nearly all large-scale architecture had a religious motive—the West in the mediaeval Christian period demonstrated a singular lack of technical will or mentality; and when in the twelfth century there was some renewal of technical interest this again was stimulated through contact with the East—through Jews, the Crusaders, Venetian and Genoese merchants, and through translation from the Arabic. The West has developed technically in direct relationship to the decline of the Christian consciousness, for the simple reason that the "secularization" of nature, which permits it to be regarded as an object and so exploited technically, is in direct contradiction to the sacramental spirit of Christianity, wherever and whenever this is properly understood, as it was at least to some extent in the mediaeval world. Yet even after the breakdown of Christian authority in the West, technical development was slow: it was not until the eighteenth and nineteenth centuries that people began to think on any effective scale that the utilization of machines and gadgets in order to produce concrete results of a quantitative nature was a preoccupation not beneath the dignity of man. And they began to think this because they had accepted as true a philosophy which proclaimed that basically man was a two-legged terrestrial animal whose destiny and needs could best be fulfilled through the pursuit of social, political, and economic self-interest and the provision of an ever-increasing number and variety of material goods.

Hence the call to a type of human being whose role was to be regarded with increasing respect. I refer to the scientist. For the world's resources, natural and other, could not be exploited significantly unless there was a great development in the means of exploitation. So, perhaps for the first time in history, scientists—and especially scientists who would apply their knowledge—were to move into the center of the social and economic scene. By applying their expertise to achieve positive concrete results, by raising the level of man's material well-being through the exploitation of the world's natural resources, they would be in the forward van of humanity's march of progress towards a better and happier future. Scientists began to take the place of priests, initiating not of course into the kingdom of heaven but into the brave new world of more consumer goods and limitless economic growth. It was by courtesy of the scientists that the industrialists and bankers of the nineteenth century bulldozed their way to fortune and produced the devastation of the modern industrial world.

It is in a sense quite just that scientists should have been given and should have retained this exalted status in our society because it has been largely through their efforts that the worldview underpinning this society and man's place in it has been promoted, propagated, and maintained as the dominant view down to the present day. Here of course Francis Bacon is a key figure, for it was Bacon who laid down the guidelines, moral, aesthetic, and psychic, for the "new philosophy." When Bacon concluded that his *novum organum* should apply "not only to natural but to all sciences" (including ethics and politics) and that it is to "embrace everything," he opened the road for the all-inclusive scientific takeover of our culture and for the urban industrialism which is its brainchild. In Bacon's program is to be found a prescription for the total scientivization of our world, from the practices of the laboratory, often themselves of an indescribable cruelty, down to those, no less sinister, of the modern police state. But if Bacon is the presiding genius, the *buccinator* of this take-over, it was others—Galileo, Descartes, Newton—who perfected that mechanistic vision in accordance with which our modern world has been built. It was they who marked the advent of a new conceptual universe, who formulated the purely quantitative attitude to nature which first appears in Galileo's new approach to terrestrial mechanics and who fostered the illusion that knowledge of the world could be obtained through the application of mathematical techniques—indeed, that what could not be caught in the net of numbers was non-science, non-knowledge, and even in the end non-existent.

It was not Galileo, however, but Descartes who formulated most decisively the philosophical principles of the new science, its dream of reducing knowledge to mathematics, and of the new mathematical cosmology. Breaking the last tenuous links between God and the world He has created, Descartes virtually exiles God from the world—or, rather, exiles the world from God. For Descartes, God is no longer symbolized by the things He has created; his thought does not leave room even for the scholastic idea of analogy between God and the world: there are no *imagines* or *vestigia Dei in mundo*—except what Descartes calls the soul and which he identifies purely and simply with the human reason and the sparse complement of clear and distinct ideas with which God has endowed it. The Cartesian world is but a strictly uniform mathematical world, a world of geometry in which there is nothing else but extension and motion; and if God had any reasons for creating it, these are known only to Himself and we have not and cannot have the slightest idea of them or of any other divine or teleological realities, for the simple reason that, according to Descartes, we possess no faculty through which we are capable of apprehending them. This of course meant the expulsion from scientific thought of all considerations based on value, perfection, harmony, meaning, beauty, purpose, for these considerations are now regarded as merely subjective and so as irrelevant to a scientific understanding of the real "objective" world—the world of quantity, of reified geometry, of a nature that is dead, alien, and purely functional. With the Newtonian mechanistic synthesis, this new attitude is virtually achieved. The world-picture, with man in it, is flattened and neutralized, stripped of all sacred or spiritual qualities, of all hierarchical differentiation, and spread out before the human observer like a blank chart on which nothing can be registered except what is capable of being measured. For Newton, the celestial spheres are a machine; for Descartes, animals are machines; for Hobbes, society is a machine; for La Mettrie, the human body is a machine; eventually for Pavlov and his successors human behavior is like that of a machine. Everything, including the mind of man, is aligned on the model of a machine constructed out of dissections, analyses, and calculations. And a worldview founded on the model of a machine brings after it a mechanistic world. The machines of the dark satanic mills of our urban industrial society are eloquent reflections of the philosophy of Descartes and his peers and successors; and the mentality (also satanic) that degrades men and women to work with such machines is one which is the necessary and logical consequence of this philosophy.

At this point I would like to forestall a possible criticism. It might be said that the mechanistic worldview of Newtonian physics has long since been discarded by scientists themselves, relegated to that rubbish-dump of exploded theories which constitutes the history of modern science. The quantum and relativity theories proposed at the turn of the twentieth century might be cited in support of this, cited in support of the claim that the scientific worldview has radically changed. In addition, it could be pointed out that philosophers of science like Ernst Mach or Henri Poincaré—to mention but two of the more intelligent positivists—have shown that the theories and explanatory concepts of science are no more than convenient intellectual tools by means of which scientists handle their data and reduce it to comparative order, and that they should be valued for their utility and convenience only and not as statements of truth about reality. Mach certainly, and Poincaré probably, would go on to say that there are no ultimate truths about reality in any case, although those of science are as near as any we are likely to get. And more recently, other philosophers of science such as Michael Polanyi have spoken of how impossible it is for the scientist not to be influenced by purely subjective factors such as what he expects to see, what other people have persuaded him he should see, and so on—factors which mean that measurements of temporal and spatial intervals are not just given to the mind but are given to a particular mind deeply and inextricably involved with its own subjective personal prejudices and requirements.

In short, it could be argued that scientists themselves now admit that the best of their theories are but hypotheses, and that these, far from being reached inductively on the basis of objective data, as the old-fashioned empiricist would have it, are for the most part simply postulated as the most probable explanation or interpretation of certain data in accordance with a specific model which the scientist in question happens to have accepted. Thus, Le Verrier postulated by purely mathematical means the then unknown planet Venus, or more recently Watson and Crick proceeded in a similar manner when developing their theory of the genetic code. All this, it might be concluded, means that the old closed, rigid, cast-iron mechanistic picture of the universe, in which man was seen as a mere cog in a vast cosmic machine, has now gone for ever, and that science, the new science, is open, flexible, indefinite, and much more aware of its limitations than was previously the case. Indeed, it is even thought, both by some scientists and by some theologians, that it might now be possible to reconcile science and religion in a new religio-scientific conception of things.

Some of this is no doubt true, just as it is no doubt true that many scientists, aware of the crushing inhumanity of their discipline, are desperately looking for something which would appear to allow the human and even the religious element to be affirmed within it. For a whole range of phenomena in atomic physics and astronomy the old machine model is inadequate and scientists working in these areas are forced to revise their observational methods, to invent new and more flexible models, and to develop more subtle mathematical procedures for construing their experimental data. But, first, though these modifications have taken place in relation to these areas, nonetheless the old physics is still to all intents and purposes the physics of an equally wide range of phenomena, of all those phenomena which belong to what might be called our local environment, of ordinary space and ordinary time. Where the so-called life sciences are concerned, scientific thought is in fact more crudely mechanistic than ever. In biology, the cell is a "chemical factory," ribosomes are directed by a "programming machine," RNA is like "a worker in a multi-copying industry who duplicates the program of an automatic machine on the keyboard of a key punch," and so on. "In science," as Joseph Needham puts it, "a man is a machine, or if he is not, then he is nothing,"[3] and as if to confirm his words, and to illustrate what I have already said to the effect that the type of mind needed for science can be the most average and characterless from the point of view of normal human intelligence, Francis Crick, the Nobel prize-winner, discoverer of the bihelical structure of DNA, can write: "I myself, like many scientists, believe that the soul is imaginary and that what we call our mind is simply a way of talking about the function of our brains"; and can add: "once one has become adjusted to the idea that we are here because we have evolved from simple chemical compounds by a process of natural selection, it is remarkable how many of the problems of the modern world take on a completely new light."[4]

The real reason, however, invalidating the claim that the modern scientific outlook is fundamentally different from that of Galileo and Descartes and Newton and so is more susceptible to humanization goes much deeper than this continuing adherence to the machine metaphor. Scientists may well dispense with this metaphor and adopt some other in its place. That is not fundamentally very significant. But what they cannot do, without admitting their total bankruptcy and irrelevance, is to dispense with the assumptions on which modern science itself is based. And by assumptions I mean epistemological assumptions. Modern scientists may protest that their theories are mere hypotheses, more or less useful and convenient. They may admit that the old empiricist epistemology—according to which knowledge can be obtained only by observation—was inadequate and even false, and that into any act of observation or any formulation of theory enter factors—hereditary, cultural, subjective—which the scientist cannot specify and of which indeed he may be largely unaware. But—at least not without making nonsense of their work—they cannot reject the very premises of scientific thought itself. And these premises, these underlying assumptions, are the same today as they were for the scientists of the seventeenth century. And the reason why scientists,

---

[3] Joseph Needham, *Man a Machine* (London, 1927), p. 93. Cited at p. 184 of Theodore Roszak, *Where the Wasteland Ends* (London, 1973), a book to which I am here indebted.

[4] Francis Crick, *Of Molecules and Men* (University of Washington Press), pp. 87, 93. Cited by Roszak, *Where the Wasteland Ends*, p. 188.

however much they may wish to, cannot humanize science is because inhumanity is built into these very premises on which modern science itself is based.

It is here that we approach the crux of the matter, or what might be called the question of questions for our generation. It may seem presumptuous to try to reduce the premises of what is called scientific knowledge to a few sentences. But I think it can be done. Basically, scientific theories, or hypotheses, or explanations—what in common ill-formed language are still called scientific truths—are statements which either can be verified with reference to empirical evidence or experiment or at least cannot be shown to be false with reference to such evidence or experiment. In other words, scientific knowledge presupposes two terms or poles. The first is the faculty capable of formulating scientific statements; and the second is an "objective" world of phenomena that supplies the raw material of evidence and experiment against which these statements can be directly or indirectly checked. This is not to say that these two terms are symmetrical or of equal importance. It is only to say that they are posited as the prerequisites of scientific knowledge. Without either, there could be no knowledge as modern science understands the word. In fact, it is quite clear that the two terms are not symmetrical or of equal importance. It is the first—what I have called the faculty capable of formulating scientific statements—which is decisive. It is decisive not only because it is the formulating agent but also because it is the faculty which observes and which provides the criteria determining what is observed, as well as of the relevance or irrelevance, the compatibility or incompatibility, of the information it amasses as a result of its observation. Indeed, it is this faculty alone which is the supreme arbiter of scientific knowledge. It is therefore crucial, if one is to assess the value of this knowledge, to know what this faculty itself is, and how it works; for what it is and the laws that govern its structure will determine the whole character of its formulations.

Here I might revert to the opening paragraph of this paper. For the faculty by which modern science is so exclusively determined is precisely that which philosophers who deny man's capacity for metaphysical or spiritual knowledge assert to be the sole faculty of knowing that man possesses. It is the faculty of the reason. The question before us therefore is one of examining and determining the characteristics and limitations of the reason; for the one thing scientists cannot do, if they are to claim that their knowledge amounts to anything at all, is to say that it is not a rational knowledge. Again it may appear presumptuous to try to describe the characteristics of the reason in a few sentences. But again I think it can be done.

The reason is that faculty which is capable of dissecting, analyzing, and classifying material which is given to it and of forming conceptions by means of analytical or analogical logic, measurement, and mechanical connection. This is to say that the scope of the reason is limited to the material it receives and to the conceptions which refer to this material without necessarily arising directly from it. The reason knows this material only according to how it appears to it and not as it is in itself, and similarly it knows the conceptions only as logical possibilities and not as realities in themselves. As for this material—the data with which the reason operates—this it derives from a source outside itself. It could—granted that this is a possibility—receive this material from "above," through direct illumination from God or through supernatural revelation; or it can receive it from "below," through sense-impressions of the phenomenal world. In either case, it is this material which constitutes the "facts" with which the reason works. But if it closes itself to receiving these facts from above—from God or through supernatural revelation—either because it denies the possibility of receiving them from this source or because it has not the capacity so to receive them, then it will be compelled to derive them exclusively from below, from the phenomenal world. In this case its conceptions will refer to the finite and temporal world alone, to the world of change and impermanence. It is this world which will then constitute what it calls reality—which will then be for it the real world.

Moreover, in interrogating this world—in interrogating the "facts of nature"—what the reason perceives will be only that which its own limitations allow it to perceive, and what it receives by way of information will be only, so to speak, echoes of its own voice. Indeed, the conceptions it formulates as it analyzes and classifies sense-impressions according to its criteria and according to its inherent mode of operation will represent nothing more than a display of ventriloquism in which the so-called external world is the dummy. The reason is not, and cannot be, a neutral element on to which objects can project themselves in such a way that they reveal their own intrinsic nature. Rather it is the opposite which is the case: that the reason imposes its inherent nature on the objects which it observes. This is to say that, when the reason turns exclusively to the phenomenal world for its information, not only do its conceptions refer solely to the finite and temporal world, but also they refer merely to those aspects of it that are susceptible to measurement and mechanical connection. Any aspects of it not susceptible to measurement and mechanical connection must in the nature of things transcend the limits of what the reason can observe and so cannot form any part of the knowledge which it formulates. In addition to this, as its raw material must now be derived from a world of change and impermanence, the knowledge it formulates cannot itself be other than changing and impermanent, and consequently it will be led to deny the validity of all knowledge that is other than changing and impermanent—that is stable and eternal. In the end it is compelled either into a position of pure relativism, to a position of saying that every opinion is equally false or equally true; or—in order to escape from this relativism—to establish some official authoritative body to prescribe what is to be maintained and what is to be denied, what is allowed to be thought and what is to be rejected as in conflict with the authorized official version of things. It is no accident that among the most cherished of the present theories of modern science one is that of evolution, another is that of relativity, and a third is that of indeterminacy—although all three will sooner or later be jettisoned on to that rubbish dump of discarded theories which, as I said, constitutes the history of modern science; for all modern scientific theories are in the end not the product of empirical observation and experiment but the inevitable logical consequence of the premises on which modern scientific thought itself is based; and, these premises being what they are, the supercession of these theories is as inevitable as their original appearance. It is no accident either that the age of modern science is the age *par excellence* of the totalitarian ideological state.

For modern science has its starting-point in a revolution in consciousness, or revolt against heaven, that has resulted in the reason first ignoring, then denying, and finally closing itself to the source of knowledge which is above it; and this has meant that it has been forced to turn for its knowledge exclusively to that which is below it—to the "external" world of sense-data and sense-impression. As a consequence, the conceptions of modern science—that which constitutes its knowledge—are of the type whose features I have just described. They refer, that is to say, only to what is temporal and finite and they reflect merely the logical and mechanical criteria and characteristics of the innate structure of the reason. As I have remarked, the reason is not a neutral element on which an object can imprint its identity and so reveal its essential or inherent nature. When you take a photograph of a person, certain inherent qualities of that person are eliminated from the photograph by the very nature of the material on which the image is projected. To go no further, a photograph of a person eliminates the actual physical warmth of that person, or the softness of his skin, not to mention all his mental and emotional qualities. In other words, the material of the film interposes itself between the person photographed and the living reality of that person; and the kind of knowledge you can form from a photograph of a person will be purely abstract and have little value when compared with a direct knowledge of the living reality of that person—that reality which is precisely what the photograph has excluded.

A similar process takes place when the reason turns exclusively to the facts of the so-called external world for its information: it is compelled to eliminate from its perception of those facts the qualities of which, because of its inherent nature, it is incapable of receiving the imprint. This is to say that it cannot avoid imposing its own laws on the material it perceives. In fact, these laws act as a selector conditioning what it perceives and what it does not and cannot perceive. In other words, the reason cannot avoid interposing itself between us and the objects it purports to examine. Nor is the situation altered by the addition of instruments between the reason and these objects: however sophisticated and sensitive the instrument, the information it conveys cannot transcend or escape the inherent limitations of the actual observing faculty itself, which in this case is the reason. In other words, the kind of knowledge the reason is now capable of forming on the basis of its observation—what we call scientific knowledge—is but a reflection of the intrinsic limitations and characteristics of the reason itself and of the presuppositions it has adopted, and has little or nothing to do with what things are in themselves, in their living reality. Indeed, all the reason can now do is to shut man up in himself and fetter him to his own prejudices and opinions and condemn him to rest satisfied with what at best are but the external appearances of things. What things are in themselves, in their living reality, is something the reason can never know. It is something consequently that modern science can never know.

Modern science, since it is based on and limited to the sphere of the rational, can never reach a knowledge of anything in itself, no matter how much it concerns itself with experiment and observation or how far it carries its function of dissection and analysis. This is the situation to which modern science has condemned itself and in which it continues to be inextricably trapped. And it is because those qualities which essentially make a human being what he or she is are neither temporal nor finite, or such that can be measured or analyzed by the reason, that it may be said that an inhumanity is built into the very premises on which modern science itself is based. In other words, to reduce man to the level of what the reason can perceive or understand about him is to dehumanize him. When further it is remembered that the qualities which essentially make every single living thing what it is similarly transcend the sphere of the rational, one begins to get a measure of the terrifying mutilation which the scientific worldview represents. I am not denying or denigrating the legitimate function of the reason or saying that there cannot be a science of phenomena. Far from it. But when the reason is set up as the supreme arbiter of human knowledge and denies or ignores principles and qualities which transcend its competence, then it necessarily degenerates into a mechanical, inhuman, and godless faculty; and the picture of the universe it projects and the character of the world it fabricates in accordance with that picture are equally mechanical, inhuman, and godless. Needless to add, this picture also represents an appalling lie.*

None of this would be very important if modern science, like chess or trapeze artistry, was but the pursuit of a few specialists. Unfortunately, this is not the case. Whether we like it or not, the scientific attitude has permeated and vitally affected virtually every aspect of our public and private activity and thinking. It is not simply that our governments pour millions of pounds annually, through schools, universities, research projects, and multitudinous other ways, into its promotion and dissemination. It is more serious than that. The scientific conception of knowledge has become virtually equated with the only way of knowing there is. Not only does it dominate its own offspring, such as the social sciences and anthropology—a bastard progeny if ever there was one—but it has invaded also the classical fields of the humanities, a fact which makes a proper understanding of poetry, for instance, almost inaccessible to the modern student. Philosophy has long since capitulated and now has become identified with little more than such peripheral and graceless mental gymnastics as logical analysis or even mere information theory.

---

* Editors' Note: See also the chapter of Frithjof Schuon, "Rationalism, Real and Apparent," in *Logic and Transcendence* (London: Perennial Books, 1975), pp. 33-55, for a comprehensive analysis of the role of reason in relation to the spiritual Intellect and the empirical senses. As Schuon says elsewhere, reason can both help to actualize a virtual intellection, and give expression to an effective intellection.

Far more serious, however, and more insidious, is the capitulation of the one discipline which should from the start have exposed the limitations of the modern scientific mentality. I refer to theology. Here it is sufficient to remark that, taking refuge in a fiction, proposed by Aquinas and reaffirmed by philosophers such as Kant, to the effect that although the reason can have no direct apprehension of the realities of revelation in themselves, nevertheless its mode of cognition and its conclusions are quite valid with respect to the phenomenal world—the world of nature—theologians for the most part have lulled themselves into a completely false security. Even worse, they have felt obliged to modify their own doctrine where this has run counter to the various theories which scientists have put forward from time to time about the origin of the universe, the evolution of man, and so on. Because of this one is treated to the absurd spectacle of theologians trying to bring Christian doctrine up to date or to remake it in accordance with the spirit of the times or with the contemporary mind, totally forgetting that this up-to-dateness and this spirit and this mind are merely the determination of a science which by definition is destructive of the religious intelligence and its norm. The result has been that theologians have largely failed to make any radical or effective critique of scientific epistemology, have failed to elucidate the appalling consequences of making the reason the supreme and sole instrument of knowledge and to explain why this has meant a progressive falsification of our understanding both of ourselves and of the world about us. In view of this failure it is not surprising that so many students of our universities end up with no better ideology than some form of Marxist-Leninism, itself a translation into political terms of the most banal aspects of nineteenth century bourgeois scientific theory. When this same hotchpotch of rationalist-materialist banalities is taken over by—or, rather, takes possession of—the masses, then society is turned into a prison camp in which everything that gives human life its value is systematically attacked and lacerated. It should be added that it is beside the point for scientists themselves to plead, as they are often in the habit of pleading, that they are but humble practical men and women quietly getting on with their research and making no claims to setting the standards of knowledge or to any special authority, and that if others exploit the results of their research for commerce, war, or other unwholesome purposes, they are not to be blamed. That exaltation of the reason which is a prerequisite of scientific research already in itself represents a self-assertion and an arrogance that preclude all genuine humility, which must be based on truth and not on a lie; and—short of denying their integrity as human beings—scientists cannot disclaim responsibility for the consequences which, as they are fully aware, their research must inevitably set in motion. And it must be said that more and more scientists not only do not disclaim this responsibility but accept it agonizingly and with great fortitude.

At this point—if not indeed at some much earlier point—it might be objected that the picture I am painting is too bleak and that things are not so bad as I make out. First, it could be said that even if in general terms the sketch I have made of the effects of submitting to the categories of the scientific mentality is true with reference to certain spheres of activity, none the less in other spheres there have been such positive gains that these offset, if they do not totally outweigh, any disadvantages; and that in any case these disadvantages themselves can be corrected when we have a little more knowledge about them. In particular, it might be claimed that the gains in the field of medicine are so vast that these alone justify the whole scientific experiment of the last few centuries. I do not think it is so simple. The world of modern science is a single interlocking whole and it is impossible to abstract one aspect of it as if this aspect could exist independently of the other aspects. It is impossible to do this because any one process, however beneficial it may seem in itself, is inextricably involved with a thousand other processes and depends upon them. If you want a product such as a car you have to have all the rest as well, from the dereliction of the oil-rigs and refineries and the motorways down to the lead poison, the carbon monoxide, and the noise that ruins the life of our cities and the deadly boredom of those whose work it is to put these machines together. In any case, it is entirely spurious to sing the praises of, say, modern medicine when the type of society which has produced it, and which it presupposes, is one which has done so much to deprive man of the basic elements on which his health depends.

But, more seriously, it may be questioned whether the scientific takeover is quite so totalitarian as I have suggested. In the sphere of the intelligence and the imagination, there have always been those who have repudiated its pretensions: poets, for instance, such as Blake, who discerned so clearly to what the thought of Bacon, Locke, Newton was leading; or Yeats, who hated this science and called it "the opium of the suburbs"; or David Jones, who knew so well that when man's work is merely utilitarian it is also sub-human and how in the technological world man's capacity to make—his function as *poeta*—is brutalized out of recognition. The testimony of these three alone—and there are many others*—is sufficient to indicate that the creative intelligence and imagination—necessarily anti-scientific—have not been extinguished. Moreover, the smell of the rose is still as much the smell of the rose for us as it was for Plato and, in spite of all, our lives are still punctuated by moments of grace and beauty and love that go far beyond all I have been talking about. In this sense, everything is still in its place and nothing has been lost. Indeed, since the worldview of modern science is basically false, it cannot ultimately affect the truth of things, however much it may appear to do so. The norm of human and natural existence always remains. But when this is said, we must still remember man's seemingly inexhaustible capacity for being taken in by a lie, and so for turning his life into a kind of illusion. We must still remember that the social order we have built about us—our present—is one predominantly determined by the categories of this false philosophy and its practical application, and that the difference between our world and that of the human and natural norm is growing greater, not smaller, every day. Indeed, it has now become so great that it is virtually impossible for the one to understand the other. We have all but lost the capacity to measure how far we have in fact fallen below the level of the human and natural norm.[5]

For modern science has its origin in a loss of memory, a forgetfulness by man of who he is. By an ineluctable logic inherent in this origin it proceeds along a course each step of which is marked by a further fall by man into deeper ignorance of his own nature and consequently into deeper ignorance of the nature of everything else. Progressively divorced by this ignorance from the roots of his being, man, so long as he persists in this course, is doomed to advance blindly and at an ever-increasing pace towards total loss of identity, total loss of control,

---

* Editors' Note: Pre-eminently, in the twentieth century, the figures of René Guénon, Ananda K. Coomaraswamy, and Frithjof Schuon, in their devastating critique of the modern world.

[5] Modern science is now a worldwide phenomenon, and it has radically altered, even indeed threatens totally to displace, the patterns of life and the values which until its advent had characterized not only European civilization but every civilization as well. Non-Europeans have been induced to believe that the acceptance of the methodology and techniques of modern science whose mastery and manipulation can produce certain effects in the practical sphere does not lead inevitably to the disruption of the spiritual universe to which their own civilizations owe all that is sacred and human about them. They have been lulled into a state of passive acquiescence to what is really a western imperialism of a far more vicious and totalitarian nature than they have experienced in any other form.

and eventually to total self-destruction. Nothing can stop this process except a complete reversal of direction. And nothing can initiate a reversal of direction except a recovery by man of an awareness of who he is: the cure must go back to where the sickness started. To such a recovery modern science itself can contribute nothing: a science whose very categories exclude a recognition of the essential qualities of human nature clearly is not in a position to make man the subject of its investigation with any hope of telling us anything very important about him. Only a religious understanding—one that transcends the sphere of the rational—is capable of recognizing those qualities and so of assessing their significance for the living of a human life.

III

METAPHYSICS

God is Reality, the world is appearance;
the soul is not other than God.

<small>VEDANTIC MAXIM</small>

7 ORIENTAL METAPHYSICS*

René Guénon

For the subject of this essay I have taken Oriental metaphysics. Perhaps it would have been better to have said simply metaphysics unqualified, for in truth, pure metaphysics being essentially above and beyond all form and all contingency is neither Eastern nor Western but universal. The exterior forms with which it is covered only serve the necessities of exposition, to express whatever is expressible. These forms may be Eastern or Western; but under the appearance of diversity there is always a basis of unity, at least, wherever true metaphysics exists, for the simple reason that truth is one.

If this be so, what need is there to deal specifically with Oriental metaphysics? The reason is that in the present intellectual state of the Western world metaphysics is a thing forgotten, generally ignored, and almost entirely lost, while in the East it still remains the object of effective knowledge. Thus it is to the East that one must look if one wishes to discover the true meaning of metaphysics; or even if one's wish is to recover some of the metaphysical traditions formerly existing in a West which was in many respects much closer to the East than it is today, it is above all with the help of Oriental doctrines and by comparison with them that one may succeed, since these are the only doctrines in the domain of metaphysics which can still be studied directly. As for these, however, it is quite clear that they must be studied as the Orientals themselves study them and one must certainly not indulge in more or less hypothetical interpretations which may sometimes be quite imaginary; it is too often forgotten that Eastern civilizations still exist and still have qualified representatives from whom it is possible to enquire in order to discover the exact truth about the subject in question.

I have said "Eastern metaphysics" and not merely Hindu metaphysics, for doctrines of this order, with all they imply, are not only to be found in India, as some people believe who, moreover, barely grasp their true nature. The case of India is by no means exceptional in this respect; it is precisely that of all civilizations which possess what

---

* Editors' Note: The text of a lecture given at the Sorbonne in Paris on 12 December, 1925.

95

might be termed a traditional basis. On the contrary, what are exceptional and abnormal are civilizations without such a basis, and to tell the truth, the only one known to us is that of the modern West. To take only the principal Eastern civilizations: the equivalent of Hindu metaphysics is found in China (in Taoism) and is also to be found elsewhere in certain esoteric schools of Islam; it should be understood, however, that this Islamic esotericism has nothing in common with the overt philosophy of the Arabs, which is for the most part Greek-inspired. The only difference is that except in India these doctrines are reserved for a relatively restricted and closed elite. This was also the case in the West in the Middle Ages, in an esotericism comparable in many respects to that of Islam and as purely metaphysical as the Islamic one; of this the moderns, for the most part, do not even suspect the existence. In India it is not possible to speak of esotericism in the true sense of the word, because there is no doctrinal dualism of exoteric and esoteric; it can only be a matter of natural esotericism, in the sense that each goes more or less deeply into the doctrine and more or less far according to the measure of his abilities, since there are, for certain individualities, limitations which are inherent in their own nature, and which it is impossible to overcome.

Naturally, forms differ from one civilization to another; but though more accustomed myself to the Hindu forms, I have no scruple in employing others when necessary, if they can contribute to the understanding of certain points; there are no objections to this since they are only different expressions of the same thing. Once again, truth is one, and it is the same for all those who, by whatever way, have attained to its understanding.

This said, it should be made clear in what sense the word "metaphysics" is used, all the more so since I have frequently had occasion to state that everyone does not understand it in the same way. I think the best course to take with words that can give rise to ambiguity is to reduce them, as far as possible, to their primary and etymological meaning. Now, according to its composition, this word "metaphysics" means literally "beyond physics," taking the word "physics" in the accepted meaning it always had for the ancients, that is as the "science of nature" in its widest sense. Physics is the study of all which appertains to the domain of nature; metaphysics, on the other hand, is the study of what lies beyond nature. How then can some claim that metaphysical knowledge is natural knowledge, either in respect of its object, or with regard to the faculties by which it is obtained? There we have a complete misconception, a contradiction in terms;

and, what is more amazing, this confusion affects even those who should preserve some idea of the true metaphysics and know how to distinguish it clearly from the pseudo-metaphysics of modern philosophers.

But, one might say, if this word "metaphysics" gives rise to such confusion, would it not be better to abandon it and substitute something more suitable? Plainly, this would not be advisable, since, by its formation, this word meets the exact requirements; also it is hardly possible, since Western languages have no other word equally adapted to this usage. Simply to use the word "knowledge," as is done in India, because this is indeed knowledge *par excellence* and that which alone can be dignified by that name, is out of the question, for it would only make things more confusing for Occidentals who habitually associate knowledge with nothing beyond the scientific and rational. Also is it necessary to concern ourselves with the abuse to which a word is put? If we rejected all such, what would be left? Is it not sufficient to take precautions to avoid misunderstandings and misrepresentations? We are not any more enamored of the word "metaphysics" than of any other, but since a better term cannot be suggested to replace it we will continue to use it as before.

Unfortunately one comes across people who claim to "judge" that which they do not know, and who, because they apply the name "metaphysics" to a purely human and rational knowledge (which for us is only science or philosophy), imagine that Oriental metaphysics is no more and no other than that; from which they arrive logically at the conclusion that this metaphysics cannot in reality lead to any particular results. They fail to see that it is an effective guide just because it is something quite other than they suppose. What they envisage has really nothing to do with metaphysics since it is only knowledge of a natural order, an outward and profane scholarship; it is not of this that we wish to speak. Can one then make "metaphysical" synonymous with "supernatural"? We are prepared to accept such an analogy, since if one does not go beyond nature, that is to say the manifest world in its entirety (and not only the world of the senses, which is only an infinitesimal part of it), one is still in the realm of the physical. Metaphysics is, as we have already said, that which lies beyond and above nature; hence it can properly be described as "supernatural."

But an objection will undoubtedly be raised here: Is it possible to go beyond nature? We do not hesitate to answer plainly: Not only is it possible, but it is a fact. Again it might be said, is this not merely an assertion; what proofs thereof can be adduced? It is truly strange that proof is demanded concerning the possibility of a kind of knowledge instead of searching for it and verifying it for one's self by undertaking the work necessary for its acquisition. For those who possess this knowledge, what interest can there be in all this discussion? Substituting a "theory of knowledge" for knowledge itself is perhaps the greatest admission of impotence in modern philosophy.

Moreover, all certitude contains something incommunicable. Nobody can truly attain to any knowledge other than by a strictly personal effort; all that one can do for another is to offer him the opportunity and indicate the means by which to attain the same knowledge. That is why it would be vain to attempt to impose any belief in the purely intellectual realm; the best argument in the world could not in this respect replace direct and effective knowledge.

Now, is it possible to define metaphysics as we understand it? No, for to define is always to limit, and that with which we are concerned is, in itself, truly and absolutely unlimited and cannot be confined to any formula or any system. Metaphysics might be partly described, for example, by saying that it is the knowledge of universal principles, but that is not a definition in the proper sense, and only conveys a rough idea. Something can be added by saying that the scope of these principles is far greater than was thought by some Occidentals who, although really studying metaphysics, did so in a partial and incomplete way. Thus when Aristotle envisages metaphysics as a knowledge of being *qua* being, he identifies it with ontology, that is to say he takes the part for the whole. For Oriental metaphysics, pure being is neither the first nor the most universal principle, for it is already a determination. It is thus necessary to go beyond being, and it is this which is of the greatest significance. That is why, in all true metaphysical conceptions it is necessary to take into account the inexpressible: just as everything that can be expressed is literally nothing in comparison with that which surpasses expression, so the finite, whatever its magnitude, is nothing when faced with the Infinite. One can hint at much more than can be expressed, and this is the part played by exterior forms. All forms, whether it is a matter of words or symbols, only act as a support, a fulcrum for rising to possibilities of conception which far outstrip them; we will return to this later.

We speak of metaphysical conceptions for lack of any other term whereby to make ourselves understood, but it is not to be concluded from this that there is here something comparable to scientific or philosophic conceptions; it is not a question of any "abstractions," but of attaining an intuitive and immediate supra-rational knowledge. This pure intellectual intuition, without which there is no true metaphysics, has, moreover, no connection with the intuition spoken of by certain contemporary philosophers, which is, on the contrary, infra-rational. There is an intellectual intuition and a sensible intuition; one lies beyond reason, but the other is situated on its hither side; the latter can only know the world of changing and becoming, that is to say nature, or rather, an inferior part of nature. The domain of intuition, on the contrary, is the province of eternal and immutable principles; it is the realm of metaphysics.

To comprehend universal principles directly the transcendent intellect must itself be of the universal order; it is no longer an individual faculty, and to consider it as such would be contradictory, as it is not within the power of the individual to go beyond his own limits and leave the conditions which limit him *qua* individual. Reason is a specifically human faculty, but that which lies beyond reason is truly "non-human"; it is this which makes metaphysical knowledge possible, and that knowledge, one must again emphasize, is not a human knowledge. In other words, it is not as man that man can attain it, but because this being which is human in one of its aspects is at the same time something other and more than a human being. It is the attainment of effective consciousness of supra-individual states which is the real object of metaphysics, or better still, of metaphysical knowledge itself. We come here to one of the most vital points, and it is necessary to repeat that if the individual were a complete being, if he made up a closed system like the monad of Leibnitz, metaphysics would not be possible; irremediably confined in himself, this being would have no means of knowing anything outside his own mode of existence. But such is not the case; in reality the individuality represents nothing more than a transitory and contingent manifestation of the real being. It is only one particular state amongst an indefinite multitude of other states of the same being; and this being is, in itself, absolutely independent of all its manifestations, just as, to use an illustration which occurs frequently in Hindu texts, the sun is absolutely independent of the manifold images in which it is reflected. Such is the fundamental distinction between "Self" and "I," the personality and the individuality; as the images are connected by the luminous rays with their solar source, without which they would have neither existence nor reality, so the individuality, either of the human individual or of any other similar state of manifestation, is bound by the personality to the principial center of being by this transcendent intellect of which we are speaking. It is impossible, within the limits of this exposition, to develop these lines of thought more completely, or to give a more exact idea of the theory of multiple states of being;* but I think I have said enough to show the extreme importance of all truly metaphysical doctrine.

I said "theory," but here it is not a question of theory alone; this is a point which needs further explanation. Theoretical knowledge, which is only indirect and in some sense symbolic, is merely a preparation, though indispensable, for true knowledge. It is, moreover, the only knowledge which is communicable, even then only in a partial sense. That is why all statements are no more than a means of approaching knowledge, and this knowledge, which is in the first place only virtual, must later be effectively realized. Here we find another discrepancy in the more limited metaphysics to which we referred earlier, for example that of Aristotle. This remains theoretically inadequate in that it limits itself to being, and its theory seems to be presented as self-sufficient instead of being expressly bound up with a corresponding realization, as is the case in all Oriental doctrines. However, even in this imperfect metaphysics (we might be tempted to say this demi-metaphysics), sometimes statements are encountered which, if properly understood, would lead to totally different conclusions; thus, did not Aristotle specifically state that a being is all that it knows? This affirmation of identification through knowledge is the same in principle as metaphysical realization. But here the principle remains isolated; it has no value other than that of a merely theoretical statement, it carries no weight, and it seems that, having propounded it, one thinks no more about it. How was it that Aristotle himself and his followers failed to see all that here was implied? It is the same in many other cases, where apparently other equally essential things are forgotten, such as the distinction between pure intellect and reason, even after having defined them quite explicitly; these are strange omissions. Should one see in this the effect of certain limitations inherent in the Occidental mind, apart from some rare but always possible exceptions? This might be true in a certain measure; nevertheless it is not necessary to believe that Western intellectuality has always been as narrowly limited as it is in the present age. But after all, we have been speaking only of outward doctrines, though these are certainly superior to many others since, in spite of all, they comprise a part of the true metaphysics. For our part we are certain that there has been

---

* Editors' Note: See Guénon's later work dedicated to this subject, *The Multiple States of Being* (New York: Larson, 1984).

something other than this in the West during the Middle Ages and in olden times; there certainly have existed amongst an elite purely metaphysical doctrines which could be called complete, including their realization, a thing which, for most moderns, is barely conceivable. If the West has lost the memory of this completely it is because it has broken with its proper tradition, which explains why modern civilization is abnormal and deviationist.

If purely theoretical knowledge were an end in itself and if metaphysics went no further, it would still assuredly be worth something, but yet it would be altogether insufficient. In spite of conferring the genuine certainty, even greater than mathematical certainty, which belongs to such knowledge, it would yet remain, though in an incomparably superior order, analogous to that which, at an inferior level, constitutes terrestrial and human, scientific and philosophical, speculation. That is not what metaphysics is meant for; if others choose to interest themselves in a "mental sport," or suchlike, that is their affair; these things leave us cold, and moreover we think that the curiosities of psychology should be completely indifferent to the metaphysician. What he is concerned with is to know what is, and to know it in such fashion as to be oneself, truly and effectively, what one knows.

As for the means of metaphysical realization, we are well aware of such objections as can be made by those who find it necessary to challenge its possibility. These means, indeed, must be within man's reach; they must, in the first stages at least, be adapted to the human state, since it is in this state that the being now exists which subsequently will assume the higher states. Thus it is in these formal means, appropriate to this world as presently manifested, that the being finds a fulcrum for raising itself beyond this world. Words, symbolism, signs, rites, or preparatory methods of any sort have no other reason for existence and no other function; as we have already said, they are supports and nothing else. But some will ask, how is it possible that merely contingent means can produce an effect which immeasurably surpasses them and which is of a totally different order from that to which the instruments themselves belong? We should first point out that these means are, in reality, only fortuitous. The results they help to attain are by no means consequential; they place the being in the position requisite for attainment and that is all. If the above-mentioned objections were valid in this case they would be equally so for religious rites, for the sacraments, for example, where the disproportion between the means and the end is no less; some of those who have raised the above objections might have thought of this too. As for us, we do not confuse a simple means with a cause in the true sense of the word and we do not regard metaphysical realization as an effect, since it is not the production of something which does not yet exist, but the knowing of that which is, in an abiding and immutable manner, beyond all temporal succession, for all states of the being, considered under their primary aspect, abide in perfect simultaneousness in the eternal now.

Thus we see no difficulty in recognizing that there is nothing in common between metaphysical realization and the means leading to it, or, if preferred, which prepare for it. This is why, moreover, no means are strictly or absolutely necessary; or at least there is only one indispensable preparation, and that is theoretical knowledge. This, on the other hand, cannot go far without a means which will play the most important and constant part: This means is concentration. This is something completely foreign to the mental habits of the modern West, where everything tends towards dispersion and incessant change. All other means are only secondary in comparison; they serve above all to promote concentration and to harmonize the diverse elements of human individuality in order to facilitate effective communication between this individuality and the higher states of being.

Moreover, at the start, these means can be varied almost indefinitely, for they have to be adapted to the temperament of each individual and to his particular aptitudes and disposition. Later on the differences diminish, for it is a case of many ways which all lead to the same end; after reaching a certain stage all multiplicity vanishes, but by that time the contingent and individual means will have played their part. This part, which it is unnecessary to enlarge upon, is compared, in certain Hindu writings, to a horse which helps a man to reach the end of his journey more quickly and easily, but without which he would still have been able to arrive. Rites and various methods point the way to metaphysical realization, but one could nevertheless ignore them and by unswervingly setting the mind and all powers of the being to the aim of this realization could finally attain the supreme goal; but if there are means which make the effort less laborious, why choose to neglect them? Is it confusing the contingent with the absolute to take into account the limitations of our human state, since it is from this state, itself contingent, that we are at present compelled to start in order to attain higher states, and finally the supreme and unconditioned state?

After considering the teachings common to all traditional doctrines we must now turn to the principal stages of metaphysical realization. The first is only preliminary and operates in the human domain and does not go beyond the limits of the individuality. It consists of an indefinite extension of this individuality of which the corporeal modality, which is all that is developed in the ordinary man, represents the smallest portion; it is from this corporeal modality that it is necessary to start by means borrowed from the sensible order, but which, however, must have repercussions in the other modalities of the human being. The phase in question is, in short, the realization or development of all the potentialities which are contained in the human individuality, and which, comprising, as they do, manifold extensions, reach out in diverse directions beyond the realm of the corporeal and sensible; and it is by these extensions that it is possible to establish communication with the other states.

This realization of the integral individuality is described by all traditions as the restoration of what is called the "primordial state" which is regarded as man's true estate and which moreover escapes some of the limitations characteristic of the ordinary state, notably that of the temporal condition. The person who attains this "primordial state" is still only a human individual and is without effective possession of any supra-individual states; he is nevertheless freed from time and the apparent succession of things is transformed for him into simultaneity; he consciously possesses a faculty which is unknown to the ordinary man and which one might call the "sense of eternity." This is of extreme importance, for he who is unable to leave the viewpoint of temporal succession and see everything in simultaneity is incapable of the least conception of the metaphysical order. The first thing to be done by those who wish to achieve true metaphysical understanding is to take up a position outside time, we say deliberately in "non-time," if such an expression does not seem too peculiar and unusual. This knowledge of the intemporal can, moreover, be achieved in some real measure, if incompletely, before having fully attained this "primordial state" which we are considering.

It might be asked perhaps: Why this appellation of "primordial state"? It is because all traditions, including that of the West (for the Bible says nothing different) are in agreement in teaching that this state was originally normal for humanity, whereas the present state is merely the result of a fall, the effect of a progressive materialization which has occurred in the course of the ages, and throughout the duration of a particular cycle. We do not believe in "evolution" in the sense that the moderns give the word. The so-called scientific hypotheses just mentioned in no way correspond to reality. It is not possible here to make more than bare allusion to the theory of cosmic cycles, which is particularly expounded in the Hindu doctrines; this would be going beyond our subject, for cosmology is not metaphysics even though the two things are closely related. It is no more than an application of metaphysics to the physical order, while the true natural laws are only the consequences, in a relative and contingent domain, of universal and necessary principles.

To revert to metaphysical realization: Its second phase corresponds to supra-individual but still conditioned states, though their conditions are quite different from those of the human state. Here, the world of man, previously mentioned, is completely and definitely exceeded. It must also be said that that which is exceeded is the world of forms in its widest meaning, comprising all possible individual states, for form is the common denominator of all these states; it is that which determines individuality as such. The being, which can no longer be called human, has henceforth left the "flow of forms," to use a Far-Eastern expression. There are, moreover, further distinctions to be made, for this phase can be subdivided. In reality it includes several stages, from the achievement of states which though informal still appertain to manifested existence, up to that degree of universality which is pure being.

Nevertheless, however exalted these states may be when compared with the human state, however remote they are from it, they are still only relative, and that is just as true of the highest of them, which corresponds to the principle of all manifestation. Their possession is only a transitory result, which should not be confused with the final goal of metaphysical realization; this end remains outside being and by comparison with it everything else is only a preparatory step. The highest objective is the absolutely unconditioned state, free from all limitation; for this reason it is completely inexpressible, and all that one can say of it must be conveyed in negative terms by divestment of the limits which determine and define all existence in its relativity. The attainment of this state is what the Hindu doctrine calls "Deliverance" when considered in connection with the Supreme Principle.

In this unconditioned state all other states of being find their place, but they are transformed and released from the special conditions which determined them as particular states. What remains is that which has a positive reality, since herein it is that all things have their own principle; the "delivered" being is truly in possession of the fullness of its own potentialities. The only things which have disappeared are the limiting conditions, which are negative, since they represent no more than a "privation" in the Aristotelian sense. Also, far from being a kind of annihilation, as some Westerners believe, this final state is, on the contrary, absolute plenitude, the supreme reality in the face of which all else remains illusion.

Let us add once more that every result, even partial, obtained by the being in the course of metaphysical realization are truly its own. This result constitutes a permanent acquisition for the being, of which nothing can deprive it; the work accomplished in this way, even if interrupted before it is completed, is achieved once and for all since it is beyond time. This is true even of merely theoretical knowledge, for all knowledge carries its benefit in itself, contrary to action, which is only a momentary modification of a being and is always separated from its various effects. These effects belong to the same domain and order of existence as that which has produced them. Action cannot have the effect of liberating from action, and its consequences cannot reach beyond the limits of individuality considered in its fullest possible extension. Action, whatever it may be, is not opposed to, and cannot banish, ignorance which is the root of all limitation; only knowledge can dispel ignorance as the light of the sun disperses darkness, and it is thus that the "Self," the immutable and eternal principle of all manifest and unmanifest states, appears in its supreme reality.

After this brief and very imperfect outline, which can only give the merest idea of metaphysical realization, it is absolutely essential to stress one point in order to avoid grave errors of interpretation; it is that all with which we are here concerned has no connection whatever with phenomena of any sort, however extraordinary. All phenomena are of the physical order; metaphysics is beyond the phenomenal, even if we use the word in its widest sense. It follows from this, amongst other inferences, that the states to which we are referring are in no way "psychological"; this must be specifically stated since strange confusions sometimes arise in this connection. By definition psychology can only be concerned with human states, and further, what it stands for today is only a very limited part of the potentialities of the individual, who includes far more than specialists in this science are able to imagine. The human individual is, at one and the same time, much more and much less than is ordinarily supposed in the West; he is greater by reason of his possibilities of indefinite extension beyond the corporeal modality, in short, of all that refers to what we have been studying; but he is also much less since, far from constituting a complete and sufficient being in himself, he is only an exterior manifestation, a fleeting appearance clothing the true being, which in no way affects the essence of the latter in its immutability.

It is necessary to insist on this point that the metaphysical domain lies entirely outside the phenomenal world, for the moderns hardly ever know or investigate anything other than phenomena; it is with these that they are almost exclusively concerned, as is demonstrated by the attention they have given to the experimental sciences. Their metaphysical ineptitude arises from the same tendency. Undoubtedly some phenomena may occur during the work for metaphysical realization, but in a quite accidental manner. They can also have unfortunate consequences, as things of this nature are only an obstacle for those who are tempted to attach importance to them. Those who are halted or turned aside by phenomena, and above all those who indulge in search for extraordinary "powers," have very little chance of pressing on to a realization beyond the point already arrived at before this deviation occurred.

This observation leads naturally to the rectification of some erroneous interpretations on the subject of the term "yoga." Has it not been claimed that what the Hindus mean by this word is the development of certain powers latent in the human being? What we are about to say will suffice to show that such a definition should be rejected. In reality the word "yoga" is the same as that which we have translated as literally as possible by the word "union" and which, correctly defined, thus means the supreme goal of metaphysical realization; the "yogi," in the strictest sense of the term, is solely the man who attains this end. However, it is true that in a wider sense the same terms, in some cases, may be applied to stages preparatory to "union" or even to simple preliminary means, as well as to the being who has reached states corresponding to those stages which these means are employed in order to attain. But how can it be supposed that a word primarily meaning "union" applies correctly and originally to breathing exercises or other things of that sort? These and other exercises, usually based on what we might call the science of rhythm, admittedly figure amongst the most usual means for the promoting of realization; but one must not mistake for the end that which amounts to no more than contingent and accidental aids, nor must one confuse the original meaning of a word with a secondary acceptation which is more or less distorted.

Referring to the original "yoga," and while declaring that it has always meant essentially the same thing, one must not forget to put a question of which we have as yet made no mention. What is the origin of these traditional metaphysical doctrines from which we have borrowed all our fundamental ideas? The answer is very simple, although it risks raising objections from those who would look at everything from an historical viewpoint: It is that there is no origin; by which we mean no human origin subjected to determination in time. In other words, the origin of tradition, if indeed the word origin has any applicability in such a case, is "non-human," as is metaphysics itself. Doctrines of this order have not appeared at any particular moment in the history of humanity; the allusion we have made to the "primordial state," and also what we have said of the intemporal nature of all that is metaphysical, enables one to grasp this point without too much difficulty, on condition that it be admitted, contrary to certain prejudices, that there are some things to which the historical point of view is not applicable. Metaphysical truth is eternal; even so, there have always existed beings who could truly and completely know. All that changes is only exterior forms and contingent means; and the change has nothing to do with what people today call "evolution," It is only a simple adaptation of such and such particular circumstances to special conditions of some given race or epoch. From this results the multiplicity of forms; but the basis of the doctrine is no more modified and affected than the essential unity and identity of the being is altered by the multiplicity of its states of manifestation.

Metaphysical knowledge, as well as the realization that will turn it into all that it truly ought to be, is thus possible everywhere and always, at least in principle and when regarded in a quasi-absolute sense; but in fact and in a relative sense, can it be said that this is equally possible in any sphere and without making the least allowance for contingencies? On this score we shall be much less positive, at least as far as realization is concerned; which is explained by the fact that in its beginning such a realization must take its support from the realm of contingencies. Conditions in the modern West are particularly unfavorable, so much so that such a work is almost impossible and can even be dangerous in the absence of any help from the environment and in conditions which can only impede or destroy the efforts of one who undertakes such a task. On the other hand, those civilizations which we call traditional are organized in such a way that one can find effectual aid, though this is not absolutely necessary, any more than anything else of an external kind; nevertheless without such help it is difficult to obtain effective results. Here is something which exceeds the strength of an isolated human individual, even if that individual possesses the requisite qualifications in other respects; also we do not want to encourage anyone, in present conditions, to embark thoughtlessly upon such an enterprise, and this brings us to our conclusion.

For us, the outstanding difference between the East and West (which means in this case the modern West), the only difference which is really essential (for all others are derivative), is on the one side the preservation of tradition with all that this implies, and on the other side the forgetting and loss of this same tradition; on one side the maintaining of metaphysical knowledge, on the other complete ignorance of all connected with this realm.* Between civilizations which open to their elite the possibilities of which we have caught a glimpse and offer the most appropriate means for their effective realization (thus allowing of their full realization by some at least)—between those traditional civilizations and a civilization which has developed along purely material lines, what common measure can be found? And how, without being blinded by I know not what prejudices, dare one claim that material superiority compensates for intellectual inferiority? When we say intellectual, we mean by that the true intellectuality, that which is restricted by neither limitations of the human nor the natural order and which makes pure metaphysical knowledge possible in its absolute transcendence. It seems to me that only a moment's reflection on these questions leaves no doubt or hesitation as to the answer that should be given.

The material prosperity of the West is incontrovertible; nobody denies it, but it is hardly a cause for envy. Indeed one can go further; sooner or later this excessive material development threatens to destroy the West if it does not recover itself in time, and if it does not consider seriously a "return to the source," using an expression which is employed in certain Islamic esoteric schools. Today one hears from many quarters of the "defense of the West," but unfortunately it does not seem to be understood that it is against itself that the West needs to be defended, and that it is its own present tendencies which are the chief and most formidable of all the dangers which really threaten it. It would be as well to meditate deeply on this; one cannot urge this too strongly on all who are still capable of reflection. So it is with this that I will end my account; I have done my best to make it, if not

---

* Editors' Note: Recent decades, however, have seen the Orient become increasingly modernist under the pernicious influence of Western "globalization." See also Frithjof Schuon, "Between East and West," in *The Eye of the Heart* (Bloomington, IN: World Wisdom Books, 1997), pp. 63-70.

fully comprehensible, at least suggestive of that Oriental intellectuality which no longer has any equivalent in the West. This has been a sketch, even if imperfect, of the true metaphysics, of that knowledge, which, according to the sacred works of India, is alone completely true, absolute, infinite, and supreme.

8 THE DECISIVE BOUNDARY

Martin Lings

The different degrees in the hierarchy of universal existence could be subdivided again and again. But what matters doctrinally is to be aware of the main divisions, starting from the Absolute Itself which is beyond existence and beyond Being, and which alone is Real, in the full sense of the word. This is the degree of the Transpersonal Self, which transcends all relativity. Below It, but still in the domain of Divinity, is the relative Absolute,[1] that is, the Personal God, the Creator from Whom proceeds all createdness, all existence.[2] Creation marks the division between the Divine and the existent, between Worshiped and worshiper. The subsequent great division in the hierarchy is the polarization of all existence into Heaven and earth, or Spirit and soul—from our point of view this world and the next, though the last word may be taken in a wider sense to include all that transcends this world, both created and Uncreated. Finally there is the division between soul and body, between the psychic world and the material world.

Each world in the hierarchy of the universe is a reflection of the one above it, and each of its contents reflects, in the higher world, a counterpart which is the immediate source of its existence but which, in its turn, is no more than the reflection of a yet more real counterpart from a yet higher plane of existence. There is thus, for each symbol in the world of matter, a whole series of archetypes one above the other, like the rungs of a ladder, leading up to the Supreme Archetype in the Divine Essence. With regard to the term archetype however, we are obliged to make an important reservation, the reason for which can clearly be seen in the light of the significance of the *Symplegades*, the

---

[1] We owe this indispensable term to Frithjof Schuon who, no doubt more than any writer of this [i.e. the twentieth] century, has stressed the need for awareness of the distinction *in divinis* between the Absolute and the relative, a distinction which has always been known to esoterism, whatever the tradition, but which exoteric theology has refrained from divulging, more or less with impunity until now, when the widespread overactivity of minds makes its disclosure the lesser of two evils.

[2] The word is used here in its original sense of *ex-stare*, to stand out from (i.e. from an origin).

Clashing Rocks of Greek mythology. In his masterly article on these rocks,[3] Ananda Coomaraswamy shows that they have their equivalents in many other ancient traditions where the symbol takes also the form of clashing mountains, clashing icebergs, clashing waters, clashing portals and, in the temporal domain, the clashing together of day and night between which the two twilights offer narrow gates of passage. What is above all significant in our present context is the extreme difficulty and danger of the passage. It is virtually impossible to reach what lies beyond the rocks without the help of Heaven; and aspiration towards that beyond—so Coomaraswamy's article shows us—was a dominant factor in the lives of all the peoples of antiquity—we might say of all peoples except those who are typical of the modern civilization. The rocks are clearly the equivalent of the "strait gate" (Matthew 7:13-14) of the Gospel; and like that gate they are situated precisely between the soul and the Spirit, where this world ends and the next world begins. To tell of the rocks is thus to affirm that the place where they operate is what might be called a particularly crucial rung in the ladder of existence. From the human point of view, that is indeed the decisive boundary; nothing of lasting value exists or can be achieved this side of the Symplegades, while beyond them there is no evil, no suffering, and no death. It was the Fall which galvanized these rocks into activity, and they are in fact the equivalent of what barred the return of fallen man to Eden—in the words of Genesis: "Cherubims and a flaming sword which turned every way to keep the way of the tree of life" (3:24). The Tree and the Fountain mark the center of the earthly state; but a center, since it is the point of access to higher realities, is always above the rest of its domain. Thus on the one hand Eden is the Terrestrial Paradise, while on the other hand it is spoken of as if it belonged to the next world, for like its central Tree and Fountain it is beyond the flaming sword and the clashing rocks. So, analogously, is the Heart, the center of the soul; but the soul as such, together with its body, is on this side of the barrier. It ranks above the body, which is its shadow or reflection; but it shares with the body the limitation of being natural and not in any sense supernatural.

It follows by way of consequence that although every material symbol reflects its counterparts in the soul—and it may reflect more than one at different levels of the psychic domain—such counter-

---

[3] See *Studies in Comparative Religion*, Winter, 1973 [Editors' Note: Chapter 14 of the present anthology]. For a brief analysis, see Martin Lings, *The Eleventh Hour* (Cambridge, UK: Archetype, 2002), pp. 75-78.

parts are not normally referred to as archetypes. This term is strictly reserved, in traditional practice, for what lies beyond the crucial barrier that is represented by the rocks which Athene held apart for the Argonauts to pass, by "the strait gate" of which it is said "few are they that find it," and by the waters of the Red Sea[4] which opened for the children of Israel on their way to the Promised Land but which closed upon Pharaoh and his host who had no warrant to pass.

There is more than one imperative practical reason—and for practical we might say methodic—why such words as archetype should not be squandered on the psychic domain. The prefix "arch" signifies both exaltation and primacy, which confers on it also a sense of finality from the mystical standpoint of looking towards our first origins with a view to reintegration, whereas the soul is, from the same standpoint, that which has to be surpassed. There can be no advancing upon the spiritual path unless all one's aspirations and energies be concentrated on what lies beyond the ego. But there is something in the soul which shrinks, not unnaturally, from the ordeal of the dread passage, and which will snatch at any pretext for putting off "the evil day," and for enticing the spiritual traveler into its own seemingly endless labyrinthine recesses. Moreover the microcosm's fear of surpassing itself finds an ally in the unwillingness of the macrocosm, that is, all that lies on this side of the barrier, to allow any part of itself to escape from its hold. Nor, to say the least, is it for nothing that the Fall unleashed for mankind a downward and outward impetus which makes any approach to the decisive boundary a difficult upstream movement. The personifier of that impetus, whether he be called demiurge or devil, will not fail to exploit the above-mentioned disinclinations as a means of obstructing the path of return to our origins.

The modem world presents another obstacle for him to exploit, one which did not previously exist, inasmuch as psychology—in all but name—was in the hands of spiritual men. In traditional civilizations it was the priest or his equivalent, and no one else, who was thought qualified to give advice about the soul, which was never considered independently of man's final ends, that is, without reference to the higher degrees of reality. The ego could not turn a blind eye to its own limitations because it was never allowed to forget its place in the hierarchy of existence. Moreover those responsible for "the cure

---

[4] That is, if the Exodus be interpreted, beyond its literal sense, according to its esoteric or anagogical significance as an image of the spiritual path, of which the ultimate goal is symbolized by the Promised Land.

of souls" could take for granted a general knowledge of the doctrine of original sin. It was as if every patient had been told in advance, to use the language of our theme, "you are on the wrong side of the boundary, and until you are able to reach the other side you will continue to be somewhat subhuman and must expect the consequences." All advice was given on that basis of realism.

Modern psychology, on the contrary, dismisses the doctrine in question and with it the "rocks." The higher reaches of the universe are relegated to the realm of mere supposition, and the microcosm, soul and body, is isolated from all that transcends it. The soul is thus treated as the highest known thing. The average psychoanalyst may not deliberately set out to inflate it with self-importance, but in fact his so-called science acts like a conspiracy in that direction. Another closely related illusion inculcated by it is that of being self-sufficient and normal. The soul is made unrealistically expectant of freedom from problems which are bound to beset it, and the absence of which would be discreditable.[5]

The point to be made here however, is that although modern psychology is eager to throw metaphysics to the winds, it is not prepared to impoverish its own vocabulary by abstention from high-sounding words of metaphysical import. Consequently "archetype" and "transcendent," to mention only two examples,[6] are currently used in relation to things which, while being higher than others, none the less belong to the domain of nature which is by definition untranscendent and therefore not capable of being the repository of archetypes.[7]

[5] See, in this respect, Frithjof Schuon, *Survey of Metaphysics and Esoterism,* (Bloomington, IN: World Wisdom Books, 1986) p. 197.

[6] We are not considering here the words "intellect" and "intellectual," since these have already been in misuse since the so-called "Enlightenment." Modern psychology did not inaugurate this violation, though it can be blamed for failing to react against it.

[7] Jung is particularly insidious in his misuse of this term—see Titus Burckhardt, *Mirror of the Intellect* (Cambridge, UK: Quinta Essentia, 1987) pp. 58-67.

9 SCIENTIA SACRA*

Seyyed Hossein Nasr

The Good Religion is Innate Wisdom: and the forms and virtues of Innate
Wisdom are of the same stock as Innate Wisdom itself.
Dēnkard

A fund of omniscience exists eternally in our heart.
Tipiṭaka

Scientia sacra is none other than that sacred knowledge which lies
at the heart of every revelation and is the center of that circle which
encompasses and defines tradition. The first question which presents
itself is, how is the attainment of such a knowledge possible? The
answer of tradition is that the twin source of this knowledge is revelation and intellection or intellectual intuition which involves the
illumination of the heart and the mind of man and the presence in
him of knowledge of an immediate and direct nature which is tasted
and experienced, the sapience which the Islamic tradition refers to
as "presential knowledge" (*al-ʿilm al-ḥuḍūrī*).[1] Man is able to know
and this knowledge corresponds to some aspect of reality. Ultimately
in fact, knowledge is knowledge of Absolute Reality and intelligence
possesses this miraculous gift of being able to know that which is and
all that partakes of being.[2]

Scientia sacra is not the fruit of human intelligence speculating
upon or reasoning about the content of an inspiration, or a spiritual
experience which itself is not of an intellectual character. Rather, what
is received through inspiration is itself of an intellectual nature; it is
sacred knowledge. The human intelligence which perceives this mes-

* Editors' Note: A slightly abridged version of chapter 4 of Seyyed Hossein Nasr's
Knowledge and the Sacred (the 1981 Gifford Lectures), expressly approved by the
author for publication in the present anthology.

[1] On the meaning of this term see Nasr, *Islamic Science: An Illustrated Study* (London:
World of Islam Festival Publishing, 1976), p. 14.

[2] "All knowledge is by definition knowledge of Absolute Reality; which is to say that
Reality is the necessary, unique, and essential object of all possible knowledge" (Frithjof
Schuon, *The Eye of the Heart* [Bloomington, IN: World Wisdom, 1997], p. 13).

sage and receives this truth does not impose upon it the intellectual nature or content of a spiritual experience of a sapiential character. The knowledge contained in such an experience issues from the source of this experience which is the Intellect, the source of all sapience and the bestower of all principial knowledge, the Intellect which also modifies the human recipient that the Scholastics called the potential intellect. Here the medieval distinction between the active and passive or potential intellect[3] can serve to elucidate the nature of this process of the illumination of the mind and to remove the error of seeing the sapiential and intellectual content of spiritual experience as being the result of the human mind meditating upon or reasoning about the content of such an experience, whereas spiritual experience on the highest level is itself of an intellectual and sapiential nature.

From another point of view, that of the Self which resides at the center of every self, the source of the *scientia sacra* revealed to man is the center and root of human intelligence itself since ultimately "knowledge of the Substance is the substance of knowledge," or knowledge of the Origin and the Source is the Origin and Source of knowledge. The truth descends upon the mind like an eagle landing upon a mountain top or it gushes forth and inundates the mind like a deep well which has suddenly burst forth into a spring. In either case, the sapiential nature of what the human being receives through spiritual experience is not the result of man's mental faculty but issues from the nature of that experience itself. Man can know through intuition and revelation not because he is a thinking being who imposes the categories of his thought upon what he perceives but because knowledge is being. The nature of reality is none other than consciousness, which, needless to say, cannot be limited to only its individual human mode.

Of course not everyone is capable of intellection or of having intellectual intuition no more than everyone is capable of having faith in a particular religion. But the lack of possibility of intellection for everyone does not invalidate the reality of such a possibility any more than does the fact that many people are not able to have faith

---

[3] Islamic as well as Jewish and Christian philosophers of the medieval period distinguished between the Active Intellect (*al-ʿaql al-faʿāl, intellectus agens, ha-sekhel hapoʾel*) which is the origin of knowledge and the potential or "material" intellect (*al-ʿaql al hayūlānī, intellectus materialis, ha-sekhel ha-hyulaʾni*) which receives knowledge, and emphasized the intellectual nature of what is received by the human mind from the Divine Intellect.

115

invalidate the reality of a religion. In any case for those who have the possibility of intellectual intuition there is the means to attain a knowledge of a sacred character that lies at the heart of that objective revelation which constitutes religion and also at the center of man's being. This microcosmic revelation makes possible access to that *scientia sacra* which contains the knowledge of the Real and the means of distinguishing between the Real and the illusory.

What we have designated as *scientia sacra* is none other than metaphysics if this term is understood correctly as the ultimate science of the Real. This term possesses certain unfortunate connotations because, first of all, the prefix *meta* does imply transcendence but not immanence and also it connotes a form of knowledge or science that comes after physics whereas metaphysics is the primary and fundamental science or wisdom which comes before and contains the principles of all the sciences.[4] Second, the habit of considering metaphysics in the West as a branch of philosophy, even in those philosophical schools which have a metaphysical dimension, has been instrumental in reducing the significance of metaphysics to just mental activity rather than seeing it as a sacred science concerned with the nature of Reality and wed to methods for the realization of this knowledge, a science which embraces the whole of man's being.[5] In Oriental languages such terms as *prajñā, jñāna, maʿrifah,* or *ḥikmah* connote the ultimate science of the Real without their being reduced to a branch of another form of knowledge known as philosophy or its equivalent. And it is in this traditional sense of *jñāna* or *maʿrifah* that metaphysics, or the "science of the Real," can be considered as identical with *scientia sacra.*

If one were to ask what is metaphysics, the primary answer would be the science of the Real or, more specifically, the knowledge by means of which man is able to distinguish between the Real and the illusory and to know things in their essence or as they are, which means ultimately to know them *in divinis.*[6] The knowledge of the

---

[4] The Platonic view which sees knowledge descending from the realm of the "ideas" to the world, or from the Principle to manifestation, is more akin to the sapiential perspective than the Aristotelian one which moves from manifestation to the Principle or from physics to metaphysics.

[5] On the distinction between metaphysics and profane philosophy see René Guénon, *Introduction to the Study of Hindu Doctrines* (London: Luzac & Co., 1945), pp. 108ff; and "Oriental Metaphysics," in Needleman (ed.), *Sword of Gnosis* (Baltimore, MD: Penguin, 1974), pp. 40-56. [Editors' Note: Chapter 7 of the present anthology.]

[6] This element comprises the heart of all traditional doctrine while the method concerns means of attaching oneself to the Real. On the relation between doctrine

Principle which is at once the absolute and infinite Reality is the heart of metaphysics while the distinction between levels of universal and cosmic existence, including both the macrocosm and the microcosm, are like its limbs. Metaphysics concerns not only the Principle in itself and in its manifestations but also the principles of the various sciences of a cosmological order. At the heart of the traditional sciences of the cosmos, as well as traditional anthropology, psychology, and aesthetics stands the *scientia sacra* which contains the principles of these sciences while being primarily concerned with the knowledge of the Principle which is both sacred knowledge and knowledge of the sacred *par excellence*, since the Sacred as such is none other than the Principle.

The Principle is Reality in contrast to all that appears as real but which is not reality in the ultimate sense. The Principle is the Absolute compared to which all is relative. It is Infinite while all else is finite. The Principle is One and Unique while manifestation is multiplicity. It is the Supreme Substance compared to which all else is accident. It is the Essence to which all things are juxtaposed as form. It is at once Beyond Being and Being while the order of multiplicity is comprised of existents. It alone *is* while all else becomes, for It alone is eternal in the ultimate sense while all that is externalized partakes of change. It is the Origin but also the End, the alpha and the omega. It is Emptiness if the world is envisaged as fullness and Fullness if the relative is perceived in the light of its ontological poverty and essential nothingness.[7] These are all manners of speaking of the Ultimate Reality which can be known but not by man as such. It can only be known through the sun of the Divine Self residing at the center of the human soul. But all these ways of describing or referring to the Principle possess

and method see Marco Pallis, "The Marriage of Wisdom and Method," *Studies in Comparative Religion* 1972, 6 (2), pp. 78-104. [Editors' Note: See also Marco Pallis' *A Buddhist Spectrum* (Bloomington, IN: World Wisdom, 2003), pp. 25-37, for a revised version of this article.]

[7] Some contemporary scholars such as R. Panikkar (in his *Inter-religious Dialogue* [New York, 1978]) have contrasted the Buddhist *Shunyata* and the Christian Pleroma but, metaphysically speaking, the concept of Ultimate Reality as emptiness and as fullness complement each other like the *yin-yang* symbol and both manifest themselves in every integral tradition. Even in Christianity where the symbolism of Divine Fullness is emphasized and developed with remarkable elaboration in Franciscan theology, especially that of St. Bonaventure, the complementary vision of emptiness appears in the teachings of the Dominican Meister Eckhart who speaks of the "desert of the Godhead."

meaning and are efficacious as points of reference and support for that knowledge of the Real that in its realized aspect always terminates in the Ineffable and in that silence which is the "reflection" or "shadow" of the non-manifested aspect of the Principle upon the plane of manifestation. From that unitary point of view, the Principle or the Source is seen as not only the Inward but also the Outward,[8] not only the One but also the essential reality of the many which is but the reflection of the One. At the top of that mountain of unitive knowledge there resides but the One; discrimination between the Real and the unreal terminates in the awareness of the non-dual nature of the Real, the awareness which is the heart of gnosis and which represents not human knowledge but God's knowledge of Himself, the consciousness which is the goal of the path of knowledge and the essence of *scientia sacra*.[9]

The Ultimate Reality is at once Absolute and Infinite since no finite reality can be absolute due to its exclusion of some domain of reality. This reality is also the Supreme Good or the Perfection which is inseparable from the Absolute. Reality, being at once Absolute, Infinite, and Supreme Goodness or Perfection, cannot but give rise to the world or multiplicity which must be realized for otherwise that Reality would exclude certain possibilities and not be infinite. The world flows from the infinitude and goodness of the Real for to speak of goodness is to speak of manifestation, effusion, or creation and to speak of infinity is to speak of all possibilities including that of the negation of the Principle in whose direction the cosmogonic process moves without ever realizing that negation completely, for that total negation would be nothingness pure and simple.

Goodness is also from another point of view the image of the Absolute in the direction of that effusion and manifestation which marks the descent from the Principle and constitutes the world. Herein lies the root of relativity but it is still on the plane of Divinity. It is relatively *in divinis* or what could be called, using the well-known Hindu concept, the Divine *māyā*.[10] Relativity is a possibility of that

---

[8] In one of the most difficult verses to comprehend from the exoteric point of view the Quran states, "He is the First and the Last; the Outward and the Inward" (57:3).

[9] This is the view of the Advaita Vedanta in Hinduism and of the transcendent Unity of Being (*waḥdat al-wujūd*) in Sufism which, because of the myopia of a reason divorced from the sanctifying rays of the Intellect, have been often mistaken for pantheism. See Nasr, *Three Muslim Sages* (Cambridge, Mass., 1964), pp. 104-108; also Titus Burckhardt, *Introduction to Sufi Doctrine* (London, 1976), pp. 28-30.

[10] See Frithjof Schuon, *From the Divine to the Human* (Bloomington, IN: World

Reality which is at once Absolute and Infinite; hence that reality or the Absolute gives rise to that manifestation of the good which in descending hierarchy leads to the world. The world is ultimately good, as asserted by various orthodox traditions,[11] because it descends from the Divine Goodness. The instrument of this descent is the reflection of the Absolute upon the plane of that Divine Relativity, the reflection which is none other than the Supreme Logos, the source of all cosmic perfections, the "place" of the archetypes, the "Word" by which all things were made.[12]

Since the world or manifestation or creation issues from that Reality which is at once Absolute, Infinite, and Perfection or Goodness, these Hypostases of the Real or the Divine must be also reflected in the manifested order. The quality of absoluteness is reflected in the very existence of things, that mysterious presence of each thing which distinguishes it from all other things and from nothingness. Infinitude is reflected in the world in diverse modes in space which is indefinite extension, in time which is potentially endless duration, in form which displays unending diversity, in number which is marked by endless multiplicity, and in matter, a substance which partakes potentially of endless forms and divisions. As for Goodness, it is reflected in the cosmos through quality itself which is indispensable to existence however eclipsed it might become in certain forms in the world of multiplicity which are removed as far as possible from the luminous and essential pole of manifestation. Space which preserves, time which changes and transforms, form which reflects quality, number which signifies indefinite quantity, and matter which is characterized by limitless substantiality are the conditions of existence of not only the physical world but the worlds above reaching ultimately the

---

Wisdom, 1982), Part Two, "Divine and Universal Order."

[11] The point of view of Manichaeism which sees the world as evil rather than good is primarily initiatic and not metaphysical, that is, it begins not with the aim of understanding the nature of things but of providing a way for escaping from the prison of material existence. Buddhism possesses a similar practical perspective but, of course, with a different metaphysical background since it belongs to a different spiritual universe.

[12] Islam and Hinduism join the Judeo-Christian tradition in confirming that it was by the Word that all things were made. The Quran asserts, "Verily, when He [Allah] intends a thing, His Command is, 'Be' [kun], and it is!" (36:82 [Yusuf Ali translation]). Here the imperative form of the verb "to be," namely kun, being identified with the Word or Logos.

Divine Empyrean and the Divine Hypostases of Absoluteness, Infinity, and Perfection themselves.

Since metaphysics as developed in the Occident has almost always been related to ontology, it is important to pause a moment and discuss the relation of Being to the Principle or Ultimate Reality. If Being is envisaged as the principle of existence or of all that exists, then It cannot be identified with the Principle as such because the Principle is not exhausted by its creating aspect. Being is the first determination of the Supreme Principle in the direction of manifestation, and ontology remains only a part of metaphysics and is incomplete as long as it envisages the Principle only as Being in the sense defined. But if Being is used to embrace and include the sense of Absoluteness and Infinity, then it can mean both the Supra-Being or Reality beyond Being and Being as its first determination, even if only the term *Being* is used. Such seems to be the case with *esse* as employed by certain of the Scholastics and also *wujūd* in some of the schools of Islamic philosophy and theosophy.[13]

The distinction between Being and being, Being and existence, existence and essence or quiddity and the relation between quiddity or essence and existence in existents lies at heart of medieval Islamic, Jewish, and Christian philosophy and has been discussed in numerous works of medieval thought. From the point of view of *scientia sacra* what caused this profound way of envisaging reality to become unintelligible and finally rejected in the West was the loss of that intellectual intuition which destroyed the sense of the mystery of existence and reduced the subject of philosophy from the study of the act of existence (*esto*) to the existent (*ens*), thereby gradually reducing reality

---

[13] One can interpret Thomistic metaphysics which begins and ends with *esse* as including the notion of the Real in its completely unconditioned and undetermined sense although this term could be complemented by the term *posse* to denote the All-Possibility of the Divine Principle. From this point of view one can assert that despite the sensualist epistemology of St. Thomas, criticized earlier because of its denial of the possibility of intellectual intuition, Thomism contains in its dogmatic content truths of a truly metaphysical nature which reflect knowledge of a principial order and which can serve as support for metaphysical contemplation.

In Islamic philosophy such a figure as Ṣadr al-Dīn Shīrāzī speaks about *wujūd* (which means literally "being") in such a manner that it is definitely to be identified with the Supreme Principle rather than its first self-determination. The Supreme Name of God in Islam, namely, Allah, implies also both Being and Beyond Being, both the personal Deity and the Absolute and Infinite Reality, both God and the Godhead of Meister Eckhart.

to pure "it" divorced from the world of the Spirit and the majesty of Being whose constant effusions uphold the world which appears to the senses as possessing a continuous "horizontal" existence divorced from the "vertical" Cause or Being *per se*. That Islamic philosophy did not end with that impasse which marks the study of ontology in Western philosophy is due to its insistence upon the study of Being and its act rather than existents and to the wedding of this philosophy, by Suhrawardī and those who were to follow him, to spiritual experience which made the experience of Being not only a possibility but the source for all philosophical speculation concerning the concept and reality of being.

The Ultimate Reality which is both Supra-Being and Being is at once transcendent and immanent. It is beyond everything and at the very heart and center of man's soul. *Scientia sacra* can be expounded in the language of one as well as the other perspective. It can speak of God or the Godhead, Allah, the Tao, or even *nirvāna* as being beyond the world, or forms, or *samsāra*, while asserting ultimately that *nirvāna is samsāra*, and *samsāra, nirvāna*. But it can also speak of the Supreme Self, of *Ātman*, compared to which all objectivization is *māyā*. The Ultimate Reality can be seen as both the Supreme Object and the Innermost Subject, for God is both transcendent and immanent, but He can be experienced as immanent only after He has been experienced as transcendent. Only God as Being can allow man to experience the Godhead as Supra-Being. The unitive knowledge which sees the world not as separative creation but as manifestation that is united through symbols and the very ray of existence to the Source does not at all negate the majesty of transcendence. Without that majesty, the beauty of Divine Proximity cannot be beheld and integral metaphysics is fully aware of the necessity, on its own level, of the theological formulations which insist upon the hiatus between God and man or the Creator and the world. The metaphysical knowledge of unity comprehends the theological one in both a figurative and literal sense, while the reverse is not true. That is why the attainment of that unitive knowledge is impregnated with the perfume of sanctity which always strengthens the very foundations of the religion with which the formal theology in question is concerned, while the study of formal theology can never result in that *scientia sacra* which simply belongs to another dimension and which relies upon another aspect of the functioning of the Intellect upon the human plane.

Metaphysics does not only distinguish between the Real and the apparent and Being and becoming but also between grades of existence. The hierarchic nature of reality is a universal assertion of all traditions and is part and parcel of their religious practices as well as their doctrines, whether conceived in terms of various hosts and orders of angels as described in the famous *Celestial Hierarchies* of Dionysius, or levels of light and darkness as in certain schools of Islamic esoterism, or as various orders of gods and titans as in religions with a mythological structure such as Hinduism. Even in Buddhism for which the Supreme Principle is seen as the Void or Emptiness rather than Fullness, the vast intermediate worlds are depicted with remarkable power and beauty in both Buddhist cosmological texts and Buddhist art. The emphasis upon the hierarchic structure of reality in traditional doctrines is so great that a famous Persian poem states that he who does not accept the hierarchy of existence is an infidel (*zindīq*). Here again *scientia sacra* which is concerned with the nature of reality is distinguished from theology as usually understood, which can remain satisfied with what concerns man directly and a simpler view of reality based on God and man without emphasis upon the hierarchy of existence, although even in theology many schools have not failed to take into consideration the existence if not always the full significance of the intermediate planes of reality.[14]

The relation between the various levels of reality or hierarchy of existence cannot be fully understood without taking into consideration another important notion found in one way or another in all the complete expressions of the *scientia sacra*, this notion being that of necessity to which is contrasted the notion of possibility. The distinction between necessity and possibility is the cornerstone of the philosophy of Ibn Sīnā (Avicenna) who has been called the "philosopher of being" and father of medieval ontology. But the significance of both of these terms is of a purely metaphysical order and cannot be limited to the philosophical realm, even if this be traditional philosophy. It is the fruit of intellection rather than ratiocination as are in fact many of the tenets of traditional philosophy which veil in a syllogistic garb intuitions of a purely metaphysical nature. The presence of the notions of necessity and possibility in both Hindu and Far Eastern doctrines point in fact to realities of a universal order not at all limited to one particular mode of exposition or school of metaphysics.

---

[14] In Islam such a widespread theological school as Ash'arism is characterized by its rejection of the hierarchy of existence in conformity with its atomistic and voluntaristic point of view.

Necessity is opposed to possibility conceptually but, if the meaning of possibility is understood fully, it will be seen that in one sense it complements necessity and is opposed to necessity only in one of its meanings. The root of possibility is related to potentiality and also "puissance," all three words being derived from *posse*, which means "to be able to." Possibility has in fact two meanings: one, the quality or character of something that can exist or not exist; and two, the quality or character of something which has the power and capability to perform or carry out an act. In the first sense the quiddities of things are possible, or contingent; an object can exist or not exist and there is no logical or metaphysical contradiction whether, let us say, a horse exists or not. In this sense but on a higher level, the archetypes or what Islamic metaphysics call *al-aʿyān al-thābitah* or "immutable essences"[15] are also possible beings, only God being necessary. Taken in this meaning of the term, possibility is opposed to necessity while things which do exist and therefore must exist have become necessary not through their own essence but through the Necessary Being which alone is necessary in Itself. That is why, to use the language of Islamic philosophy again, they are called *al-wājib biʾl-ghayr*, literally "that which is made necessary by other than itself," the "other" being ultimately the Necessary Being.

In the second sense of the meaning of possibility as power, it is not opposed to necessity but complements it as far as the Principle is concerned. God is Absolute Necessity and Infinite Possibility, the omnipotence of God reflected in the Divine Attribute *al-Qādir* in the Quran, meaning exactly possibility in this second sense. Whatever happens in this world is according to the Will of God but also in conformity with a Divine Possibility. God could not will what is not possibility in this sense for He would then negate His own Nature. Whatever claims a blind type of religious voluntarism might make, God's omnipotence cannot contradict His Nature and when the Gospel claims, "With God all things are possible," it is referring precisely to this Infinite Possibility of God.

Each world brought into being corresponds to a Divine Possibility and gains existence through the Divine Will which operates on different levels, sometimes appearing as contradictory to the eyes of the earthly creature. But there is never anything arbitrary about what God

---

[15] On the immutable essences see Titus Burckhardt, *Introduction to Sufi Doctrine*, pp. 62-64.

wills; His wisdom complements His Will and His Nature remains inviolable.

As far as necessity is concerned, it can be said that although the medieval philosophers called pure Being the Necessary Being, strictly speaking only the Beyond Being or Ultimate Reality is necessity in Itself and necessary with respect to Itself. Being is necessary vis-à-vis the world so that from the point of view of the world or of multiplicity, it can be legitimately considered as the Necessary Being. But Being can also be considered as Possibility as such which must be distinguished from the possibilities which are qualities of Being. These qualities possess two aspects: they are contingent or possible in relation to the Principle or Essence, that is, they can exist or not exist; and they are necessary in their content and so participate in the necessity of the Essence. From the consideration of these two aspects one can see that there are two kinds of possibilities: those which reflect necessity and those which reflect contingency. The first kind engenders objects which definitely exist and the second those which can possibly not exist.

God gives existence to possibilities which are so many reflections and reverberations of Being and from this breathing of existence upon the quiddities of possibilities the world and, in fact, the myriad of worlds are born. That Divine Relativity or *māyā*, as it is projected toward nothingness and away from the Source, produces privative modalities and inversions of these possibilities whose origin is positive reflection and inversion, polarization of light and casting of shadows, luminous Logos and dark Demiurge. Being as Possibility is Itself the supreme veil of the Reality which in Itself is not only Infinite but also Absolute, that Essence which is beyond all determination.[16]

To speak of the veil is to be concerned with one of the key concepts with which *scientia sacra* is concerned, one which, however, has not been as much emphasized in Western metaphysical doctrines as it has in the East, although it is certainly mentioned by such figures as Eckhart and Silesius who allude to the Divine Relativity and are aware of its significance for the understanding of how the roots and principles of manifestation are to be found in the Principle Itself. The veil is none other than what the Hindus call *māyā* and the Sufis *ḥijāb*. The fact that *māyā* has now become practically an English word points to the necessity of dealing with such a concept in the exposition of

---

[16] "We can discern [in the absolutely Real] a tri-dimensionality—it too intrinsically and undifferentiated, yet the harbinger of a possible unfolding: these dimensions are

traditional doctrines and the lack of an appropriate term in the English language to convey all that *māyā* signifies.

Māyā is usually translated as illusion and from the non-dualistic or Advaitist point of view *māyā* is illusion, only *Ātman*, the Supreme Self, being real. But *māyā* is also creativity and "Divine Play" (*līlā*). On the principial level she is relativity which is the source of separateness, exteriorization, and objectivization. She is that tendency toward nothingness which brings manifestation into being, the nothingness which is never reached but which is implied by the cosmogonic movement away from the Principle. Infinitude could not but include the possibility of separation, division, and externalization which characterize all that is other than the Principle. *Māyā* is the supreme veil and also the supreme theophany which at once veils and reveals.[17] God being good cannot but radiate His goodness and this tendency toward radiation or manifestation implies that movement away from the Source which characterizes cosmic and even metacosmic levels of reality away from the Origin which alone is absolutely real. *Māyā* is almost the same as the Islamic *raḥmah*, the Divine Mercy, whose "breath" existentiates the world, the very substance of the world being *nafas al-raḥmān*, the Breath of the Compassionate in the same way that one can call *māyā* the breath of *Ātman*. For Hinduism, however, the creation of the world or the casting of the veil of *māyā* upon the Absolute Self or *Ātman* is expressed as "Divine Play," while for Islam this externalization which is none other than the activity of *māyā* is envisaged as the love of God to be "known," the origin of the world being the revelation of God to Himself according to the famous tradition of the Prophet (*ḥadīth*), "I was a hidden treasure, I desired to be known, hence I created the world in order to be known."

Formal theology envisages God and the world or the Creator and the created in a completely distinct and "absolute" manner and

'Being,' 'Consciousness,' and 'Bliss.' It is in virtue of the third element—immutable in itself—that Divine Possibility overflows and gives rise, 'through love,' to that mystery of exteriorization that is the universal Veil, whose weft is made of the worlds and whose warp is made of beings" (Frithjof Schuon, *From the Divine to the Human*, p. 55).

[17] "*Māyā* is likened to a magic fabric woven from a warp that veils and a weft that unveils" (Frithjof Schuon, *Light on the Ancient Worlds* [Bloomington, IN: World Wisdom, 1984], p. 89). On the metaphysical significance of *māyā* as both veil and principle of relativization and manifestation of the Absolute, see, besides this article, the chapter "*Ātmā-Māyā*" in Frithjof Schuon's *In the Face of the Absolute* (Bloomington, IN: World Wisdom, 1990), pp. 53-64.

is therefore unable to provide answers for certain fundamental questions intellectually, questions which can be dealt with only from the perspective of the *scientia sacra* and the doctrine of *māyā* or veil which, on the highest level, implies introduction of relativity into the principial plane without, however, reaching the level of the Absolute which remains beyond all duality and relativity. Since there is a world which is relative, the roots of this world must exist in the principial order itself and this root is none other than the Divine *māyā* which veils and manifests the One upon all planes of reality. She is the Feminine, at once Mary and Eve. Evil issues from the exteriorizing activity of *māyā* but Existence which remains pure and good finally prevails over evil as Eve was forgiven for her sins by the spiritual inviolability and victory of Mary.

Māyā acts through both radiation and reverberation or reflection, first preparing the ground or plane of manifestation and then manifesting both the radiation and reverberation which take place on this plane. To use an image of Schuon,[18] if we envisage a point which symbolizes the Absolute or the Supreme Substance, the radii symbolize the radiation, the circumference the reflection or reverberation of the center, and the area of the whole circle, Existence itself,[19] or a particular level of existence in which *māyā* repeats her act. *Māyā* is the source of all duality even on the principial level causing the distinction between the Essence and the Qualities. It is also the source of the dualism between subject and object even on the highest level beyond which there is but the One, in which knower and known, or subject and object are one. But *māyā* does not remain bound to the principial level alone. She is self-projected through various levels of cosmic existence which a *ḥadīth* calls the seventy thousand veils of light and darkness and which can be summarized as the three fundamental levels of angelic, animic, and physical existence.

Māyā in its aspect of illusion is also the cause for this impossibility of encompassing Reality in a closed system of thought so characteristic of profane philosophy. The Absolute is blinding evidence or something incomprehensible to those who do not possess the eye or intuition to grasp it conceptually. In any case, ratiocination, belonging

---

[18] See "*Ātmā-Māyā*."

[19] As far as the highest level is concerned, Islamic metaphysics calls the reverberation "the most sacred effusion" (*al-fayḍ al-aqdas*) and the radii "the sacred effusion" (*al-fayḍ at-muqaddas*), the first being the archetype of all things (*al-a'yān al-thābitah*) and the second the Breath of the Compassionate which externalizes and existentiates them on various planes of reality.

to the realm of relativity, cannot be used to prove or perceive the Absolute which remains beyond the reach of all attempts of the relative to comprehend It. But intelligence can know the Absolute and in fact only the Absolute is completely intelligible. Below that level, the activity of *māyā* enters into play and brings about an element of ambiguity and uncertainty. If there were to be such a thing as pure relativity, it would be completely unintelligible. But even in the relative world which still bears the imprint of the Absolute, the element of ambiguity and unintelligibility of *māyā* enters into all mental activity which would seek to transgress beyond its legitimate function and try to enmesh the Absolute in a finite system of thought based upon ratiocination.[20] Human thought as mental activity cannot become absolutely conformable to the Real as a result of *māyā*, whereas direct knowledge or intellection has such a power. The plight of innumerable schools of modern philosophy and their failure to achieve the task of encompassing the Real through the process of purely human thought is caused by the power of *māyā* which exercises its illusory spell most upon those who would deny her reality.

Closely related to the doctrine of *māyā* is the question of evil and its meaning in the light of the absolute goodness of the Origin and Source, a question which lies at the heart of the problems of theodicy, especially as they have been discussed in the Abrahamic world over the ages. This problem, namely, how can a God who is both omnipotent and good create a world which contains evil, is insoluble on the level of both formal theology and rationalistic philosophy. Its answer can be found only in metaphysics or *scientia sacra*, the eclipse of which has caused many men to lose their faith in religion and the religious world view precisely because of their inability to gain access to a doctrine which would solve this apparent contradiction. From the metaphysical point of view there is not just the question of the omnipotence of God, there is also the Divine Nature which the Divine Will cannot contradict. God cannot will to cease to be God. Now, this Divine Nature is not limited to Being; as already mentioned, it is the Absolute and Infinite Reality which is the Beyond Being or Supra-Being of which Being is the first determination in the direction of manifestation or creation. The Divine Nature or Ultimate Reality is both infinite and good and therefore wills to radiate and manifest

---

[20] "The desire to enclose universal Reality in an exclusive and exhaustive 'explanation' brings with it a permanent disequilibrium due to the interference of *Māyā*" (Frithjof Schuon, *Light on the Ancient Worlds*, p. 91).

Itself. From this radiation issue the states of existence, the multiple worlds, hence separation, elongation from the Source from which results what manifests itself as evil on a particular plane of reality. To speak of Infinity is to speak of the possibility of the negation of the Source in the direction of nothingness, hence of evil which one might call the "crystallization or existentiation of nothingness." Since only God—who is both the Beyond Being and Being—is Good, as the Gospels assert, all that is other than God partakes of that element of privation which is the source of evil. The will of God as the Godhead or the Beyond Being is the realization of the possibilities inherent in Its Infinitude and hence that separation from the Source which implies evil. But precisely because manifestation is a possibility of Infinite Reality, the existence of the world in itself is not evil nor does the element of evil appear in any of the worlds still close to the Divine Proximity.[21] Now, the Will of God as Being operates within the radiation and reverberation caused by *māyā* and the very Nature of that Infinite Reality which is the Supra-Being. The Will of God on this level opposes concrete forms of evil according to the criteria established by various revelations and always in the light of the total good and in accordance with the economy of a particular traditional mode of life. On this level the Will of God is opposed to various types of evil without being able to eradicate existence as such, which would amount to negating the Divine Nature Itself. There are in reality two levels of operation of the Divine Will or even two Divine Wills, one related to the Absolute and Infinite Reality which cannot but manifest and create, hence, separation, elongation, and privation which appear as evil; and the second related to the Will of Being which opposes the presence of evil in accordance with the divine laws and norms which constitute the ethical structures of various traditional worlds.

To relate evil to the infinity of that Reality which is also the All-Possibility, does not mean to deny the reality of evil on a particular level of reality. The existence of evil is inseparable from the relative level in which it manifests itself. One cannot simply say that evil does not exist as do even certain traditional masters of gnosis who, gazing with constancy upon the overwhelming goodness of the Divine Principle, in a sense circumvent evil and pass it by.[22] But this is of course

---

[21] The Quranic doctrine that Iblīs [Satan] was a *jinn* and made of fire signifies that the presence of evil does not make itself felt on the cosmic plane until the descent reaches into the animic realm.

[22] The Intellect as it operates in man does not begin with a knowledge of the world but with an *a priori* knowledge of the Divine Good which it perceives before it even

not the case of all the traditional sages, many of whom have provided the metaphysical key for the understanding of evil. From the point of view of *scientia sacra*, although real on the relative plane of reality, evil has no reality as a substance and in itself as a thing or object. Evil is always partial and fragmented. It must exist because of the ontological hiatus between the Principle and manifestation but it remains always limited and bound while goodness is unlimited and opens unto the Infinite. Also as far as the Will of God is concerned, God wills evil not as evil but as part of a greater good to which this segmented reality called evil contributes. That is why evil is never evil in its existential substance but through that privation of a good which plays a role in the total economy of the cosmos and contributes to a greater good. Every disequilibrium and disorder is of a partial and transient nature contributing to that total equilibrium, harmony, and order which is the cosmos.[23]

The doctrine of *māyā* or *ḥijāb* enables us to understand the metaphysical roots of that which appears as evil. This doctrine explains evil as privation and separation from the Good and also as an element contributing to a greater good, although within a particular ambience or plane of existence, evil remains evil as a result of either privation or excess. If this doctrine is fully understood then it is possible to comprehend the meaning of evil as such. But even in this case it is not possible for man to understand such or such an evil, only God being totally and completely intelligible. In any case, although the Divine Will wills everything that exists including what appears as evil, as far as man, who is both intelligent and has a free will, is concerned, God wills for him only the good. The best way of solving the question of evil and theodicy is in fact to live a life which would make possible the actualization of the *scientia sacra* in one's being. This realization

---

comes to understand evil. That is why some metaphysicians, led through intellection to a direct understanding of the Good in itself, do not even have a desire to understand evil and pass it by as if it did not exist. There is, of course, also the experiential aspect to consider. A saint who has destroyed evil not in the whole world but around himself might be said to breathe already in the atmosphere of paradise and therefore be oblivious to the evils of terrestrial existence which do not exist as such for him. This attitude is to be found among certain of the great Sufis who assert that evil simply does not exist without bothering to provide the metaphysical evidence as to what one means by such a statement and from what point of view can one say that evil does not exist.

[23] *Cosmos* literally means "order" in Greek. The opposite of cosmos is nothing but chaos.

or actualization is the best possible way of understanding the nature of the Good and the why of terrestrial human existence which, being removed from God, cannot but be marred by the fragmentation, dissipation, and privation that appears as evil and that is as real as that plane of reality upon which it manifests itself. Evil ceases to exist, however, on a higher plane, where transient and partial disorders contribute to a greater order and privation to a greater good. Closely allied to the question of good and evil is that of free will and determinism which has also occupied philosophers and theologians in the Abrahamic world over the ages but which also is of central concern in other traditional climates such as that of India as evidenced by the discussion of correct action in the *Bhagavad Gītā*. In this question also there is no possibility of going beyond the either-or dichotomy as long as one remains on the level of formal theology or rationalistic philosophy as witnessed by centuries of debates among theologians and philosophers in Judaism, Christianity, and Islam. From the metaphysical point of view, however, the whole debate appears as sterile and fragmented through the fact that both sides attribute a quality of absoluteness to that which is relative, namely the human plane. Metaphysically speaking, only the Ultimate Reality is absolute and at once pure necessity and pure freedom. Only God is completely necessary and free, being both Absoluteness and Infinitude. Now, on the human plane, we are already on the level of relativity, therefore there cannot be either absolute determination or absolute free will. Something of both must manifest itself on the level of human relativity. If only one of these two conditions were to be present, the plane of relativity would no longer be relative but absolute. Man's freedom is as real as himself. He ceases to be free in the sense of independent of the Divine Will to the extent that he ceases to be separated ontologically from God. At the same time, man is determined and not free to the extent that an ontological hiatus separates him from his Source and Origin, for only God is freedom. Journeying from the relative toward the Absolute means at once losing the freedom of living in error and gaining freedom from the tyranny of all the psycho-material determinations which imprison and stifle the soul. In God there is pure freedom and pure necessity and only in Him is man completely free and also completely determined but with a determination which, being nothing but man's own most profound nature and the root of his being, is none other than the other face of freedom, total and unconditional.

Intelligence is a divine gift which pierces through the veil of *māyā* and is able to know reality as such. It is a ray of light which pierces through the veils of cosmic existence to the Origin and connects the periphery of existence, upon which fallen man lives, to the Center wherein resides the Self. The Intellect is itself divine and only human to the extent that man participates in it. It is a substance as well as a function; it is light as well as vision. The Intellect is not the mind nor is it reason which is the reflection of the Intellect upon the human plane, but it is the root and center of consciousness and what has been traditionally called the soul. In the technical sense, however, the soul must be considered as the equivalent of the *anima* or *psyche* in which case the Intellect is *spiritus* or *nous* from whose marriage with the passive and feminine psyche is born that gold which symbolizes the perfection of the sanctified soul.

The metacosmic principle which is the Intellect is the source of both knowledge and being, of the subjective conscience which knows and the objective order which is known. It is also the source of revelation which creates a nexus between man and the cosmos and of course the metacosmic Reality. The Logos or *Buddhi* or *ʿaql*, as the Intellect is called in various traditions, is the luminous center which is the generating agent of the world—for "it was by the Word that all things were made"—of man, and of religion. It is God's knowledge of Himself and the first in His creation. Moreover, as there is a hierarchy of cosmic existence, so are there levels of consciousness and degrees of descent of the Intellect through various levels of existence until man is reached, in whose heart the ray of Intellect still shines, although it is usually dimmed by the passions and the series of "falls" that have separated man from what he really is.

Yet, even the consciousness of fallen man and the intelligence which shines within him, although a distant reflection of the Intellect, nevertheless display something of the miracle of the Intellect which is at once supernatural and natural. Perhaps the most immediate experience of man is his subjectivity, the mystery of inwardness and a consciousness which can reflect upon itself, opening inwardly unto the Infinite which is also bliss. No less of a miracle is the power of objectivity, the power of human intelligence to know the world in an objective manner and with a categorical certitude which no amount of sophism can destroy. Finally, there is the mystery of the adequation of knowledge, of the fact that our intelligence corresponds to the nature of reality and that what man knows corresponds to aspects of the Real.[24] But these are all mysteries as long as man is cut off from the light of intellectual intuition or intellection. Otherwise, in the light of the Intellect itself both the subjective and objective powers of intelligence are perfectly intelligible.

As already stated, *scientia sacra* cannot be attained without intellection and the correct functioning of intelligence within man. That is why those who are cut off from this inner sacrament[25] not only repudiate the teachings of this sacred knowledge but also offer rationalistic arguments against them based usually on incomplete or false premises, expecting the heavens to collapse as a result of this sound and fury which metaphysically signifies nothing. Intellection does not reach the truth as a result of profane thought or reasoning but through an *a priori* direct intuition of the truth. Reasoning may act as an occasion for intellection but it cannot be the cause of intellection. For that very reason the fruit of intellection cannot be nullified or negated by any form of reasoning which, based on the limitations of the person who uses reasoning, often results in error pure and simple. This assertion does not mean of course that intellection is against logic or that it is irrational. On the contrary, there is no truth which can be considered illogical, logic itself being an ontological reality of the human state. But the role and function of reasoning and the use of logic in metaphysics and profane philosophy are completely different, as different as the use of mathematics in the rosette of the Chartres Cathedral or a cupola of one of the mosques of Isfahan and in a modern skyscraper.

Although the Intellect shines within the being of man, man is too far removed from his primordial nature to be able to make full use of this divine gift by himself. He needs revelation which alone can actualize the intellect in man and allow it to function properly. The day when each man was also a prophet and when the intellect functioned in man "naturally" so that he saw all things *in divinis* and possessed

---

[24] The principle of adequation does not negate our earlier assertion that *māyā* prevents containing and comprehending reality in a system derived from ratiocination, for we are speaking here of intellection and intelligence not ratiocination and thought of a purely human character.

[25] Not only in the Islamic tradition whose spirituality is essentially sapiential is intelligence considered as God's greatest gift to man (according to the well-known saying attributed to 'Alī ibn Abī Tālib, "God did not bestow upon His servants anything more precious than intelligence"), but even in Christianity which is primarily a way of love the Hesychasts consider the essence of the prayer of Jesus itself to be the actualization and descent of intelligence into the human heart.

a direct knowledge of a sacred character is long past. The traditional doctrines themselves emphasize that in the later unfolding of the cosmic cycle it is only revelation or *avatāric* descent that enables man to see once again with the "eye of the heart" which is the "eye of the intellect." If there are exceptions, these are exceptions which only prove the rule and in any case "the wind bloweth where it listeth."

Revelation in its esoteric dimension makes possible, through initiation, access to higher levels of man's being as well as consciousness. The appropriate rites, the traditional cadre, forms and symbols, and the grace issuing from revelation provide keys with which man is able to open the doors of the inner chambers of his being and with the help of the spiritual master to journey through the cosmic labyrinth with the result of finally attaining that treasure which is none other than the pearl of gnosis. Revelation actualizes the possibilities of the intellect, removes impediments of the carnal soul which prevent the intellect from functioning, and makes possible the transmission of an initiatic knowledge which at the same time resides within the very substance of the intellect. There is an unbridgeable hiatus between intelligence sanctified by revelation and the intelligence which, cut off from this source and also from its own root, is reduced to its reflection upon the human mind and atrophied into that truncated and fragmented faculty which is considered scientifically as intelligence.[26]

As far as the relation between the intellect and revelation is concerned, it is fundamental to say a few words on the rapport between intellectuality and sacred scripture which has been so forgotten in the modern world. Without reviving spiritual exegesis, it is not possible to rediscover *scientia sacra* in the bosom of a tradition dominated by the presence of sacred scripture. Scripture possesses an inner dimension which is attainable only through intellection operating within a traditional framework and which alone is able to solve certain apparent contradictions and riddles in sacred texts. Once intellectual intuition becomes inoperative and the mind a frozen lake over which ideas glide but into which nothing penetrates, then the revealed text also veils its inner dimension and spiritual exegesis becomes reduced to archaeology and philology, not to speak of the extrapolation of the subjective errors of the present era back into the age of the revelation in question. Clement and Origen become thus transformed into modern

---

[26] See Schuon, *In the Tracks of Buddhism* (London: George Allen & Unwin, 1968), p. 83.

exegetes for whom the New Testament is little more than an ethical commentary upon the social conditions of first-century Palestine.

In the Oriental world, including the Judeo-Christian tradition, the spiritual science of exegesis has never died out completely. The sacred text serves as the source for the formal world of the tradition in question, including its ritual and liturgical practices and its sacred art, as well as the intellectual aspect of the tradition extending from formal theology, philosophy, and the science of symbols, to *scientia sacra* itself which crowns the inner message conveyed by the sacred text and which is attained through the intelligence that is sanctified by that very sacred scripture.[27] In Islam, dominated by the blinding presence of the Quran, every aspect of the tradition has been related to the Holy Book and the category of exegetes has ranged from those concerned with the Divine Law to the gnostics who have penetrated through that spiritual hermeneutics or *ta'wīl* to the pearl of wisdom residing behind the veil of the external forms of the Holy Book. Such masterpieces of Sufism as the *Mathnawī* of Jalāl al-Dīn Rūmī are in reality commentaries upon the Quran, not to speak of the numerous esoteric commentaries of such masters as Ibn 'Arabī, Ṣadr al-Dīn al-Qūnyawī, 'Abd al-Razzāq al-Kāshānī, Rashīd al-Dīn Aḥmad Mībudī, and others. Both *scientia sacra* and all the ancillary traditional sciences in Islam may be said to issue forth from the fountainhead of the inner wisdom contained in the Quran in the same way that Hinduism considers the traditional sciences to be the limbs of the Vedas. Spiritual hermeneutics is the means whereby the intelligence, sanctified by revelation, is able to penetrate into the heart of revelation to discover that

---

[27] "From the doctrinal point of view, the most urgent need at present is to rediscover the spiritual science of exegesis, that is to say the metaphysical and mystical interpretation of the Scriptures. The principles of this science, which for its handling presupposes on every count a highly intuitive intelligence and not simply a mental acuteness, have been expounded, for Christendom, by Origen and others, and put into practice by the Fathers and the greatest saints. In other words, what the West lacks is an intellectuality founded, not on academic erudition and philosophical skepticism, but upon intellectual intuition as actualized by the Holy Spirit on the basis of an exegesis that takes into account all levels of reality and understanding; this exegesis itself implies the science of symbolism which, for its part extends into all the realms of formal expression and especially into sacred art; the latter includes the liturgical art, in the broadest sense, as well as art properly so-called. Since the traditional East has never departed from this manner of regarding things, a proper comprehension of its metaphysical teachings, its commentaries, its symbolisms, and its arts would be, for the West, of vital interest" (Frithjof Schuon, *Language of the Self* [Madras: Ganesh, 1959], pp. 228-229).

principial truth which is the very root and substance of intelligence itself. In this process the microcosmic manifestation of the Intellect, which is the source of inner illumination and intellection, unveils the inner meaning of that macrocosmic manifestation of the Intellect which is revelation or more specifically, sacred scripture. Moreover, the same truth pertains *mutatis mutandis* to the interpretation of the inner meaning of that other revealed book which is the cosmos itself.

Scientia sacra envisages intelligence in its rapport not only with revelation in an external sense but also with the source of inner revelation which is the center of man, namely the heart. The seat of intelligence is the heart and not the head, as affirmed by all traditional teachings. The word *heart*, *hṛdaya* in Sanskrit, *Herz* in German, *kardia* in Greek, and *cor/cordis* in Latin, have the root hrd or krd which, like the Egyptian Horus, imply the center of the world or a world.[28] The heart is also the center of the human microcosm and therefore the "locus" of the Intellect by which all things were made. The heart is also the seat of sentiments and the will, the other elements of which the human being is constituted. Profound emotions as well as will have their origin in the heart as does intelligence which constitutes the apex of the microcosmic ternary of powers or faculties. It is also in the heart that intelligence and faith meet and where faith itself becomes saturated with the light of sapience. In the Quran both faith (*īmān*) and intelligence (*'aql*) are explicitly identified with the heart (*al-qalb*), while in Hinduism the Sanskrit term *śraddhā*, which is usually translated as faith, means literally knowledge of the heart.[29] In Latin also the fact that *credo* and *cor/cordis* are derived from the same root points to the same metaphysical truth. This traditional exegesis of language reveals not only the relation of principial knowledge to the heart but also the important metaphysical principle that integral intelligence is never divorced from faith but that, on the contrary, faith is necessary in the actualization of the possibilities of intellection within the cadre of a revelation. That intelligence which is able to attain to

---

[28] See René Guénon, "The Heart and the Cave," in *Studies in Comparative Religion* 1971, 4, pp. 69-72. [Editors' Note: This article also appears in Guénon's *Fundamental Symbols: The Universal Language of Sacred Science* (Cambridge, UK: Quinta Essentia, 1995), pp. 145-148.]

[29] This issue has been dealt with in detail by W. C. Smith in his *Faith and Belief*. Smith draws attention quite rightly to the fact that, before modern times, belief as opinion was not a religious category and faith was related to knowledge not to belief in the tentative sense in which this term is used today. This does not mean that the more traditional sense of the term belief which is still alive cannot be fully resuscitated.

the knowledge of the sacred is already sanctified and rooted in the center of the human state where it is never divorced from either faith or love. In the heart, knowledge in fact always coincides with love. Only when externalized does knowledge become related to the mind and the activity of the brain, and love to that substance which is usually called the soul.

This externalization of the intelligence and its projection upon the plane of the mind is, however, a necessary condition of human existence without which man would not be man, the creature who is created as a thinking being. Dialectical intelligence identified with the mind is not in itself negative; in fact, human intelligence in its fullness implies the correct functioning of both the intelligence of the heart and that of the mind, the first being intuitive and the second analytical and discursive. The two functions together make possible the reception, crystallization, formulation, and finally communication of the truth. Mental formulation of the intuition received by the intelligence in the heart becomes completely assimilated by man and actualized through the activity of the mind. This in fact is one of the main roles of meditation in spiritual exercises, meditation being related to the activity of the mind. Through this process also the light received by the heart is communicated and transmitted, such an activity being necessary because of the very nature of the content of the intuition received by the intelligence residing in the heart, the content which, being good, has to give of itself and, like all goodness, shine forth.[30] The human being needs to exteriorize certain inner truths in order to be able to interiorize, to analyze in order to synthesize, synthesis needing a phase of analysis. Hence, the need of man for language which proceeds from holy silence and returns again to it, but which plays a vital role in the formulation of the truth issuing from the first silence and in preparing man for return to the second silence which is synthesis after analysis, return to unity after separation.

Symbolically, the mind can be considered as the moon which reflects the light of the sun which is the heart. The intelligence in the heart shines upon the plane of the mind which then reflects this light upon the dark night of the terrestrial existence of fallen man.

---

[30] In traditional Islamic educational circles the ability to teach metaphysics is considered as the sign of the teacher's complete assimilation of the subject in such a manner that his intellect has reached the level of al-'aql bi'l-malakah (*intellectus habitus*) and the knowledge in question has become for him *bi'l-malakah*, that is, completely digested and assimilated.

Scientia sacra which issues from the total intelligence of the heart, therefore, also includes the dialectic of the mind. In fact, some of the greatest dialecticians in both East and West have been metaphysicians who have realized the supreme station of knowledge. What tradition opposes is not the activity of the mind but its divorce from the heart, the seat of intelligence and the location of the "eye of knowledge," which the Sufis call the eye of the heart (*'ayn al-qalb* or *chishm-i dil*) and which is none other than the "third eye" of the Hindu tradition. It is this eye which transcends duality and the rational functioning of the mind based upon analysis and which perceives the unity that is at once the origin and end of the multiplicity perceived by the mind and the mind's own power to analyze and know discursively. That is why the Sufis chant:

> Open the eye of thy heart so that thou wilst see the Spirit
> So that thou wilst see that which cannot be seen.

The attempt of the rational mind to discover the Intellect through its own light is seen by tradition to be futile because the object which the rational faculty is trying to perceive is actually the subject which makes the very act of perception by the rational faculty possible. A mind which is cut off from the light of the intelligence of the heart and which seeks to find God is unaware that the light with which it is seeking to discover God is itself a ray of the Light of God. Such a mind cannot but be like a person wandering in the desert in the brightness of day with a lamp in his hand looking for the sun. Blindness does not issue from reason but from reason being cut off from the intellect and then trying to play the role of the intellect in the attainment of knowledge. Such an attempt cannot but result in that desacralization of knowledge and of life that one already observes in members of that segment of humanity which has chosen to take its destiny into its own hands and live on the earth as if it were only of this earth.

Since *scientia sacra* is expressed outwardly and does not remain only on the level of the inner illumination of the heart, it is necessary to understand something of the kind of language it employs. The formal language used for the expression of *scientia sacra*, and in fact nearly the whole spectrum of traditional teachings, is that of symbolism. *Scientia sacra* can be expressed in human words as well as in landscape paintings, beating of drums, or other formal means which convey meaning. But in all cases symbolism remains the key for the understanding of its language. Fortunately, during this century much has been written on the veritable significance of symbols, and it has been shown, especially in works identified with the circle of traditional writers, that symbols are not man-made signs, but reflections on a lower level of the existence of a reality belonging to the higher order. Symbols are ontological aspects of a thing, to say the least as real as the thing itself, and in fact that which bestows significance upon a thing within the universal order of existence. In the hierarchic universe of traditional metaphysics, it can be said that every level of reality and everything on every level of reality is ultimately a symbol, only the Real being Itself as such. But on a more limited scale, one can say that symbols reflect in the formal order archetypes belonging to the principial realm and that through symbols the symbolized is unified with its archetypal reality.[31]

There are, moreover, symbols which are "natural" in the sense of being inherent in the nature of certain objects and forms through the very cosmogonic process which has brought forth these forms upon the terrestrial plane. There are other symbols which are sanctified by a particular revelation that is like a second creation. The sun is "naturally" the symbol of the Divine Intellect for anyone who still possesses the faculty of symbolic perception and in whom the "symbolist spirit" is operative. But the same sun is sanctified in a special manner in solar cults such as Mithraism and gains a special significance in a particular traditional universe as has wine in Christianity or water in Islam. The Sufi poets may use the symbolism of wine in the first sense of symbol but it is the Christic descent which has given that special significance to wine in the Eucharist as a sanctified symbol that remains bound to the particular world which is Christian.[32]

---

[31] For primordial man the symbolized was in fact the symbol since he still lived in the unfragmented reality of the paradisal state. Something of this primordial point of view has survived among some of the so-called primitive peoples among whom the "symbolist spirit" is still alive and who identify in their perception of things the object symbolized and the symbol. This is the reverse of idolatry which reduces the symbol to the physical object which is supposed to symbolize it, while in the perspective in question the object symbolizing an archetypal reality is "elevated" to the level of that reality and becomes a transparent form through which that reality is reflected and manifested.

[32] "Natural symbolism, which assimilates, for example, the sun to the divine Principle, derives from a 'horizontal' correspondence; revealed symbolism, which makes this assimilation spiritually effective—in ancient solar cults and before their 'petrifaction'—derives from a 'vertical' correspondence; the same holds good for gnosis, which reduces phenomena to 'ideas' or archetypes. Much might be said here on the natural symbolism of bread and body—or of body and blood—and their 'sacramentalization'

Scientia sacra makes use of both types of symbolism in the exposition of its teachings but is always rooted in its formal aspect in the
tradition in which it flowers and functions and by virtue of which the
very attainment of this sacred knowledge is possible in an operative
manner. Sufism may draw occasionally from Hindu or Neoplatonic
formulations and symbols, but its formal world is that of the Quran
and it is the grace issuing from the Quranic revelation which has made
the attainment of gnosis in Sufism possible. It is in fact the living tradition that molds the language of discourse of metaphysics and that
chooses among the symbols available to it those which best serve its
purpose of communicating a doctrine of a sapiential and sacred nature.
On the one hand, symbolism can be fully understood only in the light
of a living spirituality without which it can become a maze of riddles;
on the other hand, symbols serve as the means whereby man is able
to understand the language of *scientia sacra*.

Finally, it must be emphasized that traditional metaphysics or
scientia sacra is not only a theoretical exposition of the knowledge of
reality. Its aim is to guide man, to illuminate him, and allow him to
attain the sacred. Therefore, its expositions are also points of reference, keys with which to open certain doors and means of opening
the mind to certain realities. In their theoretical aspect they have a
provisional aspect in the sense of the Buddhist *upāya*, of accommo-
dating means of teaching the truth. In a sense, *scientia sacra* contains
both the seed and the fruit of the tree of knowledge. As theory it is
planted as a seed in the heart and mind of man, a seed that if nurtured
through spiritual practice and virtue becomes a plant which finally
blossoms forth and bears fruit in which, once again, that seed is contained. But if the first seed is theoretical knowledge, in the sense of
theoria or vision, the second seed is realized gnosis, the realization of
a knowledge which being itself sacred, consumes the whole being of
the knower and, as the sacred, demands of man all that he is. That is

by Christ; likewise the sign of the Cross, which expresses with its two dimensions the
respective mysteries of the Body and Bread and the Blood and Wine, has, of course,
always had its metaphysical sense but received its quasi-sacramental virtue—at least
in its specifically Christian form—through the incarnated Word, in other terms, it
is necessary for the *Avatāra* to 'live' a form in order to make it 'effective,' and that
is why sacred formulae or divine Names must come from Revelation in order to be
capable of being 'realized'" (Frithjof Schuon, *Stations of Wisdom* [Bloomington, IN:
World Wisdom, 1995], pp. 90-91).

why it is not possible to attain this knowledge in any way except by being consumed by it.

> The result of my life can be summarized in three words;
> I was immature, I matured, and I was consumed.
>
> Rūmī

10 UNDERSTANDING AND BELIEVING

Frithjof Schuon

It is generally recognized that man is capable of believing without understanding; one is much less aware of the inverse possibility, that of understanding without believing, and it even appears as a contradiction, since faith does not seem to be incumbent except on those who do not understand. Yet hypocrisy is not only the dissimulation of a person who pretends to be better than he is; it also manifests itself in a disproportion between certainty and behavior, and in this respect most men are more or less hypocritical since they claim to admit truths which they put no more than feebly into practice. On the plane of simple belief, to believe without acting in accordance with the dictates of one's belief corresponds, on the intellectual plane, to an understanding without faith and without life; for real belief means identifying oneself with the truth that one accepts, whatever may be the level of this adherence. Piety is to religious belief what operative faith is to doctrinal understanding or, we may add, what sainthood is to truth.

If we take as a starting point the idea that spirituality has essentially two factors, namely discernment between the Real and the illusory and permanent concentration on the Real, the *conditio sine qua non* being the observance of traditional rules and the practice of the virtues that go with them, we shall see that there is a relationship between discernment and understanding, on the one hand, and between concentration and faith, on the other; faith, whatever its degree, always means a quasi-existential participation in Being or in Reality; it is, to take a basic *hadīth*, "to worship God as if thou sawest Him, and if thou seest Him not, yet He seeth thee". In other terms, faith is the participation of the will in the intelligence; just as on the physical plane man adapts his action to the physical facts which determine its nature, so also, on the spiritual plane, he should act in accordance with his convictions, by inward activity even more than by outward activity, for "before acting one must first be", and our being is nothing else but our inward activity. The soul must be to the intelligence what beauty is to truth, and this is what we have called the "moral qualification" that should accompany the "intellectual qualification".

There is a relationship between faith and the symbol; there is also one between faith and miracles. In the symbolic image as in the miraculous fact, it is the language of being, not of reasoning, which speaks; to a manifestation of being on the part of Heaven, man must respond with his own being, and he does so through faith or through love, which are the two aspects of one and the same reality, without thereby ceasing to be a creature endowed with thought. In plain terms, one might wonder what basis or justification there can be for an elementary faith which is disdainful, or almost so, of any attempt at comprehension; the answer has just been given, namely that such faith is based on the illuminating power which belongs in principle to the symbols, phenomena, and arguments of Revelation;[1] the "obscure merit" of this faith consists in our not being closed to a grace for which our nature is made. There is room for differences, on the human side, as regards the modes or degrees of receptivity and also the intellectual needs; these needs do not in any sense mean that the thinking man lacks faith, they merely show that his receptivity is sensible to the most subtle and most implicit aspects of the Divine Message; now what is implicit is not the inexpressible but the esoteric, and this has the right to be expressed.[2] Attention has already been drawn to the relationship between faith and miracles; in fact, perfect faith consists in being aware of the metaphysically miraculous character of natural phenomena and, as a result, in seeing in them the trace of God.

The demerit of unbelief or lack of faith does not therefore lie in a natural lack of special aptitudes, nor is it due to the unintelligibility of the Message, for then there would be no demerit; it lies in the passionate stiffening of the will and in the worldly tendencies which bring about this stiffening. The merit of faith is fidelity to the "super-naturally natural" receptivity of primordial man; it means remaining as God made us and remaining at His disposition with regard to a Message from Heaven which might be contrary to earthly experience,

---

[1] The "signs" (*āyāt*) of which the Koran speaks, and which may even be natural phenomena envisaged in the light of the revealed doctrine. A remark which should be made in this context is that the insensibility of the believers of any intrinsically orthodox religion to the arguments of another religion does not in any sense come into question here, since the motive for refusal is in that case a positive factor, namely an already existing faith which is in itself valid.

[2] It goes without saying that the implicit is to be found even on the plane of the literal meaning, but this mode of indication causes practically no problems and is not in question here.

while being incontestable in view of subjective as well as objective criteria.[3]

It is related that Ibn Taymiyyah[4] once said, while coming down from the pulpit after a sermon: "God comes down from Heaven to earth as I am coming down now";[5] there is no reason to doubt that he meant this to be taken literally, with a literalism defying all interpretation, but his attitude has nonetheless a symbolic value which is independent of his personal opinions. The refusal to analyze a symbol by discursive and separative thought—in order to assimilate it directly and as it were existentially—does in fact correspond to a perspective which is possible and therefore valid in the appropriate circumstances. "Blind faith" may be seen to coincide here with an attitude which is its opposite while being at the same time analogous, namely the assimilation of truth through the symbol and by means of the whole soul, the soul as such.

*   *   *

Faith as a quality of the soul is the stabilizing complement of the discerning and as it were explosive intelligence; without this complement, intellectual activity—not pure intellection— lets itself be carried away by its own movement and is like a devouring fire; it loses its balance and ends either by devouring itself in a restlessness without issue or else simply by wearing itself out to the point of sclerosis. Faith implies all the static and gentle qualities such as patience, gratitude, confidence, generosity; it offers the mercurial intelligence a fixative element and thus realizes, together with discernment, an equilibrium which is like an anticipation of sainthood. It is to this polarity, at its

---

[3] To say that Abraham and Mary had the merit of great faith means that they were sensible to the Divine criteria despite the apparent impossibility of the Message; this means also that the men of old were by no means credulous, if we may be allowed to make this remark in a context which goes beyond the level of ordinary humanity, since we are speaking of prophets.

[4] Arab theologian of the thirteenth century, Hanbalite by origin and the protagonist of an extreme exoterism.

[5] With reference to the *hadīth* of "the Descent" (*an-Nuzūl*): "Our Lord—blessed and exalted be He—cometh down each night unto the nethermost heaven (*as-samā' ad-dunyā*, a Koranic term which signifies, not the lowest of the seven Heavens, but the terrestrial firmament) while the last third of the night yet remaineth, and He saith: 'Who calleth upon Me, that I may answer him? Who asketh of Me, that I may give unto him? Who seeketh My forgiveness, that I may forgive him?'"

highest level, that the complementary terms "blessing" (or "prayer", *salāh*) and "peace" (or "greeting", *salām*) are applied in Islam.

It must be stressed again that an intellectual qualification is not fully valid unless it be accompanied by an equivalent moral qualification; herein lies the explanation of all the fideist attitudes which seem bent on limiting the impetus of the intelligence. The upholders of tradition pure and simple (*naql*) in the first centuries of Islam were deeply conscious of this, and Ashari himself must have sensed it—although it took him in the opposite direction since he ventured on to the plane of theological reasoning—when he attributed to God an unintelligibility which, in the last analysis, could only signify the precariousness of man's intellectual means in the face of the dimension of absoluteness.

One can meditate or speculate indefinitely on transcendent truths and their applications (that is moreover what the author of this book* does, but he has valid reasons for doing it, nor does he do it for himself). One can spend a whole lifetime speculating on the suprasensorial and the transcendent, but all that matters is the "leap into the void" which is the fixation of spirit and soul in an unthinkable dimension of the Real; this leap, which cuts short and completes in itself the endless chain of formulations,[6] depends on a direct understanding and on a grace, not on having reached a certain phase in the unfolding of the doctrine, for this unfolding, we repeat, has logically no end. This "leap into the void" we can call "faith"; it is the negation of this reality that is the source of all philosophy of the type that may be described as "art for art's sake", and of all thought that believes it can attain to an absolute contact with Reality by means of analyses, syntheses, arrangements, filtrations, and polishings—thought that is mundane by the very fact of this ignorance and because it is a "vicious circle" which not merely provides no escape from illusion, but even reinforces it through the lure of a progressive knowledge which in fact is inexistent.[7]

In view of the harm that the prejudices and tendencies of ordinary piety can sometimes do to metaphysical speculations, we might be tempted to conclude that piety should be abandoned on the threshold

---

* Editors' Note: the author refers to his book *Logic and Transcendence* (London: Perennial Books, 1975), of which the present article is a chapter.

[6] But for this completion there would be no such thing as doctrines, these being by definition forms, delimitations, mental coagulations.

[7] A valid doctrine is a "description" which is based on direct, supramental knowledge,

of pure knowledge, but this would be a false and highly pernicious conclusion; in reality, piety—or faith—must never be absent from the soul, but it is only too clear that it must be on a level with the truths that it accompanies, which implies that such an extension is perfectly in its nature, as is proved by the Vedantic hymns, to take just one particularly conclusive example.

The Hindus have been reproached for being inveterate idolaters and for finding in the least phenomenon a pretext for idolatry; we are referred, for example, to an animal festival at which, so it seems, the artisan gathers his tools together in order to worship them. The truth is that the Hindu refuses to become rooted in outwardness: he readily looks to the Divine substratum of things, whence his acute sense of the sacred and his devotional mentality; this is the last thing that modern man wants, monstrously "adult" as he has become in conforming to the worst illusion that has ever darkened the human outlook. The reflection of the sun may not be the sun but it is nonetheless "something of the sun", and in this sense it is not wrong to speak elliptically of a kind of identity, the light being always the one light and the cause being really present in the effect. Whoever does not respect the effect makes himself incapable of respecting fully the cause, apart from the fact that the cause withholds itself from whoever despises its reflections; whoever understands the cause perceives it also in its earthly traces. The sense of the sacred: this word felicitously expresses a dimension which should never be absent either in metaphysical thought or in everyday life; it is this which gives birth to the liturgies, and without it there is no faith. The sense of the sacred, with its concomitances of dignity, incorruptibility, patience, and generosity is the key to integral faith and to the supernatural virtues which are inherent in it.

*   *   *

If one adopts the distinction made by the alchemists between a "dry path" and a "moist path", the former corresponding to "knowledge" and the latter to "love", one should also be aware that the two poles

and the author is therefore under no illusion as to its inevitable formal limitations; on the other hand, a philosophy which claims to be a "research" is a mere nothing and its apparent modesty is no more than a pretentious negation of true wisdom, which is absurdly called "metaphysical dogmatism". There is clearly no humility in saying that one is ignorant because everyone is ignorant.

"fire" and "water", which these paths represent respectively, are both reflected in each path, so that "knowledge" has necessarily an aspect of "moisture", and "love" an aspect of "dryness".

Within the framework of a path of love, this aspect of "dryness" or of "fire" is doctrinal orthodoxy, for it is well known that no spirituality is possible without the implacable and immutable bulwark of a Divine expression of the saving Truth; analogously and inversely, the aspect of "moisture" or of "water" which, being feminine, is derived from the Divine Substance (*Prakriti*, the *Shakti*) is indispensable to the path of "knowledge" for the evident and already mentioned reasons of equilibrium, stability, and effectiveness.

When comparing the quality of "knowledge" with fire, one is aware that this comparison cannot perfectly and exhaustively account for the metaphysical reaches of the intelligence and for its activity of realization: fire in itself, besides its qualities of luminosity and ascension, has in fact an aspect of agitation and destructiveness, and it is this aspect—the very one that the fideist opponents of *kalām* have in mind—which proves that the "fiery" element in knowledge is not self-sufficient and that it has in consequence an imperative need of a "moist" element, which is none other than faith with all its fixative and appeasing virtues.[8] Even the most penetrating intelligence, if it relies too much on its own strength, runs the risk of being abandoned by Heaven; forgetting that the Subject, the Knower, is God, it closes itself to the divine influx. Profane thought is not confined to thought which is ignorant of metaphysical and mystical truths,[9] but also includes thought which, while knowing these truths well enough in theory, has nonetheless a disproportionate approach to them, an approach that is unaccompanied by a sufficient adaptation of the soul; not that such thought is profane by definition as in the case of ignorant thought, but it is so secondarily or morally and lies in grave danger of error, for man is not merely a mirror, he is a cosmos which is both complex and fragile. The connection, often affirmed by tradition, between Knowledge and Peace, shows in its own way that in pure

---

[8] "There is no lustral water like unto knowledge," says the *Bhagavad Gītā*: it is here water, not fire, which is related to *jñāna*.

[9] "Metaphysical": concerning universal realities considered objectively. "Mystical": concerning the same realities considered subjectively, that is, in relation to the contemplative soul, insofar as they enter operatively into contact with it.

intellectuality the mathematical element is not everything, and also that fire by itself could not be the symbol of intellectuality.[10]

The two principles "fire" and "water" come together in "wine", which is both "liquid fire" and "igneous water";[11] liberating intoxication proceeds precisely from this alchemical and as it were miraculous combination of opposite elements. It is thus wine, and not fire, which is the most perfect image of liberating *gnosis*, envisaged not only in its total amplitude but also in the equilibrium of its virtual modes, for the equilibrium between discernment and contemplation can be conceived at every level. Another image of this equilibrium or of this concordance is oil; it is moreover through oil that fire is stabilized and that it becomes the calm and contemplative flame of the lamps in sanctuaries. Like wine, oil is an igneous liquid, which "shineth even though the fire have not touched it", according to the famous Verse of Light (*Āyat an-Nūr*).

From a certain elementary point of view, there is a connection between the emotional path of "warriors" and water, which is passive and "feminine", just as there is a connection between the intellectual path of "priests" and fire, which is active and "masculine"; but it remains abundantly clear that water has a sacerdotal aspect of peace, and that fire has a warlike aspect of devouring activity, and that each path has necessarily a "dry" pole and a "moist" pole.

All these considerations converge on the problem of the relation-ships between speculative intelligence and faith: faith is a pure and calm "water", intelligence is an active and discriminating "fire". To say that water is pure amounts to saying that is has a virtual quality of luminosity, that it is thus predisposed to be a vehicle for fire and to be transmuted into wine, as at the marriage in Cana; when considered with regard to its possibilities, water is a virtual wine since it already possesses luminosity by reason of its purity, and in this sense it is

---

[10] Shankara, affirming his identity with "inward Wisdom", calls it: "That which is the stilling of mental agitation and the supreme appeasement. . . . That which is the pool Manikarnika. . . . That which is the Ganges . . ." images referring to water, not to fire. Islam, for its part, associates coolness, the color green, and streams with Paradise.

[11] When the Red Indians called alcohol "fire-water", they were expressing, without knowing it, a profound truth: the alchemical and almost supernatural coincidence of liquidity and ignition. According to the *Brihadaranyaka Upanishad* and the *Shatapatha Brāhmana*, the Divine Fire (*Agni*) is engendered in the undifferentiated Self (*Ātmā*) by the tension between igneous Energy (*tejas*) and the Water of Life or the Elixir (*rasa*); *Agni* is "churned" and "born of the Waters", or "born of the Lotus"; he is the Lightning hidden in the Celestial Waters.

comparable to oil; like wine, oil is igneous by its very nature, but at the same time it does not correspond exactly to wine except when combined with the flame that it feeds, whereas wine has no need of any complement to manifest its nature.

*   *   *

It follows from all that has been said so far that faith and intelligence can each be conceived at two different levels: faith as a quasi-onto-logical and premental certitude ranks higher than the discerning and speculative aspects of intelligence,[12] but intelligence as pure Intellec-tion ranks higher than that faith which is no more than sentimental adherence; it is this ambivalence which is the source of numerous misunderstandings, but which makes possible at the same time an exo-esoteric language that is both simple and complex. Faith in its higher aspect is what we might call *religio cordis*: it is the "inward religion" which is supernaturally natural to man and which coincides with *religio caeli*—or *perennis*—that is, with universal truth, which is beyond the contingencies of form and time. This faith can be satisfied with little. Unlike an intelligence which is all for exactness but never satisfied in its play of formulations—moving from concept to concept, from symbol to symbol, without being able to settle on any—the faith of the heart is capable of being satisfied by the first symbol that providentially comes its way,[13] and of living on it until the supreme Meeting.

The faith in question, which we have called *religio cordis*, the sub-jective and immanent side of *religio caeli*, has two poles, in conformity with the distinction between the "dry" and the "moist" paths; they are represented in the Buddhism of the North by Zen and *Jōdo* respec-tively. Both turn away from verbal comprehension, the one to plunge

---

[12] This higher faith is something altogether different from the irresponsible and arrogant taking of liberties so characteristic of the profane improvisers of Zen or of *Jñāna*, who seek to "take a short cut" by stripping themselves of the essential human context of all realization, whereas in the East, and in the normal conditions of ethical and liturgical ambience, this context is largely supplied in advance. One does not enter the presence of a king by the back door.

[13] In the lives of the saints, the spiritual career is often inaugurated by an outward or inward incident which throws the soul into a particular and definitive attitude with regard to Heaven; the symbol here is not the incident itself, but the positive spiritual factor that the incident serves to bring out.

into our very being and the other to plunge into faith. For Zen, truth must coincide with reality and this is our substratum which is both existential and intellectual, whereas for *Jōdo*, truth-reality is attained in perfect faith, the giving up of oneself to the universal Substance which is Mercy and which is manifested in some Sign or some Key.[14]

The spiritual dimension symbolized by wine or intoxication is represented, in the *Mahāyāna*, by the union of the two poles *Vajra* ("Lightning" or "Diamond") and *Garbha* ("Matrix"); or *Mani* ("Jewel") and *Padma* ("Lotus"); or by the conjunction of expressed Truth (*Upāya*) and liberating Gnosis (*Prajñā*); the "great Bliss" (*Mahāsukha*) which results from the union of the two poles evokes the Beatitude (*Ānanda*) of *Ātmā*, wherein is the meeting of "Consciousness" (*Chit*) and "Being" (*Sat*). According to its most outward acceptation, this directly or indirectly sexual symbolism expresses the equilibrium between mental knowledge and virtue; on this basis, the equilibrium may be that between doctrinal investigation and spiritual practice, or that between doctrine and method. All these modes can be brought back to a confrontation between a "knowing" and a "being", or between an intellectual objectivation and a volitive or quasi-existential participation, or, we might say, between a mathematical or architectural dimension and an ethico-aesthetic, or musical dimension, in the vastest sense that these terms can have, bearing in mind that phenomena have their roots in the Divine. It is true that from a certain point of view, the element "being" is more than a complement, inasmuch as it combines the elements "knowing" and "willing"; and in this case it represents the synthesis of holiness that underlies the polarity "intelligence-beauty", which brings us back to the symbolism of love and wine, and to the mystery of the coincidence of faith and *gnosis*.

The cult of a Goddess, of a *Shakti*, of a Tara—of a "Lady" one might simply say—may indicate the predominance of a perspective of love, or of dogmatic and methodic *bhakti*, but it may equally well be the sign, even within a perspective of *gnosis* or of *jñāna*, that emphasis is being placed on the element of "faith" in the higher sense of the term in which Zen and *Jōdo* conceive it, the one according to the "dry path", and the other according to the "moist path". This is also what

---

[14] In Amidism faith is ultimately based on intuition of the essential Goodness of Reality which is Divinely "the Other" in relation to the existence-bound subject; in Zen, on the contrary, what we call "faith" is based on intuition of the essential reality of our "Self", of our subjective essence in its Nirvanic Transpersonality.

Ibn Arabi meant—and in his case there cannot be the slightest doubt that the perspective was that of *gnosis*—by the "religion of Love", which he identified with *al-islām,* the essential conforming of the intelligence and the soul to the divine nature, which is beyond forms and oppositions.

IV

SYMBOLISM

That which is below is like that
which is above,
and that which is above is like that
which is below.

<small>HERMES TRISMEGISTUS</small>

11 THE SYMBOL

Martin Lings

Seest thou not how God citeth a symbol: "A good word is as good
as a good tree, its root set firm and its branches in heaven, giving
its fruit at every season by the leave of its Lord"?
God citeth symbols for men that they may remember.
Qur'ān, 14:24-25

The Eternal (*al-bāqī*) is the All-Embracing (*al-muḥīṭ*): He is not only
as it were after all time but also before all time, being the Ancient of
Days (*al-qadīm*); and so the journey to extinction in the Truth of Certainty (*ḥaqqu 'l-yaqīn*)* is likened to an act of remembrance. The same
applies by analogy to the attainment of the lesser spiritual degrees,
for each degree embraces or envelops the degrees which are below
it. Thus time itself, which belongs to the lowest degree of all, that of
earthly existence, is enveloped by all that lies above, so that the next
world in its entirety, with all its spiritual degrees, is before time as
well as after it; and this is expressed in an utterance of the Prophet
referring to the creation of Adam's body which is at the beginning of
time, and to his own prophethood which is of the next world: "I was
a Prophet while Adam was still betwixt water and clay." It can thus
be said that man has behind him not only a historical and "horizontal"
past but also a spiritual and "vertical" past. A merely theoretic doctrinal knowledge is a horizontal remembrance: we remember what
we have been taught in time; and apart from lessons in the narrower
sense, the facts of the horizontal plane, that is, of this world, when
looked at objectively, without prejudice, make us inclined to believe
what the doctrine teaches us about the world beyond. But insofar
as there is any certainty in this belief, a vertical element has been
added to the horizontal; we are only certain about something because
we have seen it to be true. Thus, even if we are unaware of it, the
least particle of certainty that can be had about the next world must
necessarily have come down from above; it does not belong to horizontal remembrance but to vertical remembrance which is nothing
other than intellectual intuition or—what in a sense amounts to the

---

* Editors' Note: The supreme degree of spiritual realization in Islamic mysticism.

same—spiritual love. We can thus say that the initial act of this way is to awaken, in the erring faculties of intuition, the vertical remembrance which is theirs by rights and which alone can draw them from the outer part of the soul to its center, where the vertical is to be found in all its fullness, that is, in the Tree of Immortality. It is such remembrance[1] that is meant by the Arabic world *dhikr*, the general name given in Islam to all the different means of reminding man of his original state; and in every *dhikr* it is a symbol which is used to prompt the memory.

The outer world of earthly existence corresponds in all its details to the inner world of man's soul, and there is a similar correspondence between the Garden of the Heart and the Garden of the Soul;* but these are only two particular instances of the general truth that all the different domains in the Universe correspond to each other in that each is an image of the Universe itself. The ancient sciences sprung from a knowledge of these correspondences, which was one of man's original endowments. For example, the sciences of medicine were based on a knowledge of the correspondences or likenesses between the domain of the body and other earthly domains such as those of plants and minerals. But the work of the spiritual path does not necessarily call for a knowledge of cosmic or "horizontal" likenesses such as these; when, in connection with the *dhikr*, the Qur'ān speaks of the *mathal*—"example" or "symbol"—it is referring to the essential or "vertical" likenesses between higher and lower domains, such as those between the Heart and the soul. A symbol is something in a lower "known and wonted" domain which the traveler considers not only for its own sake but also and above all in order to have an intuitive glimpse of the "universal and strange" reality which corresponds to it in each of the hidden higher domains. Symbols are in fact none other than the illusory perfections of creation which are guides and incentives to the traveler upon his journey, and they have power to remind him of their counterparts in higher worlds not through merely incidental resemblance but because they are actually related to them

---

[1] This recalls the words of Jesus at the institution of the rite of the bread and wine: "Do this in memory of me." For his body, represented by the bread, is the fruit of the Tree of Immortality, just as his blood, represented by the wine, is the water of the Fountain.

* Editors' Note: The Garden of the Soul is what in the monotheistic religions is called the Garden of Eden; the Garden of the Heart is the innermost precinct of the Garden of Eden where can be found the Tree of Life and the Fountain of Immortality.

in the way that a shadow is related to the object which casts it. There is not the least thing in existence which is not such a shadow, as is implied in the Chapter of the Cow: "Verily God disdaineth not to cite as symbol even a gnat or something smaller" (Qur'ān, 2:20).

Nor is there anything which is any more than a shadow. Indeed, if a world did not cast down shadows from above, the worlds below it would at once vanish altogether, since each world in creation is no more that a tissue of shadows entirely dependent on the archetypes in the world above. Thus the foremost and truest fact about any form is that it is a symbol, so that when contemplating something in order to be reminded of its higher realities the traveler is considering that thing in its universal aspect which alone explains its existence.

Thanks to the true relationship between this world and the next, the "known and wonted" objects have always, for the spiritual man, something of the marvelously "strange." Inversely, the Qur'ān tells us that the higher realities have, for the blessed souls in Paradise, something of the "known and wonted," inasmuch as those souls have had experience, on earth, of the shadows of the realities: "Whensoever they are given to eat of the fruits of the garden, they say: 'This is that which was given us aforetime'; and it was given them in a likeness thereof" (Qur'ān, 2:25).

What is true of earthly objects applies also to acts: an earthly act is the last of a hierarchy of corresponding shadows which spans the whole Universe. Figuratively speaking, if each series of corresponding shadows or reflections throughout the different worlds be likened to the series of the rungs of a ladder, an earthly act is as the lowest rung, or rather as the support upon which rests the foot of the ladder, and to stand at the foot in upward aspiration is precisely what constitutes an act of remembrance in the sense of the word *dhikr*. The traveler may thus sanctify all his acts[2] in seeking to remember, through them, the Divine Qualities in which they are rooted. The fundamental acts of life which were given to man at his creation are as it were the primordial rites; but in view of human decadence Providence has added

---

[2] The intention to ritualize all one's actions necessarily means avoiding those actions which are too remote from the Truth to serve as reminders of it. For example, murder is in itself, that is, as an act of slaying, the shadow of a Reality. It is this Reality, expressed by His Name the Slayer (*al-mumīt*), which makes possible the ritual sacrifice of an animal. But in Truth the Slayer is not to be separated from His other Names, whereas murder, unlike sacrifice, constitutes a kind of separation, reflecting nothing of the Divine Mercy, Benevolence, and Serenity; the murderer is thus only a very indistinct and fragmentary shadow of the Slayer.

to these the rites revealed to the Prophets which are rites in the strict sense of the term. Each of these is as the foot of a ladder which the Divine Mercy has let down into the world as a vehicle of Grace and, in the upward direction, as an eminent means of remembrance. Such is the ladder which appeared in a dream to Jacob, who saw it stretching from Heaven to earth with Angels going up and down upon it; and it is also "the straight path" (*aṣ-ṣirāṭu 'l-mustaqīm*), for indeed the way of religion is none other than the way of creation itself retraced from its end back to its Beginning.

The ladder as a symbol of the true rite and all that this rite implies recalls the tree which is mentioned in the opening quotation as a symbol of the good word; for indeed the best example of a good word is a Divine Name uttered as a *dhikr* in upward aspiration towards the Truth. The firm-set root of the tree is the *dhikr* itself uttered with firm-set purpose; the Heaven-reaching branches represent the tremendous impact of the *dhikr* as it passes upwards throughout the whole Universe; and the fruit of the tree is the Reality in Whose memory the *dhikr* is performed.

The images of the tree and the ladder may help to explain why the Revealed Books, which have been sent down directly from Heaven, necessarily admit of several different interpretations. These are in no sense contradictory, each being right at its own level.[3] Ranged in hierarchy like the rungs of a ladder, they are what might be called the vertical dimension of the Book in question. This dimension is in the nature of things: like a star that falls from the sky, every Revelation leaves behind it a luminous trail of higher truths. A profane book, on the contrary, has only one meaning and therefore no vertical dimension at all. "A bad word is as a bad tree which lies uprooted on the surface of the earth" (Qur'ān, 14:26).

---

[3] In general only one interpretation of what is quoted from the Qur'ān is given here. But it goes without saying that this interpretation is not exclusive of others. As an example of different levels of interpretation, let us consider the story of the three messengers who were sent to a city to preach there the Truth (Qur'ān 26:13-29). According to the literal historical meaning, the city is Antioch and the messengers are Peter and two others of the companions of Jesus. Also macrocosmic, but higher in virtue of its universality, is the interpretation according to which the city represents mankind, whereas the three messengers are Moses, Jesus, and Muhammad. Higher still is the microcosmic interpretation: the city is the human soul, its inhabitants the different psychic elements, and the three messengers the Heart, the Spirit, and the Intellect.

12 THE TRADITIONAL DOCTRINE OF SYMBOLISM

Ghazi bin Muhammad

The first thing to be said about the traditional doctrine of symbolism is
that it is a single doctrine, which is to say that despite vast theological,
cultural, social, racial, linguistic, and historical differences there was
more or less one common, unified understanding of the question of
symbolism the world over in all non-secular—"traditional" precisely—
societies up to the time of the Renaissance. Now this is perhaps not
as surprising as it might initially seem, for three obvious reasons:
first, because man was (and still is) everywhere essentially the same.
Second, because the world was (and still is) everywhere essentially
the same. Third, because belief in the Creator necessarily imposes a
hierarchical worldview or *Weltanschauung*: that is, a cosmology which
comprises varying ontological degrees, from Absolute Reality "down"
to the material world. Indeed, such a traditional cosmological scheme
can be independently found, *mutatis mutandis*, in most ancient
religions[1]—from Platonism to the three great Monotheistic religions

---

[1] According to the traditional cosmological scheme of creation, manifestation as such
comprises three great Worlds created successively by God (in descending order of
ontological reality and "closeness" to God): "the World Spirit," "the World Soul," and
"the World Body." Now the World Spirit, or the World of the Spirit, is also called
the "World of Ideas" (by Plato); the "World of Archetypes"; the Universal Spirit; the
Kingdom of Heaven; the Realm of Supra-formal Manifestation; the World of Essences;
the World of the Domination (in Christianity); the *'Alam al-Jabarut* or *'Alam al-Ruh*
(in Islam); the *Olam Haberiyah* (in Judaism); *Svar* (in Hinduism), and so on. It is said
to "contain" the Archangels, the eternal Archetypes of all things in Creation, and the
"individual" spirits of men, but strictly speaking it *is* each spirit, each Archetype,
and each Archangel, for in it there is no "separation" or "difference" (although of
course there are "distinctions") between subject, object, and their union; between
the knower, the known, and knowledge; between the lover, the beloved, and love,
and so on.

The World Soul, or the World of Souls, is also called the World of Formation; the
Subtle World; the Psychic World; the Grave; the World of the Imagination; the World
of Exemplars; the Intermediary World; the Isthmus; the World of the Dominion (in
Christianity); the *'Alam al-Malakut* or *Barzakh* (in Islam); the *Olam Hayetsirah* (in
Judaism); *Bhuvas* (in Hinduism), and so on. It is ordinarily hidden to (fallen) man, but
it contains the individual souls of all men (as well as the genii or *jinn*, the fairies, and
the other "psychic beings") *distinctively* in much the same way as individual bodies

(Judaism, Christianity, and Islam) to Hinduism—and it is above all precisely this which enables one to speak of "a traditional doctrine of symbolism" for, as will later be seen, traditional symbolism relies upon the correspondences between the different levels of reality.

The next thing to be said about traditional symbolism is that it has nothing, absolutely nothing whatsoever, to do with twentieth century *ersatz* ideas about symbolism, or even with the nineteenth century French poetic movement with the same name. Nor does it have anything to do with metaphor, simile, metonymy, synecdoche, allegory, irony, or any of the other literary tropes[2] with which it was associated during the twentieth century, much less with the putatively real "symbols" so ubiquitous and familiar during that century, the majority of which (e.g. flags) were associated with the paraphernalia of nation-states or other large organizations. This is because modern "symbolism" and the other literary tropes to which it is related, envisages (explicitly or implicitly) an exclusively arbitrary, conventional, or man-made relation between the symbol and what it symbolizes, even when the two naturally resemble each other, and does not assume any particular underlying notions about their "reality," or even about "reality" as such. Traditional symbolism on the other hand—like the Platonic distinction *form* and *substance*, the Aristotelian distinction between *substance* and *accident*, and the Thomist distinction between *essence*

---

are contained in that third great World, the World Body or Physical Universe (the Corporeal World; the *'Alam al-Mulk wal Shahadah* in Islam; *Olam Ha'asiyah* in Judaism; *Bhu* in Hinduism) which is obviously none other than the world that all men ordinarily know through their physical, bodily senses.

[2] A "metaphor" is nowadays generally taken to mean a figure of speech which is not literally true, but somehow correlates to the thing meant (e.g. "my castle" for "my house"); "metonymy," contrasted with "metaphor" by the Russian Formalist Roman Jakobson in the early twentieth century, is generally taken to mean a figure of speech which substitutes or shifts the name of an attribute, an adjunct, or an association for that of the thing meant (e.g. "crown" for "king"); a "synecdoche" is a figure of speech wherein a part is mentioned in *lieu* of—but indicating—the whole (e.g. "there are new faces here"); a "simile" is a descriptive, often lyrical, comparison, usually involving such prepositions as "like" or "as" (e.g. "brave as a lion"); an "allegory" is either a story with a deliberate, pointed meaning or a "moral" (exactly like a "fable" with the difference that it need not necessarily be fictitious or imaginative), or a literary personage or object embodying and representing an idea, however nebulously (e.g. "lady liberty"); and finally, "irony" from the Ancient Greek *eiron* meaning "mask," is the communication of an intention which dissembles and at the same time intends that its dissembling be understood as such: a mask has a certain face which is not that of its wearer, and yet poses as a real face, albeit without intending absolute verisimilitude.

and *form* (none of these pairs having exactly the same connotations despite a certain correspondence between them, and their individual meaning anyway changing diametrically depending on who is using them)—presupposes a *real*, that is, a fully *ontological* relation between the symbol and what it symbolizes.[3]

Now what exactly does it mean to say that traditional symbolism presupposes—and indeed depends on—"an ontological relationship between the symbol and what it symbolizes"? It means, remembering our universal and traditional cosmology as discussed earlier, that a true symbol is merely the manifestation on a "lower" level of reality of precisely that same "higher object," or Archetype, or ultimately Divine Quality (or "matrix" of Qualities) which it "symbolizes." In other words, the "essence" and the immediate "principle of manifestation" of a symbol is, if not what the symbol symbolizes, then certainly something else with the same "essence" as its symbol albeit "higher" than it. A symbol and what it symbolizes are thus "one," on a certain level of reality, and a symbol is thus something real in itself—albeit not "as real" as what it symbolizes—and not something that merely indicates something else.

Now the metaphysics of this doctrine of traditional symbolism are extremely complex,[4] but we will nevertheless address the subject here as succinctly as possible. Let it first be said then that the existence

---

[3] Thus: «[E]n parlant du symbole, la Tradition et les modernes ne parlent pas de la même chose. Toutes les difficultés ou les bizarreries de la symbologie [moderne] viennent de là.» [When speaking of the symbol, Tradition and the modernists do not mean the same thing. This is at the origin of all the difficulties and oddities of the (modern) science of symbolism] (Jean Borella, *La Crise du Symbolisme Religieux* [Lausanne: L'Âge d'Homme/Delphica, 1990], p. 11).

[4] We will briefly say, however, that traditional symbolism generally consists of four "component parts": (i) the "objective" sign; (ii) what is "subjectively" understood by it; (iii) what it indicates; and (iv) its Archetype (evidently, sometimes these last two can be one and the same): «[L']appareil symbolique [traditionel est] constitué par la relation vivante qui unit le *signifiant*, le *sens* et le *référent* particulier—c'est ce qu'on appelle le ‹triangle sémantique›—sous la juridiction d'un quatrième élément que nous dénommons *référent métaphysique* (ou transcendant), en qui les trois premiers trouvent leur principe d'unité: le signifiant (ou ‹symbolisant›) est généralement de nature sensible; le sens, de nature mentale, s'identifie à l'idée que le signifiant évoque à notre esprit, naturellement ou culturellement; le référent particulier, c'est l'objet non visible (accidentellement ou essentiellement) que le symbole, en fonction de son sens, peut désigner (la désignation du référent, ou accomplissement du sens, est la tâche propre de l'herméneutique, ou science de l'interprétation); quant au référent

159

of symbolism arises from the universal, inherent "logic of creation": that is to say that since God created the Universe from Qualities and Attributes which are necessarily comprised within His Infinite Self, then the elements within the universe must—at least in so far as they have positive qualities and thus real attributes—reflect God's Qualities and Attributes. Now to reflect something, or rather to be a reflection of something, means also to be a symbol of it. Thus on one level everything real in Creation is a symbol, ultimately, of the Creator (we quote for brevity only from the Bible and the Quran):[5]

> The heavens declare the glory of God; and the firmament showeth his handiwork. Day unto day uttereth speech, and night unto night showeth knowledge. There is no speech nor language, where their voice is not heard. Their line is gone out through all the earth, and their words to the end of the world (Psalms 19:1-3).

> Lo! in the difference of the day and night and all that God hath created in the heavens and the earth are portents, verily, for folk who ward off [evil] (Quran 10:6).

métaphysique, toujours oublié et pourtant fondamental, puisque c'est lui qui fait du signe un véritable symbole, c'est l'archétype—ou le principe métacosmique—dont le signifiant, le sens et le référent particulier ne sont que des manifestations distinctes » [The traditional symbolic apparatus lies in the living relationship which unifies the *signifier*, the *meaning*, and the specific *referent*—this is called the "semantic triangle"—under the jurisdiction of a fourth element, which we call the *metaphysical* (or transcendent) *referent*, in which the three first elements find their unifying principle: the signifier (or "symbolizer") generally addresses the senses; the meaning addresses the mind, by identifying itself with the idea that the signifier evokes in our mind, naturally or culturally; the specific referent is the non-visible object (accidentally or essentially) that the symbol, in function of its meaning, may designate (the designation of the referent, or the fulfillment of the meaning, is the proper task of hermeneutics, or the science of interpretation); as to the metaphysical referent, which is always forgotten despite the fact that it is fundamental, since it is by it and through it that the referent is made a true symbol, it is the archetype—or the metacosmic principle—of which the signifier, meaning, and specific referent are but distinctive manifestations] (Jean Borella, *La Crise du Symbolisme Religieux*, p. 9).

[5] It is perhaps also worth mentioning here that Plato, in his famous allegory of the Cave at the beginning of Book VII of the *Republic*, likens the things of the Physical World to "shadows of puppets of real things," and the things of the Subtle World to the "puppets of real things" (the "real things" thus being the Archetypes, the contents of the Spiritual World), and this along with his cosmology in the beginning of the main section of his *Timaeus* where the world is described as being "modeled" on the Creator, echoes the idea of "universal symbolism," and indeed established it for Platonists and Neoplatonists thereafter.

And of His portents is this: The heavens and the earth stand fast by His command. . . . Unto Him belongeth whosoever is in the heavens and the earth. . . . He it is who produceth creation, then reproduceth it. . . . His is the Sublime Exemplar in the heavens and in the earth. He is the Mighty, the Wise (Quran 30:25-27).

It must be said, however, that whilst everything in creation is in principle "symbolic" of the Qualities of the Creator, not everything in creation is accessible to every man as a "symbol" as such. One Quranic commentator writes:

"The seven heavens and the earth and all that is therein glorify Him, nor is there anything but glorifieth Him with praise; yet ye understand not their glorification" (Quran 17:44). The above verse is an answer to the question [what is symbolism?]; it also justifies to a certain extent, in its last sentence, the writing of this chapter, for a thing's glorification of God—which "ye understand not"—is precisely its symbolism. This may be deduced from the Islamic "holy utterance," so called because in it the Divinity speaks on the tongue of the Prophet [Muhammad]: "I was a Hidden Treasure and I loved to be known, and so I created the world." Thus the universe and its contents were created in order to make known the Creator, and to make known the good is to praise it; the means of making it known is to reflect it or to shadow it; and a symbol is the reflection or shadow of a higher reality. . . .

Since nothing can exist except in virtue of its Divine root, does that mean that everything is a symbol? The answer is yes and no— yes for the reason just given, and no because "symbol" means "sign" or "token," which implies an operative power to call something to mind, namely its Archetype. In the light of the initially quoted verse "Nor is there anything but glorifieth Him with praise," we could say that whether this or that can rightly be called symbolic depends on whether its "praise" is powerful or faint. The word symbol is [traditionally] normally reserved for that which is particularly impressive in its "glorification". . . .

Since we are concerned with what is symbolic and what is not, it should be understood that we are not considering here disparities such as those between the animal, vegetable, and mineral kingdoms or between sections of the same kingdom—mammals, birds, and insects, for example. The lion, the eagle, and the bee are all true symbols, each being a summit in its own domain. . . . It is in the nature of things [however] that some of the contents of the world that is furthest from the Principle should bear signs of that remoteness.[6]

*   *   *

All true symbols can be divided into three main, self-evident categories: those manifested to human beings primarily[7] in the Physical
World, those manifested to human beings primarily in the Subtle
World, and those manifested in both simultaneously. Taking the last
first, all that needs to be said is that these consist quite simply of
human beings, which have bodies in the Physical World and souls in
the Subtle World, and which are not only quite obviously symbols,
but even the greatest of all symbols since according to the Bible:
"God created man in His own image,"[8] and according to the Prophet
Muhammad: "Verily God created Adam in His own image."[9]

Turning to the symbols of the Physical World, these too are obvious;
they consist first of the great "natural symbols" of creation (the sun, the
sky, the seas, the mountains, fine trees, great animals, and so on), and
second of the symbols of "sacred art" (icons, calligraphy, and so on—at
least insofar as these are "physical"). As regards the symbols of "sacred
art" these need no explanation—because obviously the very purpose
of "sacred art" is to furnish man with "sacred symbols" (which are
not only true symbols *per se* but "complete true symbols" as it were,
symbols significantly capable of transmitting aspects of the Divine
to fallen man) for religious contemplation. The reason why "sacred
art" is traditionally bound by particular rules, proportions, colors,

---

[6] Martin Lings, *Symbol & Archetype: A Study of the Meaning of Existence* (Cambridge,
UK: Quinta Essentia, 1991), pp. 1-8. The author also adds, in a footnote, the following
illuminating comments: "To take examples from the world of mammals in addition
to the lion, with whom other members of the cat family are to be included, we may
mention, as being truly symbolic in their different ways, the elephant, the camel, the
horse, and the wolf. On the other hand, in contrast with these sacred animals, the
hippopotamus, the giraffe, and the hyena are uninspiring, by which we mean, to revert
to our liminal quotation, that their 'praise' is too faint to earn for them, as such, the
title of symbol in the higher and more exclusive sense of the word, though as animals,
that is, in their life and their consciousness, they are symbolic, as also in their very
existence" (Ibid., p. 8).

[7] Evidently, everything in the Physical World has its direct principle in the Subtle
World, and, conversely, many things pertaining to the Subtle World have their
"prolongations" in the Physical World ("sacred words," for example, have physical
sounds, as will be discussed below).

[8] Genesis 1:27.

[9] *Musnad Ibn Hanbal*, 2: 244, 251, 315, 323 etc.; *Sahih Bukhari, Kitab Al-Isti'than*,
chapter 1, *et passim*.

materials, scales, harmonies, etc. (in short, specific *forms*) can now be clearly understood: it is precisely to ensure that "sacred symbols" are produced that can really help fallen man contemplate, that is, to participate in a direct vision of higher realities *through* forms, rather than be confined within the limits of forms as such. As regards the natural symbols of creation, however, we quote from "the Seraphic Doctor," St. Bonaventure:

> The *origin* of things, according to their creation, distinction, and embellishment, as the work of the six days, proclaims the divine power that produces all things from nothing, the divine wisdom that clearly distinguishes all things, and the divine goodness that lavishly adorns all things. The *magnitude* of things, in the mass of their length, width, and depth; in their great power extending in length, width, and depth as appears in the diffusion of light; in the efficiency of their operations which are internal, continuous, and diffused as appears in the operation of fire—all this clearly manifests the immensity of the power, wisdom, and goodness of God. . . . The *multitude* of things in their generic, specific, and individual diversity in substance, form or figure, and efficiency—beyond all human calculation—clearly suggests and shows the immensity of the three previously mentioned attributes in God. The *beauty* of things, in the variety of light, shape, and color in simple, mixed, and even organic bodies—such as heavenly bodies, and minerals (like stones and metals), and plants, and animals—clearly proclaims the three previously mentioned attributes. . . . Whoever, therefore, is not enlightened by such splendor of created things is blind; whoever is not awakened by such outcries is deaf; whoever does not praise God because of all these effects is dumb; whoever does not discover the First Principle from such clear signs is a fool.[10]

Finally, as regards the symbols of the Subtle World, these too can be divided into two main categories:[11] words (or rather "sacred words" as will be discussed shortly) and visions (or rather their contents, when indeed it is a questions of visions or visionary dreams as such, and not *gnosis* or spiritual knowledge which are beyond visions). To take visions first, since they are easier to explain, let it be said from the

---

[10] Bonaventure, *The Soul's Journey into God*, trans. Ewert Cousins (Mahwah NJ: Paulist Press, 1978), chapter 1: 14-15; pp. 65-67.

[11] There are also of course other "categories" of "contents of the Subtle World"—such as the "exemplars" or "daemons" of objects of the Physical World, and *genii*—which are *not* symbols as such, simply because they are not "normally" accessible to men.

outset that these are traditionally distinguished from ordinary dreams (which are merely a kind of psychic "playback" and "reprocessing" of the day's memories, imaginings, emotions, sensations, associations, and so on) by their clarity; by their extraordinary reality; by their lasting effects and "imprint"; by the coherence of their content, and by their occurring at "sacred moments," all of which are signs, precisely, of "events" occurring in the "ontologically superior" Subtle World. In other words, visionary dreams, unlike ordinary "psychic dreams," consist of sacred forms or symbols actually present—and seen by the dreamer—in an objective, supra-psychic subtle domain (but, as with all symbols, rooted in a higher source). The traditional "sacred science" concerned with the interpretation of such "visionary" dreams and their symbolic contents is known as Oneirology and it was (and perhaps still is) to be found in practically all religious lore. Indeed, the Bible and the Quran (not to mention the Platonic Tradition of course, witness Macrobius' *The Dream of Scipio*) are strewn with references to visionary dreams and their interpretation, as with those of the Prophets Abraham, Jacob, and Joseph (among others), and even the Prophet Muhammad.[12] We quote from al-Ghazali a true story about arguably the most famous dream interpreter in history (certainly in Islamic history, excluding the Prophets themselves, of course), Ibn Sirin, the seventh-eighth century author of the seminal *Tafsir al-Ahlam* (*The Interpretation of Dreams*):

> A certain man dreamt that there was a ring in his hand with which he was sealing the mouths of men and the genitals of women. Ibn Sirin [in interpretation] said: "You are the man who calls out to prayer in the lunar month of Ramadan[13] before dawn." The man said "Yes." Another man dreamt he was pouring oil into olive oil. Ibn Sirin said to him: "If you have a slave woman she is in fact your mother; she was captured in a war [enslaved] and sold, and you bought her without knowing [your relationship with her]." This was in fact true. Observe, then, that sealing of mouths and genitals with a ring agrees with calling out to prayer before dawn, in respect of the essence of the ring which is prohibition, although the former differs

[12] The Prophet Muhammad said: "The visionary dream of the faithful believer is one part of the forty-six parts of prophecy" (*Sahih Bukhari, Kitab al-Ta'bir,* chapter 4, *et passim*).

[13] In Ramadan Muslims abstain from all food, drink, and sexual contact from sunrise to sunset; at these two times—as well as the other times for the five prayers—the call to prayer is ritually enacted by a muezzin, a man permanently appointed to carry out this function.

from the latter in respect of form. . . . Everything has a definition, a reality, which is its essence.[14]

Turning now to words, it should first of all be said that although these have phonetic and scriptural "forms" which render them tangibly accessible to humans, they essentially pertain to the Subtle World, for obviously it is only by the intelligence—which is situated, in the first instance, within the soul and thus belongs to the subtle level of existence—that they are "received" and understood. Then it should be said that words in (*originally* revealed or inspired) "sacred languages" (like Arabic, Hebrew, Sanskrit, and even Ancient Greek) are traditionally viewed as being the *exact* symbolic phonetic and scriptural equivalents[15] of the things they naturally and inherently "symbolize" on their own "planes"—modern languages, however, obviously contain many words which are the creations of mere arbitrary phonetic conventions, as de Saussure rightly saw (although he then mistakenly generalized this observation so as to include *all* languages). It should also be clear that the existence of more than one sacred language is no impediment to this, since symbols can symbolize more than one thing, and since one thing can be symbolized by more than one symbol:

> Socrates: A name is an instrument of teaching and of distinguishing natures, as the shuttle is of distinguishing the threads of the web. . . . As to names, ought not our legislator [the inventor of the Greek language] also know how to put the true natural name of each thing into sounds and syllables, and to make and give all names with a view to the ideal name, if he is to be a namer in any true sense? And we must remember that different legislators will not all use the same syllables. For neither does every smith, although he may be making the same instrument for the same purpose, make them all of the same iron [alloy]. The form must be the same, but the material may vary, and still the instrument may be equally good of whatever iron made, whether in Hellas or in a foreign country—there is no difference. . . . Cratylus is right in saying that things have names by nature, and that not every man is an artificer of names, but [only] he who looks to the name which each thing by nature has, and is able

---

[14] Abu Hamid al-Ghazali, *The Jewels of the Quran* (*Kitab Jawahir al-Quran*), trans. M. Abul-Qasem (London: Kegan Paul International, 1977), pp. 50-51.

[15] Every letter (and consequently every word) in sacred languages was also traditionally identified with a number and this relation formed the basis of many a scripture-based traditional science—such as *gematria* and *jafr*—particularly in Jewish *Kabbalah*, Islamic Sufism, and in the works of such seminal Christian mystics as John of Ruysbroeck.

to express the true forms of things in letters and syllables. . . . Now that you and I have talked over the matter, a step has been gained, for we have discovered that names have by nature a truth, and that not every man knows how to give a thing a name.[16]

Now we do not want to dwell on the problems of understanding the operation of language, for it is undoubtedly one of the most complex problems in all philosophy—indeed twentieth century philosophy is all but exclusively dedicated to it, without for all that making the distinction between sacred and "conventional" language as mentioned above—and it would take us too far from our present inquiry.[17] We will, however, briefly say that the symbolic nature of words is attested to not only by Adam's giving names to all creatures (according to both the Bible and the Quran[18]), but also *a priori* by the "Hypostasis" of the Uncreated Divine Word both in itself[19] and as the "Creative Power."[20] Moreover, the very fact that so many religions admit—or rather are based

---

[16] Plato, *Cratylus* 388c-390-b, trans. Benjamin Jowett, in *Plato: The Collected Dialogues*, ed. E. Hamilton and H. Cairns, Bollingen Series LXXI (Princeton University Press, 1961), pp. 426-429.

[17] There is a plethora of learned modern books about the operation of language, but one of the few that studies the difference between the operation of sacred language and conventional language seriously is Umberto Eco's *The Search for the Perfect Language*. Whilst Eco ultimately rejects the idea of the sacred and of objective truths, his scholarship does point in many useful directions, even as regards traditional hermeneutics and linguistic symbolism.

[18] "And He taught Adam all the names, then showed them to the angels, saying: Inform me of the names of these, if ye are truthful. They said: Be glorified! We have no knowledge saving that which Thou hast taught us. Lo! Thou, only Thou, art the Knower, the Wise. He said: O Adam! Inform them of their names, and when he had informed them of their names, He said: did I not tell you that I know the secret of the heavens and the earth?" (Quran 2:31-33). "And out of the ground the Lord God formed every beast of the field, and every fowl of the air; and brought them unto Adam to see what he would call them: and whatsoever Adam called every living creature, that was the name thereof. And Adam gave names to all the cattle, and to the fowl of the air, and to every beast of the field" (Genesis 2:19-20).

[19] "In the beginning was the Word, and the Word was with God, and the Word was God" (John 1:1). It is also worth noting that orthodox Muslims fought many wars early in Islamic history with the Mu'tazilites over the question of whether the Quran, the Word of God revealed in the Arabic language, was created or Uncreated (the orthodox position being of course that it was Uncreated).

[20] "But His command, when He intendeth a thing, is only that He saith unto it: Be! And it is" (Quran 36:81). "And God said: Let there be light, and there was light" (Genesis 1:3).

on—holy scriptures of Divine origin, and that their founders so often spoke in oral parables,[21] betokens a universal traditional recognition of the symbolism of words, for obviously Revelation necessarily implies not merely perfect content but also apposite and perfect form (since its Source is Omnipotent and Omniscient). Finally, it is the symbolic nature of words that explains why, for so many ancient peoples, there was no distinction between words (in their own, sacred languages) and the objects they refer to; why words were "mysteriously one" with the things named:

> Another distinction lacking to ancient Egypt was the one most of us make automatically between the name and the thing [named]. For the ancient Egyptian the name *was* the thing; the real object we separate from its designation was identical with it.[22]

*   *   *

The following verses from the Holy Quran can now be properly pondered and expounded, for they contain and summarize the entire traditional doctrine of symbolism:

> Seest thou not how God coineth a similitude: A goodly word, [is] as a goodly tree, its roots set firm, its branches reaching into heaven, giving its fruit at every season by permission of its Lord? God coineth the similitudes for mankind in order that they may reflect (14:24-25).

God gives a symbol ("a goodly tree") for a symbol ("a goodly word") thereby showing the ubiquity of symbols in creation and their universality.

---

[21] "And the disciples came, and said unto him, Why speakest thou in parables? He answered and said unto them, Because it is given unto you to know the mysteries of the kingdom of heaven, but to them it is not given. . . . Therefore I speak to them in parables: because they seeing see not; and they hearing hear not, neither do they understand" (Matthew 13:10-11, 13). In fact the whole doctrine of symbolism is contained within these verses, sacred parables being (as will shortly be seen) as it were "double symbols"—symbolic both by the forms of their words as such and by the analogies their contents evoke.

[22] J. M. Roberts, *The Penguin History of the World* (London: Penguin Books, 1990), p. 88.

- He does this through what? Through symbols; specifically, through "goodly words"—of which the Quran obviously consists *par excellence*—showing not only the infinite mirror-play of the symbols of creation, but also, and perhaps more poignantly, the impossibility of escaping from symbols in communication.
- What kind of symbols? All kinds: a physical symbol ("a goodly tree") is given for a subtle symbol ("a goodly word") showing the equivalence of all true symbols, whether subtle or physical.
- For whom? For "mankind in order that they may reflect"; in other words, there is an epistemological gap between (cognitive) subjects and objects, and the purpose of symbolism lies in bridging this gap through the *contemplation* of symbols (and not through reason or logic), and thus in these latter's "human" and "operational" efficacy inherent in such symbols.
- Why? So that symbolism may give "its fruit" (intuition, enlightenment, and ultimately salvation) "at every season" (with every different person who contemplates symbols) "by permission of its Lord" (only through the Grace of God).
- How? Because "its roots set firm," are sunk in the depths the spirit of whosoever properly contemplates symbols, and "its branches reaching into heaven" open unto the World Spirit through this contemplation.

Now we could easily comment further on these two verses, as so many have before us, for they are themselves what they describe—infinite, "reaching into heaven"—but it should be clear by now that they contain the entire traditional doctrine of symbolism with all its implications and ramifications as we have been discussing it thus far in this essay (not to mention the secret of ritual orison), and thus contain as much, in two lines, as the whole of twentieth-century semiotics, with its countless books, studies, essays, and dissertations!

That this doctrine should not be more specifically and systematically expounded should not be surprising, first because symbols were *intuitively* understood and contemplated by ancient man, who was closer to the Divine and to what reflects It on earth, and second because ancient religions were obviously not in the business of expounding academic treatises, but rather of saving souls (the majority of whom anyway were *academically* unlearned) and giving practical instructions to that end:

> Primordial man did not . . . need, in any negative sense of that word, a science of symbols. . . . Otherwise expressed, beneath the Supreme Beatitude of Gnosis, that is, the consciousness of identity with the Absolute Infinite One, his happiness as a soul in bliss coincided with symbols, that of Paradise itself and of all that it contained including himself and other holy microcosms.[23]

Nevertheless, it must be said that there are obviously clear, if pithy, indications of this doctrine in traditional sources in all religions, because religions nevertheless must needs contain the seeds of every essential idea (for potential future doctrinal exposition):

> For the invisible things of Him from the creation of the world are clearly seen, being understood by the things that are made, even His eternal power and Godhead; so that they [men] are without excuse (Romans 1:20).

> The sensory world is a ladder[24] to the Spiritual World, for, if there were no connection and relationship between the two, the way to ascending to the Spiritual World would be blocked. If ascending were impossible, travel to the presence of Lordship and nearness to God would also be impossible. . . . The visible world is a ladder to the Spiritual World, and traveling on "the Straight Path" [Quran 1:6] consists of climbing this ladder. One may refer to this traveling as "religion" and the "way-stations of guidance." If there were no relationship and connection between the two worlds, ascending from one world to the other would be inconceivable. The Divine Mercy made the sensory world parallel to the Spiritual World; there is nothing in this world [the sensory world] that is not a similitude of something in that world [the Spiritual World].[25]

---

[23] Martin Lings, *Symbol & Archetype*, p. 9.

[24] The image of the symbol as ladder is also to be found in Christianity and Judaism, and indeed comprises one of the interpretations given to Jacob's famous dream in Genesis 28:12: "And he dreamed, and beheld a ladder set up on the earth, and the top of it reached to Heaven: and behold the angels of God ascending and descending on it."

[25] Abu Hamid al-Ghazali, *Mishkat al-Anwar*, chapter 2, 6-9 (our own translation). *Mishkat al-Anwar* is al-Ghazali's commentary on the Verse of Light (Quran 24: 35).

The object of wisdom is no particular being, but all the beings, absolutely; and it should not begin to seek the principles of an individual being, but the principles common to all. The object of wisdom is all the beings, as the object of sight is all visible things. The function of wisdom is to see all the beings in their totality, and to know their universal attributes, and that is how wisdom discovers the principles of all beings.[26]

*   *   *

In conclusion then, the traditional doctrine of symbolism can be summarized—and recapitulated—as follows:

Symbolism is a language and a precise form of thought; a hieratic and a metaphysical language and not a language determined by somatic or psychological categories. Its foundation is in the analogical correspondence of all orders of reality and states of being or reference; it is because "This world is in the image of that, and vice versa" (AB VIII.2 and KU IV.10[27]) that it can be said *Coeli enarrant gloriam Dei* [the heavens declare the glory of God].[28]

Symbolism seems to us to be quite specially adapted to the needs of human nature, which is not exclusively intellectual but which needs a sensory basis from which to rise to higher levels. . . . Fundamentally, every expression, every formulation, whatever it may be, is a symbol of the thought which it expresses outwardly. In this sense, language itself is nothing other than symbolism. There can be no opposition, therefore, between the use of words and the use of figurative symbols; rather these two modes of expression should be complementary one to another (moreover, they may in fact be combined, for primitively writing is ideographic and sometimes, as in China, it has retained this characteristic). Generally speaking, the form of language is analytical and "discursive," as is human reason of which it is the true and fitting instrument and the flow of which it reproduces as

[26] *The Pythagorean Sourcebook and Library*, comp. and trans. Kenneth Sylvan Guthrie (Michigan: Phanes Press, 1987), p. 182. The particular passage quoted is from *The Fragments of Archytas*, Archytas being a contemporary and friend of Plato, and one of the earliest Pythagoreans.

[27] AB = *The Aitareya and Kausitaki Brahmanas of the Rigveda*, ed. A. B. Keith (Cambridge, Mass., 1920, Harvard Oriental Studies, XXV). KU = *Katha Upanishad*, in *The Thirteen Principal Upanishads*, ed. R. E. Hume (2nd ed., London, 1931).

[28] *Coomaraswamy 1: Selected Papers, Traditional Art and Symbolism*, ed. Roger Lipsey, Bollingen Series LXXXIX (Princeton University Press, 1977), p. 174.

exactly as possible. On the contrary, symbolism in the strict sense is synthetic and thereby as it were intuitive, which makes it more apt than language to serve as a support for intellectual intuition which is above reason, and which must not be confused with that lower intuition to which numerous contemporary philosophers so often refer. . . .

We have often said, and we cannot repeat it too often: every real symbol bears its multiple meanings within itself, and this is so from its very origin; for it is not constituted as such in virtue of human convention but in virtue of the law of correspondence which links all the worlds together. If some see these meanings while others do not, or see them only partially, they are none the less really there: it is the "intellectual horizon" of each person that makes all the difference. Symbolism is an exact science and not a daydream in which individual fantasies can have a free run.[29]

---

[29] René Guénon, *Fundamental Symbols: The Universal Language of Sacred Science*, trans. Alvin Moore, Jr. (Cambridge, UK: Quinta Essentia, 1995), pp. 13, 29.

13 THE LANGUAGE OF THE BIRDS

René Guénon

Wa-ṣ-ṣāffāti ṣāffan,
Faz-zājirāti zajran,
Fat-tāliyāti dhikran. . . .
By those ranged in ranks,
And who drive away, repulsing,
And who recite the invocation. . . .
Qurʾān 37:1-3

There is often mention, in diverse traditions, of a mysterious language called "the language of the birds"—a designation that is clearly symbolic, for the very importance that is attributed to the knowledge of this language, as the prerogative of a high initiation, does not allow us to take it literally. We read, for example, in the *Qurʾān*: "And Solomon was David's heir. And he said, O mankind! Lo! we have been taught the language of the birds (*ullimnā manṭiq aṭ-ṭayr*) and have been given abundance of all things" (27:16). Elsewhere we read of heroes who, having vanquished the dragon, like Siegfried in the Nordic legend, instantly understand the language of the birds; and this makes it easy to interpret the symbolism in question. Victory over the dragon has, as its immediate consequence, the conquest of immortality, which is represented by some object the approach to which is guarded by the dragon; and this conquest essentially implies the reintegration into the center of the human state, that is, into the point where communication is established with the higher states of the being. It is this communication which is represented by the understanding of the language of the birds; and in fact birds are frequently taken as symbols of the angels, that is, precisely, of the higher states. We have had occasion elsewhere[1] to cite the Gospel parable that refers, in this very sense, to "the birds of the heavens" which come and rest in the branches of the tree, the same tree that represents the axis which passes through the center of each state of the being and links all the states with each other.[2]

[1] *Man and His Becoming according to the Vedānta*, chap. 3.

[2] In the Medieval symbol of the *Peridexion* (a corruption of the word *Paradision*), one sees the birds on the branches of the tree and the dragon at its foot (cf. *The Sym-*

172

In the Qur'ānic text given above, the term *aṣ-ṣāffāt* is taken as meaning literally the birds, but as denoting symbolically the angels (*al-malā'ikah*); and thus the first verse signifies the constitution of the celestial or spiritual hierarchies.[3] The second verse expresses the fight of the angels against the demons, the celestial powers against the infernal powers, that is, the opposition between higher and lower states.[4] In the Hindu tradition this is the struggle of the *Devas* against the *Asuras* and also, according to a symbolism which comes very close to the symbolism of our theme, the combat of *Garuda* against the *Nāga* which is, moreover, none other than the above mentioned serpent or dragon. The *Garuda* is the eagle, and elsewhere it is replaced by other birds such as the ibis, the stork, the heron, all enemies and destroyers of reptiles.[5] Finally, in the third verse, the angels are said to be reciting the *dhikr* which is generally interpreted as meaning here the *Qur'ān;* not the *Qur'ān* that is expressed in human language, needless to say, but its eternal prototype inscribed on the "Guarded Tablet" (*al-lawḥ al-maḥfūẓ*), which like Jacob's ladder extends from the heavens to the earth, and therefore throughout all the degrees of universal existence.[6] Likewise, it is said in the Hindu tradition

---

bolism of the Cross, chap. 9). In a study on the symbolism of the "bird of Paradise" (*Le Rayonnement intellectuel*, May-June 1930) Charbonneau-Lassay has reproduced a sculpture in which this bird is represented by only a head and wings, a form frequently used to depict the angels (cf. *Le Bestiaire du Christ*, chap. 46, p. 425).

[3] The word *ṣaff* or "rank," is one of those many words which have been suggested as the origin of the word *ṣūfī* and *taṣawwuf;* and although this derivation does not seem acceptable from a purely linguistic point of view, it is none the less true, as with many other derivations of the same kind, that it represents one of the ideas really contained in these terms: for the "spiritual hierarchies" are essentially identical with the degrees of initiation.

[4] This opposition is expressed in each being by the two tendencies, ascending and descending, called respectively *sattva* and *tamas* by the Hindu doctrine. It is also that which Mazdeism symbolizes by the antagonism between light and darkness, personified respectively by *Ormuzd* and *Ahriman*.

[5] See on this subject the remarkable works of Louis Charbonneau-Lassay on the animal symbols of Christ (cf. *Le Bestiaire du Christ*). It is important to note that the symbolic opposition of bird and serpent does not apply except when the serpent is considered under its malefic aspect; on the contrary, under its benefic aspect it sometimes is united with the bird as in the case of *Quetzalcohuatl* of the ancient Meso-American traditions. Moreover, one also finds in Mexico the combat of the eagle with the serpent. As regards the association of bird and serpent, we can recall the Gospel text: "Be ye wise as serpents and guileless as doves" (Matt. 10:16).

[6] On the symbolism of the book to which this directly relates, see *The Symbolism of the Cross*, chap. 14.

that the *Devas*, in their fight against the *Asuras*, protect themselves (*achhandayan*) by the recitation of the hymns of the *Veda*, and that it is for this reason that the hymns received the name of *chhandas*, a word which denotes "rhythm." The same idea is contained in the word *dhikr* which, in Islamic esoterism, is used of rhythmic formulas that correspond exactly to Hindu *mantras*. The repetition of these formulas aims at producing a harmonization of the different elements of the being, and at causing vibrations which, by their repercussions throughout the immense hierarchy of states, are capable of opening up a communication with the higher states, which in a general way is the essential and primordial purpose of all rites.

This brings us back directly and very clearly to what was said above about the "language of the birds," which we can also call "angelic language," and of which the image in the human world is rhythmic speech; for the "science of rhythm," which admits of many applications, is the ultimate basis of all the means that can be brought into action in order to enter into communication with the higher states. That is why an Islamic tradition says that Adam, in the earthly Paradise, spoke in verse, that is, in rhythmic speech; this is related to that "Syrian language" (*lughah suryāniyyah*) of which we spoke in our previous study on the "science of letters,"* and which must be regarded as translating directly the "solar and angelic illumination" as this manifests itself in the center of the human state. This is also why the Sacred Books are written in rhythmic language which, clearly, makes of them something quite other than the mere "poems," in the purely profane sense, which the anti-traditional bias of the modern critics would have them to be. Moreover, in its origins poetry was by no means the vain "literature" that it has become by a degeneration resulting from the downward march of the human cycle, and it had a truly sacred character.[7] Traces of this can be found up to classical antiquity in the West, when poetry was still called the "language of the Gods," an expression equivalent to those we have indicated, in as

---

* Editors' Note: See "The Science of Letters," in René Guénon, *Fundamental Symbols: The Universal Language of Sacred Science*, chap. 8.

[7] It can be said, moreover, in a general way, that the arts and sciences have become profane by just this kind of degeneration which deprives them of their traditional nature and, by way of consequence, of any higher significance. We have spoken of this in *The Esoterism of Dante*, chap. 2, and *The Crisis of the Modern World*, chap. 4 [Editors' Note: See also René Guénon, *The Reign of Quantity and the Signs of the Times*, chap. 8].

much as the Gods, that is, the *Devas*,[8] are, like the angels, the representation of the higher states. In Latin, verses were called *carmina*, a designation relating to their use in the accomplishment of rites; for the word *carmen* is identical to the Sanskrit *karma* which must be taken here in its special sense of "ritual action";[9] and the poet himself, interpreter of the "sacred language" through which the divine Word appears, was *vates*, a word which defined him as endowed with an inspiration that was in some way prophetic. Later, by another degeneration, the *vates* was no longer anything more than a common "diviner,"[10] and the carmen (whence the English word *charm*) no more than a "spell," that is, an operation of low magic. There again is an example of the fact that magic, even sorcery, is what subsists as the last vestige of vanished traditions.*

These few indications should be enough to show how inept it is to mock at stories that speak of the "language of the birds." It is all too easy and too simple to disdain as superstitions everything that one does not understand. But the ancients, for their part, knew very well what they meant when they used symbolic language. The real "superstition," in the strictly etymological sense (*quod superstat*), is that which outlives itself, in short, the "dead letter." But even this very survival, however lacking in interest it may seem, is nevertheless not so contemptible; for the Spirit, which "bloweth where it listeth" and when it listeth, can always come and revivify symbols and rites, and restore to them, along with their lost meaning, the plenitude of their original virtue.

---

[8] The Sanskrit *Deva* and the Latin *deus* are one and the same word.

[9] The word "poetry" also derives from the Greek *poiein* which has the same signification as the Sanskrit root *kri*, whence comes *karma*, which is found again in the Latin *creare* understood in its primitive acceptation; at the beginning, therefore, it was a question of something altogether different from a mere artistic or literary production in the profane sense that Aristotle seems to have had uniquely in view in speaking of what he called the "poetic sciences."

[10] The word "diviner" itself is no less deviant from its meaning; for etymologically it is nothing else than *divinus*, signifying here "interpreter of the Gods." The "auspices" (from *aves spicere*, "to observe the birds"), omens drawn from the flight and song of birds, are more closely related to the "language of the birds," understood in this case in the most literal sense but nevertheless still identified with the "language of the Gods," who were thought to manifest their will by means of these omens. The birds thus played the part of "messengers," analogous—but on a very low plane—to the part that is generally attributed to the angels (whence their very name, for this is precisely the meaning of the Greek *aggelos*).

* Editors' Note: On this question of the origins of magic and sorcery, see René Guénon, *Fundamental Symbols*, chap. 22, "Seth," the final paragraph.

14 SYMPLEGADES*

Ananda K. Coomaraswamy

Beyond the Clashing Rocks in the Other World,
Beauty most marvelous is, Life's Herb, Life's Water.
Karl von Spiess

All waits undreamed of in that region, that inaccessible land.
Walt Whitman

The distribution of the motif of "Clashing Rocks"[1] is an indication
of its prehistoric antiquity, and refers the complex pattern of the
Urmythos of the Quest to a period prior at least to the population of
America. The signs and symbols of the Quest of Life which have so
often survived in oral tradition, long after they have been rationalized
or romanticized by literary artists, are our best clue to what must have
been the primordial form of the one spiritual language of which, as
Jeremias says (*Altorientalischen Geisteskultur*, Vorwort) "the dialects
are recognizable in the divers existing cultures." Here, for the sake of
brevity, we are considering only a single component of the complex
pattern, that of the "Active Door."[2] It has been quite generally recognized that these Wandering Rocks, "to pass between which thou must
thyself find a means" (Jülg), are the "mythical forms of that wonder-
door beyond which lie Oceanus, the Islands of the Blessed, the
Kingdom of the Dead" and that they divide "this known world from
the unknown Beyond" (Jessen in Wilhelm Heinrich Roscher, *Aus-
führliches Lexikon der griechischen und römischen Mythologie* [Leipzig,
1884]): that, as Cook, endorsing Jessen, says, they "presuppose the
ancient popular belief in a doorway to the Otherworld formed by
clashing mountain-walls." The Planktai Petrai, in other words, are
the leaves of the Golden Gates of the Janua Coeli,[3] of which in the

* Editors' Note: This edition of Ananda K. Coomaraswamy's article is a slightly
abridged version prepared by Dr. Martin Lings for publication in the British journal
Studies in Comparative Religion 1973, 7 (1). The numerous Latin, German, French,
and Italian passages were translated by Dr. Lings into English, while the Greek was
transliterated. The extensive footnotes have been changed to endnotes to facilitate a
smoother reading of the main text. The fundamental thesis of the article is summed
up in the final section at pp. 188-189.

Christian tradition, St. Peter, appointed by the Son of Man, is now the Keeper.

We begin with the problems of distribution of the motif, of which the meaning will develop as we proceed. In certain contexts, as pointed out by Cook (pp. 988-991) "dancing reeds" replace the floating or dancing islands, and although there is no indication in the classical sources of the notion of a dangerous passage between a pair of dancing reeds, this appears elsewhere, and it can hardly be doubted that it belongs to the original form of the story. Dr. Murray Fowler[4] has called attention to an Indian context (*Śatapatha Brāhmaṇa* III.6.2.8, 9) where Soma, the plant, bread, or water of life, is to be brought down from above by the aquiline Gāyatrī (Suparṇī, Vāc), Agni's vocal and metrical power, and we are told that it had been "deposited [for safe-keeping] within, i.e., behind, two golden leaves,[5] that were razor-edged, and snapped together[6] at every winking of an eye." She tears out these leaves, and appropriates the life-giving power, which Indrāgnī "extend for the generation of offspring" (*Śatapatha Brāhmaṇa* III.6.2.13). In other words, the Falcon, successful Soma-thief, passes safely between these "two Gandharva Soma-wardens" and returns with the rescued prisoner, viz., that King Soma who "was Vṛtra" (*Śatapatha Brāhmaṇa* III.4.3.13, etc.) and now "made to be what he actually is,[7] the Sacrifice is now himself a God restored to the Gods" (*Śatapatha Brāhmaṇa* III.6.3.16, 19). From the point of view of the Titans this translation of the "imprisoned, strictly-guarded Soma-Haoma"[8] is a theft, but from that of the Gods a rescue and a disenchantment.[9]

It will be recognized immediately that the Falcon's Quest—and we use this word deliberately to imply that this is, in fact, a Grail Quest—is identical with that of the doves that fetch ambrosia[10] for Father Zeus from beyond the Planktai Petrai, always at the price of one of their number, caught on the way as they pass the Clashing Rocks (*Odyssey* XII.58ff): and that it corresponds at the same time to the Quest of the Golden Fleece, where it is, indeed, a winged "ship" that Athena (Goddess of Wisdom) drives between the Clashing Rocks that she holds apart, but it is like a bird that *Argo* flies through the air, and even so can only escape with the loss of her stern-ornament (or, as we might almost say, "tail-feather"), after which the rocks remain in close contact, barring the way to other mortal voyagers (*Argonautica* II.645 ff). The door is thus normally "closed"; for as we shall presently realize, it is one that can only be opened, in what would otherwise seem to be a smooth and impenetrable wall, by a more than normally human wisdom.[11]

An example of this "Open Sesame" motif (best known in connection with Aladdin's Cave) can be cited from Southern Africa: "In one of Schultze's [Hottentot] stories the fleeing heroine drops food behind her, delaying the pursuing Lion, who eagerly devours it. When the pursuer endeavors to follow, the rock closes and kills him. The opening and closing rock occurs in various combinations in South African mythology" (from a review of J. Schultze, *Aus Namaland und Kalahari* [Berlin, 1907], in *Journal of American Folklore* XXXXI (1908), p. 252). In such a sequence it is easy to recognize in the heroine, Psyche, and in the pursuer, Death.

To return now to the Cutting Reeds, we can cite an American Indian myth in which, amongst the series of living obstacles that bar the way of the hero Nayaṇezgani there are not only "Crushing Rocks" which he stays apart, but also "Cutting Reeds" which "tried to catch him, waving and clashing together." We are also told of these Cutting Reeds that "when anyone passed through them, the reeds moved and cut the person into little pieces and ate him" (M. C. Wheelwright, *Navajo Creation Myth* [Santa Fe, 1942], pp. 71, 96). Another reference to the "Slicing Reeds" will be found in the Franciscan Fathers' *Ethnologic Dictionary of the Navaho Language* (St. Michael's, Arizona, 1910), p. 358.

The Cutting Reeds are, of course, only one of the many forms of the Active Door, of which the passage is so dangerous. We shall consider now some of the other forms of the Wonder Door, and to begin with the Clashing Rocks or Mountains themselves. Different forms of the Door may be associated in one and the same story. In a more elaborate Indian text, parallel to that of the Brāhmaṇa already cited, the "golden blades" are represented by "two sleepless, watchful, razor-edged lightnings, striking from every side," and it is asked "How did the Vulture [Garuda, Eagle, Soma-thief] transgress these Soma-wardens, 'Fear' and 'No-Fear'?" (*Suparṇādhyāya* 24.2, 3). These names of the Soma-wardens, also to be thought of as snakes or dragons, are significant because, as we shall presently come to see more clearly, the two leaves or jambs of the Active Door are not merely affronted by the very nature of a door, but at the same time stand for the "pairs of opposites" or "contraries" of whatever sort, between which the Hero must pass in the Quest of Life, without hope or fear, haste, or delay, but rather with an equanimity superior to any alternative. When Alexander sought he did not find what Khizr found unsought (*Sikandar Nāma* LXIX.75). Taken superficially, "Seek, and ye shall find" is a very comfortable doctrine; but it should be understood that whoever has not found has never really sought (cf. *Nafaḥātu'l Uns* as cited by Nicholson, *Diwani Shams-i-Tabrīz* [1898], p. 329).

In the same context (25.5) we find an obstacle described as consisting of "two razor-edged restless mountains." The text is obscure and admittedly in need of emendation,[12] but there is a clearer reference, the importance of which has been hitherto completely overlooked, in *Śaṅkhāyana Āraṇyaka* IV.13 (= *Kauṣītaki Upaniṣad* II.13), to moving mountains: here we are told of the Comprehensor of the doctrine that the powers of the soul are an epiphany of Brahma, that "verily, even though both mountains, the northern and the southern, were to roll forth against him, seeking to overcome him instantly, indeed, they would not be able to devour him."[13] The immediate reference may be to the Himālayas and Vindhyas, normally separated by the Gangetic Madhya-deśa, but must be indirectly to Sky and Earth, who were originally "one," or "together," and can be reunited. The door of the world of heavenly light is to be found, indeed, "where Sky and Earth embrace" and the "Ends of the Year" are united (*Jaiminīya Upaniṣad Brāhmaṇa* I.5.5; I.35.7-9; IV.15.2-5).[14] The Expert, for whom the antitheses are never absolute values but only the logical extremities of a divided form (for example, past and present of the eternal now), is not overcome by, but much rather transits their "north-and-south-ness" or, as we should say, "polarity," while the Empiricist is crushed or devoured by the perilous alternatives (to be or not to be, etc.) that he cannot evade.[15]

An unmistakable reference to the Clashing Rocks is to be found in *Ṛgveda*, VI.49.3, where the "Rocks" are *times*, viz., Day and Night, described as "clashing together and parting" (*mithasturā vicarantī*); *mithas* here (√*mith*, to unite, alternate, dash together, understand, and also kill, cf. *mithyā*, contrarily, and *mithuna*, pairing) in combination with *turā* (√*tur*, to hasten, rush, overpower, injure), corresponding to *tustūrṣamāṇau* (*Śaṅkhāyana Āraṇyaka* IV.13 = *Kauṣītaki Upaniṣad* II.13), rendered above by "seeking to overcome instantly" in connection with the two "rolling mountains." This is an important case, whether we consider Day and Night as *times* or as *light and darkness*—Mitrāvaruṇau. Its bearing will be realized if we recall that the Vedic Hero's greatest feat is performed at Dawn; Indra has agreed that he will not slay Namuci (Vṛtra, and Buddhist Māra) "either by day or by night," and keeps his word to the letter by lifting his head at dawn, thus dividing heaven from earth and making the sun rise (for references see *Journal of the American Oriental Society* XV.143ff. and LV.375)—dividing the light from the darkness, and day from night.

It is no wonder, then, that the Mahāvīra's feat is so often described as having been performed "suddenly" and "once for all" (*sakṛt*, etc.), for whatever is done when it is neither Day nor Night (cf. *Ṛgveda* X.129.3) is done *ex tempore, sub specie aeternitatis* [in time and in eternity], and forever.

Conversely, for those who are already in time and would be liberated, would "become eternal," Day and Night are as it were two impassible, revolving Seas or wandering Pillars, and one should not perform the Agnihotra (Sacrifice of the Burnt-Offering) either by Day or by Night but only at dusk after sunset and before dark, and at dawn after dark and before sunrise (*Jaiminīya Brāhmaṇa* I.5).[16] "Night and Day are the Sea that carries all away, and the two Twilights are its fordable crossings; and as a man would cross over it by its fordable crossings, so he sacrifices [performs the Agnihotra] at Twilight[17]. . . . Night and Day, again, are the encircling arms of Death; and just as a man about to grasp you with both arms can be escaped [*atimucyeta*] through the opening [*antareṇa*] between them, so he sacrifices at Twilight. . . . This is the sign (*ketu*) of the Way-of-the-Gods [*devayāna*], which he takes hold of, and safely reaches Heaven" (*Kauṣītaki Brāhmaṇa* II.9).[18] In the same way for Philo, Day and Night, Light and Darkness, are archetypal contraries, divided in the beginning "lest they should be always clashing" by median boundaries, Dawn and Dusk, which are not sensible extents of time but "intelligible forms [*ideai*] or types" (*De opificio mundi* 33); and though he does not say so, it is evident that if anyone would return from the chiaroscuro of this world to the "supercelestial" Light of lights he will only be able to do so—if he *is* able—by the way of these "forms" in which the Day and Night are *not* divided from one another.

Thus the Way "to break out of the universe" (Hermes Trismegistus, *Lib.* XI.2.9, see note 48) into that other order of the Divine Darkness[19] that Dionysius describes as "blinding by excess of light" and where the Darkness and the Light "stand not distant from one another, but together in one another" (Jacob Boehme, *Three Principles*, XIV.78) is the single track and "strait way" that penetrates the cardinal "point" on which the contraries turn; their unity is only to be reached by entering in there where they actually coincide. And that is, in the last analysis, not any where or when, but within you; "World's End is not to be found *by walking*, but it is within this very fathom-long body that the pilgrimage must be made" (*Samyutta Nikāya* I.62)—

Our soul is, as it were, the day, and our body the night;
We, in the middle, are the dawn between our day and night.[20]

H. Rink[21] records from Greenland the myth of the Eskimo hero Giviok, whose way to the Otherworld, in which he finds his dead son living, is confronted by "two clashing icebergs," with only a narrow passage between them, alternately opened and closed. He cannot circumnavigate them because, when he tries to do so, *they always keep ahead of him* ("for there is no approach by a side path here in the world," *Maitri Upaniṣad* VI.30!). He therefore speeds between them, and has barely passed when they close together, bruising the stern-point of his kayak. As Professor Cook sees, this is "a mariner's version of the gateway to the Otherworld." In this northern setting, the floating islands are naturally thought of as icebergs.

In a more recent collection of Eskimo folktales[22] the Clapping Mountains are connected, significantly, with the migrations of birds. "All of the birds who fly south must pass between them. Every little while they clap together, just as you clap your hands, and anyone caught between them is crushed to death." This dangerous passage is an ordeal appointed by the Great Spirit, and "any geese that cannot fly fast will be crushed." Whether or not the narrator "understood his material" we have no means of telling but it is impossible to doubt that the talking geese originally represented souls or that amongst them those who could not fly fast represented the uninitiated.

"Rocks-That-Come-Together" are well known all over America. They are mentioned by the Franciscan Fathers' *Ethnologic Dictionary* as "cliffs which bound together [crushing]"; in Fr. Berard Haile, *Origin Legend of the Navaho Enemy Way* (London, 1938), p. 125, as "two rocks that clap together"; and in Wheelwright's *Navajo Creation Myth* as "crushing rocks" between which the Hero must pass. Other examples of the motif are cited from American sources by Paul Ehrenreich;[23] in the South American Tupi saga of the heavenly ascent of two brothers, respectively human and divine; the way leads between clashing rocks, by which the mortal is crushed. In one North American version the door of the king of heaven is made of the two halves of the Eagle's beak, or of his daughter's toothed vagina, and with this Ehrenreich compares the Polynesian tale of Maui's brother crushed between the thighs of the Night Goddess. Ehrenreich holds that the "clashing rocks" are heaven and earth, the cleft between them being that at the horizon.[24] Franz Boas[25] cites the North American Indian story of the heavenly ascent of two brothers, who on their way must strike out the wedges from certain cloven tree trunks, by which they will be in danger of being crushed as the sides spring together. T. Waltz records that the Mexican dead "had to pass between clashing mountains"

(*Anthropologie der Naturvölker* [Leipzig, 1864], IV.166); and in Codex Vindobonensis (leaf 21) there is a picture of two individuals climbing over a succession of mountains, of which two are cloven and no doubt to be understood as "clapping," which might illustrate this deathway.

The notion itself of "Floating Islands" is typically, although not by any means exclusively, Indian. The "worlds" or states of being are often spoken of as "islands" (*dvīpa*), India, for example, being Jambudvīpa. That Earth in particular is such an island, originally submerged, and brought up in the beginning from the depths, is the basis of the adequate symbolism of Earth by a lotus flower or leaf, expanded upon the surface of the cosmic waters in response to the light of and as a reflection of the Sun, "the one lotus of the sky": hence the lotus or, lotus-petal molding (which becomes in late Greek art the "egg-and-dart") represents the archetypal "support" of existence. By the same token the terrestrial Agni is "lotus-born" (*abja-ja*);[26] and that the manifested Gods and the Buddha are represented with lotus-pedestals,[27] thrones, or footstools (as in the parallel case of the Egyptian Horus) is as much as to say that their feet are firmly based upon a ground that is really an "island" floating upon and surrounded by an ocean of all the possibilities of manifestation from which the particular compossibles of any given world must have been derived. For all this, moreover, there is a close parallel in the case of Rhodes, the "Island of the Rose"; for, as has often enough been demonstrated, the rose is the precise equivalent in European symbolism of the lotus in Asiatic, and Rhodes, a land that rose from the depths of the sea, is preeminently the Island of the Sun, who made her his wife and begot seven sons upon her (Cook, p. 986). The famous Colossus of Rhodes was of course an image of the Sun, and however late the legend may be that the legs (*jambes!*) of this image straddled the harbor, to form the *jambs* of a mighty door through which every ship must pass on entering or leaving port, the figure is manifestly that of a Sundoor.

It is a highly characteristic feature of the "Active Door" that whoever or whatever passes through it must do so with all speed and suddenly, and even so may be docked of its "tail"; which tail may be, in the examples already considered, either the stern-point of a boat, or one of two brothers, or if there is a flock of birds (doves of Zeus or Eskimo geese) then the last of the line; or if the Hero wins through his pursuer may be caught. Striking examples of these features can be cited in the widely diffused art and folktale motif of the "Hare and Hounds." We need hardly say that the Hare is one of the many crea-tures ("birds," men, or animals)[28] that play the part of the Hero in the life-quest, or that the Dog is one of the many types of the defender of the Tree of Life; whatever details are suited to the symbolism of the robbery of a defended "garden enclosed" or "castle" are to be found amongst our variants. The hare-hunt has been discussed at length by the great folklorist Karl von Spiess,[29] who cites a riddle, of Greek origin, but also widely diffused in Europe. It runs: "A wooden key, a watery lock; the Hare runs through, the Dog was caught." One modern answer is: bucket and sea. But the original reference is to the crossing of the Red Sea, Moses being the Hare and the Pharaoh the Dog. It will be seen immediately that the divided sea is a type of the Active Door (cf. above, on Day and Night) which in this case closes upon the pursuer. But the Hare does not always escape scot-free. Then, in the words of von Spiess, "This is the situation, viz., that the Hare has run into another world to fetch something—the Herb of Immortality. Thereupon the guardian Dog, pursuing the Hare, is hard upon it. But just where both worlds meet, and where the Dog's domain ends, it is only able to bite off the Hare's tail, so that the Hare returns to its own world docked. In this case the Dog's jaws are the 'Clapping Rocks.'" In the other and more typical case in which the Hero is a "bird," and the Defender an archer,[30] the "minor penalty" is represented by the loss of a feather or a leaf of the herb, which falls to earth and takes root there, to spring up as a terrestrial tree of life and knowledge; in this case the Hero's wound is in his foot, and his vulnerability in this respect is related to the motif of "Achilles' heel."

Whoever seeks to interpret myths in a purely rationalistic way, and considers the story of the Hare by itself, might argue that it represents no more than an aetiological myth of popular origin. But actually, that such myths are transmitted, it may be for thousands of years, by the folk to whom they have been entrusted, is no proof of their popular *origin*; it is in quite another sense than this that *Vox populi vox Dei* [the voice of the people is the voice of God]. As von Spiess clearly saw, the Hare is not only to be equated with the heroic "bird," but also with the human and knightly heroes of otherworld adventures. We have, in fact, introduced the Hare at this point in order to lead up to the remarkable Celtic forms of the motif of the Active Door, in which the Hero escapes from its closing jaws almost literally by the skin of his teeth. In a typical form the story occurs in Chrétien's *Iwain* (vv. 907-969).[31] Iwain is riding in pursuit of the Defender of the Fountain Perilous, whom he has already wounded, and reaches the gateway of his palace, which was very high and wide, "yet it had such a narrow entrance-way that two men or two horses could scarcely enter abreast without interference or great difficulty; for it was constructed just like a trap which is set for the rat on mischief bent, and which has a blade above ready to fall and strike and catch, and which is suddenly released whenever anything, however gently, comes in contact with the spring. In like fashion, beneath the gate, there were two springs connected with a portcullis up above, edged with iron and very sharp. . . . Precisely in the middle the passage lay as narrow as if it were a beaten (single) track. Straight through it exactly the (wounded) knight rushed on, with my lord Iwain madly following him apace, and so close to him that he held him by the saddle-bow behind. It was well for him that he was stretched forward, for had it not been for this piece of luck he would have been cut quite through; for his horse stepped upon the wooden spring which kept the portcullis in place. Like a hellish devil the gate dropped down, catching the saddle and the horse's haunches, which it cut off clean. But, thank God, my lord Iwain was only slightly touched when it grazed his back so closely that it cut both his spurs off even with his heels."[32]

Another variant occurs in *La Mule sans Frein*;[33] here Gawain has crossed the Perilous Bridge of Dread (by which the Active Door is always approached) and reaches the castle from which he is to recover the stolen bridle; the castle is always revolving, like a mill-wheel or top, and the gate must be entered as it comes round; he succeeds, but the side of the moving gate cuts off a part of the mule's tail; and in any case, as A. C. L. Brown justly remarks, "a revolving barrier, or an active door of some kind, was a widespread motive of Celtic Otherworld story . . . before the time of Chrétien." So, too, for Kittredge, "these traits are not the personal property of Chrétien."[34]

The Sky is, of course, the "revolving barrier" (cf. Philo, *De confusione linguarum* 100, and *De opificio mundi* 37), and the Sun the "active door." It should be superfluous to emphasize that the traditional symbols are never the inventions of the particular author in whom we happen to find them: "the myth is not my own, I had it from my mother." Euripides, in these words, shows that he knew better than such naive scholars as Sir J. G. Frazer and A. A. Macdonell, of whom the former saw in the theme of the Clashing Rocks "a mere creation of the storyteller's fancy" and the latter in the related and almost equally widely distributed motif of the Fallen Feather "probably a mere embellishment added by the individual poet"! Our scholars, who think of myths as having been invented by "literary men," overlook that the traditional motifs and traditional themes are inseparately connected. The traditional raconteur's figures, which he has not invented, but has received and faithfully transmits, are never figures of speech, but always figures of thought; and one cannot ask which came first, the symbol or its significance, the myth or its ritual enactment. Nor can anything be called a *science* of folklore, but only a collection of data, that considers only the formulae and not their doctrine, "che s'asconde sotto 'l velame dei versi strani" [that is hidden under the veil of the strange lines].* The materials collected even in the present short article should suffice to convince the reader that, as the late Sir Arthur Evans once wrote, "The coincidences of tradition are beyond the scope of accident."

"The whirling castle," as Kittredge says, "belongs to the same general category as perpetually slamming doors and clashing cliffs [symplegades]. . . . The turning castle has also its significance with respect to the Other World." This Otherworld is at once a Paradise and the World of the Dead,[35] and in post-Christian folklore to be identified with Fairyland; it may be located overseas to the West, or Underwave, or in the Sky, but is always in various ways protected from all but the destined Hero who achieves the Quest. It is the Indian "Farther Shore" and Brahmaloka, and we are especially reminded of the latter by the fact that it is so often called the "land of no return" or "Val sans Retour." This Otherworld can be regarded either as itself a revolving castle or city, or as a castle provided with a perpetually closing or revolving door. A notable example of the turning castle can be cited in the *Fled Bricrend*,[36] where it belongs to Cu Roi (to be equated with Mananan mac Lir and the Indian Varuṇa) and revolves as fast as a millstone, while that its gateway is really the Sundoor is clearly indicated by the fact that the entrance "was never to be found after sunset." The protection of the Otherworld and its treasures may consist in whole or part of a rampart of fire;[37] and whether it be the Empyrean or, more rarely, the Terrestrial Paradise, the Door itself has terrible defenders, of types including Scorpion-men, sleepless and baleful Serpents or Dragons, Centaurs (notably "Sagittarius"), Gandharvas, Cherubim (Genesis III.24, etc.) and in many cases armed Automata.

Here we are primarily concerned with the Active Door itself and its significance. We shall conclude with a brief reference to the type

---

* Editors' Note: the author makes reference to the lines of Dante's *Divine Comedy*: "O voi ch'avete li'ntelletti sani, mirate la dottrina che s'asconde sotto 'l velame de li versi strani" [Ye that are of sane intellect, note the doctrine that is hidden under the veil of the strange lines] (*Inferno*, IX, 61-63), an explicit reference by the Florentine poet to the deeper meaning of his poem.

of the Active Door that is described as a Wheel. A western example can be cited in *Wigalois*:[38] here, in pursuit of the magician Rōaz—"a parallel figure to Curoi" (Brown, *Iwain*, p. 81)—Wigalois reaches a castle, with a marble gate, in front of which there turned a wheel "set with sharp swords and clubs." The *Mahābhārata* (Pūna ed., I. ch. 29) describes what is assuredly the same Wheel much more fully: "There before the Soma Garuḍa beheld a razor-edged Wheel [*cakra*] of steel, covered with sharp blades, and continually revolving, as terribly bright as the sun, an engine [*yantra*] of unspeakably dreadful aspect, fitly devised by the Gods for the cutting to pieces of Soma-thieves; the Skyfarer [*khecara*][39] seeing an opening therein, hovered, and making a cast of his body suddenly [*kṣaṇena*][40] darted through between the spokes . . . flew off with the Water of Life" (*amṛta*, Soma). So, too, in the *Suparṇādhyāna* (25.3, 4) there is a mind-made Wheel of Indra's, ever revolving faster than the winking of an eye, which Garuḍa, the Soma-thief, with his "more than speed," passes (no doubt, through) and leaves behind him. To this very Wheel there is an illuminating reference in the much later *Kathā Sarit Sāgara* (Bk. VI, ch. 29, in C. H. Tawney's version [Calcutta, 1880], I.257-259). Here Somaprabhā is a daughter of the Asura Maya, the well-known Titan "artificer of the Gods" (to be identified with Tvaṣṭṛ, described in *Ṛgveda* X.53.9 as *māyā*[41] *vet*, Sāyaṇa *devaśilpi*—and in the last analysis with Thaumas, father of Iris [Hesiod *Theogony* 265, cf. Plato, *Theatetus* 155 D], and with such *black*smiths[42] as Daedalus, Hephaistos, Vulcan, Wayland and Regin). Somaprabhā ("Soma-Radiance") assumes a human form and entertains her mortal friend Kalingasenā with a variety of Automata, described as "self-empowered wooden puppets."[43] There she explains to Kalingasenā's father as follows: "O King, these cunning engines, etc., in their endless variety, are works of art that were made by my father of old. And even as this great engine, the world, is in essence a product of the five elements, so are these engines. Hear about them, one by one: that one of them in which Earth is the basis is that which closes doors and the like, and even Indra could not open what it has closed; the forms that are produced from the Water-device seem to be alive; the engine that is wrought of Fire gives forth flames; the Air engine performs such acts as coming and going; the engine of which Ether is the constitution utters language distinctly.[44] All these I got from my father. But the Wheel-engine that guards the Water of Life that he only, and no one else, understands." Here it is highly significant that the magician, master of the Active Door, is also a maker of Automata, and further, that he is not originally a God, but a Titan.

The Automata in this context are significant because, as remarked by J. Douglas Bruce,[45] the European "mediaeval automata . . . are created for some special function, usually to guard an entrance." In the *Perlesvaus*, for example, Gawain comes to a turning castle, the door of which is guarded by two men "made by art and necromancy," while in the prose Lancelot the gate of the Dolorous Garde is defended by copper figures of armed knights.

The sun-bright Wheel that guards the supra-solar Otherworld is, naturally the Wheel of the Sun himself which Indra tears away from the Great Fiend when either he, or the Falcon for him, robs the Scorcher of "all life's support" (*Rgveda* IV.28.2, etc.).[46] It is also, in other words, the sparkling sun-hued Brahma Wheel of Fire of *Maitri Upaniṣad* VI.24; and the guarded Sundoor of *Jaiminīya Upaniṣad Brāhmaṇa* I.3, 5 and 6, where the "opening in the sky" is covered all over (concealed) by rays (the spokes of the "Wheel") and it is only by his Truth that the Comprehensor "is enabled to pass through the midst of the Sun" and is thus "altogether freed," attaining that Immortality, or Water of Life that rises in the Land of Darkness "beyond the Sun." Hence also the invocation, "Disperse thy rays and gather in thy radiance, that he-whose-norm-is-truth may see thy fairest form" (*Iśa Upaniṣad* 15, 16, etc.). "Disperse"; because these rays are the multitude of his powers by which all things are quickened and moved, and collectively the actuality or truth by which the "Truth of the truth" is concealed (*Bṛhadāraṇyaka Upaniṣad* I.6.3, II. 1.20, with *Jaiminīya Upaniṣad Brāhmaṇa* as above), just as also for Philo (*De opificio mundi* 71) and Dionysius the uncreated is hidden "by the piercing splendor and rushing torrent of the rays."[47] The Sundoor itself, thus hidden by the dazzling rays that illumine and enliven every living being, in whom they operate as the "powers of the soul," is precisely the "point" at the center of the fiery Wheel, at which they intersect; and since, in the most general case, the sun is "seven-rayed,"[48] and is situated in the middle, whence the six directions of the cosmic cross (*trivṛd vajra*) extend, so that the universe is "filled" with light, it will be seen that the way in by what is called the "seventh and best ray," viz., that which passes through the solar disk and so out of the dimensioned universe, leads as before in the case of the Clapping Rocks between contrary pairs, in this case East and West, North and South, Zenith and Nadir. The Way is always a "Middle Way," or as Boethius expresses it, "Truth is a mean between contrary heresies" (*Contra Evtychen* VII).

*   *   *

It remains only to consider the full doctrinal significance of the Symplegades. What the formula states literally is that whoever would transfer from this to the Otherworld, or return, must do so through the undimensioned and timeless "interval" that divides related but contrary forces, between which, if one is to pass at all, it must be "instantly." The passage is, of course, that which is also called the "strait gate" and the "needle's eye." What are these contraries, of which the operation is "automatic"? We have already seen that the antithesis may be of Fear and Hope, or North and South, or Night and Day. These are but particular cases of the polarity that necessarily characterizes any "conditioned" world. A "world" without pairs of opposites—good and evil, pleasure and pain, love and hate, near and far, thick and thin, male and female, positive and negative, "all these pairs" (*Kauṣītaki Upaniṣad* I.4, cf. Philo, *Heres* 132, 207-214)—would be an "unconditioned" world, a world without accidents, change, or becoming, logically inconceivable and of which experience would be impossible.

It is, then, precisely from these "pairs" that liberation must be won, from their conflict that we must escape, if we are to be freed from our mortality and to be as and when we will: if, in other words, we are to reach the Farther Shore and Otherworld, "where every where and every when are focused," "for it is not in space, nor hath it poles" (*Paradiso* XXIX.22 and XXII.67). Here, under the Sun, we are "overcome by the pairs" (*Maitri Upaniṣad* III.1): here, "every being in the emanated-world moves deluded by the mirage of the contrary-pairs, of which the origin is in our liking and disliking. . . . But to those who are freed from this delusion of the pairs . . . freed from the pairs that are implied by the expression 'weal and woe,' these reach the place of invariability" (*Bhagavad Gītā* VII.27.28 and XV.5), i.e., the place of their coming together or coincidence (*samayā*), through their midst or in between (*samāya*) them.

It is then deeply significant that in the Greenland saga, the Hero, on his way to the Otherworld in which he finds his "dead" son "living," cannot circumvent the paired bergs (which are the "lions in his path"), for they "always get ahead of him" however far he goes to either side. It is inevitably so, because the contraries are of indefinite extension, and even if we could suppose an equally indefinite journey to the point at which "extremes meet,"[49] this would be still a meeting place of both extremes, and there would be no way through to a beyond or a within except at their meeting point; a cardinal "point" that has no fixed position, since the distinction of the correlated members of any pair of contrary qualities (e.g., long and short) is only to be found where we actually make it; and without extent, seeing that it is one and the same "limit" that simultaneously unites and divides the contraries of which it is no part—"strait is the gate and narrow is the way, which leadeth unto life, and few there be that find it" (Matthew VII.14). It is for the same reasons that the passage must be made so "suddenly": it is from the world of time (i.e., past and future) to an eternal Now, and between these two worlds, temporal and timeless, there can be no possible contact but in the "moment without duration" that for us divides the past from the future, but for the Immortals includes all times.

The "moment" has come at last to understand the poignant words of Nicolas of Cusa in the *De visione Dei* (ch. IX, fin.): "The wall of the Paradise in which Thou, Lord, dwellest, is built of contradictories, nor is there any way to enter but for one who has overcome the highest Spirit of Reason who guards its gate," and to recall the promise, "To him that overcometh will I give to eat of the Tree of Life, which is in the midst of the Paradise of God" (Rev. II.7).[50] In this doctrine and assurance are reaffirmed what has always been the dogmatic significance of the Symplegades and of the Hero's Quest—"I am the Door," and "No man cometh to the Father but by Me."

Notes

[1] The subject of "Clashing Rocks" is dealt with at considerable length by A. B. Cook in *Zeus* (Cambridge, 1914-1940) III, ii, Appendix P, "Floating Islands," pp. 975-1016.

[2] Here, in addition to A. B. Cook's references and those given below, we can only cite from the vast literature of the whole subject such works as G. Dumézil, *Le festin d'immortalité* (Paris, 1924); J. Charpentier, *Die Suparnasaga* (Uppsala, 1920); S. Langdon, *Semitic Mythology* (Boston, 1931); J. L. Weston, *From Ritual to Romance* (1920); R. S. Loomis, *Celtic Myth and Arthurian Romance* (New York, 1927); A. C. L. Brown, *The Origin of the Grail Legend* (Cambridge, 1943); E. L. Highbarger, *The Gates of Dreams* (Baltimore, 1940).

[3] For other material on this subject see my "Symbolism of the Dome," *Indian Historical Quarterly* XIV (1938), pp. 1-56, and the "*Svayamātṛṇṇa*, Janua Coeli," *Zalmoxis*, ii (1939), pp. 3-51. [Editors' Note: These essays can also be found in *Coomaraswamy 1: Selected Papers, Traditional Art and Symbolism*, edited by Roger Lipsey, Bollingen Series LXXXIX (Princeton, NJ: Princeton University Press, 1977), pp. 415-464 and pp. 465-520 respectively.]

[4] "Ambrosiai Stelai," *American Journal of Philology*, LXIII, pp. 215-216.

[5] These *kuśī* (or -*kuśyau*) are primarily a pair of "leaves" or "blades" as of sword-grass, at the same time that they are in effect the two "leaves" or possibly "jambs" of an active Door; and in this connection it is not insignificant that Kuśī is also a synonym

of Dvārakā, Krishna's "City of the Door." In *Śatapatha Brāhmaṇa* the *hiraṇmayau kuśyau* (V.1) are said to be *dīkṣā* (initiation) and *tapas* (ardor). Cf. *Śatapatha Brāhmaṇa* III.1.2.20; III.4.3.2 where it is *in* these as a "new garment" that the Sacrificer is qualified to enter the Sadas, analogically the Otherworld.

[6] "Snapping together," for a door is also a "mouth" and our "leaves" or "rocks" are really the fiery Jaws of Death; as in *Ṛgveda* X.87.3 where the same verb is used of the bite of Agni's iron teeth, the upper and the lower. Cf. *Kauṣītaki Upaniṣad*, II.13, where the rolling mountains "do not devour" the Comprehensor.

In *Ṛgveda* VIII.91.2 (cf. IX.1.6) and the Brāhmaṇa versions, *Śatyāyana Brāhmaṇa* and *Jaiminīya Brāhmaṇa* 1.220 (translated by H. Oertel in *Journal of the American Oriental Society*, 1897, XVIII, pp. 26-30); also *Pañcaviṁśa Brāhmaṇa* VIII. 4.1, Apālā (alias the Daughter of the Sun = Śraddhā, Faith; Gāyatrī; Akupārā, etc.), prepares Soma (as *kawa* is prepared in the South Sea Islands) by chewing and Indra takes it directly from her mouth—"and whoever is a Comprehensor thereof, if he kisses a woman's mouth, that becomes for him a draught of Soma." Thus *in divinis*; in the ritual mimesis, where the Soma (substituted plant) is crushed in a pestle and mortar or more usually between two stones (as it were "clashing rocks"), and two sides of the Soma-press are "jaws," the stones are "teeth" and the skin on which they move is the "tongue," while the other "mouth" into which the juice is poured is that of the sacrificial altar in which also the Sacrificer, identifying himself with the victim, offers up himself. Thus the gates of entry (birth, from the human standpoint, death from the divine) and exit (death from the human point of view, birth from the divine) are both equally "jaws"—"the soul—every great soul—in its cycle of changes must pass twice through the Gate of Ivory" (Highbarger, *The Gates of Dreams*, p. 110). The Sacrifice is always a prefigured heavenly ascent; it is not that one does not wish to be "swallowed up" by the deity *by* whom one must be assimilated if one would be assimilated *to* him (cf. my *Hinduism and Buddhism*, pp. 23, 24, and *Ṛgveda*, VII.86.2: "When at last shall we come to be again *within* Varuṇa?"), but that one would not be demolished by the "upper and the nether *mill*stones" through which the way leads; and hence "the Brahmans of yore were wont to wonder, Who will today escape Leviathan's jaws?" and it is actually only by the substitution of a "victim" (—a "sop to Cerberus"—) that one "comes safely through his maw" (*Jaiminīya Brāhmaṇa* I.174). On the Jaws of Death see further my "*Svayamātṛṇṇa, Janua Coeli*," p. 23, note 6.

[7] The bringing down of Soma to earth, which is his coming into his kingdom, involves a passion and a resurrection. He comes forth in triumph: "even as Ahi, slipping out of his inveterated skin, Soma flows like a prancing steed" (*Ṛgveda* IX.86.44).

[8] L. von Schroeder, *Herakles und Indra* (Vienna, 1914), p. 45.

[9] The contrary values are very clearly developed in the *Argonautica*, where the Rape of the Fleece and carrying off of Medea are, from her father's point of view, the acts of a high-handed marauder; and (IV.1432 ff) Herakles' slaughter of the Serpent and theft of the Golden Apples are from the point of view of Jason's companions heroic feats, but from the point of view of the Hesperides themselves acts of wanton violence. In the same way, as Darmetester says, "In the Vedic mythology the Gandharva is the keeper of Soma, and is described now as a God, now as a fiend, accordingly as he is a heavenly Soma-priest or a jealous possessor who grudges it to man" (*Sacred Books of the East*, Vol. 23, 63, note 1). In such contexts, however, "grudge" is not the word; it is not with malice that the Cherub "keeps the way of the Tree of Life," or invidiously that St. Peter keeps the Golden Gates, or that Heimdallr guards the Bridge, or that the

door is shut against the foolish virgins, but only to protect the fold against the wolves who have no right to enter.

The opposing interests of Gods and Titans are only reconciled when, as in the Vedic and Christian traditions, the Sacrifice is indeed a victim, but not an unwilling victim. It is only from our temporally human point of view that "good and evil" are opposed to one another, but "to God all things are good and fair and just" (Heracleitus, *Fragment* 61), "to him in all conflicts both sides are right" (*Ṛgveda* II.7.15); and this is the essential meaning of the Clashing Rocks, that whoever would return home must have abandoned all judgment in terms of right and wrong, for *there*, as Meister Eckhart says, in full agreement with Chuang Tzu, the Upaniṣads and Buddhism, "neither vice nor virtue ever entered in." The Gods and Titans are the children of one Father, and have their appointed parts to play, if there is to be a "world" at all (cf. Heracleitus, *Fragment* 43, 46), and though one of these parts may be ours "for the time being," the Comprehensor must act without attachment, dispassionately, remaining above the battle even while participating in it.

[10] On *ambrosia* and *amṛta* see M. Fowler, "A Note on *ambrotos*," *Classical Philology*, XXXVII (1942), pp. 77-79.

[11] The door as an obstacle is the "barricade of the sky" (*avarodhanam divaḥ, Ṛgveda* IX.113.8), which divides the world of mortality under the Sun from the world of immortality beyond him; the Sundoor is the "Gateway of Truth" (*Īśā Upaniṣad* 15, etc.), and as such "a forwarding for the wise and a barrier to the foolish" (*Chāndogya Upaniṣad* VIII.6.5); cf. Matthew 25:1-12, Luke 11:9, John 10:9, etc., and also my "*Svayamātṛṇṇa*, Janua Coeli," notes 23, 31, 51.

In marriage, the bride is assimilated to Sūryā, the married couple's journey to a heavenly ascent (even the crossing of a "river" is provided for), and their new home (in which they are to "live happily ever afterwards") to the Other-world of Immortality. An analogy of the doorway to the dangerous Janua Coeli naturally follows, and we find that when it is reached the incantation is employed, "Injure her not, ye god-made pillars, on her way," these pillars being, of course the jambs of "the door of the divine house" (*Atharva Veda* XIV.1.61, 63). No doubt it is for the same reason that the bride must not step on the threshold as she enters (*Āpastamba Gṛhya Sūtra* II.6.9), for, evidently, to do so might release the trap, and therefore the bride must step over the threshold without touching it. There can be no question but that the European custom of carrying the bride across the threshold has an identical significance; the husband plays the part of psychopomp, and it is easy to see why it should be regarded as most unlucky if he stumbles and does not clear the threshold safely.

[12] The text has *parvatāṣṭhirāḥ* which, although it could mean "mountain domes," is implausible. Charpentier's suggestion of *parvataḥ sthirāḥ* ("stable mountains") contradicts the required sense. I have assumed *parvataḥ asthirāḥ* (an equally possible resolution of the crasis), "restless mountains"; the following *subudhnyaḥ* need not imply "firmly grounded," but rather "deeply rooted," which is not inconsistent with motion, as will be obvious if we remember that our "floating islands" are, as it were, lotus leaves or flowers, not detached from their stems, but swinging upon them, as the leaves of doors swing on hinges.

[13] "No one becomes immortal in the flesh" (*Śatapatha Brāhmaṇa* X.4.3.9), and whoever reaches the Other-world and the attainment of all desires does so "going in the spirit" (*ātmany etya, Śatapatha Brāhmaṇa* I.8.1.31 and *Jaiminīya Upaniṣad Brāhmaṇa*

III.33.8), "having shaken off his bodies" (*Jaiminīya Upaniṣad Brāhmaṇa* III.30.2-4)—the Platonic *katharsis* (*Phaedo* 67C).

[14] On the Doors of the Year, and World's End see further "*Svayamātṛṇṇa*, Janua Coeli," notes 4 and 26 and "The Pilgrim's Way," *JBORS*, XXIII (1937), pp. 452-471 and XXIV (1938), pp. 118-119 [Editors' Note: also available in Ananda K. Coomaraswamy, *What is Civilization? and Other Essays* (Ipswich: Golgonooza Press, 1989), pp. 107-120]. The "Year" is Prajāpati, the Imperishable World, and, like a house is only his "who knows its doors" (*Śatapatha Brāhmaṇa* 1.5.3.2, 3, 1.6.1.19) or "ends," Winter and Spring. The end of the Year is also its beginning, so that the Year is endless or infinite (*ananta*) like a wheel (*Aitareya Brāhmaṇa* III.43). "The great symbol of the serpent biting its own tail represents the aeon" (Jeremias, *Der Antichrist in Geschichte und Gegenwart* [1930], p. 4).

[15] On the one hand, "everything composed of contraries is necessarily subject to corruption" (St. Thomas Aquinas, *Summa Theologica* I.80.1; cf. *Phaedo* 78 C and *Dīgha Nikāya* II.144), on the other, "The notions even of contraries are not contrary in the intellect for they belong to one and the same knowledge. Therefore it is impossible that the intellective soul should be corruptible" (*Summa Theologica* I.75.6). That, in fact, "the knowledge which knows one thing knows also its opposite" (*Summa Theologica* I.14.8) is remarkably illustrated by the fact that in the oldest languages we so often meet with words that embody contrary meanings. On this important subject see Karl Abel, *Über den Gegensinn der Urworte* (Leipzig, 1885) (also in his *Sprachwissenschaftlichen Abhandlungen* [Leipzig 1885]; Freud's discussion in *Jahrbuch f. Psychoanalytische und Psychopathologische Forschungen*, II, 1910, contributes nothing); R. Gordis, "Effects of Primitive Thought on Language," *American Journal of Semitic Languages and Literature*, LV (1938), p. 270ff; B. Heimann, "Plurality, Polarity, and Unity in Hindu Thought," *Bulletin of the School of Oriental and African Studies*, IX, pp. 1015-1021, "Deutung und Bedeutung indischer Terminologie," *XIX Congr. Internaz. d. Orientalisti*, and "The Polarity of the Indefinite," *Journal of the Indian Society of Oriental Art*, V (1937), pp. 91-94; Chuang Tzu, Ch. 2 and *passim*; my "Tantric Doctrine of Divine Biunity," *Ann. Bhandarkar Or. Res. Inst.*, XIX, pp. 173-183 [Editors' Note: also available in *Coomaraswamy 2: Selected Papers, Metaphysics*, edited by Roger Lipsey, Bollingen Series LXXXIX (Princeton, NJ: Princeton University Press, 1977), pp. 231-240]; M. Fowler, "The Role of Surā in the Myth of Namuci," *Journal of the American Oriental Society*, LXII, pp. 36-40 (esp. note 19), and "Polarity in the *Rigveda*," *Rev. of Religion*, VII (1943), pp. 115-123. Also, on the *enantia* generally, Plato, *Theatetus* 157B, etc., and Philo, *Heres* 207, 215, etc., as discussed by E. R. Goodenough in *Yale Classical Studies*, III (1932), pp. 117-164.

For example, one Egyptian sign stands for "strong-weak," which is meant depending on the determinant employed; one Chinese ideogram, "big-small," means "size," and generally speaking, abstract nouns are combinations of two opposites. So zero (Sanskrit *kha*, see my "Kha and Other Words Denoting Zero," in *Bulletin of the School of Oriental and African Studies*, VII, 1934 [Editors' Note: also available in *Coomaraswamy 2: Selected Papers, Metaphysics*, pp. 220-230]) is the totality of + and – numerical series and, accordingly (like God), *et unicum et nihil et plenum* [at one and the same time one, nothing, and all].

That in so many of the oldest languages (with survivals in some modern) the same roots often embody opposite meanings, only distinguishable by the addition of determinants, is an indication that the movement of "primitive logic" is not abstractive (from an existing multiplicity) but deductive (from an axiomatic unity). The same synthetic bias can be recognized in the old duals (e.g., Mitrāvaruṇau) that denote, not the mere association of *two* "persons," but the biunity of *one*. Many of our profoundest religious dogmas (e.g., that of the divine procession *ex principio vivente conjuncto* [from a living principle with which it remains united]) stem from these insights.

[16] Similarly in *Śatapatha Brāhmaṇa* II.3.9.1, 36; and in the *Avesta* (Weber, *Indische Studien*, IX [1853], ch. 9, p. 292), where the *daevayaśna* is to be performed after dark and before sunrise. The contrary argument of *Aitareya Brāhmaṇ* V.29, seems to me illogical. Indra had also agreed not to slay Namuci "with anything moist or anything dry," and does so with "foam." Both formulae recur in *Taittirīya Saṃhitā* VI.4.1.5. and 2.4, where the heart of the sacrificial victim is deposited "at the junction of wet and dry," and the sacrificial waters, originally liberated when Vṛtra was slain, are to be collected "at the junction of shade and shining," viz., of night and day. The first of these actions "atones" or sacrifices the contraries, the second secures the "color of both" at once; and that is, of course, the "color" of the Otherworld, Brahmaloka or Empyrean in which the darkness and light are not separated, but dwell together in one another (*Katha Upaniṣad* III.1 and VI.5 and Jacob Boehme, *Three Principles* XIV.76), and of Dionysius' "Divine Darkness, blinding by excess of light."

[17] The parallel to the crossing of the Red Sea, from the Egyptian Darkness of this world to a Promised Land, will be obvious. The Agnihotra performed at twilight is a "Passover" in Philo's sense. By the same token, *brahma-bhūti*, "becoming Brahma," "theosis," is also "Dawn."

[18] The return is obviously to the primordial condition of *Ṛgveda* X.129.1-3, where all is One, without distinction of Day and Night. *Kauṣītaki Brāhmaṇa* continues, describing Night and Day as the Dark and the Dappled (*śyāmā-śabarau*, the "Dogs of Yama"): an important datum for the iconography of Cerberus, but one that cannot be further discussed here.

[19] "Of every land, that Dark Land is the best, In which there is a Water, the Giver-of-Life" (Nizāmu'd Dīn, *Sikandar Nāma*, LXVIII.18). "There shines not sun, nor moon, nor any star. . . . His shining only all this world illuminates" (*Kaṭha Upaniṣad* V.15); "There neither sun, nor moon, nor fire give light; those who go there do not come back again; that is My supreme abode" (*Bhagavad Gītā* XV.6); "There shine no stars, nor sun is there displayed, there gleams no moon; (and yet) no darkness there is seen" (*Udāna* 9). "When sun and moon have gone home, when fire is doused and speech is hushed, what is this person's light? The Spirit (*ātman*, Self) is his light" (*Bṛhadāraṇyaka Upaniṣad* IV.3.6, cf. *Jaiminīya Upaniṣad Brāhmaṇa* III.1): "And the city had no need of the sun, neither of the moon, to shine in it: for the glory of God did lighten it, and the Lamb is the light thereof" (Rev. 21:23).

[20] Rūmī, *Diwani Shams-i Tabrīz*, cited in Nicholson's "Additional Notes," p. 239.

[21] *Tales and Traditions of the Eskimo* (London, 1875), pp. 157-161.

[22] C. E. Gillum, *Beyond the Clapping Mountains, Eskimo Stories from Alaska* (New York, 1943).

[23] "Die Mythen und Legenden der Sudamerikanischen Urvölker und ihrer Beziehungen zu denen Nordamerikas und der alten Welt," *Zeit. f. Ethnologie*, XXXVII (1905), Supplement.

For some other parallels see S. Thompson, "European Tales among the North American Indians," *Colorado College Pub., Language Series*, II (1919), pp. 319-471; A. H. Gayton, "The Orpheus Myth in North America," *Journal of American Folklore*, XLVIII (1935), pp. 263-293; my "Sun-kiss," pp. 46-67 (esp. 55-57), and comment by M. Titiev, *Journal of the American Oriental Society*, LX (1940), p. 270. Many or most of these parallels have to do with the metaphysics of light, the progenitive power (see "Sun-kiss," note 13 for some of the references). One of the most remarkable is that of the Jicarilla Apache birth rite "where a cord of unblemished buckskin, called in the rite 'spider's rope,' is stretched from the umbilicus of the child towards the sun" (M. E. Opler, *Myths and Tales of the Jicarilla Apache Indians* [New York, 1938], p. 19). This combines the Indian symbolism of the Sun as a spider (cf. *Journal of the American Oriental Society*, LV, pp. 396-398) whose threads are rays (*sūtrātman* doctrine), with the concept of the Sun equated with the vivifying Spirit, at the same time that it corresponds exactly to the Orthodox Christian conception of the Nativity, where (as at Palermo and in many Russian icons) the Madonna is evidently the Earth Goddess, and a (seventh) ray of light extends directly from the (otherwise six-rayed) Sun to the Bambino.

Independent origins for such complex patterns are almost inconceivable: we are forced to suppose that we are dealing with a mythology of prehistoric and presumably neolithic antiquity. This is a consideration that will present no difficulty to anthropologists such as Father W. Schmidt, Franz Boas, Paul Radin, or Josef Strzygowski, who recognize no distinction of mental ability as between "primitive" and modern man, who, if capable at all of such abstract vision, is radically disinclined for it, and certainly does not found his art and literature upon it.

[24] Cf. *Bṛhadāraṇyaka Upaniṣad* III.3.2 where, at the ends of earth, there is an interspace "as thin as the edge of a razor." This seems to mean at the horizon; but it is normally at the Sundoor that one reaches "world's end" and "breaks out of the universe."

[25] *Indianischer Sagen von der Nordwestkuste Amerikas* (Berlin, 1905), p. 335.

[26] In this connection cf. L. von Schroeder, *Arische Religion* II (1923), pp. 555-557. Von Schroeder justly assimilates Loki, "Sohn der Laufey, d.h. der 'Laub-insel'" i.e., son of Leaf-island as his Mother, to Agni, the lotus-born, and to Apollo of Delos, an island that, having arisen from the sea, might be compared to the "water-born" (*abja* = lotus). Von Schroeder also compares Loki "Nadelsohn" to Agni *saucika* but cannot make out what the "Needle" is; it is, in fact, the Father, viz., the Thunderbolt, *vajra* (*keraunos*), lightning from above, "leaf" (Earth) and "needle" (Axis Mundi) being the lower and upper "fire-sticks" in this generation. For the "needle" as the "tool" with which the Mother Goddess "sews" her work see *Ṛgveda* II.32.4.

[27] How such a figure could have been imagined can well be realized from Durer's woodcut of the Angel whose "face was as the sun and his feet as pillars of fire: And he had in his hand a little book open: and he set his right foot upon the sea, and his left foot on the earth" (Rev. 10:1ff). This revelation was made to St. John in Patmos, also an island risen from the sea. For a reproduction of Durer's cut and its later imitations see *Jahrbuch f. Hist. Volkskunde*, II, p. 153ff.

[28] For example, the Boar, "thief of the Fair" (*vāma-moṣa*), i.e., of Soma, *Taittirīya Saṃhitā* VI.2.4.2. An excellent Rumanian version explains "Why the Stork has no Tail": the Water of Life and Death can only be reached by passing between two constantly clashing mountains into a valley beyond them; it is fetched by a stork, who on

his return barely escapes with the loss of his tail (F. H. Lee, *Folktales of All Nations* [London, 1931], pp. 836-838).

[29] "Die Hasenjagd" in *Jahrbuch f. Hist. Volkskunde*, V, VI (1937), pp. 243-267. Cf. L. von Schroeder, *Arische Religion* (Leipzig, 1923), II, p. 664ff. The Hare is normally the Hero, but may be the Dragon in disguise (A.H. Wratislaw, *Sixty Folk-Tales, Exclusively from Slavonic Sources* [London, 1889], no. 43). See also John Layard, *The Lady of the Hare* (London, 1945), and my review in *Psychiatry*, VIII (1945); and Philostratus, *Vit. Ap.* 3.39.

[30] For a part of this material, which I propose to discuss more fully elsewhere in a paper on "The Early Iconography of Sagittarius-Kṛsānu," see Karl von Spiess, "Der Schuss nach dem Vogel" in *Jahrbuch f. Hist. Volkskunde*, V, VI (1937), pp. 204-235. [Editors' Note: The author's unfinished article "The Iconography of Sagittarius" was published as part of a collection of his unpublished writings, entitled *Guardians of the Sundoor: Late Iconographic Essays*, edited by Robert Strom (Louisville, KY: Fons Vitae, 2004).]

[31] W. W. Comfort, *Chrétien de Troyes* (London, 1913), p. 192. Cf. G. L. Kittredge, *Gawain and the Green Knight* (Cambridge, Mass., 1916), p. 244, and A. C. L. Brown, *Iwain* (Boston, 1903), p. 80.

The Russian hero Ivan is, doubtless, Gawain-Iwain; at any rate, a Prince Ivan brings back two flasks of the Water of Life, from where it is kept between two high mountains that cleave together except for a few minutes of each day, and as he returns, they close upon him and crush his steed's hind legs (W. R. Ralston, *Russian Folk-tales* [New York, 1873], p. 235ff). Cf. A. H. Wratislaw, *Sixty Folk-Tales*, pp. 280, 283.

[32] Motif of Achilles' heel. Cf. *Aitareya Brāhmaṇa* III.27, where the Soma-guardian, Kṛsānu (Sagittarius) cuts off a claw from Gāyatrī's foot.

[33] See A. C. Brown, *Iwain*, pp. 80, 81, with other "variants of what may be called the active door type": and "The Knight of the Lion," *Publications of the Modern Languages Association*, XX (1905), pp. 673-706. Incidentally, we consider that "Symplegades" (= Sanskrit *mithasturā*) is the best "catch-word" for our motif, because the contraries involved are not always "rocks," or even always the leaves of a door in the most literal and restricted sense of the word.

[34] G. L. Kittredge, *Gawain and the Green Knight*, pp. 244, 245. On the Bridge, *Harvard Journal of Asiatic Studies*, VIII (1944), p. 196ff.

[35] "Or Zeus or Hades, by whichever name thou wouldst be called" (Euripides, Nauck, fr. 912); Plato, *Laws* 727D, "Hades . . . realm of the Gods yonder"; cf. *Phaedo* 68AB, "Hades," where and where only is pure wisdom to be found. The distinction of Heaven from Hell is not of places but in those who enter; the Fire, as Jacob Boehme is fond of saying, is one and the same Fire, but of Love to those who are lovers, and of Wrath to those who hate. So in the Celtic mythology, Joyous Garde and Dolorous Garde are one as places, differing only according to our point of view. This is important for the iconography of the "Door."

[36] Ed. G. Henderson, Irish Texts Society (London, 1899), II, 103, § 80; cf. Loomis, *Celtic Myth and Arthurian Romance*, p. 365; Brown, *Iwain*, pp. 51-55; Kittredge, *Gawain and the Green Knight*, pp. 244-245.

[37] *Imran Maeile Dúin*, § p 32; William Larminie, West Irish tale of "Morraha" in *West Irish Folk-Tales and Romances* (London, 1893); *Mahābhārata* (Pūna ed.) I.29; Suparṇādhyāya, XXVI.5; Dante, *Purgatoria.*

[38] Ed. Pfeiffer (Leipzig, 1847); see Brown, *Iwain*, p. 80.

[39] *Khe-cara* here, however, with special reference to the penetration of the *kha* (= *ākāśa*, *aither*, *claritas*, *quinta essentia*) of the Sundoor ("like the hole in the chariot-wheel," *yathā ratha-cakrasya kham*, *Bṛhadāraṇyaka Upaniṣad* V.10; cf. *Jaiminīya Upaniṣad Brāhmaṇa* I.3.6 and *Ṛgveda* VIII.91.7), an aperture that as Void or Space-absolute is to be equated with Brahma (*Chāndogya Upaniṣad* III.12.7, IV.10.4, *Bṛhadāraṇyaka Upaniṣad* V.1 and see above, note 15); and is "within you" (*Maitri Upaniṣad* VII.11). "This turning disc is unique of heaven with the sun was the oldest divine symbol of the primordial religion—and also of the Chinese religion" (R. Schlosser, "Der Ursprung des chinesischen Käsch," *Artibus Asiae*, V (1935), p. 165): "I saw Eternity the other night, Like a great Ring of pure and endless light. . . . Some . . . soar'd up into the Ring" (Vaughn).

[40] The "moment" (*kṣaṇa*) of transition here corresponds to the "single moment of full awakening" (*eka-kṣaṇa-abhisambodha*) which in Prajñāpāramitā (Mahāyāna Buddhist) doctrine is the last step of the Via Affirmativa (*śaikṣa mārga*) and is an awakening to "Non-duality" (*advaya*), i.e., from the illusion of Duality, followed immediately by the attainment of Buddhahood (see E. Obermiller, "The Doctrine of Prajñāpāramitā," *Acta Orientalia*, XI (1932), pp. 63, 71, 81). Cf. Acts 2:2 (the "sound" of the Holy Ghost signifies suddenness). All spiritual operations are necessarily "sudden," because whatever is eternal is also immediate; "the now that stands still is said to make eternity" (St. Thomas Aquinas, *Summa Theologica*, I.10.2). So mythical events are eternal (*nitya*), "once for all" (*sakṛt*), "today" (*sadya*) or "now" (*nu*) (*Ṛgveda* passim); and this "once for all" is what is really meant by the "long ago" and "once upon a time" of our fairy-tales. In any ease, the passage of an interval that is "not a sensible extent of time" must be "instantaneous" by hypothesis XXVI.5.

[41] Māyā (√*mā*, measure, fashion, make), the "Art" or "Power" of creation and trans-formation, is an essentially *divine* property and can be rendered by "Magic" only in Jacob Boehme's sense (*Sex Puncta Mystica*, V.1, see my *Hinduism and Buddhism*, note 257). In connection with the Titan Maya, Māyā must be identified with his wife Līlāvatī, who can be called "Illusion" only in the literal and etymological sense of the word, as being the "means" of the divine Līlā, and the "Wisdom" who finds out the knowledge of "witty inventions" and belonged to the Lord "in the beginning of his way, before his works of old" (Proverbs 8:12 ff).

The creation is always conceived in these terms, viz., as *māyā-maya*, a "product of art"; this Vedantic *māyā-vada* doctrine must not be understood to mean than the world is a "delusion," but that it is a *phenomenal* world and as such a theophany and epiphany by which we are deluded if we are concerned with nothing but the wonders themselves, and do not ask "Of what?" all these things are a phenomenon.

When Indra himself is the Soma-thief and Grail-winner it is by overcoming the "devices" (*māyāḥ*) of the Titans that he makes the Soma "his alone" (*Ṛgveda* VII.98.5): and wielding this "power" himself "he casts appearances upon his own life-thread" (*Ṛgveda* III.53.8). It is by his Art (*māyayā*) that the Lord ("this is the mover in the hearts of mortal things") moves all these elemental-beings "that are mounted on their engines"; at the same time the Operator himself is concealed by the Art in which he is "wrapt up" and that is very "hard to penetrate," but which those who reach him are said to "cross over" (*Bhagavad Gītā* XVIII.61, VII.14.25). It is in this way precisely that Rājyadhara in *Kathā-Sarit-Sāgara* VII.9 populates his "city"; this man and this world being the stages on which the archetypal Thaumaturgus and Playwright exhibits himself. There can be no greater mistake than to suppose that such stories as those of *Kathā-Sarit-Sāgara* were composed only to amuse; it is a form of the pathetic fallacy that likewise explains the forms of primitive and popular art as products only of a "decorative" instinct. On *māyā*, cf. *Journal of the American Oriental Society* LXVI (1946), p. 152, note 28.

[42] In connection with "smiths," compare the ballad of the "Two Magicians" (Child, no. 44), "then she became a duck, and he became a drake," etc., with *Bṛhadāraṇyaka Upaniṣad* I.44, "she became a mare, and he became a stallion," etc.,—a good illustration of the fact that "collective memory preserves sometimes . . . archaic symbols which are in essence purely metaphysical . . . especially those symbols which are related to 'theories,' even if these theories are no longer understood" (Mircea Eliade, in *Zalmoxis*, II [1939], p. 78). The "catchwords" of Folklore are, in fact, the signs and symbols of the *Philosophia Perennis*.

[43] For Automata in analogous western literature see note 46, and M. B. Ogle, "The Perilous Bridge and Human Automata" in *Modern Language Notes* XXV (1920), pp. 129-136. N. M. Penzer, in discussing Automata (*The Ocean of Story* [*Kathā-Sarit-Sāgara*], III [1925], pp. 56-59 and IX [1928], p. 149) rather misses their "point" and so fails to make them move; that is, he considers them only from the standpoint of the historian of literature, and makes no attempt at exegesis. Even here we can only deal with the theme very briefly. Not only is the world itself an "engine" devised by the Great Engineer (from whom, as St. Augustine says, all human *ingenium* derives), but all its inhabitants are in the same way wooden (hylic) engines driven by his power (cf. *Maitri Upaniṣad* II.6)—"wooden," because the "material" of which the world is made is a "wood" (*dāru, vana = hule*); and for the same reason the Artist "through whom all things were made" is inevitably a "carpenter" (*takṣa, tektōn, armostes*).

From this point of view the myth of the City of Wooden Automata in the *Kathā-Sarit-Sāgara* (*The Ocean of Story*) VII.9 can be understood if we compare its wordings with those of *Maitri Upaniṣad* II.6 where Prajāpati (the biunity of the Sacerdotium and Regnum, represented in *Kathā-Sarit-Sāgara* by the carpenter brothers Prāṇadhara and Rājyadhara) beholds his conceptions (*prajāḥ*), as it were, as stones or stocks until he enters into them, and from within their heart, by means of his rays-or-reins (*raśmayaḥ = aktines*, Hermes Trismegistus, *Lib.* X.22, cf. XVI.7), operates and governs them, as the potter or charioteer drives his wheel or vehicle—"This is the mover in the hearts of mortal things" (Dante, *Paradiso* I.116). Rājyadhara's city is assuredly the same as that of the *Tripurārahasya* (Hemacuda section V.119-124), where the Prime Mover "though single, multiplies himself, manifests as the city and the citizens, and pervades them all, protects and holds them. Without him, they would all be scattered and lost like pearls without the string of the necklace (cf. Bhagavad Gītā VII.7). . . . If that city decays, he collects the inmates together, leads them to another, and remains their master" (as in *Bṛhadāraṇyaka Upaniṣad* IV.4.3-4). Alike for the Vedic tradition and Plato, Man is the "City of God" (*brahmapura*), and there can be no doubt that it is to this city that the myth of *Kathā-Sarit-Sāgara* really points.

Śaṅkarācārya often explains the Aupaniṣada formulations of the "thread-spirit" (*sūtrātman*) doctrine, to which the "string of the necklace" refers, by the metaphor of the "wooden puppet" (*dāru-putrikā*, in comment on *Bṛhadāraṇyaka Upaniṣad* III.4.1

and 7.1), as in *Kathā-Sarit-Sāgara*. It is in the same way that for Plato (*Laws* 644-645, 803-804) God is the Puppeteer and men his toys ("and as regards the best in us, that is what we really are"), and that for Philo (*De opificio mundi*, 117) we are puppets of which the strings are moved by the immanent Duke. This operation of his toys on the world stage is precisely what is called God's "Game" or "Sport" (*līlā*), and it is by no means accidentally that *Kathā-Sarit-Sāgara* describes the working of his puppets as Rājyadhara's "royal game";

> All this is a game that the Divinity maketh for Itself;
> For Its own sake hath It devised created things.
> (Angelus Silesius, *Cherubinische Wandersmann* II.198)

For further references see my *"Līlā"* in *Journal of the American Oriental Society*, XLI (1941), pp. 98-101 and "Play and Seriousness" in *Journal of Philosophy*, XXXIX (1942), pp. 550-552. [Editors' Note: both essays are contained in *Coomaraswamy 2: Selected Papers, Metaphysics*, pp. 148-155, and pp. 156-158 respectively.]

[44] The natural connection; cf. *Jaiminīya Upaniṣad Brāhmaṇa* I.23.1, "the Voice speaks from the Ether" (*ākāśāt*); so also *Mahābhārata* III.156.13, "an incorporeal Voice from the Ether" (*ākāśāt*). Cf. *Jaiminīya Upaniṣad Brāhmaṇa* I.28.3-4; Acts 2:3-4.

[45] "Human Automata in Classical Tradition and Mediaeval Romance," *Modern Philology*, X (1913), p. 524 ff.

[46] See also *Ṛgveda* IV.30.4; IV.31.4; V.29.10; VI.20.5, 6; VII.98.10.

[47] *Jaiminīya Upaniṣad Brāhmaṇa* I.3.5, "through the midst of the Sun, concealed by rays," corresponds exactly to Plato, *Phaedrus* 247B, "the Immortals proceed steeply upwards to the top of the vault of Heaven and take their stand beyond, outside it."

[48] For the "seven-rayed" Sun see my "Symbolism of the Dome," *Indian Historical Quarterly*, XIV (1938), pp. 7-9 [Editors' Note: this essay is also contained in *Coomaraswamy 1: Selected Papers, Traditional Art and Symbolism*, pp. 415-464; see especially pp. 420-422 on the seven-rayed sun], and *Jaiminīya Upaniṣad Brāhmaṇa* I.28-29. Cf. note 23. This pattern, again, is one of almost worldwide distribution; it is represented, for example, in the "seven gifts of the Spirit" and by the "seven eyes" of the Lamb, and those of Cuchullain. Note that the "seventh and best ray," passing through the center of the Sun-wheel to "break out of the dimensioned universe, intersecting everything" (Hermes Trismegistus, *Lib* XI.2.9) and so "bursting through the Sundoor," as *Maitri Upaniṣad* VI.30 expresses it ("for there is no approach by a side path"), bisects the three pairs of contrary spatial diameters; coinciding also, throughout its extent as Axis Mundi, vertical of the Stauros, and Vedic *skambha*, it "divides all things of the right hand from those of the left." This "seventh ray," is then, precisely the principle that is represented by Philo's (probably Pythagorean) "Severing Word" (*logos tomeus*) (*Heres, passim*); and, accordingly, by "the central and seventh light" of the seven-branched golden Candlestick, which "divides and separates the threes," and corresponds to the Sun attended by the other six planets (*Heres* 215ff).

It follows naturally from these lucid formulations that the point at which the severing Axis intersects whatever plane of reference will be the "Sundoor" of the realm next below it, and so on through the ascending hierarchy of the worlds until we reach the capstone of the cosmic roof which is the "*harmony* of the whole edifice" (Pausanias IX.38.3; cf. "through the harmony," Hermes Trismegistus, *Lib*. I.14.25), "like a great *Ring*" (Vaughn) or Flower (Pāli *kaṇṇikā*), through which the Way leads on to the "Plain of Truth" of which there can be no true report in terms of human speech (*Phaedrus* 247C, *Kena Upaniṣad* I.2-8, etc.). In other words, the Severing Logos is at once the narrow path that must be followed by every Hero, the Door that he must find, and the logical Truth and Highest Spirit of Reason that he must overcome if he would enter into the eternal life of the land "East of the Sun and West of the Moon." This is also the "Logos of God," the trenchant Word that like a two-edged sword, "sunders" soul from Spirit (Hebrews 4:12); "sunders," because whoever enters must have left himself (Achilles' heel, all that was vulnerable in him) behind him; our sensitive soul being the "mortal brother" and the "tail" or "appendage" of which the Master Surgeon's knife—Islamic Dhu'l-fiqār—relieves us, if we are prepared to submit to his operation.

[49] "That eternal Point where all our lines begin and end" (Ruysbroeck, *The Seven Cloisters*, ch. 19); Dante's "point at which all times are present" (*Paradiso* XVII.17); Meister Eckhart's "the point of the circle" (Pfeiffer ed. p. 503).

[50] "It is not for you to know the times and the seasons, which the Father hath put in his own power" (Acts 1:7).

V

THE PERENNIAL
PHILOSOPHY

Truth is one; the sages call it by many names.

ṚGVEDA 1.164.46

15 THE SPIRIT OF THE TIMES

Martin Lings

According to worldwide tradition, the "life" of the macrocosm con-sists of thousands of years of spiritual prosperity leading gradually down, from Golden Age to Silver Age to Bronze Age, until it reaches a relatively short final period[1] in which the prosperity is increasingly marred by its opposite. This period, the Iron Age or, as the Hindus term it, the Dark Age, is the late autumn and the winter of the cycle, and it roughly coincides with what is called "historic" as opposed to "prehistoric." All old age, both macrocosmic and microcosmic, has its ills. But normal old age has also its wisdom; and half hidden behind the negative signs which we see on all sides, our day has also something positive to offer which is characteristic of no previous era and which is, as such, yet another sign of the times.

Needless to say, this is not a claim that old age alone is endowed with wisdom, or that, analogously, our times excel in that respect—far from it. Humanity is the heart of the macrocosm and the four ages of the cycle are what they are according to the state of mankind. The pre-excellence of the Golden Age derives from the spirituality—which implies wisdom—of mankind in general. This whole was subsequently reduced to being no more than a majority which was then reduced to a minority, ultimately a small one. It can none the less be said that there is a mode of wisdom which belongs to old age in particular, and which is even susceptible of being assimilated, to a certain degree, by those who were not wise in youth and middle age. The old age of the cycle is bound to be a congenial setting for it; and the following passage gives us a hint of a collective or macrocosmic wisdom which belongs to our times precisely by reason of their lateness.

---

[1] According to Hinduism, which has the oldest and most explicit doctrine of the cycles, the first age is the longest and the fourth is the shortest. The Genesis com-mentaries and the Jewish apocryphal books make it clear that there is no mutual contradiction between the perspective of the monotheistic religions and the pre-bib-lical doctrine of four ages (see Martin Lings, *Ancient Beliefs and Modern Superstitions* [Cambridge, UK: Archetype, 2001], pp. 22-23 [Editors' Note: the final section of Chapter 4 in the present anthology]).

The usual religious arguments, through not probing sufficiently to the depth of things and moreover not having previously had any need to do so, are psychologically somewhat outworn and fail to satisfy certain requirements of causality. If human societies degenerate on the one hand with the passage of time, they accumulate on the other hand experiences in virtue of old age, however intermingled with errors these may be. This paradox is something that any pastoral teaching intended to be effective should take into account, not by drawing new directives from the general error, but on the contrary by using arguments of a higher order, intellectual rather than sentimental.[2]

In the phrase "human societies" the plural reminds us that the modern world is not the only human world that has degenerated with the passage of time. Each of the four ages may be said to constitute in itself a lesser cycle, beginning with a "youth" and ending with an "eld"; and there are yet lesser cycles within them—for example, the civilization of ancient Egypt, or that of ancient Rome. In all these lesser cycles there must have been in some degree, towards the end, an accumulation of "experience in virtue of old age." The twentieth century, together with the decades which immediately follow it, would appear to constitute the final phase of that particular human society which may be said to have been established in Europe—with eventual prolongations—about 1500 years ago. It is also, in a parallel way, the final phase of many other societies—Hindu, American Indian, Jewish, Buddhist, and Islamic—which have been partially merged into one with the Western world by the superimposition of its way of life over their own traditional differences from it and from each other. But at the same time we are living at the very end of one of the four ages; and since it is the last of the four, its end will be the end of the great cycle of all four ages taken as a whole. In other words, we are now participating in the extreme old age of the macrocosm, which is to be followed by a new cycle of four ages.

It may be objected that in view of the immense length of the cycle the macrocosm could be said to have reached its old age long before the twentieth century. That is true, but the old age in question was overlaid by the youth of subsidiary cycles. Two thousand years ago, the incipient twilight of the great cycle receded before the dawn of

[2] Frithjof Schuon, *In the Face of the Absolute* (Bloomington, IN: World Wisdom Books, 1994), pp. 89-90.

Christianity, which was followed later by the dawn of Islam; and even as recently as 700 years ago there took place what has been called the "second birth" of Christianity: it was the time of the building of the great cathedrals and the founding of many of the orders of mysticism. Christendom had been allowed a "fresh flowering," precariously set though it was within the old age of the great cycle. It could not last: all too quickly and easily it was drawn into the main cosmic current of degeneration. The same applies to the "second birth" of Islam which partly coincided in time with that of Christianity inasmuch as Christendom took considerably longer to develop than the civilization of Islam. It is true that the younger religion still retained something of its youth when its elder sister could no longer be called young in any sense. But today there is nothing to modify the greater cycle's old age which is, on the contrary, reinforced by the old age of all the lesser cycles which it contains. It can therefore be said, macrocosmically speaking, that all men alive today, whatever their years, are "old"; and the question arises, for each individual, which aspect of old age, the positive or the negative, will he or she represent in the macrocosm, that is, in the human collectivity taken as a whole, and how active or passive will each be in this respect.

As regards what Schuon says about pastoral teaching that is no longer effective, the dogma that there is only one valid religion, namely "ours," may serve as an example of an argument that is "psychologically somewhat outworn." Such teachings "fail to satisfy certain requirements of causality" because they are now seen to defeat one of the main ends of religion which is to bestow a sense of the Glory of God. Modern man cannot help having a broader view of the world than his ancestors had, partly through the destruction of the protective walls of the different traditional civilizations—in itself a tragedy—and partly through the enormously increased facilities of travel and the corresponding increase of information which is poured into his mind through various channels. This broader view may enable him to be impressed by religions other than his own, and at the very least it compels him to see that their existence makes the worldwide spread of his own religion impossible. If they were false, what of the Glory of Him who allowed them to establish themselves, with their millennial roots, over so vast an area?

For those who are not prepared to sacrifice that Glory to human prejudices, it has become abundantly clear that none of the so-called "world religions" can have been intended by Providence to establish itself over the whole globe. The question does not arise with those forms of worship like Hinduism and Judaism which are specifically for one people only. But Buddhism, Christianity, and Islam, though each is virtually open to everybody, have also beyond doubt their particular sectors of humanity; and though the frontiers may be difficult to define, and though Islam, the most recently revealed of the three, is in the nature of things likely to continue gaining ground in many directions, it seems probable to say the least that the three sectors will remain largely the same until the end of the age. But if such an objective view of religion is widespread, this is not for the most part due to an increase in acuity in the intelligence, but rather to the fact that an "old man" cannot help being "experienced." Otherwise expressed, it is due to a mainly passive participation in the positive aspects of the present age. For anyone who is intellectually active however, this universal outlook is a secondary accompanying asset—albeit none the less necessary—of what may be called "the spirit of the times."

To see what is meant by this, let us consider in more detail the characteristics of old age. To speak of the "old age" of the macrocosm is not merely to speak in metaphor. According to a doctrine that is to be found, variously expressed, in all religions, there is a real analogical correspondence between macrocosm and microcosm, a correspondence which is implicit in these terms themselves, "great world" and "little world." This universal doctrine enables us to grasp certain elusive aspects of the macrocosm through the corresponding aspects of the microcosm; and the ambiguous, dividedly dual nature of our times can be better understood if we consider in more detail the old age of the microcosm or, more precisely, of the normal microcosm, for he alone is the true counterpart of the macrocosm.

The word normal is used here in its strict sense, as the epithet of that which is a norm: only man as he was created, or one who has regained the primordial state, True Man as the Taoists call him, can be considered as a full microcosm, whose life corresponds to the "life" of the macrocosm, that is, to the cycle of time which is now nearing its close; and by extension from True Man, that is, from the Saint, we might include in the human norm every truly spiritual man who has at least a virtual wholeness, even if it be not yet fully realized.

Like the macrocosm, the normal microcosm is subject in old age to the tension of two opposite tendencies, a contradiction which in the first part of life was relatively latent and from which, in the Earthly Paradise, man was altogether exempt. This contradiction is due to the imprisonment of an immortal soul in a mortal body, a soul which is moreover in communion with the Spirit. The body is an

image of the soul, of which it is also a prolongation. In youth, generally speaking, the body appears as a purely positive symbol and there
is perfect harmony between it and the soul. Analogous to this is the
harmonious homogeneity of the earlier ages of the macrocosmic cycle.
But gradually, in the microcosm, the body begins to show that it is
merely a symbol, and that "merely" becomes more and more aggra-
vated with the passage of time. On the one hand, therefore, there is a
gradual bodily deterioration which ends with death; on the other hand
there is a mellowing of spirituality. The serene and objective wisdom
which is the central characteristic of normal old age outweighs, by
its transcendence, the many ills which are the inevitable result of
increasing decrepitude,[3] and in a certain sense it may be said to thrive
on them. The corresponding ills of the macrocosm likewise create a
climate which is not unfavorable to wisdom on condition that they
are seen as ills. Detachment is an essential feature of the sage, and this
virtue, which in better times could only be acquired through great
spiritual efforts, can be made more spontaneous by the sight of one's
world in chaotic ruins. / — great one liner !

There is yet another feature of normal old age, the most positive of
all, which likewise has its macrocosmic equivalent, in virtue of which
our times are unique. It is sometimes said of spiritual men and women
at the end of their lives that they have "one foot already in Paradise."
This is not meant to deny that death is a sudden break, a rupture of
continuity. It cannot but be so, for it has to transform mortal old age
into immortal youth. None the less, hagiography teaches us that the
last days of sanctified souls can be remarkably luminous and transparent. Nor is it unusual that the imminence of death should bring
with it special graces, such as visions, in foretaste of what is to come.
The mellowing of spirituality, which is the highest aspect of old age
in itself, is thus crowned with an illumination which belongs more
to youth than to age; and it is to this synthesis, or more precisely to
its macrocosmic counterpart, that the title of our chapter refers; for
analogously, in the macrocosm, the nearness of the new Golden Age
cannot fail to make itself mysteriously felt before the end of the old
cycle; and such an anticipation has been predicted in various parts of
the globe. We have here, in this junction of ending with beginning,

---

[3] By way of example we may consider on the one hand the blindness which befell
both Isaac and Jacob in extreme old age, and on the other hand their inward illumination.

yet another reason, perhaps the most powerful of all, why "the last shall be first."

The decrepitude of the macrocosm in its old age has given rise to the many pseudo-esoterisms and heresies with which the modern world is rife, and which make it easier to go astray than ever before. Despite these, thanks to what is most positive in this day of conflicting opposites, the highest and deepest truths have become correspondingly more accessible, as if forced to unveil themselves by cyclic necessity, the macrocosm's need to fulfill its aspect of terminal wisdom. This same need—for to speak of wisdom is to speak of esoterism—was bound to cause an inward movement away from error and towards these truths. That it has in fact done so is shown, apart from more direct but less accessible signs, by the greatly increased publication of relevant books, for a minority no doubt but none the less on a scale to which esoterism has long been unaccustomed. The complex nature of the spirit of the times can explain facts which could otherwise be difficult to account for. In this meeting of estuary and source, finality derives from primordiality a certain aspect of abruptness, an initiative which is not typical of old age itself. Needless to say, the movement in question could not be lacking in the necessary traditional continuity; but neither could it be a smooth transition, an ordinary sequel from something that has gone before; and this explains also the widespread lack of preparation for it. Amongst those who in themselves are truly qualified for an esoteric path, it is inevitable that not a few should stand in need of a certain initial enlightenment by reason of their upbringing and education in the modern world.

This applies in yet greater measure to others, less qualified and more numerous, who in an earlier age would probably have remained in exoterism and who appear to owe their eventual qualification for esoterism partly to the fact of their birth in the present age. The following quotation will help to explain this paradox:

> Exoterism is a precarious thing by reason of its limits or its exclusions; there comes a moment in history when all kinds of experiences oblige it to modify its claims to exclusiveness, and it is then driven to a choice: escape from these limitations by the upward path, in esoterism, or by the downward path, in a worldly and suicidal liberalism. As one might have expected, the civilizationist exoterism of the West has chosen the downward path, while combining this incidentally with a few esoteric notions which in such conditions remain inoperative.[4]

This lower choice, officially ratified by Vatican II for the Catholic Church and already characteristic of the other Churches of Western Europe, does not prevent individuals from choosing the upward path, that of esoterism. Some of those who would not have been qualified in the past are now given access to it in virtue of a truly positive attitude, severely put to the test by the present spiritual crisis, and amply verified by the choice of the higher rather than the lower. On the one hand, the foundering of certain exoteric vessels is bound in the nature of things to enlarge the responsibilities of esoterism, which cannot refuse to take on board those in the sea about it who ask for a lifeline to be thrown to them and who have no means of salvation else. On the other hand, obtusenesses which in the past would have proved to be disqualifications can be modified or even partially dissolved by the virtues inherent in "old age." Whatever the circumstances may be, a suppliant hand held out from the modern chaos in the direction of right guidance is an indication that its owner cannot be relegated to the spiritually passive majority.

In connection with the widespread need for initial enlightenment, it must be remembered that esoterism presupposes the sense of the Absolute. More precisely, since there is no soul which is not virtually imbued with this sense, esoterism presupposes that it be actual and operative, at least to a certain degree. On that basis it can be further actualized by indirect contact with the Absolute, that is, with Its "overflows," if one may use such a term, into the various domains of this world. One such "overflow" is the esoteric doctrine itself, and this is indispensable; but its effect upon the soul may be reinforced by other earthly manifestations of the Absolute. The argument of beauty, for example, may be a powerful ally to the arguments of truth.

In the theocratic civilizations, the spiritual authority and the temporal power saw to it that the beauty of nature was not unduly desecrated by man, and that parallel to nature there were objects of sacred art that conformed to a style which had come as a gift from

---

[4] Frithjof Schuon, *Esoterism as Principle and as Way* (Pates Manor, Bedfont: Perennial Books, 1981), pp. 19-20. By way of example, the acceptance of religions other than one's own is esoterically operative if it be based on intellectual discernment between the true and the false, that is, if it be recognition of orthodoxy to the exclusion of everything else. But acceptance of other religions on the basis of the widely predominant sentimental pseudo-charity of our day is not merely inoperative in any positive sense but it is exceedingly harmful, for where discernment is not the guiding factor the door to error is inevitably opened, and the true religions are dishonored by being placed on a level with heretical sects.

Heaven, and which was never a merely human invention. In the rigorous sense of the term, which is all we are considering here, sacred art is as a crystallization of sanctity, a spiritual presence which has power to purify and to enlighten and which, unlike ascetic practices of a similar power, makes no demands of man which run counter to his natural bent. "It[5] sets up, against the sermon which insists on what must be done by one who would become holy, a vision of the cosmos which is holy through its beauty; it makes men participate naturally and almost involuntarily in the world of holiness."[6]

Today, despite the desecrations, nature still remains an inexhaustible treasury of reminders to man of his true heritage, reminders which may become operative in the light of the doctrine; and parallel to virgin nature, even if the Christian civilization may have gone without possibility of recall, many of its landmarks still remain. Some of these, the cathedrals for example, are monuments of overwhelming beauty which bear witness to the spiritual exaltation of the age which produced them. In addition to their power as sacred art, they are eloquent exponents—and never more so than when seen from today's abyss—of spirituality's universal rule; "Seek ye first the Kingdom of Heaven and all the rest shall be given unto you," and its parallel "Unto him that hath shall be given." At the same time, their presence is yet another demonstration of the truth that "from him that hath not shall be taken away even that which he hath." As material objects, they proclaim the spiritual man's mastery over matter, whereas the inability of the modern world to produce anything like them betrays the materialist's impotence precisely where he might have been expected to excel. He it is "that hath not," having rejected the Transcendent; and "that which he hath," namely matter, is taken away from him in the sense that he cannot really be said to possess it, having no qualitative dominion over it. We have only to approach a town like New York to have an alarming impression that matter has taken possession of man and quantitatively overwhelmed him. But standing in front of Durham, Lincoln, or Chartres Cathedral we see that our mediaeval ancestors were able to dominate matter to the point of compelling it to excel itself and to become vibrant with the Spirit.

---

[5] Sacred art, and in particular the architecture of mediaeval Christendom.

[6] Titus Burckhardt, *Sacred Art in East and West* (Louisville, KY: Fons Vitae/Bloomington, IN: World Wisdom, 2001), p. 61. The message of this book is centrally typical of the wisdom of the age both in virtue of its universality and of its finality.

What has been said about Christian art applies also to the arts of other sacred civilizations; and for the great loss of the experience of a traditional way of life, there can now be, for those capable of taking it, a certain compensation in the gain of access to the spiritual riches of traditions other than one's own. Religions in their outermost aspects have often been represented as different points on the circumference of a circle, the center of which is the Divine Truth. Every such point is connected to the center by a radius which stands for the esoterism of the religion in question. The more a radius approaches the center, the nearer it is to the other radii, which illustrates the fact that the esoteric paths are increasingly close to each other, however far the respective exoterisms may seem to be. Now sacred art, although it does not withhold its blessings from any sector of the community, is in itself a purely esoteric phenomenon, which means that it is central and therefore universal. Needless to say, there are degrees to be observed in this respect; but all that is best in sacred art virtually belongs to everyone who has "eyes to see" or "ears to hear," no matter what his faith or his race; and this virtuality can be actualized today as never before.

The nearer a work is to the center the more universal it is, but also, at the same time, the more concentratedly it represents the world of its own particular provenance. What could be more universal than the Bharata Natyam temple dancing of India and the music that accompanies it, the landscape paintings of China and Japan, the Romanesque and Gothic cathedrals of Western Europe, and the mosques of Andalusia, Egypt, Persia, and Turkestan, to mention only a few examples? And what, respectively, could give us a more concentrated sense of the unique spiritual fragrance of each of the four ways in question, Hinduism, Taoism, Christianity, and Islam? To add a fifth, exactly the same may be said of the statuary of Buddhism, from Ajanta to Kyoto. Taken together, the summits of sacred art give us in little, that is, in an easily assimilated form, a faithful view of the immense variety of the great religions and their civilizations, a pageant which can be for some as a semi-transparent veil that both hides and reveals the Transcendent Source of these wonders.[7] This comprehensive view may be considered as an aspect of that wisdom which is the theme of our chapter; for although it is a potential feature of every sage, no

---

[7] In the Islamic litany of the 99 Names of God, one of the names which this context recalls is *al-Badī*, the Marvelously Original.

matter when he lives, it withheld itself as an actuality from all other epochs, and offers itself now to him who seeks.[8]

What has been said about the crystallization of holiness in art may be said to hold good for incarnations of holiness, the sainthoods which exemplify the primordial nature that is hidden in fallen man by second nature. Some men can be initially penetrated and won more easily by a personal perfection, a human summit, than by any other mode of excellence; and there can now be added, to the Saints of one religion's calendar, their glorious counterparts from every other religion: We are speaking here of an initial penetration, and of indirect contacts with holy men such as can be made through the reading of hagiographies. It goes without saying that at a later stage the living personal perfection of the Spiritual Master[9] will necessarily take precedence, while at the same time it will make these other examples of sainthood more accessible.

As to the doctrine, it is indispensable both in itself and to throw its light on other motivations. It is also needed today as a protection: if esoteric truths continued to be kept secret as in the past on account of their danger, this would not prevent the spread of pseudo-esoterism, a poison to which the best antidote is true esoterism whose dangers are thus outweighed by its powers to safeguard against its own counterfeits; and beyond these it is needed for the refutation of more general errors.

> We live in an age of confusion and thirst in which the advantages of communication are greater than those of secrecy; moreover only esoteric theses can satisfy the imperious logical needs created by the philosophic and scientific positions of the modern world. . . . Only esoterism . . . can provide answers that are neither fragmentary nor compromised in advance by a denominational bias. Just as rationalism can remove faith, so esoterism can restore it.[10]

---

[8] The quantities of lavishly illustrated books now available, and their equivalents for the auditive arts, are yet another sign of the times inasmuch as they spring from what might be called the archival aspect of finality.

[9] It is a universal axiom that anyone who is truly qualified to follow an esoteric path will find, if he "seeks" and, if he "knocks," the master he needs. For more ample considerations on this subject, see Appendix B in Martin Lings, *The Eleventh Hour: The Spiritual Crisis of the Modern World in the Light of Tradition and Prophecy* (Cambridge, UK: Archetype, 2002), pp. 98-101.

[10] Frithjof Schuon, *Esoterism as Principle and as Way*, pp. 7-8.

In order to follow an esoteric path it is not necessary to make a quantitative study of the doctrine; it is enough to know the essentials, which are centered on the nature of God and the nature of man. The symbolism of the elementary numbers is always enlightening, and in this case it is the number three which holds, as it were, the keys to understanding the relationship between the Creator and His human image. The presence of certain triads in the world, such as that of the primary colors, is the proof of a triplicity in the Divine Nature Itself, the Supreme Archetype of all that exists. In *From the Divine to the Human*, Schuon dwells at some length on this triplicity which is nothing other than the Absolute Infinite Perfection of God Himself, these three supreme transcendences being the intrinsic dimensions of Divine Reality. Perfection is, as he remarks, "the Sovereign Good"; and having reminded us of St Augustine's saying that "the good tends essentially to communicate itself," he adds: "As Sovereign Good, the Absolute-Infinite cannot not project the world."[11] But he goes on to remind us that It remains in Itself totally unaffected by this projection: "Being what it is, the Absolute cannot not be immutable, and It cannot not radiate. Immutability, or fidelity to itself; and Radiation, or gift of Itself; there lies the essence of all that is."[12]

The Absolute Infinite Perfection is One. It transcends all multiplicity while being its root, and it is only at a lower level that we can begin to differentiate between the three terms of the triad. This is the level of what Schuon has called "the relative Absolute"—a term which is applicable to the Christian Trinity and to Hinduism's analogous ternary Being-Consciousness-Beatitude.[13] At the same level, in Jewish and Islamic doctrine, are the non-essential Divine names such as Creator, which already implies the duality Creator-creature. Without being as yet manifested, the "Hidden Treasure" is on the way to manifesting Itself.

If the Good is that which is to be manifested or communicated, the means of radiation is derived from the Infinite. These two intrinsic aspects of Reality are reflected by the Second and Third Persons of the Trinity, and, for Hinduism, by the corresponding Consciousness and

---

[11] This same truth is expressed in Islam as the tradition: "I was a hidden treasure, and I loved to be known, and so I created the world."

[12] Frithjof Schuon, *From the Divine to the Human* (Bloomington, IN: World Wisdom Books, 1982), p. 42.

[13] *Sat-Chit-Ānanda.*

Beatitude. "It could be asked what relationship there is between the Good and Consciousness (*Chit*); now the Good, from the moment that It springs as such from the Absolute—which contains It in an undifferentiated or indeterminate manner—coincides with the distinctive Consciousness which the Absolute has of Itself; the Divine Word, which is the 'Knowledge' that God has of Himself, cannot but be the Good, God being able to know Himself as Good only."[14]

The Divine triplicity is reflected throughout the Universe in innumerable ways,[15] being especially intense in man himself. "Man, 'made in the image of God,' has an intelligence capable of discernment and contemplation; a will capable of freedom and strength; a soul, or a character, capable of love and virtue."[16] In the light of the quotation which precedes this, it is clear that intelligence corresponds to Perfection, the Sovereign Good. The same applies to doctrine, the content of the intelligence; all theology derives from the Divine Perfection by way of the Divine Word. Will and soul are rooted in the Absolute and the Infinite respectively. The psychic substance is the "space" in which man deploys his faculties, and the primordial soul is no less than a vast presence. As to the primordial will—the will that is "for God" in the most powerful sense these words have—it is irresistibly overwhelming:[17] no obstacle can stand in its way.

> Man may know, will, and love; and to will is to act. We know God by distinguishing Him from whatever is not He and by recognizing Him in whatever bears witness to Him; we will God by accomplishing whatever leads us to Him and by abstaining from whatever removes us from Him; and we love God by loving to know and to will Him, and by loving whatever bears witness to Him, around us as well as within us.[18]

---

[14] Frithjof Schuon, *From the Divine to the Human*, p. 39.

[15] Since the primary colors have been mentioned, we may say, in passing, that it is the right of the Absolute that we should know which is its color before we have time to think. As to the Infinite, its right is, with regard to the same question, that our thoughts should unfold in the direction of its two great earthly symbols, the sky and the ocean. Nor is it difficult to see that Perfection, the Sovereign Good, is the Supreme Archetype of gold.

[16] Frithjof Schuon, *Esoterism as Principle and as Way*, p. 101.

[17] Even when perverted, the will retains something of the imprint of the Absolute, whence the terrible dangers inherent in ambition.

[18] Frithjof Schuon, *Esoterism as Principle and as Way*, pp. 95-96.

Man's three faculties, intelligence, will, and soul, thus correspond to the equally interdependent ternary of doctrine, method, morals, or faith, practice, virtue, or "comprehension, concentration,[19] conformation." It follows from the above quotations that to be effective the doctrine's initial appeal to the intelligence must include within its scope also the will and the soul. There can be no spirituality—or in other words no microcosm worthy of the name—without wholeness, that is, without sincerity, which means the harmonious cooperation of all these three faculties towards the common end. Nor indeed can there be any advance upon the esoteric way if the truth that is addressed to the mind does not lead to practice, and if both are not supported by virtue.

> Obviously the most brilliant intellectual knowledge is fruitless in the absence of the realizing initiative that corresponds to it and in the absence of the necessary virtue; in other words, knowledge is nothing if it is combined with spiritual laziness and with pretensions, egoism, hypocrisy. Likewise the most prestigious power of concentration is nothing if it is accompanied by doctrinal ignorance and moral insufficiency; likewise again, natural virtue is but little without the doctrinal truth and the spiritual practice which operate it with a view to God and which thus restore to it the whole point of its being.[20]

The movement towards the inward, which we are considering here may be said to represent the highest aspect of the extreme old age of the macrocosm. As such, in virtue of all that the times stand for in a positive sense, the esoterism in question could not be other than what the Hindus call *jñāna-mārga*, the way of knowledge or, more precisely, of gnosis. It was fated to be so, for such a way presupposes a perspective of truth rather than love[21] and it is objective regard for

---

[19] The quintessence of esoteric practice is concentration on the Real. One of the most direct methodic supports for this is the invocation of the Divine Name, an orison said by Hinduism to be, for the whole of the Dark Age, the greatest means of Deliverance (*moksha*) and thus of Union (*yoga*) with the Divine Self, the One Real "I" of which all subjectivities are reflections.

[20] Frithjof Schuon, *Esoterism as Principle and as Way*, p. 169.

[21] Needless to say, it is not a question of mutually exclusive alternatives but of emphasis. Both elements must be present in every spiritual path.

truth which characterizes the wisdom of old age.[22] It is beyond doubt significant in this respect that the last religion of the cycle, Islam—and therefore Sufism its esoteric dimension—should be dominated by the perspective of truth.

The mention of *jñāna* does not necessarily mean, in this context, a movement towards Hinduism. For each seeker the way in question could be, in principle, any one of the orthodox esoteric paths which are now operative. But before a way can be followed there must be an aspiration, and the word "movement" is used here to mean the initial setting in motion of individuals in search of spiritual guidance and not the way itself, though this is bound to follow if the aspiration be a true one.

[22] Even the many pseudo-esoterisms with which the modern age is rife purport to be ways of knowledge, no doubt in the awareness that otherwise they would be without attraction for contemporary seekers.

16 PATHS THAT LEAD TO THE SAME SUMMIT

Ananda K. Coomaraswamy

There is no Natural Religion. . . . As all men are alike (though infinitely
various), so all Religions, as all similars, have one source.
William Blake

There is but one salvation for all mankind,
and that is the life of God in the soul.
William Law

The constant increase of contacts between ourselves, who for the
purposes of the present essay may be assumed to be Christians, and
other peoples who belong to the great non-Christian majority has
made it more than ever before an urgent necessity for us to understand the faiths by which they live. Such an understanding is at the
same time intrinsically to be desired, and indispensable for the solution by agreement of the economic and political problems by which
the peoples of the world are at present more divided than united. We
cannot establish human relationships with other peoples if we are
convinced of our own superiority or superior wisdom, and only want
to convert them to our way of thinking. The modern Christian, who
thinks of the world as his parish, is faced with the painful necessity of
becoming himself a citizen of the world; he is invited to participate
in a symposium and a *convivium*; not to preside—for there is Another
who presides unseen—but as one of many guests.

It is no longer only for the professed missionary that a study of
other religions than his own is required. This very essay, for example,
is based upon an address given to a large group of schoolteachers in a
series entitled "How to Teach about Other Peoples," sponsored by the
New York School Board and the East and West Association. It has, too,
been proposed that in all the schools and universities of the postwar
world stress should be laid on the teaching of the basic principles of
the great world religions as a means of promoting international understanding and developing a concept of world citizenship.

The question next arises, "By whom can such teaching be properly given?" It will be self-evident that no one can have understood,
and so be qualified to teach, a religion, who is opposed to all religion;
this will rule out the rationalist and scientific humanist, and ultimately

all those whose conception of religion is not theological, but merely ethical. The obvious ideal would be for the great religions to be taught only by those who confess them; but this is an ideal that could only be realized, for the present, in our larger universities. It has been proposed to establish a school of this kind at Oxford.

As things are, a teaching about other than Christian faiths is mainly given in theological seminaries and missionary colleges by men who do believe that Christianity is the only true faith, who approve of foreign missions, and who wish to prepare the missionary for his work. Under these conditions, the study of comparative religion necessarily assumes a character quite different from that of other disciplines; it cannot but be biased. It is obvious that if we are to teach at all it should be our intention to communicate only truth: but where a teaching takes for granted that the subject matter to be dealt with is intrinsically of inferior significance, and the subject is taught, not *con amore* [with love], but only to instruct the future schoolmaster in the problems that he will have to cope with, one cannot but suspect that at least a part of the truth will be suppressed, if not intentionally, at least unknowingly.

If comparative religion is to be taught as other sciences are taught, the teacher must surely have recognized that his own religion is only one of those that are to be "compared"; he may not expound any "pet theories" of his own, but is to present the truth without bias, to the extent that it lies in his power. In other words, it will be "necessary to recognize that those institutions which are based on the same premises, let us say the supernatural, must be considered together, our own amongst the rest," whereas "today, whether it is a question of imperialism, or of race prejudice, or of a comparison between Christianity and paganism, we are still preoccupied with the uniqueness . . . of our own institutions and achievements, our own civilization."[1] One cannot but ask whether the Christian whose conviction is ineradicable that his is the only true faith can conscientiously permit himself to expound another religion, knowing that he cannot do so honestly.

*   *   *

We are, then, in proposing to teach about other peoples, faced with the problem of tolerance. The word is not a pretty one; to tolerate is to put up with, endure, or suffer the existence of what are or appear

---

[1] Ruth Benedict, *Patterns of Culture* (1934), p. 5.

to be other ways of thinking than our own; and it is neither very pleasant merely "to put up with" our neighbors and fellow guests, nor very pleasant to feel that one's own deepest institutions and beliefs are being patiently "endured." Moreover, if the Western world is actually more tolerant today than it was some centuries ago, or has been since the fall of Rome, it is largely because men are no longer sure that there is any truth of which we can be certain, and are inclined to the "democratic" belief that one man's opinion is as good as another's, especially in the fields of politics, art, and religion. Tolerance, then, is a merely negative virtue, demanding no sacrifice of spiritual pride and involving no abrogation of our sense of superiority; it can be commended only in so far as it means that we shall refrain from hating or persecuting others who differ or seem to differ from ourselves in habit or belief. Tolerance still allows us to pity those who differ from ourselves, and are consequently to be pitied!

Tolerance, carried further, implies indifference, and becomes intolerable. Our proposal is not that we should tolerate heresies, but rather come to some agreement about the truth. Our proposition is that the proper objective of an education in comparative religion should be to enable the pupil to discuss with other believers the validity of particular doctrines,[2] leaving the problem of the truth or falsity, superiority or inferiority, of whole bodies of doctrine in abeyance until we have had at least an opportunity to know in what respects they really differ from one another, and whether in essentials or in accidentals. We take it for granted, of course, that they will inevitably differ accidentally, since "nothing can be known except in the mode of the knower." One must at least have been taught to recognize equivalent symbols, e.g., rose and lotus (Rosa Mundi and Padmāvatī); that Soma is the "bread and water of life"; or that the Maker of all things is by no means accidentally, but necessarily a "carpenter" wherever the material of which the world is made is *hylic.* The proposed objective has this further and immediate advantage, that it is not in conflict with even the most rigid Christian orthodoxy; it has never been denied that some truths are embodied in the pagan beliefs, and even St. Thomas Aquinas was ready and willing to find in the works of the pagan phi-

---

[2] To illustrate what I mean by "discussion" here, I refer the reader to my article entitled, "On Being in One's Right Mind," in the *Review of Religion,* Vol. VII, New York, 1942, pp. 32-40 [Editors' Note: This article is also published in Ananda Coomaraswamy's *What is Civilization? And Other Essays* (Ipswich: Golgonooza Press, 1989)]. Although in fact by one author, this article is in effect a collaboration of Christian, Platonist, and Hindu, expounding a doctrine held in common.

losophers "extrinsic and probable proofs" of the truths of Christianity. He was, indeed, acquainted only with the ancients and with the Jews and some Arabians; but there is no reason why the modern Christian, if his mental equipment is adequate, should not learn to recognize or be delighted to find in, let us say, Vedantic, Sufi, Taoist, or American Indian formulations extrinsic and probable proofs of the truth as he knows it. It is more than probable, indeed, that his contacts with other believers will be of very great advantage to the Christian student in his exegesis and understanding of Christian doctrine; for though himself a believer, this is in spite of the nominalist intellectual environment in which he was born and bred, and by which he cannot but be to some degree affected; while the Oriental (to whom the miracles attributed to Christ present no problem) is still a realist, born and bred in a real-istic environment, and is therefore in a position to approach Plato or St. John, Dante or Meister Eckhart more simply and directly than the Western scholar who cannot but have been affected to some extent by the doubts and difficulties that force themselves upon those whose education and environment have been for the greater part profane.

Such a procedure as we have suggested provides us immediately with a basis for a common understanding and for cooperation. What we have in view is an ultimate "reunion of the churches" in a far wider sense than that in which this expression is commonly employed: the substitution of active alliances—let us say of Christianity and Hin-duism or Islam, on the basis of commonly recognized first principles, and with a view to an effective cooperation in the application of these principles to the contingent fields of art (manufacture) and pru-dence—for what is at present nothing better than a civil war between the members of one human family, children of one and the same God, "whom," as Philo said, "*with one accord* all Greeks and Barbarians acknowledge together."[3] It is with reference to this statement that Professor Goodenough remarks that, "So far as I can see Philo was telling the simple truth about paganism as he saw it, not as Christian propaganda has ever since misrepresented it."

It need not be concealed that such alliances will necessarily involve an abandonment of all missionary enterprises such as they are now; interdenominational conferences will take the place of those proselytizing expeditions of which the only permanent result is the secularization and destruction of existing cultures and the pulling up

---

[3] Philo Judaeus, *De specialibus legibus* II, 65; E. R. Goodenough, *Introduction to Philo Judaeus* (1940), pp. 105, 108.

of individuals by their roots. *You* have already reached the point at which culture and religion, utility and meaning, have been divorced and can be considered apart, but this is not true of those peoples whom you propose to convert, whose religion and culture *are one and the same thing* and none of the functions of whose life are necessarily profane or unprincipled. If ever you should succeed in persuading the Hindus that their revealed scriptures are valid only "as literature," you will have reduced them to the level of your own college men who read the Bible, if at all, only as literature. Christianity in India, as Sister Nivedita (Patrick Geddes' distinguished pupil, and author of *The Web of Indian Life*) once remarked, "carries drunkenness in its wake"[4]—for if you teach a man that what he has thought right is wrong, he will be apt to think that what he has thought wrong is right.

We are all alike in need of repentance and conversion, a "change of mind" and a "turning round": not, however, from one *form* of belief to another, but from unbelief to belief. There can be no more vicious kind of tolerance than to approach another man, to tell him that "We are both serving the same God, you in your way and I in His!" The "compassing of sea and land to make one proselyte" can be carried on as an institution only for so long as our ignorance of other peoples' faiths persists. The subsidizing of educational or medical services accessory to the primary purpose of conversion is a form of simony and an infringement of the instruction, "Heal the sick . . . provide neither gold nor silver nor brass in your purses, nor scrip for your journey . . . [but go] forth as sheep in the midst of wolves." Wherever you go, it must be not as masters or superiors but as guests, or as we might say nowadays, "exchange professors"; you must not return to betray the confidences of your hosts by any libel. Your vocation must be purged of any notion of a "civilizing mission"; for what you think of as "the white man's burden" here is a matter of "white shadows in the South Seas" there. Your "Christian" civilization is ending in disaster—and you are bold enough to offer it to others! Realize that, as Professor Plumer has said, "the surest way to betray our Chinese allies is to sell, give or lend-lease them our [American] standard of living,"[5] and that the hardest task you could undertake for the present and immediate future is to convince the Orient that the civilization of Europe is in

---

[4] *Lambs among Wolves* (1903). See also my "Christian Missions in India" in *Essays in National Idealism* (1st ed., 1909; or 2nd ed.).

[5] J. M. Plumer, "China's High Standard of Living," *Asia and the Americas*, February, 1944.

any sense a Christian civilization, or that there really are reasonable, just, and tolerable Europeans amongst the "barbarians" of whom the Orient lives in terror.

The word "heresy" means choice, the having opinions of one's own, and thinking what we *like* to think: we can only grasp its real meaning today, when "thinking for oneself" is so highly recommended (with the proviso that the thinking must be "100 per cent"), if we realize that the modern equivalent of heresy is "treason." The one outstanding, and perhaps the only, real heresy of modern Christianity in the eyes of other believers is its claim to exclusive truth; for this is treason against Him who "never left himself without a witness," and can only be paralleled by Peter's denial of Christ; and whoever says to his pagan friends that "the light that is in you is darkness," in offending these is offending the Father of lights. In view of St. Ambrose's well-known gloss on I Corinthians 12:3, "all that is true, *by whomsoever it has been said*, is from the Holy Ghost" (a dictum endorsed by St. Thomas Aquinas), you may be asked, "On what grounds do you propose to distinguish between your own 'revealed' religion and our 'natural' religion, for which, in fact, we also claim a supernatural origin?" You may find this question hard to answer.

The claim to an exclusive validity is by no means calculated to make for the survival of Christianity in a world prepared to prove all things. On the contrary, it may weaken enormously its prestige in relation to other traditions in which a very different attitude prevails, and which are under no necessity of engaging in any polemic. As a great German theologian has said, "human culture [*Menschheitsbildung*] is a unitary whole, and its separate cultures are the dialects of one and the same language of the spirit."[6] The quarrel of Christianity with other religions seems to an Oriental as much a tactical error in the conflict of ideal with sensate motivations as it would have been for the Allies to turn against the Chinese on the battlefield. Nor will he participate in such a quarrel; much rather he will say, what I have often said to Christian friends, "Even if you are not on our side, we are on yours." The converse attitude is rarely expressed; but twice in my life I have met a Roman Catholic who could freely admit that for a Hindu to become a professing Christian was not essential to salvation. Yet, could we believe it, the Truth or Justice with which we are all alike

---

[6] Alfred Jeremias, *Altorientalische Geisteskultur*, Vorwort. "A long metaphysical chain runs throughout the world and connects all races" (Johannes Sauter, in *Archiv für Rechts- und Sozialphilosophie*, Berlin, October, 1934).

and unconditionally concerned is like the Round Table to which "al the worlde crysten and hethen repayren" to eat of one and the same bread and drink the same wine, and at which "all are equal, the high and the low." A very learned Roman Catholic friend of mine, in correspondence, speaks of Śrī Rāmakrishna as "another Christ . . . Christ's own self."

* * *

Let us now, for a moment, consider the points of view that have been expressed by the ancients and other non-Christians when they speak of religions other than their own. We have already quoted Philo. Plutarch, first with bitter irony disposing of the Greek euhemerists "who spread atheism all over the world by obliterating the Gods of our belief and turning them all alike into the names of generals, admirals and kings," and of the Greeks who could no longer distinguish Apollo (the intelligible Sun) from Helios (the sensible sun), goes on to say: "Nor do we speak of the 'different Gods' of different peoples, or of the Gods as 'Barbarian' and 'Greek,' but as common to all, though differently named by different peoples, so that for the One Reason (Logos) that orders all these things, and the One Providence that oversees them, and for the minor powers [i.e., gods, angels] that are appointed to care for all things, there have arisen among different peoples different epithets and services, according to their different manners and customs."[7] Apuleius recognizes that the Egyptian Isis (our Mother Nature and Madonna, Natura Naturans, Creatrix, Deus)

---

[7] Plutarch, *Isis and Osiris*, 67 (*Moralia*, 377). So William Law, in continuation of the citation above, "There is not one [salvation] for the Jew, another for the Christian, and a third for the heathen. No, God is one, human nature is one, and the way to it is one; and that is, the desire of the soul turned to God." Actually, this refers to "the baptism of desire," or "of the Spirit" (as distinguished from baptism by water, which involves an actual membership in the Christian community) and only modifies the Christian dogma *extra Ecclesiam nulla salus* [outside the Church there is no salvation]. The real problem is that of the proper meaning of the words "Catholic Church"; we say that this should mean not any one religion as such, but the community, or universe of experience, of all those who love God. As William Law says also: "The chief hurt of a sect is this, that it takes itself to be necessary to the truth, whereas the truth is only then found when it is known to be of no sect but as free and universal as the goodness of God and as common to all names and nations as the air and light of this world."

Cf. F. W. Buckler: "The layman, Dissenter, schismatic, or the heathen, who wittingly or unwittingly has taken up his Cross, is a child of the kingdom of God on earth and a "is adored throughout the world in divers manners, in variable customs and by many names."[8]

The Muslim Emperor of India, Jahāngīr, writing of his friend and teacher, the Hindu hermit Jadrūp, says that "his Vedānta is the same as our Taṣawwuf":[9] and, in fact, Northern India abounds in a type of religious literature in which it is often difficult, if not impossible, to distinguish Muslim from Hindu factors. The indifference of religious forms is indeed, as Professor Nicholson remarks, "a cardinal Sufi doctrine." So we find Ibn al-'Arabī saying:

> My heart is capable of every form: it is a pasture for gazelles
>   and a convent for Christian monks,
> And idol-temple and the pilgrim's Ka'ba [Mecca],
>   and the tables of the Torah and the book of the Koran;
> I follow the religion of Love, whichever way his camels take;
>   my religion and my faith is the true religion.[10]

That is to say that you and I, whose religions are distinguishable, can each of us say that "mine is the true religion," *and* to one another that "yours is the true religion"—whether or not either or both of us be truly religious depending not upon the form of our religion but upon ourselves and on grace. So, too, Shams-i-Tabrīz:

> If the notion of my Beloved is to be found in an idol-temple,
>   'Twere mortal sin to circumscribe the Ka'ba!

---

khalīfah of our Lord, as the priest or bishop, who has not taken up his Cross, however unquestionable his Apostolic continuity, is not" (*The Epiphany of the Cross* [1938]). It should also be borne in mind that (as the last mentioned author has often shown) the Christian concept of the "kingdom of God" cannot be properly understood except in the light of the Oriental theory of Kingship and Divine Right.

[8] Apuleius, *Golden Ass*, XI, 5. Cf. Alfred Jeremias, *Der Kosmos von Sumer* (*Der Alte Orient*, 32, Leipzig, 1932), chapter III, "*Die eine Madonna.*"

[9] *Tūzuk-i-Jahāngīrī* (Memoirs of Jahāngīr), in the version by Rogers and Beveridge (1905), p. 356.

[10] R. A. Nicholson, *Mystics of Islam* (1914), p. 105. Similarly, "If he [the follower of any particular religion] understood the saying of Junayd, 'The color of the water is the color of the water containing it,' he would not interfere with the beliefs of others, but would perceive God in every form and in every belief" (Ibn al-'Arabī, Nicholson, *Studies in Islamic Mysticism* [1921], p. 159). And, "Henceforth I knew that there were not many gods of human worship, but one God only, who was polyonomous and polymorphous, being figured and named according to the variety of the outward condition of things" (Sir George Birdwood, *Sva* [1915], p. 28).

The Ka'ba is but a church if there His trace be lost:
My Ka'ba is whatever "church" in which His trace is found.[11]

Similarly in Hinduism; the Tamil poet-saint Tāyumānavar, for example, says in a hymn to Śiva:

Thou didst fittingly . . . inspire as Teacher millions of religions. Thou didst in each religion, while it like the rest showed in splendid fullness of treatises, disputations, sciences, [make] each its tenet to be the truth, the final goal.[12]

The *Bhaktakalpadruma* of Pratāpa Siṁha maintains that "every man should, as far as in him lieth, help the reading of the Scriptures, whether those of his own church or those of another."[13]

In the *Bhagavad Gītā* (VII, 21) Śrī Krishna proclaims: "If any lover whatsoever seeks with faith to worship any form [of God] whatever, it is I who am the founder of his faith," and (IV, 11), "However men approach Me, even do I reward them, for the path men take from every side is Mine."[14]

We have the word of Christ himself that he came to call, not the just, but sinners (Matthew 9:13). What can we make out of that, but that, as St. Justin said, "God is the Word of whom the whole human

---

[11] R. A. Nicholson, *Diwānī Shams-i-Tabrīz*, 1898, p. 238, cf. 221. Cf. Farīd ad-Dīn 'Attar, in the *Mantiq at-Tayr*. "Since, then, there are different ways of making the journey, no two [soul-] birds will fly alike. Each finds a way of his own, on this road of mystic knowledge, one by means of the *mihrāb* [prayer niche], and another through the idol."

[12] Sir P. Arunachalam, *Studies and Translations* (Colombo, 1937), p. 201.

[13] Translation by Sir George Grierson, *Journal of the Royal Asiatic Society*, 1908, p. 347.

[14] Schleiermacher rightly maintains (*Reden*, V) that the multiplicity of religions is grounded in the nature of religion itself, and necessary for its complete manifestation—"*Nur in der Totalität aller solcher möglichen Formen kann die ganze Religion wirklich gegeben werden* [Only in the totality of all such possible forms can the whole religion be truly given]." But Schleiermacher claims the highest position for Christianity—on the grounds of its freedom from exclusiveness!

Una veritas in variis signis varie resplendeat [Let the one truth shine variously in various forms]: and in the words of Marsilio Ficino, "Perhaps, indeed, this kind of variety, ordained by God himself, displays a certain admirable adornment of the universe" (*De christiana religione*, c. 4).

Cf. also Ernest Cassirer's exposition of Pico della Mirandola's "defense of the *libertas credendi*," in the *Journal of the History of Ideas*, III, 335.

race are partakers, and those who lived according to Reason are Christians even though accounted atheists. . . . Socrates and Heracleitus, and of the barbarians Abraham and many others." So, too, Meister Eckhart, greatest of the Christian mystics, speaks of Plato (whom the Muslim Jīlī saw in a vision, "filling the world with light") as "that great priest," and as having "found the way ere ever Christ was born." Was St. Augustine wrong when he affirmed that "the very thing that is now called the Christian religion was not wanting amongst the ancients from the beginning of the human race, until Christ came in the flesh, after which the true religion, which already existed, began to be called 'Christian'"? Had he not retracted these brave words, the bloodstained history of Christianity might have been otherwise written!

We have come to think of religion more as a set of rules of conduct than as a doctrine about God; less as a doctrine about what we should *be*, than one of what we ought to *do*; and because there is necessarily an element of contingency in every application of principles to particular cases, we have come to believe that theory differs as practice must. This confusion of necessary means with transcendent ends (as if the vision of God could be earned by works) has had unfortunate results for Christianity, both at home and abroad. The more the Church has devoted herself to "social service," the more her influence has declined; an age that regards monasticism as an almost immoral retreat is itself unarmed. It is mainly because religion has been offered to modern men in nauseatingly sentimental terms ("Be good, sweet child," etc.), and no longer as an intellectual challenge, that so many have been revolted, thinking that *that* "is all there is to" religion. Such an emphasis on ethics (and, incidentally, forgetfulness that Christian doctrine has as much to do with art, i.e. manufacture, making, what and how, as it has to do with behavior) plays into the skeptic's hands; for the desirability and convenience of the social virtues is such and so evident that it is felt that if that *is* all that religion means, why bring in a God to sanction forms of conduct of which no one denies the propriety? Why indeed?[15] At the same time this excessive emphasis upon the moral, and neglect of the intellectual virtues (which last

---

[15] The answer can be given in the words of Christopher Dawson: "For when once morality has been deprived of its religious and metaphysical foundations, it inevitably becomes subordinated to lower ends." As he also says, the need for a restoration of the ethics of vocation has become the central problem of society—"vocation" being that station of life to which it has pleased God to call us, and not the "job" to which our own ambitions drive.

alone, in orthodox Christian teaching, are held to survive our dissolution) invite the retorts of the rationalists who maintain that religion has never been anything but a means of drugging the lower classes and keeping them quiet.

Against all that, the severe intellectual discipline that any serious study of Eastern, or even "primitive," religion and philosophy demands can serve as a useful corrective. The task of cooperation in the field of comparative religion is one that demands the highest possible qualifications; if we cannot give our best to the task, it would be safer not to undertake it. The time is fast coming when it will be as necessary for the man who is to be called "educated" to know either Arabic, Sanskrit, or Chinese as it is now for him to read Latin, Greek, or Hebrew. And this, above all, in the case of those who are to teach about other peoples' faiths; for existing translations are often in many different ways inadequate, and if we are to know whether or not it is true that all believing men have hitherto worshiped and still worship one and the same God, whether by his English, Latin, Arabic, Chinese, or Navajo names, one must have searched the scriptures of the world—never forgetting that *sine desiderio mens non intelligit* [without love the mind cannot understand].

Nor may we undertake these activities of instruction with ulterior motives: as in all other educational activities, so here the teacher's effort must be directed to the interest and advantage of the pupil himself, not that he may do good, but that he may be good. The dictum that "charity begins at home" is by no means necessarily a cynicism: it rather takes for granted that to do good is only possible when we are good, and that if we are good we shall do good, whether by action or inaction, speech or silence. It is sound Christian doctrine that a man must first have known and loved himself, his inner man, before he loves his neighbor.

It is, then, the pupil who comes first in our conception of the teaching of comparative religion. He will be astounded by the effect upon his understanding of Christian doctrine that can be induced by the recognition of similar doctrines stated in another language and by means of what are to him strange or even grotesque figures of thought. In the following of the *vestigia pedis* [footprints], the soul "in hot pursuit of her quarry, Christ," he will recognize an idiom of the language of the spirit that has come down to us from the hunting cultures of the Stone Age; a cannibal philosophy in that of the Eucharist and the Soma sacrifice; and the doctrine of the "seven rays" of the intelligible Sun in that of the Seven Gifts of the Spirit and in the "seven eyes" of the Apocalyptic Lamb and of Cuchulainn. He may find himself far less inclined than he is now to recoil from Christ's harder sayings, or those of St. Paul on the "sundering of soul from spirit." If he balks at the command to hate, not merely his earthly relatives, but "yea, and his own soul also," and prefers the milder wording of the Authorized Version, where "life" replaces "soul," or if he would like to interpret in a merely ethical sense the command to "deny himself," although the word that is rendered by "deny" means "utterly reject"; if he now begins to realize that the "soul" is of the dust that returns to the dust when the spirit returns to God who gave it, and that equally for Hebrew and Arabic theologians this "soul" (*nefesh, nafs*) imports that carnal "individuality" of which the Christian mystics are thinking when they say that "the soul must put itself to death"; or that our existence (distinguishing *esse* from *essentia,* γένεσις [*genesis*] from οὐσία [*ousia*], *bhū* from *as*) is a crime; and if he correlates all these ideas with the Islamic and Indian exhortation to "die before you die" and with St. Paul's "I live, yet *not I,*" then he may be less inclined to read into Christian doctrine any promise of eternal life for any "soul" that has been concreated with the body—and better equipped to show that the spiritualists' "proofs" of the survival of human personality, however valid, have no religious bearings whatever.

The mind of the democratic student to whom the very name of the concept of a "divine right" may be unintelligible is likely to be roughly awakened if he ever realizes that, as Professor Buckler often reminds us, the very notion of a *kingdom* of God on earth "depends for its revelation on the inner meaning of eastern kingship," for he may have forgotten in his righteous detestation of all dictatorships, that the classical definition of "tyranny" is that of "a king ruling in his own interests."

Nor is this a one-sided transaction; it would not be easy to exaggerate the alteration that can be brought about in the Hindu's or Buddhist's estimate of Christianity when the opportunity is given him to come into closer contact with the quality of thought that led Vincent of Beauvais to speak of Christ's "ferocity" and Dante to marvel at "the multitude of teeth with which this Love bites."

"Some contemplate one Name, and some another? Which of these is the best? All are eminent dues to the transcendent, immortal, unembodied Brahma: these Names are to be contemplated, lauded, and at last denied. For by them one rises higher and higher in these worlds; but where all comes to its end, there he attains to the Unity of the Person" (*Maitri Upaniṣad*). Whoever knows this text, but nothing of Western technique, will assuredly be moved by a sympathetic understanding when he learns that the Christian also follows a *via affirmativa* and a *via remotionis*! Whoever has been taught a doctrine of "liberation from the pairs of opposites" (past and future, pleasure and pain, etc., the Symplegades of "folklore") will be stirred by Nicholas of Cusa's description of the wall of Paradise wherein God dwells as "built of contradictories," and by Dante's of what lies beyond this wall as "not in space, nor hath it poles," but "where every where and every when is focused." We all need to realize, with Xenophon, that "when God is our teacher, we come to think alike."

For there are as many of these Hindus and Buddhists whose knowledge of Christianity and of the greatest Christian writers is virtually nil, as there are Christians, equally learned, whose real knowledge of any other religion but their own is virtually nil, because they have never imagined what it might be to *live* these other faiths. Just as there can be no real knowledge of a language if we have never even imaginatively participated in the activities to which the language refers, so there can be no real knowledge of any "life" that one has not in some measure lived. The greatest of modern Indian saints [Ramakrishna] actually practiced Christian and Islamic disciplines, that is, worshiped Christ and Allah, and found that all led to the same goal: he could speak from experience of the equal validity of all these "ways," and feel the same respect for each, while still preferring for himself the one to which his whole being was naturally attuned by nativity, temperament, and training. What a loss it would have been to his countrymen and to the world, and even to Christianity, if he had "become a Christian"! There are many paths that lead to the summit of one and the same mountain; their differences will be the more apparent the lower down we are, but they vanish at the peak; each will naturally take the one that starts from the point at which he finds himself; he who goes round about the mountain looking for another is not climbing. Never let us approach another believer to ask him to become "one of *us*," but approach him with respect as one who is already "one of *His*," who *is*, and from whose invariable beauty all contingent being depends!

17 MYSTICISM

William Stoddart

Except by those who reject it or are ignorant of it entirely, it is generally understood that mysticism claims to be concerned with "Ultimate Reality." The relationship in question is mostly taken to be of an "experiential" kind, and the phrase "mystical experience" is often used—the assumed object of the experience being, precisely, "Ultimate Reality," which is allegedly transcendent and hidden in regard to our ordinary senses. This mystical experience is held to be "incommunicable" and, particularly when doubt is cast on the alleged object of the experience, it is often said to be, in a pejorative sense, purely subjective.

Nevertheless, it would generally be admitted that, as well as "mystical experience," there is also "mystical doctrine." There is thus at least something that can be communicated (for this is what doctrine means), and at the same time something that is "objective," for whatever can be transmitted must needs be objective, even should the object in question prove to be illusory. The subjective as such cannot be transmitted,[1] but its object can—at least in conceptual terms. To say: "I have experienced something indescribable and incommunicable" is already a description and a communication. As such it can be considered objectively by a third party and, depending on the adequacy of the description, the sensitivity of the hearer, and the reality of the object, it can even stir within him a responsive chord. This means that in favorable circumstances it can, to a greater or lesser degree, stimulate in the hearer a similar intuition or "experience."

The assumed object of both "mystical experience" and "mystical doctrine" is Ultimate Reality. Mystical doctrine may call this the One, the Absolute, the Infinite, the Supreme Self, the Supreme Being, or some other name, and mystical experience is deemed to be union

---

[1] In modern subjectivism, what is expressed is only a subject that is already relative, namely the passional, sentimental, and imaginative ego; in order to express itself, it necessarily makes use of objective elements which it chooses arbitrarily, while separating itself arrogantly and foolishly from objective reality. The "purely subjective," in the modern world, can only announce its presence by gasps and howls, and this is the very definition of modern "avant-garde" poetry.

therewith, to whatever degree and in whatever mode. With this end in view, one also speaks of the "mystical way" or the "mystical path." This is the process of "unification" with the One, the Supreme Self, or the Supreme Being,—all of these being names given to Ultimate Reality.

From all of this, it clearly emerges that mysticism or mystical experience has two poles, namely mystical doctrine and the mystical way or path. Thus in mysticism, as in other spheres, it is a question of doctrine and method, or theory and practice. These twin elements of mysticism will be examined in detail in the course of this essay. The validity and justifiability of mysticism, let it be said right away, depend on the validity and justifiability of its object. If this be a reality, the experience is valid and, in the manner described, capable of being communicated to, and evoked in, a third party.

*   *   *

As is often done, I have spoken of mysticism in a manner that might give the impression that mysticism is an independent entity capable of existing in a vacuum. Such an impression would be false, however, since in practice mysticism only makes its appearance within the framework of one or other of the revealed religions. Indeed it would be true to say that mysticism constitutes the inward or spiritual dimension of every religion. Mysticism is esoterism, while the outward religious framework is the respective exoterism. The exoterism is for all, but the corresponding esoterism is only for those who feel a call thereto. Esoterism, unlike exoterism, cannot be imposed. It is strictly a matter of vocation.

It has been said that "all paths lead to the same summit." In this symbol, the variety of religions is represented by the multiplicity of starting-points around the circumferential base of a cone or mountain. The radial, upward, pathways are the mystical paths. The oneness of mysticism is a reality only at the point that is the summit. The pathways are many, but their goal is one. As they approach this goal, the various pathways more and more resemble one another, but only at the Summit do they coincide. Until then, in spite of resemblances and analogies, they remain separate, and indeed each path is imbued with a distinctive perfume or color—Islamic mysticism is clearly not Christian mysticism—but at the Summit these various colors are (still speaking symbolically) reintegrated into the uncolored Light. Islamic mysticism and Christian mysticism are one only in God.

It is this point of "uncolored Light," where the different religions come together, that is the basis of the *philosophia perennis* or *religio perennis*. This is the supra-formal, divine truth which is the source of each religion, and which each religion incorporates. The heart of each exoterism is its corresponding esoterism, and the heart of each esoterism is the *religio perennis*—or esoterism in the pure state.

In all the religions, the goal of mysticism is God, who may also be given such names as the One, the Absolute, the Infinite, the Supreme Self, the Supreme Being.[2] In sapiential or "theosophic" mysticism, the goal is said to be the Truth, conceived as a living Reality capable of being experienced. Mysticism thus has three components: the doctrine concerning God or Ultimate Reality ("mystical doctrine"), "oneness" with God or Ultimate Reality ("mystical experience"), and the movement that leads from the former to the latter ("the mystical path"). In other words: the doctrine of Unity, the experience of Union, and the path of Unification.

Mystical doctrine is one and the same as metaphysics or mystical theology. Mystical experience, when present in a total or at least sufficient degree, is salvation or liberation. And the purpose of the mystical path is "spiritual realization," i.e., the progression from outward to inward, from belief to vision, or (in scholastic terms) from Potency to Act.

* * *

Many people are familiar with the three fundamental modes of spiritual realization proclaimed by Hinduism: *karma-mārga* (the "Way of Action"), *bhakti-mārga* (the "Way of Love"), and *jñāna-mārga* (the "Way of Knowledge"). These correspond to the three degrees or dimensions of Sufism: *makhāfa* ("Fear"), *maḥabba* ("Love"), and *maʿrifa* ("Knowledge" or "Gnosis").[3]

---

[2] This also includes the "non-theistic" religion of Buddhism, since here too Ultimate Reality, variously referred to in different contexts as *Dharma* ("Law"), *Ātmā* ("Self"), *Nirvāna* ("Extinction"), or *Bodhi* ("Knowledge"), is seen as transcendent and absolute.

[3] This word is used purely etymologically, and does not hark back to the current, in the early history of Christianity, known as "gnosticism." "Gnosis," from the Greek, is the only adequate English rendering for the Sanskrit *jñāna* (with which in fact it is cognate) and the Arabic *maʿrifa*.

Strictly speaking, it is only *bhakti* and *jñāna* (i.e., *maḥabba* and *ma'rifa*) that constitute mysticism: mysticism is either a way of Love, a way of Knowledge, or a combination of both. One will recall the occasion in the life of Christ when he was received in the house of the sisters Martha and Mary. What has come to be known in Christianity as the "Way of Martha" is paralleled by the Hindu *karma-mārga*, the way of religious observance and good works. The contemplative or mystical way, on the other hand, is the "Way of Mary," which comprises two modes, namely, *bhakti-mārga* (the "Way of Love") and *jñāna-mārga* (the "Way of Knowledge"). *Karma* as such is purely exoteric, but it is important to stress that there is always a karmic component within both *bhakti* and *jñāna*. The Way of Love and the Way of Knowledge both necessarily contain an element of Fear or conformity. Likewise, the Way of Knowledge invariably contains within it the reality of Love. As for the Way of Love, which is composed of faith and devotion, it contains an indirect element of *jñāna* in the form of dogmatic and speculative theology. This element lies in the intellectual speculation as such, not in its object, the latter being limited by definition,[4] failing which it would not be a question of *bhakti*, but of *jñāna*. In spite of the presence in each Way of elements of the two others, the three Ways *karma*, *bhakti*, and *jñāna* (or *makhāfa*, *maḥabba*, and *ma'rifa*) represent three specific and easily distinguishable modes of religious aspiration.

As for the question as to which of these paths a given devotee adheres to, it is overwhelmingly a matter of temperament and vocation. It is a case where the Way chooses the individual and not the individual the Way.

Historically speaking, Christian mysticism has been characterized in the main by the "Way of Love," whereas Hindu mysticism and Islamic mysticism comprise both the "Way of Love" and the "Way of Knowledge." The language of the "Way of Love" has a remarkably similar ring in whichever mysticism it crops up, but the more jñānic formulations of Hinduism and the more "gnostic" formulations of Sufism tend to strike a foreign note in the ears of those who are

---

[4] In the Way of Love (*bhakti* or *maḥabba*), God is envisaged at the level of "Being" (which has as consequence that the Lord and the worshiper always remain distinct). In the Way of Knowledge (*jñāna* or *ma'rifa*), on the other hand, God is envisaged at the level of "Beyond-Being" or "Essence."

familiar only with Christian, or at any rate bhaktic, forms of spirituality.[5]

* * *

The goal of religion, in all its varieties, is salvation. What, then, is the difference between exoterism and esoterism? Exoterism is formalistic, but faith and devotion can give it depth. Esoterism is "deep"—supra-formal—by definition, and is the apanage only of those with the relevant vocation. Here forms are transcended, in that they are seen as symbolic expressions of the essence. In esoterism too faith is essential, but here it has the meaning of sincerity and total commitment—effort towards "realization." It means the acquisition of the essential virtues of humility and charity, and the opening of the soul to Divine grace. Metaphysically, the difference between exoterism and esoterism, or between formalism and supra-formalism, lies in how the final Goal is envisaged: in exoterism (and in esoterism of the "bhaktic" type), God is envisaged at the level of "Being" (the Creator and the Judge): no matter how deep, how sublime, the exoterist's fervor, Lord and worshiper always remain distinct. In "jñānic" esoterism, on the other hand, God is envisaged at the level of "Beyond-Being" (the Divine Essence). At this level, it is perceived that Lord and worshiper (the latter known to be created in the image of the former) share a common essence, and this opens up the possibility of ultimate Divine Union.

* * *

Reference was made earlier to "subjective" and "objective," and it may be useful to indicate precisely whence these two concepts derive. The most direct key in this regard is the Hindu appellation for the Divinity: *Sat-Chit-Ānanda*. This expression is usually translated as "Being-Consciousness-Bliss." This is accurate, and enables one to see that "Being" is the Divine Object (God Transcendent or Ultimate Reality), "Consciousness" is the Divine Subject (God Immanent or the

---

[5] Those who, by way of exception, have manifested the "Way of Knowledge" in Christianity include such great figures as Dionysius the Areopagite, Meister Eckhart, Albertus Magnus, and Angelus Silesius. It is precisely the works of *jñānins* such as these that have tended to cause ripples in the generally bhaktic climate of Christianity.

Supreme Self), while "Bliss"—the harmonious coming-together of the two—is Divine Union. The most fundamental translation therefore of *Sat-Chit-Ānanda* is "Object-Subject-Union." This is the model, or origin, of all possible objects and subjects, and of the longing of the latter for the former.[6]

This trinitarian aspect of the Divinity is universal, and is found in all religions. In Christianity it is the central dogma: God the Father, God the Son, and God the Holy Spirit. The analogy between the Christian Trinity and "Being-Consciousness-Bliss" can be seen from certain doctrinal expositions of the Greek Fathers and also from St. Augustine's designation of the Christian Trinity as "Being-Wisdom-Life." In Islam, although it is above all the religion of strict monotheism, certain Sufi formulations evoke the selfsame trinitarian aspect of the Divinity. Reference will be made later to the question of spiritual realization, but in Sufism this is essentially mediated by the invocation (*dhikr*) of the Name of God. In this connection it is said that God is not only That which is invoked (*Madhkūr*), but also That within us which invokes (*Dhākir*), and even the invocation itself, since, in the last analysis, this is none other than the internal Act (*Dhikr*) of God.[7] We thus have the ternary *Madhkūr-Dhākir-Dhikr* ("Invoked-Invoker-Invocation"), which is yet another form of the basic ternary "Object-Subject-Union." This cardinal relationship is the very essence of the theory and practice of mysticism, for this "Union" *in divinis* is the prefiguration of and pattern for the union of man with God.[8] Hindu, Christian, and Sufi doctrine coincide in elucidating just why this is so.

*   *   *

One of the most significant characteristics of mystical doctrine stemming from several of the great religions—and made explicit, for example, in the treatises of jñānic or gnostic mystics such as Shankara, Eckhart, and Ibn 'Arabī—is the distinction made, within God Himself, between God and the Godhead, between "Being" and "Essence,"

---

[6] *Sat-Chit-Ānanda* may also be interpreted as "Known-Knower-Knowledge" or "Beloved-Lover-Love."

[7] That this Divine Act should pass through man is the mystery of salvation.

[8] It will easily be seen that it is also the prefiguration of every other union under the sun, for example, conjugal union.

or between "Being" and "Beyond-Being."[9] In ordinary theological doctrine, the fundamental distinction is between God and man, or between the Uncreated and the created. Mystical or esoteric doctrine, on the other hand, makes a distinction within each of these two terms. Thus, within the Uncreated (viewed as the "Divine Essence" or "Beyond-Being"), there is already a *prefiguration* of creation, and this is God as "Being." "Beyond-Being" is the principle of "Being," and God as Being (the immediate Creator of the world) is the principle of existence or creation.

Within creation—itself relative—there is also a distinction to be made, for within creation there is a *reflection* of the Uncreated (the Absolute) in the form of Truth and Virtue, Symbol and Sacrament, Prophet or Redeemer. Once again mystical doctrine renders explicit the reality of mystical union, for it is by uniting himself with the "created" Symbol or Sacrament (for example, in truth, in beauty, in virtue, in the Eucharist, or in the invocation of a Divine Name), that the mystic realizes his union with (or reintegration into) the uncreated Divinity. Only through the sacramental perfecting of the created, can one reach the Uncreated. This is what is meant in Christianity by "the imitation of Christ," or in Islam by the observance of the *Sunna*.

This exposition is taken from the writings of Frithjof Schuon,[10] who has explained how "Being" (the *prefiguration* of the relative in the Absolute) is the uncreated Logos, whereas the *reflection* of the Absolute in the relative (namely: truth, beauty, virtue, Prophet, Savior) is the created Logos. Without this "bridge" (the Logos with its created and uncreated aspects), no contact whatsoever between created and Uncreated, between man and God, would be possible:[11] the gulf between the two would be unbridgeable. This would be "dualism," not "Non-Dualism" (or *Advaita*, to use the term from Shankaran metaphysics), and the very opposite of mysticism.

---

[9] The same distinction is also made by St. Gregory Palamas in his doctrine of the Divine Essence and the Divine Energies.

[10] See especially *Esoterism as Principle and as Way* (London: Perennial Books, 1981).

[11] The error of deism is precisely that it has no concept of the role of the Logos and envisages no such bridge.

The doctrine of the Logos, and its cardinal relevance to the mystical path, can be summarized in diagrammatic form as follows:

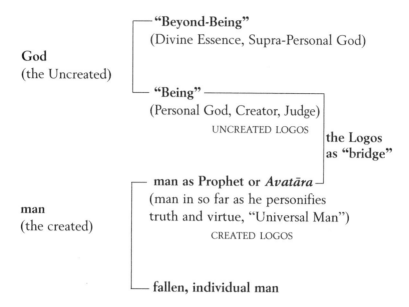

Within each religion, the Founder is the personification of the Logos, and his role as such is always made explicit. Christ said: "No man cometh to the Father but by me." The Prophet Mohammed said: "He that hath seen me, hath seen God." The Buddha said: "He who sees the *Dharma* sees me, and he who sees me sees the *Dharma*." Mystical union is realized only through the Logos.

This brings us directly to the three classical "stages" (*maqāmāt* in Arabic) recognized by all mysticisms:

I.   Purification (or Purgation),
II. Perfection (or Illumination), and
III. Union.

The second stage, "Perfection," corresponds precisely to the aspirant's assimilation to the created Logos. In Christianity, this takes the form of the "imitation of Christ" and in Islam, the observance—inward and symbolically total—of the "Wont of the Prophet" (*Sunna*). Prayers such as the "Hail Mary" (*Ave Maria*) in Catholicism and the "Blessing on the Prophet" (*ṣalāt ʿalā 'n-Nabī*) in Islam, which contain the names of the created Logos (*Jesus* and *Muhammad* respectively), are instrumental to the end in view.

*   *   *

As we have seen, mysticism includes both mystical doctrine and mystical experience. Mystical experience is the inward and unitive "realization" of the doctrine. This is the domain of spiritual method. In Hinduism spiritual method is represented by *yoga*—not the physical exercises derived from *hatha-yoga* now widely experimented with in the West, but *raja-yoga*, the "royal art" of contemplation and union. If, in Hinduism, the *veda* (knowledge) is the *scientia sacra*, then *yoga* (union) is the corresponding *ars sacra* or *operatio sacra*. Here the saying of the Medieval French architect Jean Mignot applies with fullest force: *ars sine scientiā nihil*. One cannot meaningfully or effectively practice anything, if one does not know what one is doing. Above all, one cannot practice a spiritual method except on the basis of previously comprehended spiritual doctrine which is both the motivation and the paradigm for the spiritual work to be undertaken. If doctrine without method is hypocrisy or sterility, then method without doctrine means going astray, and sometimes dangerously. This makes clear why doctrine must be "orthodox"—that is, in essential conformity with the subtle contours of truth. Here it must be noted that pseudo-doctrine, born of nothing more than human invention, is one of the most powerful causes of going astray.

These points have to be stressed, because in the present age many of those attracted by mysticism are eager at all costs for "experience"—without caring to ask themselves: experience of what—and without the safeguards either of conforming to the discipline of a religious tradition or of receiving permission and guidance from a spiritual authority. It is precisely this illegitimate wresting of method from doctrine that is harmful. The more real and effective the spiritual method appropriated, the more dangerous it can be for the appropriator. There are many recorded cases of psychological and spiritual damage resulting from the unauthorized use (i.e., the profanation) of religious rites and sacraments.

In the past, it was the opposite fault that was most likely: to know the truth, but—through weakness, passion, or pride—to fail to put it into practice; in other words, it was a question of hypocrisy, and not the heresy—most commonly in the shape of a "false sincerity"—characteristic of modern times. How typical of the age we live in that, here as elsewhere, it stands on its head! The new shortcoming is infinitely worse than the earlier one. It is forgotten that every "quest" inevitably has an object and, whether one cares to recall it or not, the object of a mystical or spiritual quest is Ultimate Reality or God. With such an object one cannot trifle with impunity.

Yoga is the way or method of union with God, through a dedicated concentration on Him. A particularly direct form of this is (in Hindu terms) *japa-yoga*, which involves the enduring invocation of a *mantra* (a Divine Name or a formula containing a Divine Name). *Mutatis mutandis*, this spiritual method plays a central role in all mysticisms. In Mahāyāna Buddhism, for example, it occurs in the form of the Tibetan *Mani* and the Japanese *Nembutsu*. In Islam, nothing is more enjoined on the spiritual aspirant than *dhikr Allāh*, the "remembrance of God" through the invocation of His Name. In Hesychasm (the mysticism of Eastern Christianity), invocation of the Divine Name takes the form of the "Prayer of Jesus," a practice vividly described in *The Way of a Russian Pilgrim*.[12] The analogous method in Western Christianity is the cult of the Holy Name. This flourished in the Middle Ages, and was also preached with poignancy and single-mindedness in the sixteenth century by St. Bernardino of Siena: "Everything that God has created for the salvation of the world is hidden in the Name of Jesus." The practice was revived, in the form of the invocation *Jesu-Maria*, in the revelations made to Sister Consolata, an Italian Capuchin nun, in the earlier part of this century.[13]

This method of concentrating on a revealed Divine Name indicates clearly that mysticism is the very opposite of giving free rein to man's unregenerate subjectivity. In fact, it is the exposing of his unregenerate subjectivity to the normative and transforming influence of the revealed Object, the Sacrament or Symbol of the religion in question. It was in this respect that St. Paul could say: "Not I, but Christ in me." At the same time, and even more esoterically, it is the exposing of our paltry egoism, seen in turn as an "object," to the withering and yet quickening influence of the divine Subject, the immanent Self.[14] This possibility is envisaged in Islam in the *hadīth qudsī* (a "Divine saying" through the mouth of the Prophet Muhammad): "I (God) am

---

[12] *The Way of a Pilgrim* (London: S.P.C.K., 1954).

[13] *Jesus Appeals to the World* (Staten Island NY: Alba House [Society of St. Paul], 1971).

[14] This synthesis of the dual aspect of realization or method is taken from the writings of Frithjof Schuon. See especially *The Eye of the Heart* (Bloomington, IN: World Wisdom Books, 1997), chapter "Microcosm and Symbol."

the hearing whereby he (the slave) heareth."[15] The vehicle of both processes is the Invocation of a Divine Name (which is both Subject and Object), within a strictly traditional and orthodox framework, and with the authorization of an authentic spiritual master. In this domain, there is no room for curiosity and experiment.

*   *   *

In the mysticisms of several religions, the soul's quest for God is symbolized in terms of the mutual longing of the lover and the beloved. St. John of the Cross, for example, makes use of this symbolism in his mystical poetry, from which the following verses are quoted:

> *Oh noche que guiaste*
> *Oh noche amable más que el alborada:*
> *Oh noche que juntaste*
> *Amado con amada*
> *Amada en el Amado transformada!*

> O night that led'st me thus!
> O night more winsome than the rising sun!
> O night that madest us,
> Lover and lov'd as one,
> Lover transformed in lov'd, love's journey done!
>   (translated by Professor E. Allison Peers)

> *Descubre tu presencia,*
> *Y máteme tu vista y hermosura;*
> *Mira que la dolencia*
> *De amor que no se cura*
> *Sino con la presencia y la figura.*

> Reveal your presence clearly
> And kill me with the beauty you discover,
> For pains acquired so dearly
> From love, cannot recover

---

[15] A similar thought is echoed in the words of St. Teresa of Ávila: "Christ has no body now on earth but yours, no hands but yours, no feet but yours; yours are the eyes through which is to look out Christ's compassion on the world; yours are the feet on which he is to go about doing good, and yours are the hands with which he is to bless us now."

Save only through the presence of the lover.
(translated by Roy Campbell)

As a child of the sixteenth century, St. John of the Cross sought to convey his "subjective" experiences rather than objective doctrine, as the mystics of a few centuries earlier had done. And yet he never wavered from the Divine Object of all mystical striving. At the practical level, in an instruction for aspirants, he said, for example: "All goodness is a loan from God." The soul's subjectivity is uncertain; only the objective reality, that comes from beyond it, is absolutely certain.

* * *

Mysticism was earlier defined as the inward or spiritual dimension contained within every religion—each religion being understood as a separate and specific Divine Revelation. Religion comprises a "periphery" and a "center," in other words, an exoterism and an esoterism. The exoterism is the providential expression or vehicle of the esoterism within it, and the esoterism is the supra-formal essence of the corresponding exoterism. This is why mysticism or esoterism—erroneously regarded by some as "unorthodox"—can in no way subvert the religious formalism of which it is the sap.

On the other hand, "essence" so far transcends "form," that inevitably it sometimes "breaks" it. Conflicts have at times occurred between the purest mysticism and the respective exoteric authority; the cases of Meister Eckhart in medieval Christendom and Al-Ḥallāj in Islam—the one leading to condemnation and the other to martyrdom—provide striking examples. Nevertheless Eckhart enunciated this shattering of forms in a positive way when he said: "If thou wouldst reach the kernel, thou must break the shell." It is hardly necessary to add that such a "transcending" of forms is at the very antipodes of heresy, which is a crude violation of the forms of a religion at their own level. Forms can be transcended only "from above" (or "from within"). To violate—or even simply to neglect—forms "from below" (or "from without") is the very opposite of transcending them. Outwardly man must observe traditional forms as perfectly as possible. This is required for the aspirant's assimilation to the created Logos, as has been explained above. Man can only offer to God—and so transcend—what he has perfected.

Mysticism is the reality of man's love for God and man's union with God. It is a hymn to Subjectivity, a hymn to Objectivity, a hymn to Joy or Union—these three Divine Hypostases being one. It has been stressed how, contrary to certain appearances and contrary to a commonly heard opinion, mysticism is always a flowering within an orthodox framework. But, since mysticism transcends forms "from above" (or "from within"), mysticism knows no bounds. Its essence is one with the Absolute and the Infinite. Let us therefore give the last word to Jalāl ad-Dīn Rūmī, one of the greatest mystics of Islam and one of the greatest mystical poets of all time:

> I am neither Christian nor Jew nor Parsi nor Moslem. I am neither of the East nor of the West, neither of the land nor of the sea. . . . I have put aside duality and have seen that the two worlds are one. I seek the One, I know the One, I see the One, I invoke the One. He is the First, He is the Last, He is the Outward, He is the Inward.

18 THE PERENNIAL PHILOSOPHY

Frithjof Schuon

The term *philosophia perennis*, which has been current since the time of the Renaissance and of which neo-scholasticism made much use, signifies the totality of the primordial and universal truths—and therefore of the metaphysical axioms—whose formulation does not belong to any particular system. One could speak in the same sense of a *religio perennis*, designating by this term the essence of every religion; this means the essence of every form of worship, every form of prayer, and every system of morality, just as the *sophia perennis* is the essence of all dogmas and all expressions of wisdom. We prefer the term *sophia* to that of *philosophia*, for the simple reason that the second term is less direct and because it evokes in addition associations of ideas with a completely profane and all too often aberrant system of thought.

The key to the eternal *sophia* is pure intellection or in other words metaphysical discernment. To "discern" is to "separate": to separate the Real and the illusory, the Absolute and the contingent, the Necessary and the possible, *Ātmā* and *Māyā*. Accompanying discernment, by way of complement and operatively, is concentration, which unites: this means becoming fully aware—from the starting point of earthly and human *Māyā*—of *Ātmā*, which is both absolute and infinite.

According to certain Fathers of the Church, "God became man so that man might become God"; an audacious and elliptical formula which we might paraphrase in a Vedantic fashion by saying that the Real became illusory so that the illusory might become real; *Ātmā* became *Māyā* so that *Māyā* might realize *Ātmā*. This is the very definition of Revelation and of the Revealer; of *Dharma* and of the *Avatāra*.

*   *   *

The decisive error of materialism and agnosticism is the failure to see that the daily experiences of our lives are immeasurably below the stature of our human intelligence. If the materialists were right, this intelligence would be an inexplicable luxury; without the Absolute, the capacity to conceive it would have no cause. The truth of the Absolute coincides with the very substance of our spirit; the various religions actualize objectively what is contained in our deepest subjectivity. Revelation is in the macrocosm what intellection is in the microcosm; the Transcendent is immanent in the world, otherwise the world would not exist, and the Immanent is transcendent in relation to the individual, otherwise It would not surpass him.

What we have said about the scope of human intelligence also applies to the will, in the sense that free-will proves the transcendence of its essential end, for which man was created and because of which man is man; the human will is proportioned to God, and it is only in God and through Him that it is totally free.

One could make an analogous observation in the case of the human soul: our soul proves God because it is proportioned to the divine nature, and it is so by compassion, disinterested love, generosity—and therefore, in the last analysis, by objectivity, the capacity to transcend itself; it is this, precisely, that characterizes the intelligence and the will of man.

And it is in these foundations of human nature—image of the divine nature—that the *religio perennis* has its root.

*   *   *

The most direct doctrinal expression of the *sophia perennis* is undoubtedly *Advaita Vedānta*, with its notions of *Ātmā*, of *Māyā*, and of *Tat tvam asi*; but this doctrine is also found, in one form or another, even if only sporadically in some cases, in the sapiential esoterisms of all the great religions, and this must necessarily be so in that every normal—and thus intrinsically orthodox—religion is itself an indirect and symbolic expression of the eternal *sophia*.

We quoted above the patristic formula which summarizes Christianity and at the same time expresses the *religio perennis*: "God became man so that man might become God." In Islam, the accent is not on the mystery of Divine Manifestation; it is put on that of Divine Oneness, and so on Divine Reality along with the consequences which this essentially comprises; the fundamental expression of this is the testimony of faith: "There is no divinity (= reality) except the (sole) Divinity (= Reality)." In Islam, what saves is not in the first place the Divine Manifestation; it is the acceptance, by the intelligence, of the Divine Oneness, then the fact of drawing from this all the consequences.

To discern the Real; to concentrate on it, or, more precisely, on so much of it as is accessible to us; then to conform morally to its nature; such is the Way, the only one there is. In Christianity, the Real is as if absorbed—with a view to the salvation of man—by its human Manifestation, Christ; concentration is realized through union with Him and through all the forms of prayer and ascesis that contribute thereto, without forgetting the sacraments which confer the corresponding graces; moral conformity demands humility and charity, and on this point Christianity cannot be distinguished from any other spiritual perspective, except by the specific sentimental coloration that it gives to these virtues.[1]

As for Judaism, it is peculiar in that it puts the whole emphasis on God as the partner of His Chosen People, the link between the two parties being the Law; one might also say that it is the latter that receives the whole emphasis since it is situated between God and Israel; if Israel is the People of God, God for His part is the God of Israel, the pact being sealed by the Sinaitic Law. The drama between God and His People reflects the drama between *Ātmā* and *Māyā*, with all its ambiguity and all its final glory, from the double point of view of cosmic rhythms and of the Apocatastasis.

Completely different from the Semitic religions, and even from the Aryan religions, is Buddhism, although it itself arose in an Aryan and theistic climate: in this perspective, the Absolute-Infinite does not take the form of an objective divinity that is at the same time transcendent, immanent, and omnipotent, but appears uniquely—at least *a priori*—under the aspect of an inward state which in reality is beyond all imaginable states, being, precisely, the absolute and infinite State. The concept of *Nirvāna*, though it is clearly non-theistic, is not for all that "atheistic" since it implies the notion of Absolute, Infi-

---

[1] The sacraments, apostolic succession, oral tradition, and the decisions of the first seven councils are essential to Christianity; by more or less rejecting or attenuating these elements, as the case may be, Protestantism seems to have placed itself in a formal position of heterodoxy. But one must not overlook the fact that this movement is the providential result of what we may call a "spiritual archetype", whose laws do not necessarily coincide with outward tradition. Baptism and a fervent piety based on the Bible, on faith, prayer, and morality may suffice for salvation, at least where there are no worldly dissipations; this reservation of course applies to Catholics as well. In any case, one must not accuse original Lutheranism or Calvinism with the faults of the "liberal" Protestantism which followed later, and it is important not to lose sight of the fact that a certain Christian esoterism, namely of Boehme and his line—not forgetting Rosicrucianism—flowered in the climate of Lutheran piety.

nite, and Perfect Reality, which could not be nothingness, except in appearance and in comparison with the world of forms and passions. From another standpoint, *Nirvāna* is objectivized in the form of the Buddha, which brings us back to the patristic formula already quoted, and which we might here paraphrase in the following terms: *Nirvāna* (the "Divine State") became *Samsāra* (= the world) so that *Samsāra* might become *Nirvāna*; now *Nirvāna* become *Samsāra* is none other than the Buddha, who is in practice God as Logos or *Avatāra*.

*　　*　　*

The very expression *philosophia perennis*, and the fact that those who have used it were mostly Thomists, and so Aristotelians, raises the question as to what, in this context, is the value of Greek wisdom, all the more so since it is generally presented as a merely human system of thought. In the first place, by Greek wisdom we mean, not just any philosophy of Classical Antiquity, but essentially Platonism with its Pythagorean root and its Plotinian prolongation; on this basis, one can even accept Aristotelianism, but on the express condition that it is combined—as in the spirit of the Muslim philosophers—with Platonism in the widest sense, of which it is then like a particular and more or less secondary dimension.[2] Then one must take account of the following, which is essential: Greek wisdom presupposes, on the one hand, initiation into the Mysteries and on the other hand the practice of the virtues; basically it pertains to gnosis—to the *jñāna* of the Hindus—even when it deals with things that have no connection with knowledge; admittedly, Aristotelianism is not a *jñāna*, but it nevertheless derives from a perspective which specifically pertains to this order. Aristotelianism is a metaphysics which made the mistake of opening itself towards the world, towards the sciences, towards experience, but which is no less logically valid for all that, whereas Platonism contemplates Heaven, the archetypes, the eternal values.

If on the one hand the Greek spirit—through Aristotelianism but also and above all through the sophists and the skeptics—gave rise to the aberration of profane and rationalistic philosophy, it also provided—especially through Platonism—elements that were highly

---

[2] As for Stoicism, one hesitates to bring it into this synthesis, in spite of the interest of its moral idealism, and in spite of the influence that it exerted for this very reason. Its pantheistic immanentism can be viewed either as an intentionally fragmentary perspective exclusively aimed at a heroic morality, or as a heterodoxy pure and simple.

useful not only for the various theologies of Semitic origin, but also for the esoteric speculations that accompany them and are superimposed upon them; we should not forget that for certain Sufis, Plato enjoys the prestige of a kind of prophet, and Meister Eckhart calls him "that great priest" who "found the way ere ever Christ was born".

*   *   *

Situated in a sense at the antipodes of Greek philosophy—and some will doubtless be surprised that we should mention them—are the disparate and highly unequal traditions that can be classed under the epithet shamanism. On the one hand, this traditional current, belated witness of the Primordial Tradition, gave birth to the ancient Chinese religion, then to its two complementary crystallizations, Confucianism and Taoism; it is to this current moreover that all the ancient Mongol religions belong, Shintōism as well as Bön, and the religion of Genghis Khan. On the other hand, this same current is manifested in the shamanism of the Indians of America, although in very different forms from those it assumes in Asia; but American shamanism has this feature in common with the Asiatic—and it is a feature moreover that characterizes all Hyperborean shamanism—namely that it is founded on the cult of the phenomena of nature and thus on a sort of immanent "pantheism",[3] in other words it envisages virgin nature as the Manifestation of the Divine Principle, and not otherwise.[4]

Obviously, the interest of shamanism does not lie in its abuse of magic and of oracles; it lies in its having its root in virgin nature and in its primordial sense of the sacred, and so in the "primordiality" of its cultic expressions, including the characteristic phenomenon of "autoprophetism", from which, moreover, the function of the shaman derives by exteriorization. The sacred Scripture of shamanism is contained, not in a book, but in the symbols of nature on the one hand and in the substance of the soul on the other, the soul moreover

---

[3] We would recall here that "pantheism"—like "polytheism"—is only an error when it is interpreted in a narrowly literal fashion, in accordance with the *Deus sive natura* of Spinoza, but not when the aspect of Manifestation presupposes and includes that of Transcendence.

[4] It is difficult to know for certain—and we have no intention of pursuing this simple question of fact—whether the traditions of the peoples who possess no writing, those of the Africans for example, also pertain to shamanism—not Mongolian of course—or whether they constitute different branches of the primordial current; this is independent of the question of their present-day level.

reflecting, and prolonging, the external world; from this it results that if on the one hand the dogmas of this religion are expressed by the signs of surrounding nature, on the other hand the soul has access to the mysteries to the extent that it is capable, morally and ritually, of detaching itself from appearances and entering into contact with its own supernatural essence.[5] All this is true in principle and virtually, and must not make us forget the degeneration of vast sectors of shamanism; but it is not the accidental human facts that matter here, it is the principle envisaged and its fundamental reality.

These survivals of the Primordial Tradition contain a message that is addressed to every man conscious of the human vocation, and this is a consciousness of the sacred character of the universal sanctuary constituted by virgin nature, which includes the most modest flower as well as the stars; it is also the consciousness of the immanence, in the depths of the heart, of the one and total Revelation. But this truth would in practice be nothing without the following one, which shamanism cannot give us, namely that the *religio perennis*, as integral Doctrine and saving Way, is inherent in the great and intrinsically orthodox traditions of humanity, and that it is in them that one must seek and not elsewhere.

---

[5] "Our Sacred Book is Nature," an American Indian told us, "and our reading is Inspiration." It is unnecessary to add that this religion is not a matter of improvisation and is not accessible—integrally and *a priori*—to every man, even if he be Indian especially in the conditions of the present-day world. We may add that Zen rests on the same principle as shamanistic autoprophetism, while on the other hand this principle gives rise in our time to the most pernicious falsifications, in contempt of the most elementary traditional rules. "Look for everything within yourselves," the false prophets tell us, without explaining how, and above all while accepting or creating conditions, which go in exactly the opposite direction; all this despite the warnings of the Logos: "Whoso gathereth not with Me scattereth," and likewise, "Without Me ye can do nothing."

VI

BEAUTY

*It is told that once Ananda, the beloved disciple of the
Buddha, saluted his master and said: "Half of the holy
life, O master, is friendship with the beautiful, association with the beautiful, communion with the beautiful."
"Say not so, Ananda, say not so!" the master replied.
"It is not half the holy life;
it is the whole of the holy life."*

<small>SAMYUTTA NIKĀYA</small>

19 FOUNDATIONS OF AN INTEGRAL AESTHETICS

Frithjof Schuon

Esoterism comprises four principal dimensions: an intellectual dimension, to which doctrine bears witness; a volitive or technical dimension, which includes the direct and indirect means of the way; a moral dimension, which concerns the intrinsic and extrinsic virtues; and an aesthetic dimension, to which pertain symbolism and art from both the subjective and objective point of view.

Exoterically, beauty represents either an excusable or an inexcusable pleasure, or an expression of piety and thereby the expression of a theological symbolism; esoterically, it has the role of a spiritual means in connection with contemplation and interiorizing "remembrance". By "integral aesthetics" we mean in fact a science that takes account not only of sensible beauty but also of the spiritual foundations of this beauty,[1] these foundations explaining the frequent connection between the arts and initiatic methods.

Aesthetics as such, being the science of the beautiful, concerns the laws of objective beauty as well as those ruling the sensation occasioned by the beautiful. Something is objectively beautiful when it expresses in a particular fashion or other an aspect of cosmic splendor which, in the final analysis, is divine splendor, and that it does so in accordance with the principles of hierarchy and equilibrium this splendor contains and requires. The perception of beauty, being a rigorous adequation and not a subjective illusion, essentially implies on the one hand a satisfaction of the intelligence and on the other a sentiment of security, infinity, and love. It implies security, because beauty is unitive and excludes, by means of a kind of musical evidence, the fissures of doubt and worry; of infinity, because beauty, by its very musicality, melts all hardness and limitations thus freeing the soul from its constrictions,

---

[1] One must not confuse aesthetics with aestheticism: the second term, used to describe a literary and artistic movement in England in the nineteenth century, means in general an excessive preoccupation with aesthetic values real or imaginary, or at any rate very relative. However, one must not too readily cast aspersions upon romantic aesthetes, who had the merit of a nostalgia that was very understandable in a world that was sinking into a hopeless mediocrity and a cold and inhuman ugliness.

be it only in a minute or remote way; and of love, because beauty in conjuring love draws the soul to union and hence to unitive extinction. All of these factors produce the satisfaction of intelligence which spontaneously divines in beauty—inasmuch as it understands it—the truth and the good, or reality and its power to liberate.

*   *   *

The Divine Principle is the Absolute and, being the Absolute, it is the Infinite; it is from Infinity that manifesting or creating *Māyā* arises; and this Manifestation realizes a third hypostatic quality, namely Perfection. Absoluteness, Infinity, Perfection; and consequently beauty, in so far as it is a manifestation, requires perfection, and perfection is realized on the one hand through absoluteness and on the other hand through infinity: in reflecting the Absolute, beauty realizes a mode of regularity, and in reflecting the Infinite, it realizes a mode of mystery. Beauty, being perfection, is regularity and mystery; it is through these two qualities that it stimulates and at the same time appeases the intelligence and also a sensibility which is in conformity with the intelligence.

In sacred art, one finds everywhere and of necessity, regularity and mystery. According to a profane conception, that of classicism, it is regularity that produces beauty; but the beauty concerned is devoid of space and depth, because it is without mystery and consequently without any vibration of infinity. It can certainly happen in sacred art that mystery outweighs regularity, or vice versa, but the two elements are always present; it is their equilibrium which creates perfection.

Cosmic Manifestation necessarily reflects or projects the Principle both according to absoluteness and according to infinity; inversely, the Principle contains or prefigures the root of Manifestation, and so of Perfection, and this is the *Logos*. The *Logos* combines *in divinis* regularity and mystery, it is so to speak the manifested Beauty of God; but this manifestation remains principial, it is not cosmic. It has been said that God is a geometer, but it is important to add that He is just as much a musician.

Absolute, Infinite, Perfection: the first could be represented by a point, the second by the radii extending from it, and the third by the circle. Perfection is the Absolute projected, by virtue of Infinitude, into relativity; it is by definition adequate, but it is not the Absolute, or in other words, it is a kind of Absolute—namely, the manifested Absolute—but not the Absolute as such; and by "manifested Absolute" one must always understand: manifested in such and such a way. The Infinite is Divine Femininity, and it is from it that Manifestation proceeds; in the Infinite, Beauty is essential, and so formless, undifferentiated, and unarticulated, whereas in and through Manifestation it coagulates and becomes tangible, not only because of the very fact of exteriorization, but also, and positively, by virtue of its content, image of the Absolute and factor of necessity, and so of regularity.

The cosmic, or more particularly the earthly function of beauty is to actualize in the intelligent creature the Platonic recollection of the archetypes, all the way into the luminous Night of the Infinite.[2] This leads us to the conclusion that the full understanding of beauty demands virtue and is identifiable with it: that is to say, just as it is necessary to distinguish, in objective beauty, between the outward structure and the message in depth, so there is a *distinguo* to make, in the sense of beauty, between the aesthetic sensation and the corresponding beauty of soul, namely such and such a virtue. Beyond every question of "sensible consolation" the message of beauty is both intellectual and moral: intellectual because it communicates to us, in the world of accidentality, aspects of Substance, without for all that having to address itself to abstract thought; and moral, because it reminds us of what we must love, and consequently be.

*   *   *

In conformity with the Platonic principle that like attracts like, Plotinus states that "it is always easy to attract the Universal Soul . . . by constructing an object capable of undergoing its influence and receiving its participation. Now the image-like representation of a thing is always capable of undergoing the influence of its model; it is like a mirror which is capable of grasping the thing's appearance."[3]

This passage states the crucial principle of the almost magical relationship between the conformity of the recipient and the predestined content or between the adequate symbol and the sacramental pres-

---

[2] According to Pythagoras and Plato, the soul has heard the heavenly harmonies before being exiled on earth, and music awakens in the soul the remembrance of these melodies.

[3] This principle does not prevent a heavenly influence manifesting itself incidentally or accidentally even in an image which is extremely imperfect—works of perversion and subversion being excluded—through pure mercy and by virtue of the "exception that proves the rule".

ence of the prototype. The ideas of Plotinus must be understood in the light of those of the "divine Plato": the latter approved the fixed types of the sacred sculptures of Egypt, but he rejected the works of the Greek artists who imitated nature in its outward and insignificant accidentality, while following their individual imagination. This verdict immediately excludes from sacred art the productions of an exteriorizing, accidentalizing, sentimentalist, and virtuoso naturalism, which errs through abuse of intelligence as much as by omission of the inward and the essential.

Likewise, and for even stronger reasons: the inadequate soul, that is to say, the soul not in conformity with its primordial dignity as "image of God", cannot attract the graces which favor or even constitute sanctity. According to Plato, the eye is "the most solar of instruments", which Plotinus comments on as follows: "The eye would never have been able to see the sun if it were not itself of solar nature, any more than the soul could see the beautiful if it were not itself beautiful." Platonic Beauty is an aspect of Divinity, and this is why it is the "splendor of the True": this amounts to saying that Infinity is in some fashion the aura of the Absolute, or that *Māyā* is the *shakti* of *Ātmā*, and that consequently every hypostasis of the absolute Real—whatever be its degree—is accompanied by a radiance which we might seek to define with the help of such notions as "harmony", "beauty", "goodness", "mercy", and "beatitude".

"God is beautiful and He loves beauty", says a *hadīth* which we have quoted more than once:[4] *Ātmā* is not only *Sat* and *Chit*, "Being" and "Consciousness"—or more relatively: "Power" and "Omniscience"—but also *Ānanda*, "Beatitude", and thus Beauty and Goodness;[5] and what we want to know and realize, we must *a priori* mirror in our own being, because in the domain of positive realities[6] we can only know perfectly what we are.

---

[4] Another *hadīth* reminds us that "the heart of the believer is sweet, and it loves sweetness (*halawah*)". The "sweet", according to the Arabic word, is at the same time the pleasing, coupled with a nuance of spring-like beauty; which amounts to saying that the heart of the believer is fundamentally benevolent because having conquered the hardness that goes with egoism and worldliness, he is made of sweetness or generous beauty.

[5] When the Koran says that God "has prescribed for Himself Mercy (*Rahmah*)", it affirms that Mercy pertains to the very Essence of God; moreover, the notion of Mercy does not do justice, except in a partial and extrinsic way, to the beatific nature of the Infinite.

[6] This reservation means that we do not know privative realities—which, precisely,

*   *   *

The elements of beauty, be they visual or auditive, static or dynamic, are not only pleasant, they are above all true and their pleasantness comes from their truth: this is the most obvious, and yet the least understood truth of aesthetics. Furthermore, as Plotinus remarked, every element of beauty or harmony is a mirror or receptacle which attracts the spiritual presence that corresponds to its form or color, if one may so express it; if this applies as directly as possible to sacred symbols, it is also true, in a less direct and more diffuse way, in the case of all things that are harmonious and therefore true. Thus, an artisanal ambience made of sober beauty—for there is no question of sumptuousness except in very special cases—attracts or favors *barakah*, "blessing"; not that it creates spirituality any more than pure air creates health, but it is at all events in conformity with it, which is much, and which, humanly, is the normal thing.

In spite of these facts, which would seem to be quite obvious and which are corroborated by all the beauties that Heaven has bestowed on the traditional worlds, some will doubtless ask what connection there can be between the aesthetic value of a house, of an interior decoration, or of a tool and spiritual realization: did Shankara ever concern himself with aesthetics or morality? The answer to this is that the soul of a sage of this caliber is naturally beautiful and exempt from every pettiness, and that furthermore, an integrally traditional environment—especially in a milieu like that of the *brahmins*—largely if not absolutely excludes artistic or artisanal ugliness; so much so that Shankara had nothing to teach—nor *a fortiori* to learn—on the subject of aesthetic values, unless he had been an artist by vocation and profession, which he was not, and which his mission was far from demanding.

To be sure, the sensation of the beautiful may in fact be only a pleasant experience, depending on the degree of receptiveness; but according to its nature and of course by virtue of its object, it offers to the intellect, in parallel with its musicality, an intellectual satisfaction, and thus an element of knowledge.

It is necessary to dissipate here an error which would have it that everything in nature is beautiful because it belongs to nature and

---

manifest unreality—except by contrast; for example, the soul understands moral ugliness to the extent that it itself is morally beautiful, and it cannot be beautiful except by participation in Divine Beauty, Beauty in itself.

everything of traditional production is likewise beautiful because it belongs to tradition; as a result, according to this view ugliness does not exist either in the animal or the vegetable kingdoms, since, it would seem, every creature "is perfectly what it should be", which has really no connection with the aesthetic question; likewise it is said that the most magnificent of sanctuaries possesses no more beauty than some tool or other, always because the tool "is everything that it should be". This is tantamount to maintaining not only that an ugly animal species is aesthetically the equivalent of a beautiful species, but also that beauty is such merely through the absence of ugliness and not through its own content, as if the beauty of a man were the equivalent of that of a butterfly, or of a flower, or a precious stone. Beauty, however, is a cosmic quality which cannot be reduced to abstractions foreign to its nature; likewise, the ugly is not only that which is not completely what it is supposed to be, nor is it only an accidental infirmity or a lack of taste; it is in everything which manifests, accidentally or substantially, artificially or naturally, a privation of ontological truth, of existential goodness, or, what amounts to the same, of reality. Ugliness is, very paradoxically, the manifestation of a relative nothingness: of a nothingness which can affirm itself only by denying or eroding an element of Being, and thus of beauty. This amounts to saying that, in a certain fashion and speaking elliptically, the ugly is less real than the beautiful, and in short that it exists only thanks to an underlying beauty which it disfigures; in a word, it is the reality of an unreality, or the possibility of an impossibility, like all privative manifestations.

* * *

The argument that aesthetic quality is far from always coinciding with moral quality and that it is consequently superfluous—an argument that is just in its observation but false in its conclusion—overlooks an obvious fact, namely that the ontological and in principle spiritual merit of beauty remains intact on its own level; the fact that an aesthetic quality may not be fully exploited does not mean that it could not and should not be, and it would then prove its spiritual potentiality and so its true nature. Inversely, ugliness is a privation even when it is allied to sanctity, which cannot make it positive, but which obviously neutralizes it, just as moral badness sterilizes beauty, but without abolishing it as far as the existential, not the volitive, aspect is concerned.[7]

The dilemma of moralists enclosed within a "black or white" alternative is resolved metaphysically by the complementarity between transcendence and immanence: according to the first perspective nothing is really beautiful because God alone is Beauty; according to the second, every beauty is really beautiful because it is that of God. Consequently every beauty is both a closed door and an open door, or in other words, an obstacle and a vehicle: either beauty separates us from God because it is entirely identified in our mind with its earthly support which then assumes the role of idol, or beauty brings us close to God because we perceive in it the vibrations of Beatitude and Infinitude which emanate from Divine Beauty.[8]

Most paradoxically, what we have just said also applies to the virtues; the Sufis insist on it. Like physical beauties, moral beauties are both supports and obstacles: they are supports thanks to their profound nature, which ontologically belongs to God, and obstacles to the extent that man attributes them to himself as merits, whereas they are only openings towards God in the darkness of human weakness.

Virtue cut off from God becomes pride, as beauty cut off from God becomes idol; and virtue attached to God becomes sanctity, as beauty attached to God becomes sacrament.

[7] There is all the difference, in a face, between the features as such and the expression, or between the form of a body and its gestures, or again, between the form of an eye and its look. Nevertheless, even the look of a morally imperfect person can have beauty when it expresses the spring of youth, or simply happiness, or a good sentiment, or sadness; but all of this is a question of degree, either in respect of natural beauty or in respect of moral imperfection.

[8] Ramakrishna, when he saw a flight of cranes, a lion, a dancing-girl, used to fall into ecstasy. This is what is called "seeing God everywhere"; not by deciphering the symbolisms, of course, but by perceiving the essences.

20 AN INTRODUCTION TO SACRED ART

Titus Burckhardt

When historians of art apply the term "sacred art" to any and every work that has a religious subject, they are forgetting that art is essentially form. An art cannot properly be called "sacred" solely on the grounds that its subjects originate in a spiritual truth; its formal language also must bear witness to a similar origin. Such is by no means the case with a religious art like that of the Renaissance or of the Baroque period, which is in no way distinct, so far as style is concerned, from the fundamentally profane art of that era; neither the subjects which it borrows, in a wholly exterior and as it were literary manner, from religion, nor the devotional feelings with which it is permeated in appropriate cases, nor even the nobility of soul which sometimes finds expression in it, suffice to confer on it a sacred character. No art merits that epithet unless its forms themselves reflect the spiritual vision characteristic of a particular religion.

Every form is the vehicle of a given quality of being. The religious subject of a work of art may be as it were superimposed, it may have no relation to the formal "language" of the work, as is demonstrated by Christian art since the Renaissance; there are therefore essentially profane works of art with a sacred theme, but on the other hand there exists no sacred work of art which is profane in form, for there is a rigorous analogy between form and spirit. A spiritual vision necessarily finds its expression in a particular formal language; if that language is lacking, with the result that a so-called sacred art borrows its forms from some kind of profane art, then it can only be because a spiritual vision of things is also lacking.

It is useless to try to excuse the Protean style of a religious art, or its indefinite and ill-defined character, on grounds of the universality of dogma or the freedom of the spirit. Granted that spirituality in itself is independent of forms, this in no way implies that it can be expressed and transmitted by any and every sort of form. Through its qualitative essence form has a place in the sensible order analogous to that of truth in the intellectual order; this is the significance of the Greek notion of *eidos*. Just as a mental form such as a dogma or a doctrine can be the adequate, albeit limited, reflection of a Divine Truth, so can a sensible form retrace a truth or a reality which transcends both the plane of sensible forms and the plane of thought.

Every sacred art is therefore founded on a science of forms, or in other words, on the symbolism inherent in forms. It must be borne in mind that a symbol is not merely a conventional sign. It manifests its archetype by virtue of a definite ontological law; as Coomaraswamy has observed, a symbol *is* in a certain sense that to which it gives expression. For this very reason traditional symbolism is never without beauty: according to the spiritual view of the world, the beauty of an object is nothing but the transparency of its existential envelopes; an art worthy of the name is beautiful because it is true.

It is neither possible nor even useful that every artist or craftsman engaged in sacred art should be conscious of the Divine Law inherent in forms; he will know only certain aspects of it, or certain applications that arise within the limits of the rules of his craft; these rules will enable him to paint an icon, to fashion a sacred vessel, or to practice calligraphy in a liturgically valid manner, without its being necessary for him to know the ultimate significance of the symbols he is working with. It is tradition that transmits the sacred models and the working rules, and thereby guarantees the spiritual validity of the forms. Tradition has within itself a secret force which is communicated to an entire civilization and determines even arts and crafts whose immediate uses include nothing particularly sacred. This force creates the style of a traditional civilization; a style that could never be imitated from outside is perpetuated without difficulty, in a quasi-organic manner, by the power of the spirit that animates it and by nothing else.

One of the most tenacious of typically modern prejudices is the one that sets itself up against the impersonal and objective rules of an art, for fear that they should stifle creative genius. In reality no work exists that is traditional, and therefore "bound" by changeless principles, which does not give sensible expression to a certain creative joy of the soul; whereas modern individualism has produced, apart from a few works of genius which are nevertheless spiritually barren, all the ugliness—the endless and despairing ugliness—of the forms which permeate the "ordinary life" of our times.

One of the fundamental conditions of happiness is to know that everything that one does has a meaning in eternity; but who in these days can still conceive of a civilization within which all vital manifestations would be developed "in the likeness of Heaven"?[1] In a theocentric society the humblest activity participates in this heavenly benediction. The words of a street singer heard by the author in Morocco are worth quoting here. The singer was asked why the little Arab guitar which he used to accompany his chanting of legends had only two strings. He gave this answer: "To add a third string to this instrument would be to take the first step towards heresy. When God created the soul of Adam it did not want to enter into his body, and circled like a bird round about its cage. Then God commanded the angels to play on the two strings that are called the male and the female, and the soul, thinking that the melody resided in the instrument—which is the body—entered it and remained within it. For this reason two strings, which are always called the male and the female, are enough to deliver the soul from the body."

This legend holds more meaning than appears at first sight, for it summarizes the whole traditional doctrine of sacred art. The ultimate objective of sacred art is not the evocation of feelings nor the communication of impressions; it is a symbol, and as such it finds simple and primordial means sufficient; it could not in any case be anything more than allusive, its real object being ineffable. It is of angelic origin, because its models reflect supra-formal realities. It recapitulates the creation—the "Divine Art"—in parables, thus demonstrating the symbolical nature of the world, and delivering the human spirit from its attachment to crude and ephemeral "facts."

The angelic origin of art is explicitly formulated by the Hindu tradition. According to the *Aitareya Brāhmana* every work of art in the world is achieved by imitation of the art of the *devas*, "whether it be an elephant in terra-cotta, a bronze object, an article of clothing, a gold ornament, or a mule-cart."* The *devas* correspond to the angels. Christian legends attributing an angelic origin to certain miraculous images embody the same idea.

The *devas* are nothing more nor less than particular functions of the universal Spirit, permanent expressions of the Will of God. The

---

[1] "Do you not know, O Asclepius, that Egypt is the image of Heaven and that it is the projection here below of the whole ordering of Heavenly things?" (*Hermes Trismegistus*, from the French translation of L. Ménard).

* Editors' Note: cf. the Divine instruction to Moses in the Jewish scriptures: "Make all things according to the pattern which was shown thee on the mount" (Exodus 25:40; cf. Hebrews 8:5).

doctrine common to traditional civilizations prescribes that sacred art must imitate the Divine Art, but it must be clearly understood that this in no way implies that the complete Divine creation, the world such as we see it, should be copied, for such would be pure pretension; a literal "naturalism" is foreign to sacred art. What must be copied is the way in which the Divine Spirit works. Its laws must be transposed into the restricted domain in which man works as man, that is to say, into artisanship.

*   *   *

In no traditional doctrine does the idea of the Divine Art play so fundamental a part as in the Hindu doctrine. For *Māyā* is not only the mysterious Divine Power which causes the world to appear to exist outside the Divine Reality, so that it is from her, from *Māyā*, that all duality and all illusion spring: she is also in her positive aspect the Divine Art which produces all form. In principle she is not other than the possibility contained in the Infinite of limiting Itself, as the object of Its own "vision," without Its infinity being thereby limited. Thus God manifests Himself in the world, yet equally He does not so manifest Himself; He expresses Himself and at the same time keeps silence.

Just as the Absolute objectivizes, by virtue of its *Māyā* certain aspects of Itself, or certain possibilities contained in Itself, and determines them by a distinctive vision, so does the artist realize in his work certain aspects of himself; he projects them as it were outside his undifferentiated being. And to the extent that his objectivation reflects the secret depths of his being, it will take on a purely symbolical character, and at the same time the artist will become more and more conscious of the abyss dividing the form, reflector of his essence, from what that essence really is in its timeless plenitude. The creative artist knows this: this form is myself, nevertheless I am infinitely more than it, for the Essence remains the pure Knower, the witness which no form can compass; but he also knows that it is God who expresses Himself through his work, so that the work in its turn surpasses the feeble and fallible ego of the man.

Herein lies the analogy between Divine Art and human art: in the realization of oneself by objectivation. If this objectivation is to have spiritual significance and not to be merely a vague introversion, its means of expression must spring from an essential vision. In other words, it must not be the "I," that root of illusion and of ignorance of oneself, which arbitrarily chooses those means; they must be borrowed from tradition, from the formal and "objective" revelation of the supreme Being, Who is the "Self" of all beings.

*   *   *

From the Christian point of view God is similarly "artist" in the most exalted sense of the word, because He created man "in His own image" (Genesis 1:27). And moreover since the image comprises not only a likeness to its model, but also a quasi-absolute unlikeness, it could not but become corrupted. The divine reflection in man was troubled by the fall of Adam; the mirror was tarnished; but nevertheless man could not be completely cast aside; for while the creature is subject to its own limitations, the Divine Plenitude on the other hand is not subject to limitation of any kind, and this amounts to saying that the said limitations cannot be in any real sense opposed to the Divine Plenitude, which is manifested as limitless Love. The very limitlessness of that Love demands that God, "pronouncing" Himself as Eternal Word, should descend into this world, and as it were assume the perishable outlines of the image—human nature—so as to restore to it its original beauty.

In Christianity the divine image *par excellence* is the human form of the Christ;* thus it comes about that Christian art has but one purpose: the transfiguration of man, and of the world which depends on man, by their participation in the Christ.

---

* Editors' Note: Elsewhere the author writes: "The tradition of the sacred image is related to established prototypes . . . handed down in Christian art, the most important [of which] is the *acheiropoietos* ("not made by human hands") image of the Christ on the *Mandilion*. It is said that the Christ gave His image, imprinted on a piece of fabric, to the messengers of the King of Edessa, Abgar, who had asked Him for His portrait. The *Mandilion* had been preserved at Constantinople until it disappeared when the town was pillaged by the Latin Crusaders. A copy of the *Mandilion* is preserved in the cathedral of Laon. . . . It may also be noted that the imprint preserved on the Holy Shroud of Turin . . . resembles in a striking way, so far as characteristic details are concerned, the *acheiropoietos* image. . . . Another prototype, no less important, is the image of the Virgin attributed to St. Luke; it is preserved in numerous Byzantine replicas. Latin Christianity too possesses models consecrated by tradition, such as for example the Holy Countenance (*Volto Santo*) of Lucca, which is a crucifix carved in wood, Syrian in style, attributed by legend to Nicodemus the disciple of Christ" (Titus Burckhardt, *Sacred Art in East and West* [Louisville, KY: Fons Vitae/Bloomington, IN: World Wisdom, 2001], pp. 88-89).

*   *   *

That which the Christian view of things grasps by means of a sort of loving concentration on the Word incarnate in Jesus Christ, is transposed in the Islamic view into the universal and the impersonal. In Islam the Divine Art—and according to the Koran God is "artist" (*musawwir*)—is in the first place the manifestation of the Divine Unity in the beauty and regularity of the cosmos. Unity is reflected in the harmony of the multiple, in order, and in equilibrium; beauty has all these aspects within itself. To start from the beauty of the world and arrive at Unity—that is wisdom. For this reason Islamic thought necessarily attaches art to wisdom; in the eyes of a Muslim, art is essentially founded on wisdom, or on science, the function of science being the formulation of wisdom in temporal terms. The purpose of art is to enable the human environment, the world in so far as it is molded by man, to participate in the order that manifests most directly the Divine Unity. Art clarifies the world; it helps the spirit to detach itself from the disturbing multitude of things so that it may climb again towards the Infinite Unity.*

*   *   *

According to the Taoist view of things the Divine Art is essentially the art of transformation: the whole of nature is ceaselessly being transformed, always in accordance with the laws of the cycle; its contrasts revolve round a single center which always eludes apprehension. Nevertheless anyone who understands this circular movement is thereby enabled to recognize the center which is its essence. The purpose of art is to conform to this cosmic rhythm. The most simple formula

---

* Editors' Note: "The prohibition of images in Islam applies, strictly speaking, only to the image of the Divinity; it stands, therefore, in the perspective of the Decalogue, or more exactly of Abrahamic monotheism, which Islam sees itself as renewing. In its last manifestation as in its first—in the time of Muhammad as in the age of Abraham— monotheism directly opposes idolatrous polytheism, so that any plastic representation of the divinity is for Islam . . . the distinctive mark of the error which 'associates' the relative with the Absolute, or the created with the Uncreated, by reducing the level of the one to the other. . . . Thus it is that portraiture of the divine messengers (*rusūl*), prophets (*anbiyā*), and saints (*awliyā*) is avoided, not only because their images could become the object of idolatrous worship, but also because of the respect inspired by their inimitability" (Titus Burckhardt, *Art of Islam: Language and Meaning* [London: World of Islam Festival Trust, 1976], p. 26).

states that mastery in art consists in the capacity to trace a perfect circle in a single movement, and thus to identify oneself implicitly with its center, while that center remains unspecified as such.*

*   *   *

In so far as it is possible to transpose the notion of "Divine Art" into Buddhism, which avoids all personification of the Absolute, it can be applied to the beauty of the Buddha, miraculous and mentally unfathomable as it is. Whereas no doctrine concerned with God can escape, as far as its formulation is concerned, from the illusory character of mental processes, which attribute their own limits to the limitless and their own conjectural forms to the formless, the beauty of the Buddha radiates a state of being beyond the power of thought to define. This beauty is reflected in the beauty of the lotus: it is perpetuated ritually in the painted or modeled image of the Buddha.*

*   *   *

* Editors' Note: "Far back in Chinese antiquity the whole of Taoist art was summarized in the emblem of a disc perforated in the center. The disc represents the heavens or the cosmos, the void in the center the unique and transcendent Essence. . . . The point of view is the same in landscape paintings of Buddhist (*ch'an*) inspiration, where all the elements, mountains, trees, and clouds, are there only in order to emphasize by contrast the Void out of which they seem to have arisen at that very instant, and from which they are detached like ephemeral islets. . . . A Far Eastern painter is a contemplative, and for him the world is as if it were made of snowflakes, quickly crystallized and soon dissolved. Since he is never unconscious of the non-manifested, the least solidified physical conditions are for him the nearer to the Reality underlying all phenomena; hence the subtle observation of atmosphere that we admire in Chinese painting in ink and wash. . . . Although Taoist-Buddhist painting does not indicate the source of light by the play of light and shade, its landscapes are none the less filled with a light that permeates every form like a celestial ocean with a pearly luster: it is the beatitude of the Void (*shūnya*) that is bright through the absence of all darkness" (Titus Burckhardt, *Sacred Art in East and West*, pp. 183, 185).

* Editors' Note: "According to tradition the *tathāgata* [the Buddha] himself bequeathed his image to posterity: according to the *Divyāvadāna*, King Rudrāyana or Udāyana sent painters to the Blessed One to take his portrait, but while they were trying in vain to capture the likeness of the Buddha, he told them that their (spiritual) laziness was preventing them from succeeding, and he caused a canvas to be brought on to which he 'projected' his own likeness. . . . The body of the Buddha and the lotus; these two forms . . . express the same thing: the immense calm of the Spirit awakened to Itself" (Titus Burckhardt, *Sacred Art in East and West*, pp. 172, 163).

In one way or another all these fundamental aspects of sacred art can be found, in varying proportions, in each of the five great traditions just mentioned, for there is not one of them that does not possess in its essentials all the fullness of Divine Truth and Grace, so that in principle it would be capable of manifesting every possible form of spirituality. Nevertheless, since each religion is necessarily dominated by a particular point of view which determines its spiritual "economy," its artistic manifestations, being naturally collective and not isolated, will reflect this point of view and this economy each in its own style. It is moreover in the nature of form to be unable to express anything without excluding something, because form delimits what it expresses, excluding thereby some aspects of its own universal archetype. This law is naturally applicable at every level of formal manifestation, and not to art alone; the various Divine Revelations on which the different religions are founded are also mutually exclusive when attention is directed to their formal contours only, rather than to their Divine Essence which is one. Here again the analogy between "Divine Art" and human art becomes apparent.

21 DO CLOTHES MAKE THE MAN?
The Significance of Human Attire

Marco Pallis

If a man does not honor his own house, it falls down and crushes him.
Greek Proverb

During an exchange of letters that took place between the late Ananda
K. Coomaraswamy and the present writer during the war years,
discussion once happened to turn on the question of traditional dress
and its neglect, a subject which had frequently occupied my mind in
the course of various journeys through the Himalayan borderlands.
We both agreed that this question was of crucial importance at the
present time, a touchstone by which much else could be judged. Dr.
Coomaraswamy (who henceforth will usually be denoted simply by
his initials A.K.C.) then informed me that his own earliest publication
on any subject other than Geology was precisely concerned with this
question of dress; the paper referred to bore the title of "Borrowed
Plumes" (Kandy, 1905) and was called forth by its author's indignation
at a humiliating incident he witnessed while staying in a remote district
of Ceylon. He further suggested that I might some day treat the same
theme in greater detail; the opportunity came for complying with
his wishes when I was asked to add my personal tribute to a worldwide symposium in honor of the seventieth birthday of that prince of
scholars, whose rare insight had made him the qualified interpreter
and champion of the traditional conception of life not only in India
but everywhere. All that remained, therefore, was for one to apply
to the subject chosen that dialectical method, so typically Indian,
with which A.K.C. himself had made us familiar in his later works:
that is to say, the question at issue had first to be presented under its
most intellectual aspect, by connecting it with universal principles;
after which it became possible, by a process of deduction, to show
the developments to which those principles lent themselves in various
contingencies; until finally their application could be extended, as
required, to the field of human action, whether by way of doing or
undoing. In the present chapter appeal will be made, all along, to the
parallel authority of the Hindu and Islamic traditions, as being the
ones that between them share the Indian scene; such reference being

primarily intended as a guarantee of traditional authenticity, as against a merely human, personal, and private expression of opinion on the part of the writer.

*   *   *

Fundamentally, the question of what kind of clothes a person may or may not wear (like any other similar question) is a matter of *svadharma*, an application of that law or norm of behavior which is intrinsic to every being in virtue of its own particular mode of existence (*svabhava*). By conforming to his norm a man *becomes what he is*, thus realizing the full extent of his possibilities; in so far as he fails, he accepts a measure of self-contradiction and disintegrates proportionally.

The late Sir John Woodroffe, in *Bharata Shakti* (Ganesh, 1921)—a work that ought to be in the hands of every Indian and more especially the young—quotes George Tyrrell as having once written: "I begin to think that the only real sin is suicide or *not being oneself.*" That author was probably thinking in individual terms only; nevertheless, his statement contains echoes of a doctrine of universal scope—from which all its relative validity at the individual level is derived—namely, that the ultimate and only sin is *not to be One Self*, ignorance (*avidya*) of *What one is*, belief that one is *other* than the Self—indeed, on that reckoning we, one and all, are engaged in committing self-murder daily and hourly and we shall continue to do so, paying the penalty meanwhile, until such time as we can finally *recollect ourselves*, thus "becoming what we are."[1]

---

[1] Following Tyrrell, we have used the word "suicide" here in its more usual and unfavorable sense, as denoting an extremity of self-abuse; it can however be taken in a different sense, when it is far from constituting a term of reproach: we are referring to the voluntary self-immolation implied in a phrase like that of Meister Eckhart when he says that "the soul must put itself to death" or in the Buddhist "*atta-m-jaho*" (= "self-noughting" in mediaeval English) which coincides, on the other hand with *bhavit' atto* (= Self-made-become). This whole doctrine, and ultimately our basic thesis in this essay, rests on the principle that "as there are two in him who is both Love and Death, so there are, as all tradition affirms unanimously, two in us; although not two of him or two of us, nor even one of him and one of us, but only one of both. As we stand now, in between the first beginning and the last end, we are divided against ourselves, essence from nature, and therefore see him likewise divided against himself and from us." This quotation is taken from A.K.C.'s two-pronged essay *Hinduism and Buddhism* (New York, 1943); the section dealing with Theology and Autology is strongly recommended to all who wish to understand the meaning of the universal

It has been said that there are three degrees of conformity (*islam*) to the truth; firstly, everyone is *muslim* from the very fact of being at all, since, do as he will, he cannot conceivably move one hairs-breadth out of the orbit of the Divine Will that laid down for him the pattern of his existence; secondly, he is *muslim* in so far as he recognizes his state of dependence and behaves accordingly—this level is represented by his conscious attachment to a tradition, whereby he is able to be informed of what he is and of the means to realize it; and thirdly, he is *muslim* through having achieved perfect conformity, so that henceforth he is identical with his true Self, beyond all fear of parting. In Hindu parlance this same doctrine might be expressed as follows: every being is *yogi* in that any kind of existence apart from the Self is a sheer impossibility, even in the sense of an illusion; that being is a *yogi*—called thus by courtesy, as it were—in so far as he, she, or it strives, by the use of suitable disciplines (*sadhana*), to realize Self-union; the selfsame being is *the Yogi* in virtue of having made that union effective. No element in life can therefore be said to lie outside the scope of *yoga*.

What individual man is, he owes, positively, to his inherent possibilities and, negatively, to his limitations; the two together, by their mutual interplay, constitute his *svabhava* and are the factors which make him uniquely qualified (*adhikari*) for the filling of a certain part in the Cosmic "Play" (*lila*), for which part he has been "cast" by the Divine Producer. Neither possibilities nor limiting conditions are of his own choice—not his either to accept, select, or evade. The relative freedom of will which he enjoys within the limits assigned to him is but a translation, into the individual mode, of that limitless and unconditional freedom which the Principle enjoys universally.

Individual responsibility, therefore, applies solely to the manner of playing the allotted part; this, however, presupposes some opportunity of comparing the individual performance throughout with its pattern as subsisting in the intellect of the dramatist; but for some means of access to this standard of comparison, all judgment must be exercised at random. The authentic source of such information can only be the

---

axiom "*duo sunt in homine* [there are two in man]." We say "Be yourself" to someone who is misbehaving: it is in fact, only the carnal self (*nafs*) or soul that *can* misbehave, the Self is infallible. Hence for the former an ultimate suicide is essential. As between the outer and inner man, only the latter is the Man (the image of God), the outer man being the "shadow" or "vehicle" or "house" or "garment" of the inner, just as the world is the Lord's "garment" (Cf. *Isha Upanishad* 1, and Philo, *Moses* II, 135).

dramatist himself, so that its communication implies the receiving of a favor or "grace" at his hands, by a handing-over of the required knowledge, either directly or through some indirect channel—in other words, an act of "revelation" is implied. As for the carrying out of the task in practice, by faithful imitation of the pattern as traditionally revealed, that is a question of using the tools one has been given, never of forging new ones. Furthermore, in so far as one has been led, from any reasons of contingent utility, to extend the range of one's natural tools by artificial adjuncts, these too must, in some sort, be treated as supplementary attributes (*upadhi*) of the individuality: whatever equipment or "ornament" (the primary meaning of both these words is the same) may be required, it must be of such a character and quality as to harmonize with the general purpose in view, which is the realization, first at an individual and then at every possible level, of what one is.

*   *   *

Of the many things a man puts to use in the pursuit of his earthly vocation there are none, perhaps, which are so intimately bound up with his whole personality as the clothes he wears. The more obviously utilitarian considerations influencing the forms of dress, such as climate, sex, occupation, and social status can be taken for granted; here we are especially concerned with the complementary aspect of any utility, that of its significance, whence is derived its power to become an integrating or else a disintegrating factor in men's lives. As for the actual elements which go to define a particular form of apparel, the principal ones are shape or "cut," material, color, and ornamental features, if any, including fastenings and also trimmings of every sort.

The first point to be noted is that any kind of clothing greatly modifies the appearance of a person, the apparent change extending even to his facial expression; this can easily be proved by observing the same individual wearing two quite distinct styles of dress. Though one knows that the man underneath is the same, the impression he makes on the bystanders is markedly different. It is evident, therefore, that we have here the reproduction of a cosmic process, by the clothing of a self-same entity in a variety of appearances; on that showing, the term "dress" can fittingly be attached to any and every appearance superimposed upon the stark nakedness of the Real, extending to all the various orders of manifestation which, separately or collectively, are included in the "seventy thousand veils obscuring the Face of

Allah." In view of this far-reaching analogy, it is hardly surprising if, at the individual level also, dress is endowed with such a power to veil (or reveal) as it has.[2]

For the human being, his choice of dress, within the limits of whatever resources are actually available to him, is especially indicative of three things: firstly, it shows what that man regards as compatible with a normal human state, with human dignity; secondly, it indicates how he likes to picture himself and what kind of attributes he would prefer to manifest; thirdly, his choice will be affected by the opinion he would wish his neighbors to have of him, this social consideration and the previous factor of self-respect being so closely bound up together as to interact continually.

According to his idea of the part he is called upon to play in the world, so does a man clothe himself; a correct or erroneous conception of the nature of his part is therefore fundamental to the whole question—the common phrase "to dress the part" is admirably expressive. No better illustration can be given of the way dress can work on the mind than one taken from that little world of make-believe called the theater: it is a commonplace of theatrical production that from the moment an actor has "put on his motley" and applied the appropriate "make-up," he tends to feel like another person, so that his voice and movements almost spontaneously begin to exhale the flavor (*rasa*) of the new character he represents. The same individual, wearing the kingly robes and crown, paces majestically across the stage; exchanging them for a beggar's rags, he whines and cringes; a hoary wig is sufficient to impart to his voice a soft and quavering sound; he buckles on a sword and the same voice starts issuing peremptory commands. Indeed, if the "impersonation" be at all complete, the actor almost becomes that *other* man whose clothes he has borrowed, thus "forgetting who he is"; it is only afterwards, when he is restored "to his right mind" that he discovers the truth of the saying that, after all, "clothes do not make the man."

Shri Ramakrishna Paramahamsa has paid a tribute to this power of dress to mold a personality in the following rather humorous saying: "The nature of man changes with each *upadhi*. When a man wears

---

[2] The concepts of change of clothes and becoming (*bhava*) are inseparable: Being (*bhuti*) only can be naked, in that, as constituting the principle of manifestation, it remains itself in the Unmanifest. Ultimately, the whole task of "shaking off one's bodies" (or garments) is involved—these including all that contributes to the texture of the outer self "that is not my Self."

black-bordered muslin, the love-songs of Nidhu Babu come naturally to his lips and he begins to play cards and flourishes a stick as he goes out for a walk. Even though a man be thin, if he wears English boots he immediately begins to whistle: and if he has to mount a flight of stairs, he leaps up from one step to another like a *sahib*."

This testimony of the sage can be matched by evidence drawn from a very different quarter. When one studies the history of various political tyrannies which, during recent centuries, have deliberately set out to undermine the traditional order with a view to its replacement by the "humanism" of the modern West, one is struck by a truly remarkable unanimity among them in respect of the policy both of discouraging the national costume and at the same time of eliminating the spiritual authority as constituted in their particular traditions. These dictators were no fools, at least in a worldly sense, and if they have agreed in associating these two things in their minds and in making them the first target for their attack, even to the neglect of other seemingly more urgent matters, that is because in both cases they instinctively sensed the presence of something utterly incompatible with the anti-traditional movement they wished to launch. As they rightly divined, the costume implied a symbolical participation (*bhakti*) in that "other-worldly" influence which the spiritual authority was called upon to represent more explicitly in the field of doctrine.

The Tsar Peter I of Russia seems to have been about the first to perceive how much hung upon the question of dress, and when he decided that his country should "face West," politically and culturally, he made it his business to compel the members of the governing classes to give up their Muscovite costume in favor of the coat and breeches of Western Europe, while at the same time he seriously interfered in the constitution of the Orthodox Church, with a view to bringing it under State control on the model of the Protestant churches of Prussia and England. Likewise in Japan, after 1864, one of the earliest "reforms" introduced by the modernizing party was the replacement of the traditional court dress by the ugly frock-coat then in vogue at Berlin, by which the Japanese officials were made to look positively grotesque; moreover, this move was accompanied by a certain attitude of disfavor towards the Buddhist institutions in the country, though government action concerning them did not take on an extreme form. In many other countries of Europe and Asia reliance was placed rather upon the force of example from above; the official classes adopted western clothes and customs, leaving the population at large to follow in its own time, further encouraged by the teaching it received in westernized schools and universities.

The classical example, however, is that afforded by the Kemalist revolution in Turkey, a distinction it owes both to its far-reaching character and to the speed with which the designed changes were effected as well as to the numbers of its imitators in neighboring countries: in that case we have a military dictator, borne to power on the crest of a wave of popular enthusiasm, as the leader in a *jihad* in which his genius earned him (falsely, as it proved) the title of *Ghazi* or "paladin of the Faith," who no sooner had overcome his foreign enemies in the field than he turned his power against the Islamic tradition itself, sweeping the *Khalifat* out of the way like so much old rubbish and plundering the endowments bequeathed to sacred use by ancient piety; while under the new legislation *dervishes* vowed to the contemplative life were classed with common vagabonds. It was another of Kemal's earliest acts to prohibit the Turkish national costume, not merely in official circles but throughout the nation, and to impose in its place the shoddy reach-me-downs of the European factories. Some thousands of *mullahs*, who dared to oppose him, earned the crown of martyrdom at the hands of the hangmen commissioned by an arak-drinking and godless "Ghazi." Meanwhile, in the rest of the Moslem world, hardly a protest was raised; in India, where the movement to defend the *Khalifat* had been of great political service to Kemal in his early days, only the red Ottoman *fez*, adopted by many sympathizers with the Turkish cause, still survives (though proscribed in its own country) as a rather pathetic reminder of the inconsistencies to which human loyalties sometimes will lead.

* * *

It may now well be asked what, in principle, determines the suitability or otherwise of any given form of clothing, and indeed what has prompted man, in the first place, to adopt the habit of wearing clothes at all? It is evident that a change so startling as this must have corresponded to some profound modification in the whole way of life of mankind. To discover the principle at issue, one must first remember that every possibility of manifestation—that of clothing for instance—has its root in a corresponding possibility of the Unmanifest, wherein it subsists as in its eternal cause, of which it is itself but an explicit affirmation. Metaphysically, Being is Non-Being affirmed, the Word is but the uttering of Silence; similarly, once Nakedness is affirmed, clothing is "invented." The principle of Clothing resides, therefore, in Nakedness. In seeking to throw light on this fundamental aspect of the doctrine, one cannot do better than refer to the cosmological myth common to the three branches issued from the traditional stem of Abraham, of *Sayyidna Ibrahim*. According to the Biblical story, Adam and Eve, that is to say, primordial mankind in the Golden Age (*Satya yuga*), were dwelling in the Garden of Eden at the center of which grew the Tree of Life or World Axis (*Meru danda*). The Axis, which "macrocosmically" is assimilated to a ray of the Supernal Sun (*Aditya*) and "microcosmically" to the Intellect (*Buddhi*), occupies the *center* of human existence, all other faculties of knowledge or action being grouped hierarchically round the Intellect as its ministers and tools, none encroaching, each keeping to its allotted work in conformity with its own norm (*dharma*); this state of inward harmony being, moreover, externally reflected in the peaceful relations existing between Man and all his fellow-creatures around him, animals, plants, and others. It is also recorded that Adam conversed daily and familiarly with God, that is to say, the individual self was always immediately receptive of the influence emanating from the Universal Self, "one-pointed" (*ekagrya*) concentration being for it a spontaneous act requiring the use of no auxiliary means. Such is the picture given of the state of normal humanity, or the Primordial State as the Taoist doctrine calls it, which corresponds to that state known as "childlikeness" (*balya*) in the Hindu or "poverty" (*faqr*) in the Islamic doctrine, the latter term betokening the fact that the being's Self-absorption is free from all competing interests, here represented by "riches"; for this state "nakedness" would not have been an inappropriate name either.

The Bible story goes on to describe the loss of that condition of human normality by telling how Eve, corrupted by the Serpent (an embodiment of the *tamasic* or obscurantist tendency), persuaded her husband to taste of the forbidden fruit of the Tree of Knowledge of Good and Evil, with fatal results; that is to say, the original unity of vision gives way to *dualism*, a schism takes place between self and Self, in which essentially consists the "original sin" of Christian theology, containing as it does the seed of every kind of opposition, of which "myself" versus "other" provides the type. And now comes a detail which is of particular interest for our thesis: the very first effect of

Adam and Eve's eating of the dualistic fruit was a feeling of "shame" at their own nakedness, a self-consciousness by which they were driven to cover their bodies with fig-leaves, thus fashioning the earliest example of human clothing.[3]

The rest of the symbolism is not hard to unravel. For one still in the state of *balya* the thought never could arise "I must be clothed," because *balya*, by definition, implies the clear recognition that the individuality, including all its sheaths (*kosha*s) variously diaphanous or opaque, is itself but a cloak for the true Self; to clothe it would be tantamount to piling dress upon dress. From this it follows that, for one who has realized that primordial state, the most natural proceeding would be to discard all clothes; one is on sure ground in saying that the unclothed ascetic or *nanga sannyasin* adequately represents the position of one who is intent on rejoining the Self.[*]

Once there has been a departure from the indistinction of this primitive nakedness, the various traditional ways part company thus producing a wide diversity of types in each of which certain aspects of the symbolism of clothing are predominant, to the partial over-shadowing of others; this, indeed, is the general principle of distinction as between any one traditional form and another, by which each is made to display a "genius" for certain aspects of the truth, leaving to its neighbors the task of emphasizing the complementary aspects.

Space does not allow of a detailed study even of the main types into which clothing can be classified; there are, however, one or two which must be mentioned: the first of these, as a letter received from A.K.C. himself once explained, represents the most characteristic constituent of Hindu clothing both ancient and modern, and consists of a length of material woven all of a piece, without joins—the "tailored" styles, as worn by Indian Muslims for instance, come into another category. In

---

[3] In connection with Adam's "shame" a Jewish traditional commentary (Philo, IA 11.55 ff) offers a strikingly concordant testimony, as follows: "The mind that is clothed neither in vice nor in virtue (i.e., does not partake of the fruit of the Tree of Knowledge of Good and Evil), but is absolutely stripped of either, is naked, just as the soul of an infant (= *balya*)." It should likewise be noted that in Judaism the High Priest entered *naked* into the Holy of Holies—"the noblest form, if stripping and becoming naked," noblest, that is to say, as distinguished from e.g., Noah's nakedness, when he was drunk. In the same connection Shri Krishna's theft of the *gopis*' clothes (*vastraharana*) has an obvious bearing.

[*] Editors' Note: Cf. the words of Lalla Yogishwari, the fourteenth century Kashmiri saint: "Dance then, Lalla, clothed but by the air: Sing then, Lalla, clad but in the sky. Air and sky: what garment is more fair? 'Cloth,' saith Custom—Doth that sanctify?"

this type of single-piece wrap as commonly worn by Hindus, therefore, we are dealing with a "seamless garment," like that of Christ.

It will be remembered that at His Crucifixion the soldiers who stripped Jesus of His raiment were unwilling to tear the seamless robe, so they cast lots for it. As for the Savior Himself, He was raised naked on the Cross, as was only fitting at the moment when the Son of Man was discarding the last remaining appearance of duality, assumed for "exemplary" reasons, and resuming the principial nakedness of the Self. Christian theologians have often pointed out that the symbolical garment of Christ is the Tradition itself, single and "without parts," like the Supreme *Guru* who reveals it; to "rend the seamless garment" is equivalent to a rupture with tradition (which must, of course, not be confused with an adaptation of its form, in a strictly orthodox sense, to meet changing conditions).

Tradition is a coherent whole, though never "systematic" (for a "system" denotes a water-tight limitation of form); once torn, the seamless garment cannot be "patched" simply by means of a "heretical" (literally "arbitrary") sewing on of elements borrowed at random—those who think of saving their tradition by compromising with a secularist outlook might well take note of the words of Christ: "No man putteth a piece of new cloth into an old garment, for that which is put in to fill it up taketh from the garment, and the rent is made worse" (Matthew 9:16).

Some mention must also be made of what might be called the "monastic habit," founded on a general type consisting of some plain material shaped to a rather austere design or even deliberately put together from rags, as frequently occurs in Buddhism. These forms of apparel are always meant to evoke the idea of poverty and may be taken to symbolize an aspiration towards the state of *balya*. To the foregoing category might be attached, but in a rather loose sense, the self-colored cotton homespun (*khaddar*) which, in Gandhi's India, had become the emblem of a certain movement. In this case, too, the idea of poverty had been uppermost; but it must be said, in fairness, that some of its supporters, possibly affected by an unconscious bias towards westernization, often were at pains to disclaim any other purpose for their hand-spinning than a purely economic one, that of helping to reclothe the many poor people who had been deprived of their vocational life and reduced to dire want under pressure of modern industrialism. This was tantamount to admitting that *khaddar* had a utilitarian purpose but no spiritual significance and that the movement to promote its use was essentially "in front of (= outside) the temple," which is the literal meaning of the word "profane." It is hard to believe, however, that such could have been the whole intention of the saintly founder of the movement, since he had never ceased to preach and exemplify the doctrine that no kind of activity, even political, can for a moment be divorced from faith in God and self-dedication in His service, a view which, more than all else, earned for him the hatred of the "progressives" of every hue, who were not slow in applying to him the (to them) opprobrious epithets of "mediaeval," "traditional," and "reactionary."

Apart from the two special examples just given, we must confine ourselves to a few quite general remarks on the subject of traditional dress, for all the great variety of types it has displayed throughout the ages and in every part of the world. By calling a thing "traditional" one thereby relates it immediately to an idea which always, and necessarily, implies the recognition of a supra-human influence: to quote a phrase from A.K.C.'s writings: "All traditional art can be 'reduced' to theology, or is, in other words, dispositive to a reception of truth." Thus, the costume which a man wears as a member of any traditional society is the sign, partly conscious and partly unconscious, that he accepts a certain view of the human self and its vocation, both being envisaged in relation to one Principle in which their causal origin (*alpha*) and their final goal (*omega*) coincide. It is inevitable that such a costume should be governed by a *canon*, representing the continuity of the tradition, the stable element, Being; within that canon there will, however, be ample room for individual adaptation, corresponding to the variable element in existence, impermanence, Becoming.

In tribal civilizations, which are most logical in these matters, the art of dress and self-adornment is carried to a point where the details of human apparel are almost exact symbolical equivalents of the draperies, head-dress and jewels that indicate its *upadhis* in a sacred image (*pratima*); moreover, such costume is usually covered with metaphysical emblems, though its wearers are by no means always aware of their precise significance; nevertheless, they reverence them greatly and undoubtedly derive a form of spiritual nourishment and power (*shakti*) from their presence. Furthermore, it is at least rather suggestive that tribal costume often entails a considerable degree of nudity, and is, in appearance, extremely reminiscent of the dresses of gods and goddesses, as portrayed in the ancient paintings and sculptures; so much so, that a friend recently suggested that the forms of tribal life in general constitute survivals from a period anterior to our present Dark Age (*Kali yuga*). It is not surprising that both

"Christian" missionaries and the apostles of modern materialism (the two seemingly contradictory motives being, indeed, not infrequently found in the same person) should be glad whenever they succeed in inducing some simple-minded peasant or tribesman to forego the natural safeguards provided for him by his native dress and customs; for after that he is only too easily demoralized and will fall a ready victim to their properly subversive persuasions.

*   *   *

One last type of clothing now remains to be considered, that specific to modern Europe and America, which is also the type that is threatening to swamp all others, to the eventual abolition of every distinction, whether traditional, racial, or even, in more extreme cases, individual. This "modern dress," through its development parallel with that of a certain conception of Man and his needs, has by now become the recognized uniform to be assumed by all would-be converts to the creed of "individualism," of mankind regarded as sufficing unto itself; it is somewhat paradoxical that partisans of a violent nationalism (which in itself is but an offshoot of individualism) have often been sworn opponents of their own national costume, just because of its silent affirmation of traditional values; some examples illustrating this point have already been given in the course of this chapter, and readers can easily find other similar cases if they but care to look around in the contemporary world.

In this context some mention should be made of a variant on human clothing of recent occurrence, that of "party uniform" as introduced in the totalitarian states of the last decades. One has but to remember the "Blackshirts" of Mussolini's Italy or the "Brownshirts" of Hitler's Germany, for instance, whose respective uniforms were so designed as to suggest ruthlessness and brutality together with a kind of boisterous "camaraderie," indicative of party loyalties. In totalitarianism of another hue, it is a wish to affirm the "proletarian ideal" that has been uppermost. A striking example of party uniform having this idea in view is provided by that in vogue among members of the Chinese Communist party which in its calculated drabness expresses its purpose in a way that verges on genius: nothing could better indicate the total subordination of the human individual to the party machine than that shapeless tunic-like jacket, buttoned up to the chin, sometimes with a most hideous cap to match such as lends a peculiarly inhuman character to any face which it happens to surmount. The most interesting point about this type of costume is that it amounts, in effect, to the parody of a monastic habit; that is to say, where the austerity of monastic dress, in all its various forms, is imposed for the purpose of affirming a voluntary effacement of the individual in the face of the Spiritual Norm, the party uniform in question likewise is meant to suggest an effacement of individuality, but one that operates in an inverse sense, in the face of the deified collective principle known as "the Masses," supposed source of authority as well as admitted object of all human worship and service. It is the ideal of a humanity minus Man, because none can be truly human who tries to ignore his own symbolism as reflecting the divine image in which he has been fashioned and to which his whole existence on earth should tend by rights. Moreover, it is no accident that all these types of uniform have been derived from western, never from a native form of clothing.

The above admittedly represent extreme perversions, not less instructive for that. When one turns again to western dress, however, under its more ordinary forms, it is at least fair to recognize that it has lent itself, more than other forms of clothing, to the expression of profane values: this has been true of it, in an increasing degree, ever since the latter half of the Middle Ages, when the first signs of things to come began to show themselves, in the midst of a world still attached to tradition—or so it seemed. It took a considerable time, however, before changes that at first were largely confined to "high society," and to the wealthier strata generally, were able seriously to affect the people as a whole. Over a great part of Western Europe the peasant costume remained traditional, and even with all the extravagances that had begun to affect the fashions of the well-to-do a certain "aristocratic" feeling remained there that it took time to undermine completely.

Now if it be asked which are the features in modern dress which correspond most closely with the profane conception of man and his estate, the answer, which in any case can but be a rather tentative one, will include the following, namely: the combining of pronounced sophistication, on the one hand, with "free and easiness," on the other, coupled with the frequent and gratuitous alterations introduced in the name of "fashion," of change for the sake of change—this, in marked contrast with the formal stability of traditional things—without forgetting either the manifold effects of machine production in vast quantities by processes which so often denature materials both in appearance and in their intimate texture—unavoidable or not, all these are factors that tell their own tale. Also chemical dyes, which have now swept across the world, are playing their part in the process of degradation and even where traditional costume still largely prevails, as in India, they and the excessive use of bleaching agents have together done much to offset such quality as still is to be found in the forms themselves; in most of the East the same would apply. Nor must such factors as the enclosing of feet formerly bare inside tight shoes or the disturbance to the natural poise of the body resulting from the introduction of raised heels be underrated. These and many other more subtle causes have operated in turning western dress into a vehicle of great psychological potency in a negative sense. Besides, there is the fact that wherever ornamental features occur in modern clothing, these never by any chance exhibit any symbolical character; in other words, ornament, at its best as at its worst, has become arbitrary and therefore profane.

An objection might, however, be raised here which is as follows: the western dress of today is, after all, but a lineal development of what formerly had been, if not a specifically Christian form of costume, at least one that was habitual in Christian Europe, one that could therefore claim to be in a certain degree traditionally equivalent to whatever existed elsewhere; it may be asked, how comes it then that its present prolongation is opposable to all other known types, so that it alone is compelled to bear the stigma of providing a vehicle for anti-traditional tendencies? Historically the fact just mentioned is incontrovertible, no need to deny it; but far from invalidating the foregoing argument it but serves to render it more intelligible: for it must be remembered that error never exists in a "pure" state, nor can it, in strict logic, be opposed to truth, since truth has no opposite; an error can but represent an impoverishment, a distortion, a travesty of some particular aspect of the truth which, to one gifted with insight, will still be discernible even through all the deformations it has suffered. Every error is *muslim*, as it were in spite of itself, according to the first of the three degrees of conformity as defined in a preceding section, and it cannot be referred back to any separate principle of its own, on pain of accepting a radical dualism in the Universe, a ditheism, a pair of alternative, mutually limiting realities. Anything can be called "profane" in so far as it is viewed apart from its principle, but things in themselves will always remain essentially sacred.

In the case of dress, this it is that explains the fact that many westerners, though now wearing a costume associated with the affirmation of secularist values, are less adversely affected thereby (which does not mean unaffected) than Asiatics, Africans, or even Eastern Europeans who have adopted that same costume; with the former, alongside anti-traditional degeneration there has been some measure of adaptation bringing with it a kind of immunity—the disease is endemic, whereas in the second case it has all the virulence of an epidemic. Furthermore, since, as we have seen, some positive elements, however reduced, must needs persist through every corruption, those to whom this form of dress properly belongs are enabled, if they will, to utilize whatever qualitative factors are still to be found there; though the reverse is equally possible as evidenced both in the case of the affectedly fashionable person and of his shoddier counterpart, the affectedly unkempt. The position of the Eastern imitator, however, is quite different—for such as he the change over to modern dress may easily involve so complete a contradiction of all his mental and physical habits as to result in a sudden violent rending of his personality, to the utter confusion of his sense of discrimination as well as the loss of all taste in its more ordinary sense. Indeed such cases are all too common.

Some people affect to believe that a movement to submerge specific differences reveals a unifying tendency in mankind, but they are suffering under a great delusion in that they mistake for true unity what is only its parody, uniformity. For any individual, the realizing in full of the possibilities inherent in his *svabhava* marks the limit of achievement, after which there is nothing further to be desired. As between two such beings, who are wholly themselves, no bone of contention can exist, since neither can offer to the other anything over and above what he already possesses; while on the supra-individual level their common preoccupation with the principial Truth, the central focus where all ways converge, is the guarantee of a unity which nothing will disturb; one can therefore say that the *maximum of differentiation is the condition most favorable to unity, to human harmony,* an immensely far-reaching conclusion which René Guénon was the first to voice in modern times, one which many may find difficult of acceptance just because of that habit of confusing unity with uniformity that we have just referred to. Against this peace in differentiation, whenever two beings are together subjected to the steamroller of uniformity, not only will both of them be frustrated in respect of some of the elements normally includable in their own personal realization, but they will, besides, be placed in the position of having to compete in the same artificially restricted field; and this can only result in a heightening of oppositions—the greater the degree of uniformity imposed, the more inescapable are the resulting conflicts, a truth which can be seen to apply in every field of human activity, not excepting the political field.

* * *

Enough has now been said to enable the reader to appreciate the general principle we have set out to illustrate: if the subject of dress was chosen, that is because it lent itself most easily to such an exposition; but it would have been equally possible to pick on some different factor pertaining to the active life, to the *karma mārga*, such as the furnishing of people's homes, or music and musical instruments, or else the art of manners; since each of these is governed by the selfsame law of *svadharma* and it is only a question of effecting an appropriate transposition of the argument to fit each particular case. Behind the widespread defection from traditional dress and customs there undoubtedly lurks a deep-seated loss of spirituality, showing itself on the surface in a corresponding diminution of personal dignity and of that sense of discrimination that everywhere is recognizable as the mark of a character at once strong and noble. In the East, as we have seen, the tendency in question has gone hand in hand with what Henry James described as "a superstitious valuation of European civilization" and this tendency, despite the much lip-service paid to the new-fangled idea of "national culture," is far from having exhausted itself. This is further evidenced by the fact that imitation rarely stops short at those things that appear indispensable to survival in the modern world, but readily extends itself to things that by no stretch could be regarded as imposed under direct compulsion of contingent necessity. The operative cause therefore is to be sought in an overpowering psychological urge, the urge to experience certain possibilities of the being which tradition hitherto had inhibited, possibilities which can only ripen in forgetfulness of God and things divine: traditional dress being a reminder of those things has to be discarded; the modern civilization being the field for realizing those possibilities has to be espoused. Naturally, when one comes to individual cases, all manner of inconsistencies and oscillations will be apparent; the inherited past is not something that can be expunged for the mere wishing. All one can do, in discussing the matter, is to treat it on broad lines, leaving any given case to explain itself.

By way of striking a more cheerful note in an otherwise depressing story, the fact should be mentioned that Indian women, with but few exceptions, continue to wear the *sari*, that most gracious form of feminine dress, both at home and abroad. Their gentle example has actually spread to unexpected quarters; many African women visitors to this country [England] have appeared clothed in an Indian *sari*, the colors and designs of which were however drawn from the African tradition itself. This adopting of a foreign traditional model instead of the ubiquitous western one, by adherents of an emergent nationalism, is hitherto quite unprecedented; in its way it is a small and heartening sign, one of which all former subjects of colonialism might well take note. Indeed, sometimes one is tempted to believe that West Africans, in these matters, have tended to show more conscious discrimination than many of their fellows belonging to other continents and this impression has been strengthened by the frequent sight of Nigerian Muslim visitors of commanding stature and of both sexes walking our streets properly clad in their splendid national costume. May this example offered by Africa find many imitators!

To finish, one can but repeat the principle governing all similar cases: one's native attire—or indeed any other formal "support" of that order—is an accessory factor in the spiritual conditioning of a man or woman and this is due both to any associations it may happen to carry and, at a higher level, to its symbolism as expressed in various ways. The assumption of modern western dress has often been the earliest step in the flight from Tradition: it would be but poetic justice for its divestment to mark the first step on an eventual path of return—too much to hope perhaps, yet the possibility is worth mentioning. In itself such action might seem little enough, for dress is not the man himself, admittedly. Nevertheless, if it be true to say that "clothes do not make the man" yet can it as truly be declared that they do represent a most effective influence in his making—or his unmaking.

VII

VIRTUE AND PRAYER

Spiritual virtue is to adore God as if thou sawest Him; and if thou seest Him not, He nevertheless seeth thee.

MUHAMMAD

Verily of all things the remembrance of God is greatest.

KORAN 29:45

22 VIRTUE AND MORALITY

Tage Lindbom

Every crisis in human existence—religious or moral, social or political—is, at root, a rupture of the equilibrium between man and the created order; for when the individual strives to enhance his freedom of action, to emancipate his ego, he comes into conflict with the created order, and this means leveling an attack against Almighty God, no matter how marginal it may seem.

Man's assault on the created order never begins with externals—attacks against his surroundings, against institutions or standards of value. The initial disturbance of equilibrium, occurs in the human soul. For man is not only an image of God—"the Kingdom of Heaven is within you"—but also an image in microcosm of the whole created order. He carries within himself not only God, but the world.

Now it is incumbent upon man to fulfill the God-given mandate of putting the world beneath his dominion, and the starting-point does not lie in externals, as moralists and reformers believe, but in the inward attitude, the inner awareness determined by divine truth. Equilibrium in the created order comes neither from outward rules and standards nor from moralistic and social activity; it is attained through man's inward state, through his certainty that his earthly mandate is a limited one subjected to the will of the Almighty.

In inward certainty, relying upon God's grace to bless our willing effort to hold fast to everything implied in the word "faith," we have strength to go out into the world without courting disaster. But even faith, "that can move mountains," may go astray. Men can devote themselves to a doctrine, and yet find the direct sincerity of that devotion threatened, and a life of faith can lose its spiritual health and vitality if sentimentality gains the upper hand. A man who seeks to shape his spiritual life aright must be guided by the twofold criterion of doctrine and life. He must build his life in the world on two pediments, the first of which is orthodoxy; but then, lest it be subverted by Pharisaism and the letter that kills the spirit, orthodoxy must be illuminated with enlivening virtue, for virtue is the second pediment.

Virtue is a meeting-point between divine perfection and human life as an ideal state. Confronting the ideal prototype, man finds himself face to face not with a moral "must" but with an "is." Virtue stands thus "midway" between God and moral imperatives. It is virtue, as the ideal prototype, that gives men their scale of moral values and their standards of behavior, and virtue must take precedence over morality, defining and determining it. But it is not, and never can be, an outward ordinance of acts and attitudes. Its life is an inward one, directed not to "spiritual goals" formulated subjectively, but to ideal archetypes as objective realities. In this sense, virtue is ontological re-integration, not the product of subjective aspirations.

This re-integration is far from being the passive contemplation of some lofty exemplar, as of a man absorbed in contemplation at the altar. Virtue is life, the will's engagement in a struggle towards the ideal prototype. As "the Word was made flesh," so also is virtue an endeavor to involve the whole man—in the deepest sense. Like faith, virtue is "synthetic," striving for wholeness; unlike morality, it is neither formal nor separative, but essential and unitive. It seeks to unite—on a spiritual plane—and not to divide, as morality does, on the plane of forms and regulations.

If this is the positive function of virtue, it has also a negative one—to destroy egoism, to be for ever actualizing our sense of nothingness in the face of God's Omnipotence. For egoism is the relentless center, within every man, from which separativity springs.

When we say that virtue is the meeting-point between Divine Perfection and human life as an ideal state, we are speaking of the aspect that concerns Infinity and Perfection. The other aspect concerns life in the world and the world's imperfection. Virtue is life, and life is to live in the world, even in the spiritual sense. It is, therefore, above all, a confrontation with our fellow men and our attitude when confronting them. The import of virtue is, not least, that we should constantly correct the false interpretations and erroneous judgments which we make when we "transpose" our nothingness before God's Omnipotence into our relationships with our fellow men.

Virtue thus has a twofold aspect, as relating to man himself and to man as a member of society; but this implies no cleavage within the concept of virtue, for there is no operative difference between the two aspects. It is certainly not one aspect acting as the source of impulsion and the other as its operative outlet. On the contrary, virtue is a spiritual and inward entity that does not "seek its own" by outward acts laying claim to merit. It is an inner striving towards the spiritual center and, at the same time, for totality. Virtue is not a striving outwards.

Like a tree, virtue has a root and a trunk from which, however, there grows a branch where the fruit ripens. The tree is now and always one and the same, but the branch and the fruit are to the tree what virtue is to the human collectivity. Virtue exists like a tree that grows and branches out to bear fruit, but it is always, and unalterably, a tree. Yet virtue is also the Divine Existence in the human will that gives it its dynamism. In will informed by virtue, man is able, like Jacob in his dream of the ladder with its summit in Heaven, to attain his spiritual goal and, at the same time, to descend into the world with all its imperfections, armed with this same virtuous will.

To qualify virtue in worldly terms—to attempt to describe all its alternating situations—would be as difficult as trying to describe and put a name to every leaf on the verdant branch. Nevertheless we can, according to Frithjof Schuon, define what is essential under the three main headings of humility, charity, and truthfulness.* The first of these, humility, is always to be aware of our nothingness before God. This awareness has also an aspect that relates to the world, including our relations with our fellow-men. Imperfection is an inherent part of our life on earth, and our awareness of our fellows' failings is imperfect likewise. We must recognize, in all moments of humbled pride and dispute, that worldly setbacks are grounded in an imperfection that we all share.

The "I" is a fragment; it can never practice righteousness. It is precisely from manifestations of the "I" that there arise manifold injustices, conflicts, and tyrannies in the world. Secular man seeks to avoid this dilemma by making shift with the concept of mutual tolerance, an utterly unreal premise which maintains that life's contradictions can be reconciled by a thoroughgoing heterodoxy. But virtuous awareness involves admitting, on the contrary, that controversy is part of our earthly imperfection, that we all share in this imperfection, that it is inevitable, and that only the soul's humility can outweigh it. The secular concept of mutual tolerance is as unreal as the awareness is real which keeps us humble.

Humility in relation to our fellow men means to be conscious of what is separative in existence. Charity on the contrary is a spiritual attitude that oversteps the bounds that hold "I" and "you" apart. Charity is to put oneself in one's neighbor's place and to crack the

---

* Editors' Note: See especially Frithjof Schuon's chapter "The Virtues in the Way," in *Esoterism as Principle and as Way* (Pates Manor, Bedfont: Perennial Books, 1981), pp. 101-115.

hard shell of egoism and self-centeredness. The romantically heedless "egotism" of a Stendhal, is countered with another attitude which aims at its opposite; unthinking indulgence of the ego, which displays all that is most transient, lacking, and fragmentary in man, gives places to an inner striving, to a realization in which one's fellow man is no longer a hindrance along the way but a very brother.

Humility and charity are intimately bound; the one cannot exist without the other. Humility leads to charity, and charity to humility. Both work to destroy egoism. Frithjof Schuon describes them as being like the two linked arms of the Cross. The third virtue, truthfulness, is simply to love truth. Both humility and charity are "subjective" in the sense that they strive for an attitude that consistently bears the stamp of the personal; our mental powers need also to be involved in our virtuous endeavors. However, these mental faculties can, in their well-intentioned efforts to sustain virtue, place excessive emphasis on sentimental aspects which, in fact, deprive it of its purity, innocent primordiality, and objectivity. The result is that man is tempted to occupy himself with worldly matters which virtue proper should leave behind.

It is the function of truthfulness to correct and objectivize the "subjective" dangers which threaten virtuous endeavor. Love and hate are passional elements which have a large place in our lives and, as such, are inevitable and necessary. But virtue cannot join them: its independence bears, in all things, the stamp of objectivity. Our attitude must be determined not by emotional motives, but by truth and reality. We must implant this impartial and objective attitude in the will, in order to be able to achieve an upright endeavor free from all considerations of passion. We can thus correct the tendency, inspired by humility and passion, to deviate towards subjective voluntarism, which leads to overestimation of oneself and to self-glorification.[1]

It is only in virtue that man attains to his inward, primordial equilibrium; it is only in virtue that God confronts the world within a man's soul; it is only in virtue that a man may go out into the world without bring corrupted. To be virtuous means "not to seek one's own." This freedom from egotistic and passional leanings gives human inwardness an entirely universal meaning. Virtue is both center and whole for the individual viewed as a microcosm. It is virtue that real-

---

[1] Frithjof Schuon, *Language of the Self* (Ganesh, 1959), pp. 84-89 [Editors' Note: pp. 52-57 in the more recent World Wisdom edition of 1999].

izes the Creator's intention at the microcosmic level—a work of love and harmony. And this is why everything that is primordial bears the stamp of equilibrium, and why all virtue strives towards primordial equilibrium as an ideal prototype.

But human existence, by reason of its worldly separativity, is constantly upsetting the equilibrium. Man is, microcosmically, a great fountain of energy, using his body, soul, and reason to protect himself against the forces of nature and to overcome them by his will, which enables him to choose and discriminate. But in so doing he disturbs cosmic equilibrium. A world without man would be a world of simple biological cycles, an uninterrupted process of growth, bloom, and decay.

Man intervenes, however, and he does so with a recognition of his place in the hierarchy of the created order, with his intelligence, will, and passion. He carries his immortality within him, is conscious of good and evil, and has free will to choose between them. But he is at the same time a part of the created world, "condemned" to be a segment of cosmic totality and, like the rest of creation, to be imperfect. He imposes himself on existence as a conqueror who "must people the earth and lay it beneath him." But in his all-conquering march, he drags his imperfections along with him. Suspended "between Heaven and earth," he carries and transmits Divine Truth, but it is he—by reason of his very rank—who also disrupts the equilibrium of the cosmos.

Man is endowed with reason, and he knows that he cannot allow himself to engage with his fellows in the anarchical power-struggle of which he is capable. The "Law of the Jungle" constrains him to abstain from such anarchy. The theorists of natural law are right to maintain that man strives to rise beyond his "state of nature," as Aristotle insists in asserting that man is a "social being." But what is more important is that man has an inner certainty and also a higher task for which his life on earth is a period of preparation and trial. On earth he can discriminate between good and evil, for he has free will, and is therefore his own law-maker.

Morality, understood here in both the private and the social sense, is not only the outward formulation of norms for human living, nor is it simply to consider means, or to cooperate, in order to promote the "conquest of nature." Morality is first of all a "descent" by Truth into formal existence, which is characterized by contradictions and imperfections. Morality belongs to the world of forms and must therefore be "made substantial" and clothed in the forms of which created existence consists. The attitude of soul that would actualize virtue must needs transform itself, on a lower, earthly plane, into norms and rules, and become a set of standards. This is the functional aspect of morality.

But morality is likewise a prolongation into the formal world of the spiritual state that has its source in the Divine and whose channel of transmission is man. Morality seeks to quicken man's awareness that, with all his imperfections, he yet carries perfection within him. Yet morality is itself imperfect, fragmentary, separative, and shot through with contradictions; which means that man, its envoy, is afflicted with these same failings. Morality is inexorable, but within narrow bounds, for its field of application in space and time does not bear the seal of infinity. Morality must therefore submit to the domination of virtue, deriving its strength, validity and, indeed, its entire *raison d'être* therefrom. Virtue is immutable, universal, absolute, beyond space and time; it is everything that morality lacks and can never acquire.

The hierarchy is, therefore, that morality is subordinate to virtue, and that virtue is the link binding earth to Heaven. If this link is lost, morality and law become a collation of expedient rules with no under-lying authority. The administration of oaths is then mere form, and a legal judgment is no more than an expression of incidental power relationships. But if, on the contrary, the hierarchical nexus between virtue and morality remains unbroken, it means that the social order retains its legitimacy in the most outward aspects, at the same time as maintaining its underlying authority; it means also that man, aware of his nothingness before Almighty God, remains conscious of his place in the cosmic order and, thus, of the limitations of his power. It is against this cosmic order that all disobedience, rebellion, and striving for the expansion of man's power are first directed.

All heresy is an attempt to upset total equilibrium to man's advantage, for greater emancipation, or freedom of action. An attack, however marginal, is thus leveled against Divine Omnipotence—and, thereby, against the hierarchical order. Heresy—using the word in its broadest sense and not in its orthodox, exoteric one—does not pit itself against moral standards; on the contrary, heresy is always imbued with moral vehemence. Nor again, does it set out to oppose Divine Omnipotence; on the contrary, the heretic frequently aims to "reinforce" God's authority, as did William of Ockham in declaring Omnipotence to be a voluntary exercise of Will—a definition which precludes necessity. Heresy does not, in fact, oppose Divine Omnipo-tence, but it opposes the cosmic order which is the support of Omnipotence. To make a parallel with the institution of monarchy, it is not the king who is being attacked, but the throne.

It is neither God nor morality that sustains the first attack of the heretic, but virtue. The first objective is to destroy virtue, and thereby to sever the link between what is of Heaven and what is of earth. The hierarchical structure, which is the throne of the Heavenly Sovereign, can no longer remain upright. The ladder in Jacob's dream, joining earth to Heaven, is pulled away. With virtue destroyed, men are "isolated" from God, and morality now opens up to the heretic a field of activity of an entirely different kind.

Humility, the foremost virtue of all, becomes cut off from virtue and transformed into something exclusively moral, most frequently into a striving self-abasement, which is quite different from humility. For humility is a virtuous attitude which includes dignity, confidence, and even pride in our spiritual gifts, for which we owe the Creator grateful acknowledgment; whereas self-abasement precludes and denies this pride and dignity, and thus amounts to ingratitude.

To be humble is, moreover, to be "poor in spirit," which is the deepest meaning of poverty. Heretical moralism makes of poverty a purely material manifestation, maintaining that it must start by being "tangible"; but this is to rob poverty of its true, inward, and spiritual context. Poverty then becomes a rule of social conduct to be adhered to with unquestioning obedience like other social standards, and it can sink down to the merely secular plane, and become the object of human society's checks and controls. Heresy limits itself to bringing men together who believe that material poverty is right and natural as a way of life; this is not poverty of the spirit but of the purse and, as such, it comes to be urged upon all.

All heresy has a single motivating impulse—a striving for inwardness, in the sense of turning one's back on the world in order to rescue spiritual values that are threatened. There is a desire—as is implied in the word "heresy" (which means "self-choice")—to cleanse spiritual life of its dross. But this inwardness is worlds apart from virtue since it aims not to destroy the ego—which is the task of virtue—but to achieve spiritual realization in and through the ego. Heretical inwardness is therefore a moralistic striving exclusively within the confines of tangible existence. Heresy seeks to realize inwardness in the very world it is turning away from, and this inwardness is, in fact, material, individualistic, rationalistic, and sentimental—narcissism in the trappings of religion. It relies on the individual's mental powers, and shifts religious experience to the realm of the ego, which is rationalistic and sentimental.

This is the process which annuls virtue and gives the heretic a "free hand," but he is then powerless to take hold of three central elements in religious experience, namely the cosmic, the hierarchical, and the symbolic; he becomes incapable of realizing that man is no more than a small component in the cosmos—the mirror in which he beholds "God's visage"—, that the cosmos itself is a hierarchically structured order which reflects the heavenly hierarchy and, finally, that the "language" in which God speaks unceasingly to His creation is the abstract imagery of symbolism, which emerges in both virgin nature and in life sanctified by religious worship.

Humility therefore becomes self-abasement, and spiritual poverty a kind of worldly egalitarianism in relation to purely material resources. Charity is confined to the field of outward activities, and truthfulness does not go beyond individual, subjective, and mental experience. The entire created order, and everything that this order bespeaks and reveals about Divine Omnipotence, is explained as a structure without any inwardness. This enables Nature, now deprived of its celestial aspect, to be treated simply as an object of exploitation. Sacred institutions and the religious hierarchy take on the appearance of self-appointed intermediaries between God and man. Man's lonely pilgrimage is then worked out in the direction of a strictly individual solution which comes to replace God's universal compassion to the cosmos. The symbolism of the sacred retreats before the pressures of collective, democratic life with its popularly elected trustees and preachers; and rationalistic, literal belief then comes to the fore with the assertion that all men are capable of interpreting the Holy Scriptures.

All heresy starts out by attempting to "purify" and "restore"; its tragic error is to open the door to worldliness, and the individual then lays claim, under the cover of religion, to greater scope for himself and his own. This prepares the ground for further secularization; no longer at home in the intuitive world of symbols, man is forced to resort more and more to rational and sentimental modes of thought; as the world of the spirit shrivels, man relapses into subjection to the letter, which makes the word into an object of rational conjecture. Heresy has "purified" nothing and "restored" nothing, but simply brought spiritual life down to a lower level.

It may seem paradoxical that heresy should strive at one and the same time for both inwardness and extroversion. It is simply that morality, in its struggle to be free of virtue, transposes religious life to the everyday world, thereby presenting heretical spirituality in two tangible contexts, the life of the mind and the senses, on the one hand, and outward actions, on the other. If virtue seeks to destroy the ego and realize human destiny on a higher plane, morality, for its part, seeks to affirm itself, when no longer linked to virtue, as an independent entity in both the inward and the outward sense. In virtue, man's immortal being is brought back to its source, man's divine prototype; in morality, the sensory world manifests itself in terms of the human ego. Virtue is spiritual realization; morality is manifestation according to tangible and sensory norms.

For the virtuous, to live in the world is to serve. A ruler too is one who serves, in the twofold sense of serving the higher power who has ordained him in his role, and serving the men and estates over which he rules; expressed in the terms appropriate to virtue, he is performing the office of a deputy. In the world of secular morality, humble service has a quite different import; it is no longer service, but servility. The servile man does not serve, for service is an inward prompting. He acts under the compulsion of behavioral patterns that impose themselves with the authority of an outward—not an inward—moral force, as if to say "observe how I abase myself, and how correct I am!" This moral compulsion smooths the path for the servile man to achieve what, in his soul, he is really aspiring to; and that is power.

Power is seized in indirect fashion by undermining the ground which supports humility, namely spiritual readiness for service, and by perverting the moral context of service to spiritual pride, which is the most calamitous of all sins in the world of virtue.

This gives righteousness a new meaning, as it does humility, charity, and truthfulness. "Seek ye first the Kingdom of Heaven and its righteousness" assigns to the realization of virtue uncompromising priority, but secular morals assert with the utmost rigor—the more secular they become—that righteousness has to do with this world, with variable emphasis and relevance. Sentimental self-pity joins hands with the resentment occasioned by the egalitarian mentality, and the result of this alliance is presented as brotherly love. In the same way, charity is transformed into an unremitting struggle on behalf of the "weak" and against the "mighty."

Servility leads to an enhancement of self-love. Governance should not then come from above—and this very concept negates virtue—but from below, from the weak and pitiable; these, in their turn, are moved to respond by asserting that it is only rule from below that is justified. This vindication has nothing to do with being "poor in spirit," for spiritual poverty can never be observed, registered, checked, or governed from below. It must depend instead upon a display of morality with its rules resting firmly in worldly legitimacy and the will of the worldly law-giver, and its execution depending on the vigilance of an earthly ruler.

God's actions are limned in beauty and love; beauty and love are all-embracing, as are also God's works. Man must recognize this cosmic totality and equilibrium. Constantly upsetting this equilibrium, he has nevertheless opportunities to re-instate primordial equilibrium in his own heart, and virtue is the means. We must be conscious that it is a limited and fragmentary re-instatement, and modest on the cosmic scale. But endeavor—the search to restore his own equilibrium—is the token of a true man, who is a microcosmic image of created wholeness, answerable, to the limit of his strength, to his Maker. The mirror-image that is revealed by all creation can be distorted and shattered, but the reflection carried by each man in his soul can, despite everything, be safeguarded. Virtue makes it possible.

24 FRITHJOF SCHUON AND PRAYER

Reza Shah-Kazemi

In the preface to one of the last books he wrote, Frithjof Schuon affords us a rare glimpse into one of the key intentions—or personal hopes—that underlay his writings:

> If our works had on the average no other result than the restitution for some of the saving barque of prayer, we would owe it to God to consider ourselves profoundly satisfied.[1]

In addition to all of the other aspects of his contribution to the revival of religion and spirituality in the contemporary world, it can be confidently asserted that the restitution of prayer has indeed been realized, and not just for some, but for many, as a direct consequence of reading and assimilating Schuon's books. It is upon this altogether fundamental theme of prayer in the corpus of Schuon's works that we intend to dwell in this essay, albeit within a compass that can do scant justice to all of its aspects and ramifications. The intention, rather, is to draw attention to the subtlety, depth, and comprehensiveness that characterize Schuon's elucidation of prayer, an elucidation which renders prayer not only an intelligible necessity for man in his quest for God, but also an irresistible summons and an inestimable gift from God to man.

It would be difficult to overstate the importance of prayer in Schuon's perspective. As is well known, this perspective is, above all, intellectual, and as such, is aimed first and foremost at the exposition of truth at all levels; but the doctrine is not intended to remain on the discursive plane alone: for "it is as though true ideas took their revenge, on anyone who limits himself to a thinking of them."[2] These ideas are intended to be realized in depth, they should "unleash interiorizing acts of the will." Now prayer is the interiorizing act *par excellence*, it is the key to realization, to "making real" that which is mentally comprehended. Without prayer—without the assimilation by the heart of the truths perceived by the mind—there is no

---

[1] *The Play of Masks* (Bloomington, IN: World Wisdom Books, 1992), p. vii.

[2] *Spiritual Perspectives and Human Facts* (London: Faber & Faber, 1954), p. 11.

realizatory will, no spiritual development; the realities provisionally expressed by doctrine will remain abstractions. Ideas that go no further than the mental faculty, far from contributing to "remembrance," on the contrary, carry the risk not only of being forgotten, but also, of further enmeshing us in our natural state of heedlessness; for if the ego is "a kind of crystallization of forgetfulness of God," the brain, for its part, is "the organ of this forgetfulness; it is like a sponge filled with images of this world of dispersion and of heaviness."[3] The heart, on the other hand, "is the latent remembrance of God, hidden deep down in our 'I.'" Part of the realizatory power of prayer—in one of its modes—consists in its temporary displacement of concepts in the mind, the better to assimilate them permanently and in depth, in the heart, precisely: "prayer is as if the heart, risen to the surface, came to take the place of the brain which then sleeps with a holy slumber; this slumber unites and soothes, and its most elementary trace in the soul is peace. 'I sleep, but my heart waketh.'"[4]

The reason why peace of soul is the "most elementary trace" of this holy slumber, induced by prayer, is that "prayer places us in the presence of God, Who is pure Beatitude."[5] To pray is to give oneself to God; and since God is pure Beatitude, prayer itself is already something of this Beatitude, whether the person praying is conscious of it or not. The awareness of what prayer is, and of what God is, imparts to the very act of prayer the capacity to bestow peace on the soul. Once this peace is "tasted," and the sense of the sacred is awoken, with the heart rendered receptive to the presence of God—then does metaphysical doctrine begin to take root in our being, conviction deepens into certitude, the "obscure merit of faith" begins to give way to the ineffable verities of gnosis.[6] At a time when "metaphysics" is all too commonly associated with occult phenomena, it is all the more important to be reminded of what is immutable and indubitable: that permanent, inalienable miracle, the Presence of God. When this Pres-

---

[3] *Understanding Islam* (Bloomington, IN: World Wisdom Books, 1994), p. 148.

[4] Ibid., p. 149.

[5] *The Transfiguration of Man* (Bloomington, IN: World Wisdom Books, 1995), p. 98.

[6] Schuon often refers to certitude as preceding and producing serenity; the relationship between the two elements is clearly one of reciprocal influence, each element deepening, and in turn being deepened by, the other. This reciprocity, as well as the principle of the hierarchical degrees of faith, is affirmed in the following verse of the Qur'an: "He it is who hath caused the Spirit of Peace (*sakina*) to descend upon the hearts of the believers, that they might add faith unto their faith" (48:4).

ence becomes the true goal of the spiritual life, it attracts and absorbs all the spiritual energy of the aspirant, imparting to his soul that "peace which passeth all understanding." In the face of this principial peace, all transient phenomena—inward and outward—lose their captivating power. "The thirst for the marvelous is one thing, and metaphysical serenity another."[7]

Prayer, then, is the key to metaphysical realization and, *a fortiori*, to human salvation; for this reason, prayer cannot be regarded simply as an individual act, it is, rather, an existential imperative: "The very fact of our existence is a prayer and compels us to prayer, so that it could be said: 'I am, therefore I pray; *sum ergo oro.*'"[8] No more succinct means of illustrating the chasm that separates the "intelligent stupidity" of Cartesianism and the metaphysical realism of Schuon's perspective can be imagined than this reformulation—and refutation—of Descartes' *cogito ergo sum*. To exist—something no sane person can doubt—is to be aware of the need for prayer, to be aware, that is, of the need to transcend existence. For if, on the one hand, universal existence is a prayer or hymn to the Creator, on the other, the very distance between the creation and God implies otherness, denial, contradiction: awareness of this hiatus between existence and its Principle impels man to rise above existence, to reach out for God, to be true to his vocation. The very fact of ex-isting—of "standing apart" from God—then, is a motive for fervent prayer:

> . . . existence means not to be God and so to be in a certain respect ineluctably in opposition to Him; existence is something which grips us like a shirt of Nessus. Someone who does not know that the house is on fire has no reason to call for help, just as the man who does not know he is drowning will not grasp the rope that could save him; but to know we are perishing means either to despair or else to pray.[9]

Schuon continues this passage with an extremely significant analogy between the subjective dream state and the macrocosmic dream, that is, the objective world and all that it contains:

[7] *Sufism: Veil and Quintessence* (Bloomington, IN: World Wisdom Books, 1981), p. 37.

[8] *Understanding Islam*, p. 155.

[9] Ibid., p. 156.

If a man has a nightmare and, while still dreaming, starts calling on
God for aid, he infallibly awakens; this shows two things: first, that
the conscious intelligence of the Absolute subsists during sleep as a
distinct personality—our spirit thus remaining apart from our states
of illusion—and secondly, that when a man calls on God he will
end by awakening also from that great dream . . . life, the world,
the ego.[10]

This "awakening" brought about through prayer—more specifically, through God's response to prayer—is effective liberation
or spiritual realization. All prayer, thus, to some degree or another,
participates in this realization which, properly speaking is the fruit of
the liberating grace of God, responding to the deepest prayer. Even the
most elementary prayer, however, can be seen as a kind of liberation
from the totalitarian grip of the world, and the suffocating pretensions
of the ego.

> Prayer—in the widest sense—triumphs over the four accidents of
> our existence: the world, life, the body and the soul; . . . It is situated
> in existence like a shelter, like an islet. In it alone are we perfectly
> ourselves, because it puts us into the presence of God. It is like a
> miraculous diamond which nothing can tarnish and nothing can
> resist.[11]

The rest of this essay will explore the way in which Schuon treats
prayer in this "widest sense," that is, by looking briefly at the modes
and degrees of prayer, beginning with the most ordinary meaning
of prayer—personal petition to God—and culminating in the most
exalted form of prayer—methodic invocation of the Name of God.
The comprehensive manner in which prayer is expounded by Schuon
reveals that, in the last analysis, prayer is something which not only
engages all that we are, but also encompasses all that is.

Four principal degrees of prayer are delineated in one of Schuon's
most impressive and important essays, "Modes of Prayer," in the book
Stations of Wisdom. What follows is based on this chapter, with additional material from other published works of Schuon being brought
in to shed further light on certain points. The four degrees of prayer
can be understood in relation to the nature of the praying subject: such
and such a man—the subject of personal, non-canonical prayer; man

---

[10] Ibid., p. 156.

[11] *Spiritual Perspectives and Human Facts*, p. 212.

as such—the subject of canonical prayer; both man and God—both being in a sense the subject of meditative prayer; and God—the true subject of invocatory prayer.

As regards the first of these, personal supplication by a given individual addressed to the Personal God, it is "the direct expression of the individual, of his desires and fears, his hopes and gratitude."[12] Despite its elementary nature, this type of prayer cannot be dismissed as something negligible, as compared to the "serious"—supra-individual—work of esoteric realization. To those who would minimize the importance of personal prayer or deny its necessity, the reply is that its importance is rooted in the need for the human person as such to have a personal, intimate, and spontaneous relationship with the "Personal" God; and the necessity of personal prayer is a consequence of the incapacity of such and such a person: "If petition is a capital element of prayer, it is because we can do nothing without the help of God; man's resolves offer no guarantee—the example of Saint Peter shows this—if he does not ask for this help."[13] Moreover, in laying bare to God the personal needs, weaknesses and desires of the soul, the aim is "not only to obtain particular favors, but also the purification of the soul: it loosens psychic knots or, in other words, dissolves subconscious coagulations and drains away many secret poisons."[14]

Schuon specifies that this form of prayer also has its own rules, even if they are not always stipulated formally, as is the case with canonical prayer. These rules are so many conditions for the integrity of the prayer, for "it is not enough for a man to formulate his petition, he must express also his gratitude, resignation, regret, resolution and praise."[15] Each of these is then defined by Schuon. While all five of these attitudes are of great importance, we should like to dwell on one in particular, that of resignation: "Resignation is the anticipated acceptance of the non-fulfillment of some request." This attitude is strongly linked to trust, of which it is the complement. It is one thing to trust in God's goodness, another to expect Him to respond immediately to each and every request we make of Him. The antidote to this unrealistic trust is resignation in advance to the possibility that God will not necessarily answer our petition when and how we would like it to be

---

[12] *Stations of Wisdom* (Bloomington, IN: World Wisdom Books, 1995), p. 121.

[13] Ibid., p. 123.

[14] Ibid., pp. 121-122.

[15] Ibid. p. 122.

answered. Such exaggerated trust—expressive of a gross worldliness masquerading as piety—is often the cause of a loss of faith: for when "vertical" trust is displaced by "horizontal" expectation, one's faith is placed not in God but the world; no longer is it nourished by the infinite goodness of God, rather, it becomes the slave of the vagaries of the life of this world. Especially in our times, many are they who have become atheist due to God's apparent refusal to answer fervent prayers for help. In previous ages, prayer was nearly always accompanied by a decisive—doubt-dissolving—intuition of the unimpeachable goodness of God, so that even if specific prayers went unanswered, this goodness was not in the least questioned; in modern times, however, this intuition "has been artificially paralyzed" by "a perfectly sterile and 'unreal' rationalism."[16]

For this reason, it is all the more important to grasp the necessity of resignation as a condition for the integrity of personal prayer. To combine fervent, trusting prayer with this quality of resignation is subtle and challenging—avoiding, on the one hand, foolhardy expectation and, on the other, apathetic fatalism—but it is also liberating: for, irrespective of the nature of the immediate response from God, every such prayer not only anticipates, but already participates in, its own fulfillment, a fulfillment whose nature will be ultimately determined by God's grace and wisdom, and not by our own desires. In such a light, one can better understand what is meant by God's promise in the Qur'an: "I answer the supplication of the suppliant when he supplicates Me" (2:186).

The following sentence by Schuon might be read as a commentary on this verse:

> God readily answers humble, charitable, reasonable, and fervent prayers, but sometimes He answers them belatedly, and sometimes in a form other than the suppliant had in view, so much so that a refusal on the part of God is an answer since it announces a better gift, to the very extent that the prayer possessed the requisite qualities.[17]

On a still more fundamental level—going beyond the vicissitudes of time and space—it might be said that the "refusal" is but a mask over an eternally present "acceptance":

[16] Ibid., p. 101.

[17] *Christianity/Islam: Essays in Esoteric Ecumenicism* (Bloomington, IN: World Wisdom Books, 1985), p. 217.

"Before" we formulated our prayers, the divine replies "were" in eternity; God is for us the eternal, omnipresent Response, and prayer can have no other function than to eliminate all that separates us from this Response which is inexhaustible.[18]

Turning now to the second mode, that of canonical prayer—such as the Lord's Prayer in Christianity and the *salat* in Islam—this is no longer the prayer of such and such an individual, but of the individual as such. It is a prayer that has God as its author, and is thus itself of a revealed substance; by this very fact it is ontologically superior to individual prayer, and, being universal, includes "eminently or in addition, all possible individual prayers." Whoever recites the canonical prayer prays "for all and in all."[19]

Again, it is folly to belittle the significance of the canonical prayer—or exoteric rites in general—out of some presumptuous notion of esoterism. Schuon repeatedly stresses throughout his writings the indispensable nature of the exoteric framework of formal religion; without this framework, all "esoteric" exercises are doomed in advance to being nothing more than "psychological exploits." He insists on distinguishing between "the function of the exoteric viewpoint as such" and "the function of exoterism as a spiritual means."[20] The viewpoint proper to exoterism is limited to that of the individual and his final ends, on the one hand, and the Personal God, at the level of Being, on the other; it is this limited perspective that esoterism transcends, in the first place, by its awareness of the immanent Self in the transpersonal essence of the soul, and then by its awareness of the transcendence of the supra-personal Essence of God, "Beyond-Being." But this opening to metaphysical truths does not absolve esoterists from the obligation to observe the exoteric rites; the exoteric framework is transcended by esoterism, as it were, from within, not abolished on its own plane; no one, in other words, can dispense with the "function of exoterism as a spiritual means." These means will be used in two ways, according to Schuon:

. . . on the one hand by intellectual transposition into the esoteric order—in which case they will act as supports of intellectual "actu-

---

[18] *The Eye of the Heart* (Bloomington, IN: World Wisdom Books, 1997), p. 165.

[19] *Stations of Wisdom*, p. 121.

[20] *The Transcendent Unity of Religions* (London: Faber & Faber, 1953), p. 24.

alization"—and on the other hand by their regulating action on the individual portion of the being.[21]

Poorly assimilated esoterism always carries the danger of pride; and this is most often expressed in the abandonment of religious rites, in the name of the supra-formal essence. Because a certain—purely mental—awareness of the supra-personal Essence is obtained, a cavalier attitude towards the personal dimensions of the spiritual life can easily develop. What Schuon stresses, on the contrary, is that the "individual portion of the being" does not cease being so simply upon the recognition of certain esoteric truths, far from it: such truths cannot be realized without the total conformity of the individual's character to these truths. Now the individual, as stated earlier, can do nothing without the help of Heaven. The performance of the exoteric rites—in a spirit of humility towards Heaven and the sacred substance of the divinely revealed Law—is of inestimable value, both in itself, and in relation to the cultivation of virtue, without which no spiritual endeavor can bear fruit. The relationship between prayer and virtue is fundamental, for the effort of the soul, on its own, to attain virtue is inadequate; a heavenly power is needed, and it is precisely this power that is attracted by prayer. Hence it can be said that to pray is "to actualize a virtue and at the same time to sow the seed of it."[22]

Moreover, the exoteric rites are the indispensable guarantee,[23] and the *conditio sine qua non*, of the efficacy of the esoteric rites of any tradition: "It is obvious that a spiritual means has significance only within the rules assigned to it by the tradition which offers it. . . . Nothing is more dangerous than to give oneself up to improvisations in this field."[24]

---

[21] Ibid., pp. 24-25.

[22] *To Have a Center* (Bloomington, IN: World Wisdom Books, 1990), p. 145.

[23] It is important to reinforce this point: "If we start from the idea that intellection and concentration, or doctrine and method, are the foundations of the Path, it should be added that these two elements are valid and effective only by virtue of a traditional guarantee, a 'seal' coming from Heaven. . . . The importance of orthodoxy, of tradition, of Revelation is that the means of realizing the Absolute must come 'objectively' from the Absolute" (*Understanding Islam*, p. 157).

[24] *Stations of Wisdom*, p. 130. This point is made after making mention of the possibility, primarily found within Hinduism and Buddhism, of outward rites being replaced by the supreme rite of invocation. But this replacement is also conditioned by rules proper to the traditional framework in question, so it cannot be used as a justification for the abandonment of rites in the context of a religious framework

Meditation is the third mode of prayer identified by Schuon in this chapter. The reason why the thinking subject in meditation cannot be regarded as man alone is that what is actually engaged in authentic meditation is the "impersonal intelligence," which is not delimited by the ego; and the goal of meditation is metaphysical knowledge, which also goes beyond the individual. The thinking subject is therefore defined by Schuon as "man and God at the same time, pure intelligence being the point of intersection between human reason and the divine Intellect." The final chapter of this book, also entitled "Stations of Wisdom," is itself a rich source of meditation—an unrivalled source, one might say, certainly for our times. Taking as its point of departure six fundamental aspects of Reality, Schuon in masterful fashion shows the application of these aspects at different levels: divine and human, cosmic and symbolic, ethical and alchemical. Through studying carefully these six "stations of wisdom" one will gain a keener insight into what Schuon understands by "meditation," the function of which he describes as follows:

> Meditation acts on the one hand upon the intelligence, in which it awakens certain consubstantial "memories," and on the other hand upon the subconscious imagination which ends by incorporating into itself the truths meditated upon, resulting in a fundamental and as it were organic process of persuasion.[25]

Schuon also refers briefly to "pure concentration" as a possible mode of orison, "on condition that it have a traditional basis and be centered on the Divine; this concentration is none other than silence which, indeed, has been called a 'Name of the Buddha,' because of its connection with the idea of the Void."[26]

---

wherein these rites are legally binding on all. Shankara's emphasis on knowledge as the sole means of deliverance is also often cited by pseudo-esoterists to support the wholesale abandonment of rites; for such pretenders it is rather inconvenient that Shankara also insists that the performance of ritual is a "cause" of knowledge insofar as it "is instrumental in extinguishing that demerit arising out of past sins which obstructs knowledge of the Absolute." Religious rites in general are *arad-upakaraka*, or "remote auxiliaries to knowledge" (*Samkara on Discipleship*, Vol. V of *A Samkara Source-Book*, trans. A. J. Alston [London: Shanti Sadan, 1989], p. 89).

[25] *Stations of Wisdom*, p. 124. The six "stations" referred to here are also treated, with slightly different accentuations, in the chapter entitled "Meditation" in *The Eye of the Heart*.

[26] Ibid., pp. 124-125.

Now whilst meditation may be readily grasped as a mode of prayer, it may not be so clear as to how the "silence" of pure concentration can be assimilated as a form of prayer. The ontological basis of the spiritual efficacy of concentration lies in its negation of negation: everything that is "other than" God—all that can take objective form, that is, all phenomena of existence, inward and outward—in a certain sense "negates" God; by eliminating from consciousness all possible objects—or, what amounts to the same, all "alterity," everything that is other than pure consciousness itself—there occurs that negation of negation which is pure affirmation. This is one of the applications of the double negation, *neti neti:*

> The negation of pleasure, of the world, or of manifestation is equivalent to the implicit affirmation of the Principle which is, in relation to the world, "void" (Sanskrit: *shunya*) and "not this" (*neti*). . . . There is no spirituality which is not founded, in one of its constituent elements, on the negation of this dream; there is no spirituality devoid of ascetic elements. Even simple mental concentration implies sacrifice. When the concentration is continuous, it is the narrow path, or the dark night, and then the soul itself, this living substance full of pictures and desires, is sacrificed.[27]

Turning finally to invocation, this refers to the methodic repetition of a divine Name, a practice that is universal; Schuon refers, at the end of the chapter, to the practice such as it is found in four traditions: the Jesus prayer in Christianity, the invocation of the Name *Allah* in Islam, *japa-yoga* in Hinduism, and the *nembutsu* in Amidist Buddhism. The universality of this mode of prayer is nowadays well known; but less well understood is the reason why it should be the "Name" of God that functions as the key sacramental support for methodic interiorization in such formally diverse spiritual worlds. Schuon, in demonstrating so convincingly the metaphysical foundations of the practice of invocation, renders the invocation all the more intelligible, and hence, its practice all the more compelling. He begins by asserting that it is God Himself who is, in a fundamental sense, the true subject of this mode of prayer:

> The foundation of this mystery is, on the one hand, that "God and His Name are one" (Ramakrishna), and on the other, that God Him-

---

[27] *Spiritual Perspectives and Human Facts*, p. 131. It might be noted in this connection that Shankara refers to concentration as the greatest form of asceticism (*tapas*).

self pronounces His Name in Himself, hence in eternity and outside all creation, so that His unique and uncreate word is the prototype of ejaculatory prayer and even, in a less direct sense, of all orison.[28]

As regards the first point, "God and His Name are one," this is found expressed in diverse traditions, in formulations analogous to Ramakrishna's, such as the Sufi maxim: "the Name is the Named." While this principle on its own is sufficient to render intelligible the practice of invocation, Schuon adds further to this intelligibility by elaborating on the divine archetype of the invocation, indicating the manner in which God may be said to "invoke" Himself, eternally:

> The first distinction that the intellect conceives in the Divine Nature is that of Beyond-Being and Being; but since Being is so to speak the "crystallization" of Beyond-Being, it is like the "Word" of the Absolute, through which the Absolute expresses Itself, determines Itself, or names Itself.[29]

It should be noted that this "Self-naming," coterminous with Self-determination, takes place *in divinis*, that is, within the Divine Nature; in "naming" Himself as Being—or, in determining Himself with a view to entering into principial relationship with manifestation—God does not cease being God. The essence of God has but expressed Itself as Person, at the level of Being. It is thus that God can be said to invoke "His Name in Himself, hence in eternity and outside all creation."

Schuon then proceeds:

> Another distinction which is essential here, and which derives from the preceding by principial succession, is that between God and the world, the Creator and the Creation: just as Being is the Word or Name of Beyond-Being, so too the world—or Existence—is the Utterance of Being, of the personal God; the effect is always the "name" of the cause.[30]

Every link in the chain of descent from the Essence down to the world is, then, the cause, or the "named," with regard to what is beneath it, and the effect or "name" of what is above it. This way of conceiving

---

[28] *Stations of Wisdom*, p. 125.

[29] Ibid., p. 125.

[30] Ibid., pp. 125-126.

of the ontological unfolding of manifestation reveals that God's "invocation" results in the world; the cosmos is the spoken "word" of God. This whole invocatory cosmogony, however, is reversed when the starting point is the invocation as performed by man. For man, being made in the image of God, reflects God both positively and inversely, as is the case with all reflected images: in one respect the image directly reflects its archetype, and in another respect it inverts the archetype, the reflection of a face in a mirror reveals the form of the face, but what is on the right of the face will appear on the left of the reflection, and vice versa. Transposed onto the vertical plane, this inversion means that descent by God is reflected by the ascent of man. Man's invocation, then, in the first respect directly reflects and participates in the eternal invocation of the Divine; and in the second, it inverts the ontological process described by its divine archetype:

> . . . man, for his part, when pronouncing the same Name, describes the inverse movement, for this Name is not only Being and Creation, but also Mercy and Redemption; in man, it does not create, but on the contrary "undoes," and that in a divine manner since it brings man back to the Principle. The divine Name is a metaphysical isthmus (in the sense of the Arabic word *barzakh*): as "seen by God," it is determination, limitation, "sacrifice"; as seen by man, it is liberation, limitlessness, plenitude. We have said that this Name, invoked by man, is nonetheless always pronounced by God; human invocation is always the "outward" effect of eternal and "inward" invocation by the Divinity. The same holds true for every Revelation: it is sacrificial for the divine Spirit and liberating for man; Revelation, whatever its form or mode, is descent or incarnation for the Creator, and ascent or "excarnation" for the creature.[31]

If the above be a description of the objective processes involved in divine descent through manifestation and human ascent through invocation, the following refers to the subjective aspect of the process, the essential function of the invocation as regards the human soul:

> The sufficient reason for the invocation of the Name is the remembering of God; and this, in the final analysis, is not other than consciousness of the Absolute. The name actualizes this consciousness and, in the end, perpetuates it in the soul and fixes it in the heart, so that it penetrates the whole being and at the same time transmutes

[31] Ibid., pp. 126-127.

and absorbs it. Consciousness of the Absolute is the prerogative of human intelligence, and also its aim.[32]

It is this perpetuation of the consciousness of the Absolute that is the supreme aim of the spiritual path. As Schuon says elsewhere: realization is an easy thing for it suffices to remember God; but it is also the most difficult, for man is by nature forgetful. The invocation of the Name of God is the key methodic support for this perpetuation of the consciousness of the Absolute. The invocation of the Name, by virtue of its unitive nature, is proportioned to the pure Absolute, whilst other prayers, differentiated and multiple, correspond to the Personal Divinity. This basic division indicates a key distinction between what Schuon calls the "initiatic" as opposed to the religious or "mystic" way. The first is active, whereas the second is passive; the activity and passivity in question being in relation to grace: for the "initiate," practicing esoteric rites, an active method is being pursued, with a view to opening up the heart to grace. In other words, "grace is actively brought into play by means of the contemplative intelligence which identifies itself more or less directly with that which it contemplates."[33] It is important to stress that this methodic activity is not based on the presumption that grace can be attained or produced simply upon the mechanical performance of the rites in question; such a presumption is excluded for two reasons, one concerning the human dimension and the other, the nature and operation of divine grace. On the human plane, as already noted above, Schuon insists that the integrity of prayer demands conformity of soul, or good character; this highest form of prayer, "leads to the highest pinnacle of perfection, on condition . . . that the activity of prayer be in agreement with all the remainder of the being's activities. . . . The virtues—or conformity to the Divine Law—constitute the *conditio sine qua non* without which the 'spiritual prayer' would be ineffective."[34]

On the divine side, grace does not so much descend in response to the human performance of the invocatory rites; rather such rites "provide a means of removing the obstacles which are opposed to the principially permanent radiation of grace."[35] Grace is never absent, in other words, it is we who are absent from grace, albeit in appearance

[32] Ibid., p. 127.
[33] *The Transcendent Unity of Religions*, p. 73.
[34] Ibid., p. 181.
[35] Ibid., p. 73.

only; the invocation makes us present to the omnipresent reality of grace, and is thus to be considered not so much as the "cause" of grace, as its "effect." It is itself constitutive of grace, the consummation of which in the human soul is properly the concern of God.

The following passage, which concludes *Stations of Wisdom*, expresses in a powerful manner the mystery of this "permanent radiation" of grace, obscured by the veils of outward existence:

> All great spiritual experiences agree in this: there is no common measure between the means put into operation and the result. "With men this is impossible, but with God all things are possible," says the Gospel. In fact, what separates man from divine Reality is but a thin partition: God is infinitely close to man, but man is infinitely far from God. This partition, for man, is a mountain; man stands in front of a mountain which he must remove with his own hands. He digs away the earth, but in vain, the mountain remains; man however goes on digging, in the name of God. And the mountain vanishes. It was never there.[36]

To conclude: Frithjof Schuon laid bare the essentials of prayer in the manner of one who spoke, not speculatively, but out of concrete experience. Neither the profundity of his exposition nor the impact of his writings on the soul can be accounted for apart from this altogether fundamental fact. One feels absolutely sure that his vivid, often poetic, descriptions of the inner unfolding of the life of prayer stemmed from a direct vision, not from imaginative genius. The authority of his tone in this, as in so many domains, bears witness, not so much to one who was simply sure that he was right, but one who was effaced in the essence of that which he spoke about, and, consequently, one through whom the communicable aspects of that essence were expressed. Having given himself to prayer, he was, one feels, "fashioned" by prayer:

> Man prays and prayer fashions man. The saint has himself become prayer, the meeting-place of earth and Heaven; and thus he contains the universe and the universe prays with him. He is everywhere where nature prays and he prays with and in her: in the peaks which

[36] *Stations of Wisdom*, p. 157.

touch the void and eternity, in a flower which scatters itself, or in the abandoned song of a bird.

He who lives in prayer has not lived in vain.[37]

In so directly helping many souls to "live in prayer"—or at least, to live *for* prayer—Frithjof Schuon certainly effected that "restitution" for which he hoped; and, by that very token, helped them to fulfill the very purpose for which they were created; for, as the Qur'an tells us: "And I created the jinn and humankind only that they might worship Me" (51:56).

---

[37] *Spiritual Perspectives and Human Facts*, p. 213.

24 A LETTER ON SPIRITUAL METHOD

Titus Burckhardt

There is no spiritual method without these two basic elements: discernment between the real and the unreal, and concentration on the real. The first of these two elements, discernment or discrimination (*vijñāna* in Sanskrit), does not depend on any special religious form; it only presupposes metaphysical understanding. The second element, however, requires a support of a sacred character, and this means that it can only be achieved within the framework of a normal tradition. The aim of method is perpetual concentration on the Real, and this cannot be achieved by purely human means or on the basis of individual initiative; it presupposes a regular transmission such as exists only within a normal tradition. For what is man? What is his puny will? How can he possibly adhere to the Absolute without first integrating his whole being into a non-individual (i.e. a supra-individual) form? To be precise: there is no spiritual path outside the following traditions or religions: Judaism, Christianity, Islam, Buddhism, Hinduism, and Taoism; but Hinduism is closed for those who have not been born into a Hindu caste, and Taoism is inaccessible.

The guarantee of a spiritual method is that it be received from a spiritual master; the guarantee of spiritual mastership, besides doctrinal orthodoxy, is the initiatic chain going back to one of the great founders of religion—or *avatāra*s, as the Hindus would say. It is the duty of the disciple to obey his master; it is the duty of the master to prove his attachment to the initiatic chain. A master has the right not to accept a disciple; he has the right to conceal his teaching from outsiders, but he does not have the right to conceal from his disciples the spiritual chain he represents or his spiritual predecessors.

The master transmits: (1) the spiritual influence which derives from the founder of the tradition and through him from God; (2) the keys for the understanding of the method or the keys to meditation; (3) the sacred supports for perpetual concentration on the Real.

The distinctive sign of a spiritual master is his awareness of the relativity of forms—as well as of their necessity. Only a man whose knowledge transcends forms knows what forms involve. A master whose spiritual outlook is limited by a particular formal or traditional framework is not a complete master (although a true master may in practice be unfamiliar with traditions other than his own); and a master who rejects all forms is a false master (although a true master may reduce traditional form to its essential elements, and he surely will). No true master puts himself outside a given tradition (or religion), for he knows its meaning and sees its divine origin.

In the spiritual life there is no place for individual experiments; they are too ruinous.

AFTERWORD:
THE REVIVAL OF INTEREST IN TRADITION

Whitall N. Perry

Since the concept *revival* is contingent upon the notion of loss through one way or another of something antecedent—in this case Tradition—it is necessary if speaking about revival, first to understand in what, exactly, this loss consists.

Religion in the current usage of the term cannot be taken as the equivalent of Tradition, for the ritual practice of Religion is a specific act done in a specific place at a specific time to the exclusion of other acts, places, and times, whereas Tradition by protraction encompasses all acts and places and times, leaving nothing outside of itself; moreover, a great deal of what passes for Religion can still be found in the world, whilst Tradition in its integral and living sense hardly at all survives. Hence it may sound paradoxical to state, as we now do, that Tradition has its origin in Religion. Reduced to a formula: Religion is Revelation from God to man, with Tradition being its application and full extension in every domain.

All Revelation, furthermore, proclaims its authenticity or orthodoxy through participation in the ternary Unity-Infinity-Perfection, these being inseparable attributes of the Absolute. Unity, in that the *unique message* every great religion promulgates in common with every other is the Reality of God and the illusoriness of the world, with a Way by which man can leave the unreal for the Real. Infinity, in that a *plenitude* of originality characterizes each revelation to the exclusion of every other: a person in a Buddhist world, for example, could never mistake it for an Islamic one, and vice versa, whereas a heterodox religion betrays its nature through aping the original source or sources from which it has deviated; it has no fresh, spontaneous "avataric perfume" of its own. As for Perfection, each true religion manifests this through the *supranatural beauty* of its forms.

Earliest humanity—in accordance with all scripture, and counter to what the evolutionists would have us believe—participated unitively in a Primordial Religion, which was a "transparent" state of beatitude where human intellection spontaneously duplicated Divine Revelation, or in Biblical parlance, where man spoke with God.

As he lost his unific vision and our cycle of humanity accordingly unfolded, there came the racial divisions, with corresponding revelations adapted to needs of the different periods and sectors of mankind. Those known to us comprise notably Hyperborean shamanism with its Taoist, Bön, and Shinto branches; the shamanism of Siberia and the indigenous peoples of the Western Hemisphere; the animistic faiths of Africa and Southeastern Asia; the Indo-Iranian and Indo-European cultures manifesting chiefly in Hinduism, Buddhism, Zoroastrianism, Orphism, and the Celto-Germanic religions—with elements from other Near-Eastern groups, mainly Egyptian Hermeticism; and then the Semitic monotheisms or Abrahamic religions: Judaism, Christianity, and Islam.

It can happen that traditional forms remain, where their religious context has expired, and the opposite is equally true. Thus, for example, Orphic currents have come down through Pythagoreanism, Platonism, and Neoplatonism into the Christian and Arab spheres. Again, Germanic forms have left their traces in European ornamentation, mythologies, superstitions—from *superstare*, meaning something that "stands over" when the "understanding" of it has been lost—and fairy tales.

Western Christianity is a prime example of a religion outliving its traditional structure, for into what during the so-called Dark Ages and later Middle Ages was a flourishing if precarious traditional civilization, the Promethean humanism of the Renaissance brought a mortal scission, sundering the Inward from the Outward, Spirit from Cosmos, Church from State. Christianity was thenceforth to be an affair of the churches and monasteries, with the rest of life more or less abandoned to a relativistic individualism that would with its analytical thought and experimental sciences explore the properties of a matter now sealed off from higher orders of Reality, thus leading to pursuits in every facet of society that were irremediably profane, and all the more so for the fascination which the new and untried works on souls.

By Christianity we do not mean the splinter cults and sects unleashed by Protestantism, although we do include the main religious currents descending from early [Lutheran] evangelicalism. And still less do we mean the Conciliar Church of John XXIII and his successors, being a work of falsification by men of whom at best it can be said that they are mindless of what is owed to a spiritual legacy of two thousand years. Lastly, the preceding paragraph does not strictly include the Eastern branches of Christianity, which managed in some measure to retain their traditional mould despite the buffetings of the

Renaissance, and which today are more in a state of dormancy than dissolution.

*   *   *

Religion has just been defined as a Revelation from God to man; the content revealed is a Doctrine, a Method, and a Way. The Supreme One through the creative Act inherent in the Bounty of its Infinity has become the many, and it is now for the many to be recollected back to Unity; the word "religion" even shares with the word "yoga" the root meaning of "to bind together." In following the basic schema put forth by Frithjof Schuon, the Doctrine is a *discernment* addressed to the Intellect concerning the distinction between the Absolute and the relative, Reality and Illusion, *Ātmā* and *Māyā*; the Method is a *technique* addressed to man's volitional powers for maintaining a concentration on the Real; and the Way is a *life* addressed to the soul for conforming itself through intelligence, virtue, and beauty to the nature of Reality.

It is the Way which is particularly the province of Tradition, since it covers every aspect of man's relationship with the Cosmos; the Way is thus a Sacrifice—in the sense of "making sacred"—of all man's acts and attitudes in accordance with Divine Exemplars ("Make all things according to the pattern which was shewn thee on the mount" [Exodus 25:40; Hebrews 8:5]—the "mount" here representing the archetypal originals which are reflected in our world by similitude).

Tradition is the continuity of Revelation: an uninterrupted transmission, through innumerable generations, of the spiritual and cosmological principles, sciences, and laws resulting from a revealed religion: nothing is neglected, from the establishment of social orders and codes of conduct to the canons regulating the arts and architecture, ornamentation and dress; it includes the mathematical, physical, medical, and psychological sciences, encompassing moreover those deriving from celestial movements. What contrasts it totally with our modern learning, which is a closed system materially, is its reference of all things back to superior planes of being, and eventually to ultimate Principles; considerations entirely unknown to modern man.

*   *   *

The ravages wreaked on traditional structures by the new humanism (revived from the residues of the Graeco-Roman decadence) were viewed on the contrary by Renaissance standards as a bold thrust towards "reality"; the shutting out of Heaven was regarded instead as an unveiling of earthly possibilities; matter was henceforth considered an inexhaustible property to be exploited and consumed as an end in itself, thus giving rise to spurious notions like Evolution and Progress which have acted as a sort of leaven to our technological and atheistically-oriented civilization.

Yet, thanks to the law of cosmic compensation which reigns throughout all vicissitudes, there certainly were not wanting men of spiritual understanding who represented those values generally being abandoned—Renaissance figures like Nicholas of Cusa, Marcilio Ficino, Paracelsus, and including numerous intellectuals turning for the continuance of traditional doctrines and practices to Hermetico-Kabbalistic currents. The seventeenth century gave us a few isolated gnostics such as Jacob Boehme and the Cambridge Platonists; and Thomas Taylor in the period following—distinguished only for its rationalism—stood out as a solitary transmitter of Hellenic gnosis.

The global spread of nineteenth-century materialism with its crass and self-complacent obduracy was bound to engender by reaction various earnest if fragmentary efforts for traditional restoration. In the aesthetic domain there was typically the challenge of William Morris against factory-produced "art," while a Viollet-le-Duc engaged his genius in preserving our Gothic heritage. Meantime, the West was gaining extensive contact with Eastern doctrines and scriptures owing to the work of Max Müller and other illustrious orientalists. And occultists ranging from the highly endowed to the frankly dubious were contributing their share as regards esoteric and pseudo-esoteric traditions. Conversely, Sri Ramakrishna's voice from the Orient was awakening people to the universal truths underlying all religions. The East moreover had its own spokesmen excoriating modernism and reminding their countrymen of neglected patrimonies, men like B. G. Tilak, Ku Hung-ming, and Okakura Kakuzo; for it must not be overlooked that Easterners by and large when confronted with Western innovations betray a fearful muddle of fascination with subservience: the West may dispense the poison, but the East all too eagerly and with a deplorable lack of critical discernment drains the cup.

What has been so far described represents on the whole an accumulation of isolated attempts to salvage the sacred, the true, and the beautiful out of a civilization where these things no longer conveyed any relevance. But it was just this apparent incompatibility between two seemingly irreconcilable attitudes—the Science versus Religion

"syndrome"—that engendered in our century a devastating and irre-
futable response, one calling for a reassessment of all values in terms of
First Principles. This witness fell on the shoulders of three metaphysical giants, whose messages—while necessarily overlapping—could
still respectively be classed under the headings of Doctrine, Way, and
Method.

*   *   *

René Guénon (1886-1951) was the first to arrive on the scene,
with articles by him appearing in *La Gnose*—a Hermetico-occultist
review—as early as 1909. Of conservative French Catholic background, Guénon from his childhood was a frail but precocious scholar
who already by his twentieth year was leaving an apprenticeship in
philosophy and mathematics to pursue learning in Parisian occultist
circles, following an interest that had been kindled by one or another
of his former instructors.

What manifested in him at this period was an uncanny genius for
seizing the essentials behind the fragments and residues of traditional
teachings that were the sole possession which the secret societies he
frequented had in common. Within three years he had managed to
comb through the milieu, including importantly its lower depths, only
to emerge all at once with a refutation of the pernicious errors, along
with a rectification of the rest on the basis of true principles. The
catalyzing element here was undoubtedly a contact, about which no
details are known, that Guénon had with a Hindu or Hindus of the
Advaita Vedānta school, just previous to the time he began writing,
the effect of which was to polarize his already considerable understanding into a real adequacy regarding the ultimate truths which are
the common property of all Revelation. Concurrent with this, moreover, were teachings he received through Westerners attached more
or less closely to Taoism and Islam.

We know by the titles of lectures he proposed to give and by
his contributions to *La Gnose* until this review ceased publication in
early 1912 that Guénon already then was virtually in possession of the
entire life-work which was to appear from 1921 onwards in the books
and articles that constitute his fame today.

To a pragmatic civilization plunged in relativity, Guénon brought
a message based on principles and certainties, and expressed in a tone
so authoritative as to repel many readers before they even examined the evidence objectively on its own grounds. He explained and

distinguished between the Absolute and the relative, Principle and manifestation, Universals and particulars, Intellect and reason. And he demonstrated the correlation between Revelation and Orthodoxy, which alone allows a legitimate foundation for concepts and practices claiming the right to infallibility.

To a materialistic society enthralled with the phenomenal universe exclusively, Guénon, taking the Vedānta as point of departure, revealed a metaphysical and cosmological teaching both macrocosmic and microcosmic about the hierarchized degrees of being or states of existence, starting with the Absolute and descending through Pure Being, then the supraformal Archetypes, after which the subtle domain, and terminating with our sphere of gross manifestation. He elucidated the much misunderstood Eastern expositions about the posthumous states of the being, those that are central and those peripheral, the paradisal possibilities and the infernal ones, the degrees of spiritual realization—including the distinction between salvation and deliverance—and the doctrine of the Supreme Identity or final Union with the Godhead. While one could say that much of this is already to be found in Dante and other Western sources, the rejoinder is, first, that Guénon being a spokesman for traditional ideas strictly disavowed saying anything new or "on his own," and secondly, that Dante is now read only as poetry, whereas Guénon is addressing his critical contemporaries in a scientific idiom suited to their understanding even if its content—due to their materialistic prejudices—is not.

Continuing further, he expounds the doctrine of Cosmic Cycles and the Four Ages of mankind in keeping with the teachings of all earlier civilizations, and he shows clearly that we are presently in the period known to Hinduism as the *Kali yuga* or Dark Age, and even in its latter throes as our cycle accelerates towards the material dissolution and temporal rupture that mark the transition between two worlds. Guénon's work from this perspective can be regarded as preparatory, as coming providentially at a cosmic moment when it is imperative that some sort of traditional restoration take place and the nucleus of an elect be formed with the dual role of reclaiming perennial values, and of acting as a counterforce to the aberrations of the modern world. For his rejection of modernism is unqualified:

> Nothing and nobody is any longer in the right place; men no longer recognize any effective authority in the spiritual order or any legitimate power in the temporal; the "profane" presume to discuss what is sacred, and to contest its character and even its existence; the

inferior judges the superior, ignorance sets bounds to wisdom, error prevails over truth, the human supersedes the divine, earth overtops heaven, the individual sets the measure for all things and claims to dictate to the universe laws drawn entirely from his own relative and fallible reason. "Woe unto you, ye blind guides," the Gospel says; and indeed everywhere today one sees nothing but blind leaders of the blind, who, unless restrained by some timely check, will inevitably lead them into the abyss, there to perish with them.

As part of his witness Guénon mercilessly exposes false sects and subversive doctrines, including the pernicious teachings rampant in modern philosophy and psychology. But this is done with the detachment of one who sees the cosmic causes behind the phenomena, by one who knows that "it must needs be that offences come."

In several of his books he weighs the different manners in which a traditional regeneration might come about. The most favorable solution for the West, he says, is if it could return to its own intellectual sources, but the sole organization constituted for such a work is the Catholic Church, and the doubts he expressed as to its competence for this, given its state of blindness at the time of his writing to perils from without and within, have since then been only too amply confirmed. In his view a more likely if less expedient outcome would be were the West to find itself obliged to turn for help to some traditional repository still extant in the East. This would entail on the part of those Westerners qualified for the task the readaptation in their world of an Eastern tradition still possessing a spiritual aristocracy fully conscious of the necessity for such a work and able to lend the support required. By its nature a response of this kind could directly concern only a very small minority, but the presence of these people alone, although unknown to the majority, would already have a leavening influence spiritually and would serve as a vehicle for the transmission of truths carrying indefinite repercussions.

Guénon's own affiliations were Islamic, and from 1930 on he lived in Egypt, but the modality of his vision remained essentially Vedantic and Hermetic. We will just add that the Orient since his death has shown itself increasingly in need of certain positive qualities that enlightened Westerners can offer, for even though the Hindu, Buddhist, and Islamic worlds retain the allegiance of countless millions, these religions are surviving more on a "horizontal" past momentum than they are on a present "vertical" awareness of all that Tradition stands for in terms of First Principles; and, lacking effectively an intellectual aristocracy, they are quasi-blind to the devastating forces of modernism which are gaining the ascendancy at this perilous cosmic moment. It is here that awakened Western intellectuals can best supply the searing critical faculties demanded, in Guénon's words, "to safeguard the 'ark' of the tradition, which cannot perish, and to ensure the transmission of all that is to be preserved."

Returning to Guénon's doctrinal teachings, he laid great emphasis throughout his writings on the science of rites and symbols: higher orders of being have their reverberations in the lower, and it is through language, rite, symbol, and image that a spiritual communication is maintained between our phenomenal universe and its heavenly Prototype. The formulas revealed in sacred languages—prayers, litanies, incantations, invocations, mantras—are so many vibrations of the primordial Word, and thus mysteriously partake of the nature of God's own substance, eucharistically speaking. This means that any translation of these formulas into vernacular tongues immediately breaks the communication and renders void their salvific power. Guénon shows us how the symbolic forms which permeated the constructions and thinking of traditional societies are representations of universal truths capable of interpretations on multiple levels of reality, and he shows how sacred images and icons have the indispensable role of conveying divine presences.

In the passage against modernism cited above from *The Crisis of the Modern World*, Guénon alludes to spiritual authority and temporal power—being concepts which are rooted in the nature of reality. He recalls that the repartition of the social order with its diversified vocations based on distinctions of caste, whether taking into account the formal system observed in India or the less rigid divisions predominating in mediaeval Europe, far from being arbitrary corresponds to intimate differences in human natures, and in fact to differences obtaining throughout creation. And the cosmological explanation for this is explicitly given in the Hindu doctrine of the *gunas*: *Prakriti*, the unmanifested primordial Substance of the Universe contains within itself three tendencies or poles of attraction, without which there would be no manifestation; the first is *sattva*, by nature ascending and luminous, the second is *rajas*, being expansive and fiery, and the third is *tamas*, the descending and obscure principle. It is these *gunas* which ultimately regulate the social order, and one cannot just wish them away; one can at most ignore the principles at stake, at the price of begetting social disorders without end.

What has been the impact of the Guénonian message upon receptive readers? The unquestionability of the doctrines exposed ought in principle to lay the groundwork for infallible spiritual responses, but in practice it is not altogether that simple. The very fact that Guénon had to address his contemporaries in a scientific vein has its built-in pitfalls. For reading him unguardedly has the tendency to turn people into "spiritual scientists," which can spell death to spirituality. The alluring dimensions of initiation and esoterism, moreover, have a proclivity to appeal to the head rather than the heart, and to make one forget that "the fear of the Lord is the beginning of wisdom" and that Tradition has no meaning apart from a way back to God—a way which has its foundations in submission, devotion, and rectitude.

Those who apotheosize Guénon by reading into his work more than it was meant to offer render him as great a disservice as do those who reject his message globally because of some factual errors compounded with certain untenable if contingent hypotheses. One has to distinguish the major ideas, which owing to their timeless, nonhuman origin are infallible, from the speculative element that attaches to what Schuon calls "the human margin." Curiously enough, in striving to stay clear of all individualism whatsoever in his writing, Guénon employed a mode of thinking that was "impersonal" to a degree almost inhuman in its one-sidedly mathematical though crystalline abstraction, and which somewhat defeats its purpose, given that the human individuality is intrinsically a legitimate factor in the total cosmic picture and must therefore be included along with the rest. But here it is also a question of a man having an altogether exceptional character, and it in no way alters the essential message.

The factual errors referred to may be an indirect consequence of Guénon's inborn metaphysical wisdom: his certitude about principles left him somewhat careless regarding the pedestrian but inescapable requirements of scholarship; and parallel with this no doubt was a certain impatience with the conventions of modern erudition which mistakes quantitative information for knowledge.

Guénon well understood the preparatory and theoretical nature of his work. "All that we shall do or say," he wrote, "will amount to giving those who come afterwards facilities which we ourself were not given; here, as everywhere else, it is the beginning of the work that is the most painful." And he asks his readers "above all to refrain from holding any doctrine responsible for the imperfections and gaps in our treatise."

*   *   *

At the time when the nascent French metaphysician was turning towards occultist circles in Paris, a graduate student from University College, London, was in Ceylon as a geologist directing the Mineralogical Survey, which won him the degree of Doctor of Science from the University of London in 1906, at the age of twenty-nine. Thus began the career of Ananda K. Coomaraswamy (1877-1947), born in Colombo to an illustrious Tamil Śaivite Hindu from Jaffna and a patrician English lady, who raised her only child in England following the premature death of her husband.

Along with his discovery in 1904 of a rare oxide which he named thorianite, the young Coomaraswamy was coming upon a neglected treasure of a magnitude such that he felt compelled to start out on a whole new footing: this was India's magnificent cultural heritage of some three thousand years, a heritage intimately linked with Ceylon's, and whose foundations were now being eroded by what Guénon calls the "proselytizing fury" of the West, with its arts more particularly succumbing before the tide of factory produce flooding in from Europe. What provoked Coomaraswamy above all was the Asiatic apathy to the transition taking place; he deplored "the lack of self-respect and self-reliance amongst a people who have learnt to look back in contempt upon their past and to admire rather indiscriminately any foreign ways they see a chance of imitating. . . . It is useless, of course, to speak of those who regard all the past of Eastern nations as merely barbarous and savage previous to the advent of Western civilization; there are many such and they remind me much of those sixteenth-century men who turned so scornfully away from England's past and England's beauty to make a degenerate copy of classical literature and art."

The young Doctor first tried his hand at social reform but soon found that this was dealing with effects rather than causes, and he next turned to a vocation for which he was to prove himself eminently qualified—that of expert on traditional Asian arts. Although he had been invested with the sacred thread in an initiation ceremony that took place in Ceylon in the year 1897, Coomaraswamy, given his East-West lineage and consequent lifestyle, could never formally be considered a Hindu, and he wrote of himself towards the end of his life, "I . . . can only call myself a follower of the *Philosophia Perennis*, or if required to be more specific, a Vedantin." By this he proclaimed his perspective to be the universality of the Sanātana Dharma and his doctrinal point of departure the Veda. Though obviously not pure Hinduism, it is clearly what Heaven intended in order that his message reach the world. And Coomaraswamy would always consider himself an Oriental spokesman, despite living in the West and addressing mainly Westerners. Early in his career he remarked:

> Religion is not in the East, as it is in the West, a formula or a doc-
> trine, but a way of looking at life, and includes all life, so that there
> is no division into sacred and profane

—a remark, be it added, that gives a very succinct definition of the comparative distinction between Tradition and Religion as propounded at the beginning of this essay.

For Coomaraswamy, the right way of looking at art was integral to this position, because traditional arts were so many reflections of immutable principles: art was a mode of spiritual knowing, both for artist and patron, or else it was nothing worthy of man's attention and moreover a vice, since false art—the bane of individualism—could only mislead man from the ends for which he was created. The mythological content of the arts he was pursuing fascinated Coomaraswamy and inspired him—with his inborn universal genius, similar to, though differently oriented, from Guénon's—to see and reveal the striking homogeneity of mythical patterns in traditions having the most diverse outward characters. Already a master linguist (with a working knowledge of some thirty basic tongues the world over), he was discovering a common vocabulary on a higher plane shared alike by all the great religions, namely, the language of the Logos or the Primordial Word:

> In the beginning was the Word, and the Word was with God, and
> the Word was God (John 1:1). Utterance (*vāk*) brought forth all
> the Universe (*Śatapatha Brāhmana* VI *passim*). From the sound
> of Vedas that supreme Divinity made all things (*Mānava-dharma-
> śāstra* I.21).

"Of all the names and forms of God," wrote Coomaraswamy, "the monogrammatic syllable Om, the totality of all sounds and the music of the spheres chanted by the resonant Sun, is the best. The validity of such an audible symbol is exactly the same as that of a plastic icon, both alike serving as supports of contemplation (*dhiyālamba*); such a support is needed because that which is imperceptible to eye or ear cannot be apprehended objectively as it is in itself, but only in a likeness. The symbol must be naturally adequate, and cannot be chosen at random."

Around the start of the thirties Coomaraswamy through the Indologist, Heinrich Zimmer, encountered the work of Guénon, and this brought a definite vertical dimension to the Doctor's vast erudition. Shortly afterwards appeared one of his most important books, *The Transformation of Nature in Art*, which was really telling about the transformation of *man's* nature *through the spiritual resonances inherent* in *sacred* art. While our universities are replete with doctoral theses on primitive and not-so-primitive cultures, practically without exception these papers are marred by a false point of departure owing to ignorance regarding man's true origins and intimate nature, and this is what Guénon and Coomaraswamy were set on rectifying "in a way that may be ignored but cannot be refuted," as the Doctor put it. He detested the practice of reading arbitrary meanings into things which already had their true meaning:

> Let us then, admit that the greater part of what is taught in the Fine Arts Departments of our Universities, all of the psychologies of art, all the obscurities of modern aesthetics, are only so much verbiage, only a kind of defense that stands in the way of our understanding of the wholesome art, at the same time iconographically true and practically useful, that was once to be had in the market place or from any good artist; and that whereas the rhetoric that cares for nothing but the truth is the rule and method of the intellectual arts, our aesthetic is nothing but a false rhetoric, and a flattery of human weakness by which we can only account for the arts that have no other purpose than to please.
>
> . . . However this may be, we also pretend to a "scientific" and "objective" discipline of the "history and appreciation of art," in which we take account not only of contemporary or very recent art but also of the whole of art from the beginning until now. . . . [Yet] I put it to you that it is not by our aesthetic, but only by their rhetoric, that we can hope to understand and interpret the arts of other peoples and other ages than our own; I put it to you that our present university courses in this field embody a pathetic fallacy, and are anything but scientific in any sense (*Figures of Speech or Figures of Thought*).

Because Coomaraswamy, like Guénon, was defending timeless but forgotten truths that were none of his own invention, he did not hesitate with his formidable intellectual apparatus to batter at the university savants with an overwhelming erudition whose point was nonetheless unalloyed and single-minded: that the rites and ceremonies, myths and symbols, legends and sagas, and arts in general of earlier civilizations which the savants made it their prerogative to elucidate were but different expressions of the language of the Spirit, and that any attempt to construe it otherwise—no matter how brilliant the scholarship—could amount to no more in the end than academic narcissism. And if his message fell on deaf ears, Coomaraswamy claimed "this is because our sentimental generation, in which the power of the intellect has been so perverted by the power of observation that we can no longer distinguish the reality from the phenomenon, the Person in the Sun from his sightly body, or the uncreated from electric light, will not be persuaded 'though one rose from the dead.'"

The Doctor's writings in his later years became increasingly centered on the *Philosophia Perennis*, and more particularly on its aspect as Way: "We must do what the Gods did erst" was a refrain he reiterated from the *Śatapatha Brāhmana*: "The Sacrifice (*yajña*) undertaken here below is a ritual mimesis of what was done by the Gods in the beginning. . . . [It] reflects the Myth; but like all reflections, inverts it. What had been a process of generation and division becomes now one of regeneration and composition." Just as "in the beginning," or *in divinis*, there had to be a "God-slaying" to "dismember" and thus liberate the possibilities dormant in the Divine Substance if there were to be any world or worlds, so now there has to be a slaying of the Outer Man by means of a Sacrifice ("making sacred") that can *re-member*—in the sense of Platonic reconnection (cp. Luke 22:19; "this do in remembrance of Me")—and restore him to his deiform Prototype:

> This conception of the Sacrifice as an incessant operation and the sum of man's duty finds its completion in a series of texts in which *each and every function of the active life*, down to our very breathing, eating, drinking, and dalliance *is sacramentally interpreted* and death is nothing but the final *katharsis*. And that is, finally, the famous "Way of Works" (*karma mārga*) of the *Bhagavad Gītā*, where to fulfill one's own vocation, determined by one's own nature, without self-referent motives, is the *way* of perfection (*Hinduism and Buddhism*, italics ours).

Coomaraswamy tended to see this Way or process of "self-naughting" as a cosmic play (*līlā*) where the Myth was the reality, with the participation of the passible human individual in the drama reduced to little more than an accident of history or illusion ("What we call our 'consciousness' is nothing but a process")—a perspective that approached Guénon's mathematically abstract view of things, and inevitably left wanting a whole human dimension to the picture which someone else would have to redeem. A traditional witness, in other words, had been given of the Doctrine and of the Way, but a concrete revelation of the Method *per se* had yet to appear. If a revival of interest in Tradition was being accomplished, there still lacked the components essential for any revival of the thing itself.

*   *   *

Frithjof Schuon, born in Basle in 1907 of German descent, had both the advantage and disadvantage of coming after his two precursors, whose careers at this moment were already under way: the advantage, in that by the time he started writing in the thirties, Guénon and Coomaraswamy had cleared an enormous amount of ground and were establishing a whole school of thought based on the *Philosophia Perennis*, namely, the core of metaphysical principles which the West had long lost from view; the disadvantage, in that people to this day persist in ranking Schuon as a follower—or even a disciple—of Guénon, when the facts are quite otherwise. Thus, in the Introduction to his *Logic and Transcendence*, which first appeared in 1970, he felt obliged to advise his readers:

> We do not necessarily subscribe to every assessment, conclusion, or theory formulated in the name of metaphysical, esoteric, or broadly traditional principles; in other words, we do not espouse any theory simply because it belongs to some particular school, and we wish to be held responsible solely for what we write ourself.

Schuon, who is what the Hindus would call a "master," by his universality eludes easy classification, but the concept to which he best answers is that of the *Sophia Perennis* or *Religio Perennis;* and the combination of wisdom with spirituality in his message certainly highlights the appropriateness of both terms, which can be synthesized in the idea of Theosophy or Gnosis, provided these words are understood in their original, etymological sense, without reference to any sect, society, or movement.

Extracts from journals he kept in his youth manifest an instinctive spiritual genius naturally gravitating towards the grandeur and beauty of the Sacred—qualities that were already well developed before he came upon the works of Guénon, in his eighteenth year. It was from North Africa, moreover, that in his mid-twenties he received his formal spiritual affiliations.

325

Endowed with an exceptional degree of artistic perception combined with a penetrating understanding of man as such, ethnologically, culturally, psychologically, and spiritually, Schuon has the gift of reconstructing from one or two elements the essentials of virtually any traditional society that has ever existed—be it the American Indians, the ancient Japanese, tribal Africans, or different sectors of the Semitic and Aryan worlds. What this comes down to in practice is a summation and evaluation of traditional currents, ideas, and spiritual truths presented with a logic and objectivity that have perhaps known no parallel since a Plato or a Śankarāchārya. Added to this is a destiny to guide and integrate souls through a traditional perspective, crucial in its immediacy, which is the very antithesis of the modern outlook, and which by a "yoga" combining intelligence with a full deployment of the virtues can lead to the plenitude of the human state. For he beholds our modern civilization as a betrayal of man's nature—not in the sense of what man can accomplish, which in its way is practically unlimited, but in the sense of what man was created to accomplish. Guénon gave the pattern; Schuon has completed the specifics. Coomaraswamy presented the mould; Schuon has filled in the colors. He says it has been his role, moreover, to restore the notion of the Absolute in a West that has fallen into an unmitigated relativism.

The present developments of this Master's work lie outside the scope of our treatise, but the manner of his Theosis is amply demonstrated in his writings, for those who will read. While there is no end to what could be cited, we offer two representative passages—the first from *Light on the Ancient Worlds*:

> The difference between ordinary vision and that enjoyed by the sage or the gnostic is quite clearly not of the sensorial order. The sage sees things in their total context, therefore in their relativity and at the same time in their metaphysical transparency; he does not see them as if they were physically diaphanous or endowed with a mystical sonority or a visible aura, even though his vision may sometimes be described by means of such images. . . . A spiritual vision of things is distinguished by a concrete perception of universal relationships and not by some special sensorial characteristic. The "third eye" is the faculty of seeing phenomena *sub specie aeternitatis* and therefore in a sort of simultaneity; to it are often added, in the nature of things, intuitions concerning modalities that are in the ordinary way imperceptible.
>
> The sage sees causes in effects, and effects in causes; he sees God in all things, and all things in God. A science that penetrates the depths of the "infinitely great" and of the "infinitely small" on the

physical plane, but denies other planes although it is they that reveal the sufficient reason of the nature we perceive and provide the key to it, such a science is a greater evil than ignorance pure and simple; it is in fact a "counterscience," and its ultimate effects cannot but be deadly. In other words, modern science is a totalitarian rationalism that eliminates both Revelation and Intellect, and at the same time a totalitarian materialism that is blind to the metaphysical relativity—and therewith also the impermanence—of matter and of the world. It does not know that the suprasensible, situated as it is beyond space and time, is the concrete principle of the world, and that it is consequently also at the origin of that contingent and changeable coagulation we call "matter." A science that is called "exact" is in fact an "intelligence without wisdom," just as post-Scholastic philosophy is inversely a "wisdom without intelligence."

The second passage is from *Logic and Transcendence*:

Human life is studded with uncertainties; man loses himself in what is uncertain instead of holding on to what is absolutely certain in his destiny, namely death, Judgment, and Eternity. But besides these there is a fourth certainty, immediately accessible moreover to human experience, and this is the present moment, in which man is free to choose either the Real or the illusory, and thus to ascertain for himself the value of the three great eschatological certainties. The consciousness of the sage is founded upon these three points of reference, whether directly or in an indirect and implicit manner through "remembrance of God". . . . The important thing to grasp here is that actualization of the consciousness of the Absolute, namely the "remembrance of God" or "prayer" . . . is already a death and a meeting with God and it places us already in Eternity; it is already something of Paradise and even, in its mysterious and "uncreated" quintessence, something of God. Quintessential prayer brings about an escape from the world and from life, and thereby confers a new and Divine sap upon the veil of appearances and the current of forms, and a fresh meaning to our presence amid the play of phenomena.

Whatever is not here is nowhere, and whatever is not now will never be. As is this moment in which I am free to choose God, so will be death, Judgment, and Eternity. Likewise in this center, this Divine point which I am free to choose in the face of this boundless and multiple world, I am already in invisible Reality.

*   *   *

Taking an overall view, what can one say has been the repercussion on the world resulting from the works of the three authors under discussion? Certainly their ideas are now known and seriously studied in academic and intellectual circles from America to Japan; their writings have been translated into a number of tongues. For many years the journal, *Études Traditionnelles*, has been an organ for these ideas in France, and there is the more recent English review, *Studies in Comparative Religion.**

Of events directly inspired by this work, the first was an interreligious colloquium that took place in Houston, Texas, in 1973 on the theme "Traditional Modes of Contemplation and Action," which, it should be stressed, had nothing to do with ecumenism as commonly understood—which is a spiritually disguised humanism corrosive to true spirituality—but rather was a question of multiple religious forces making common cause against the ravages of atheism. Then, in 1976, there was the World of Islam Festival held in London, and in 1985, a conference on Tradition was organized by the *Institute of Traditional Studies* in Lima, Peru.

In 1974, an *Imperial Iranian Academy of Philosophy* devoted to the study of philosophy as traditionally conceived was founded in Tehran under the direction of Seyyed Hossein Nasr, but in 1980, the political upheavals in Iran brought the activities of the Academy to an end including its journal, *Sophia Perennis*. In 1979, a *Sri Lanka Institute of Traditional Studies* was inaugurated in Colombo and, more recently, a U.S. *Foundation for Traditional Studies* was set up in Washington, D.C.

But this overall view still concerns renewal of *interest* in Tradition, which is one thing, whereas the actual practice of Tradition is quite another. In these degenerate times which have spawned countless pseudo religions, often Oriental in stripe, the Adversary wears as many disguises, and it seems to be archi-rare when anyone can distinguish the gulf which separates authentic teachings from the distortions made

---

* Editors' Note: Since the demise of *Studies in Comparative Religion* in 1984, the North American journals *Sophia: The Journal of Traditional Studies*, *Sacred Web: A Journal of Tradition and Modernity*, and the online journal *Vincit Omnia Veritas* (http://www.religioperennis.org) have provided a forum for Traditionalist studies in the Anglophone world, while World Wisdom, Sophia Perennis, Fons Vitae, the Foundation for Traditional Studies, Archetype, and the Islamic Texts Society have published a significant number of English language books by Perennialist authors, including several works by Guénon, Coomaraswamy, Schuon, Burckhardt, Pallis, and Lings.

of them by people like Madame Blavatsky, Krishnamurti, Aurobindo, Gurdjieff and others—and this despite the fact that Guénon, Coomaraswamy, and Schuon have tirelessly furnished all the keys necessary for such a discernment. But God knows his own, and it is not a question of numbers but strictly of a qualitative dimension within this Reign of Quantity as Guénon characterizes the cosmic moment we are now passing through.

The pertinent issue for the reader of this book is not the macrocosmic one of the possibility or impossibility of a traditional restoration—something which only an intervention from Heaven can accomplish—but rather the microcosmic one, namely, the certainty that something on the basis of this knowledge can and has to be done in each individual soul while still on this planet before that moment when it is cast onto the Cosmic Ocean where traditional considerations alone henceforth have any relevance—when the illusory veil of a self-sufficient materialism is withdrawn and one stands naked before the benefic or terrible modes of Reality.

A person who has truly found his traditional bearings will forevermore be at peace with himself and his universe, knowing, in Guénon's words, "that the 'end of a world' never is and never can be anything but the end of an illusion."

ACKNOWLEDGMENTS

The editors wish to thank the following authors, editors, and publishers for their consent to publish the articles in this anthology.

1. "Religion and Tradition": Lord Northbourne, *Religion in the Modern World*, Ghent, NY: Sophia Perennis, 2001, pp. 3-11.

2. "Modernism: The Profane Point of View": Lord Northbourne, *Religion in the Modern World*, Ghent, NY: Sophia Perennis, 2001, pp. 12-19.

3. "Looking Back on Progress": Lord Northbourne, *Looking Back on Progress*, Ghent, NY: Sophia Perennis, 1995, pp. 7-22.

4. "The Past in the Light of the Present & The Rhythms of Time": Martin Lings, *Ancient Beliefs and Modern Superstitions*, Cambridge, UK: Archetype, 2001, pp. 1-23.

5. "Evolutionism": Titus Burckhardt, *Mirror of the Intellect*, translated by William Stoddart, Cambridge, UK: Quinta Essentia, 1987, pp. 30-45.

6. "Modern Science and the Dehumanization of Man": Philip Sherrard, *Studies in Comparative Religion* 1976, 10 (2), pp. 74-93.

7. "Oriental Metaphysics": René Guénon, *Tomorrow* 1964, 12 (4), pp. 6-16, translated by J.C. Cooper.

8. "The Decisive Boundary": Martin Lings, *Symbol & Archetype: A Study of the Meaning of Existence*, Cambridge, UK: Quinta Essentia, 1991, pp. 13-18.

9. "*Scientia Sacra*" (abridged): Seyyed Hossein Nasr, *Knowledge and the Sacred*, Edinburgh: Edinburgh University Press, 1981, pp. 130-159.

10. "Understanding and Believing": Frithjof Schuon, *Logic and Transcendence*, translated by Peter N. Townsend, London: Perennial Books, 1975, pp. 198-208; revised translation by Mark Perry and Jean-Pierre Lafouge.

11. "The Symbol": Martin Lings, *The Book of Certainty: The Sufi Doctrine of Faith, Vision, and Gnosis*, Cambridge, UK: Islamic Texts Society, 1992, pp. 35-40.

12. "The Traditional Doctrine of Symbolism": Ghazi bin Muhammad, *Sophia* 2001, 7 (1), pp. 85-108.

13. "The Language of the Birds": René Guénon, *Fundamental Symbols: The Universal Language of Sacred Science*, compiled and edited by Michel Valsan, translated by Alvin Moore, Jr., revised and edited by Martin Lings, Cambridge, UK: Quinta Essentia, 1995, pp. 39-42.

14. "Symplegades" (abridged): Ananda K. Coomaraswamy, *Studies in Comparative Religion* 1973, 7 (1), pp. 35-56.

15. "The Spirit of the Times": Martin Lings, *The Eleventh Hour: The Spiritual Crisis of the Modern World in the Light of Tradition and Prophecy*, Cambridge, UK: Archetype, 2002, pp. 53-69.

16. "Paths That Lead to the Same Summit": Ananda K. Coomaraswamy, *The Bugbear of Literacy*, Pates Manor, Bedfont: Perennial Books, 1979, pp. 50-67.

17. "Mysticism": William Stoddart, *Sacred Web* 1998, 2, pp. 65-77.

18. "The Perennial Philosophy": Frithjof Schuon, in *The Unanimous Tradition: Essays on the Essential Unity of All Religions*, edited by Ranjit Fernando, translated by William Stoddart, Colombo: Sri Lanka Institute of Traditional Studies, 1991, pp. 21-24.

19. "Foundations of an Integral Aesthetics": Frithjof Schuon, *Esoterism as Principle and as Way*, translated by William Stoddart, Pates Manor, Bedfont: Perennial Books, 1981, pp. 177-182; revised translation by Mark Perry and Jean-Pierre Lafouge.

20. "An Introduction to Sacred Art": Titus Burckhardt, *Sacred Art in East and West: Its Principles and Methods*, translated by Lord Northbourne, Louisville, Kentucky: Fons Vitae/Bloomington, IN: World Wisdom, 2001, pp. 11-20.

21. "Do Clothes Make the Man? The Significance of Human Attire": Marco Pallis, *The Way and the Mountain*, London: Peter Owen, 1991, pp. 141-159.

22. "Virtue and Morality": Tage Lindbom, *Studies in Comparative Religion* 1975, 9 (4), pp. 227-235.

23. "Frithjof Schuon and Prayer": Reza Shah-Kazemi, *Sophia* 1998, 4 (2), pp. 180-193.

24. "A Letter on Spiritual Method": Titus Burckhardt, *Mirror of the Intellect*, translated by William Stoddart, Cambridge, UK: Quinta Essentia, 1987, pp. 251-252.

Afterword: "The Revival of Interest in Tradition": Whitall N. Perry, in *The Unanimous Tradition: Essays on the Essential Unity of All Religions*, edited by Ranjit Fernando, Colombo: Sri Lanka Institute of Traditional Studies, 1991, pp. 3-16.

NOTES ON CONTRIBUTORS
In order of appearance

LORD NORTHBOURNE, the Honorable Walter James, was born in 1896 and received his education at Eton Public School and Magdalen College, University of Oxford, where he took an agricultural degree, and also taught in the 1920s. A leading figure in the organic farming movement, he published several articles on agriculture, inveighing both philosophically and in practical terms against the industrialization of farming. These articles later served as the basis for his first book, *Look to the Land*. He subsequently served as Chairman and Provost of Wye Agricultural College, University of London, from 1946 to 1965. Lord Northbourne was a frequent contributor to the British journal *Studies in Comparative Religion* and a translator of important perennialist works by Frithjof Schuon, René Guénon, and Titus Burckhardt. His books *Religion in the Modern World* and *Looking Back on Progress* are considered by many to be among the most accessible introductions to the "perennialist" or "traditionalist" outlook, and exercised a considerable influence on E.F. Schumacher and Father Thomas Merton. Lord Northbourne died in 1982.

TITUS BURCKHARDT, a German Swiss, was born in Florence in 1908 and died in Lausanne in 1984. An eminent member of the perennialist school, he is perhaps best known to the general public as an art historian. He won much acclaim for producing and publishing the first successful full-scale facsimiles of the Book of Kells, a copy of which he presented to Pope Pius XII at his summer residence at Castel Gandolfo. He later acted as a specialist advisor to UNESCO, with particular reference to the preservation of the unique architectural heritage of Fez. Besides his studies in Islamic art, mysticism, and culture, such as *Introduction to Sufi Doctrine, Fez: City of Islam*, and *Moorish Culture in Spain*, his best known works are: *Sacred Art in East and West, Siena: City of the Virgin, Chartres and the Birth of the Cathedral*, and *Alchemy: Science of the Cosmos, Science of the Soul*. Two notable compendiums of his work have also been published: *Mirror of the Intellect: Essays on Traditional Science and Sacred Art* and *The Essential Titus Burckhardt: Reflections on Sacred Art, Faiths, and Civilizations*, both translated and edited by William Stoddart.

PHILIP SHERRARD was co-founder, with Keith Critchlow, Brian Keeble, and Kathleen Raine, of *Temenos*, a review dedicated to the traditional exposition of the arts and imagination. He taught at both Oxford and London Universities where he lectured on the History of the Orthodox Church, of which he was a member since 1956. He was co-translator, with G.E.H. Palmer and Bishop Kallistos Ware, of the *Philokalia*, the influential compendium of mystical writings by the spiritual fathers of the Orthodox Church. Of his many writings, two notable works are dedicated to a critique of modern scientism and its dehumanization of man: *The Rape of Man and Nature*, and *Human Image, World Image: The Death and Resurrection of Sacred Cosmology*. A wide-ranging collection of articles called *Christianity: Lineaments of a Sacred Tradition* presents a summation of his life's work, and includes a final chapter on the revival of contemplative Hesychast spirituality in the modern world. Philip Sherrard died in London in 1995.

RENÉ GUÉNON was born in Blois, France in 1886 and was to become the forerunner-cum-originator of the perennialist school of thought. Frithjof Schuon said of him that he had "the central function of restoring the great principles of traditional metaphysics to Western awareness," and he added that Guénon "gave proof of a universality of understanding that for centuries had no parallel in the Western world." Guenon's powerful indictment of the modern world is to be found in his works of civilizational criticism, *Crisis of the Modern World* and *The Reign of Quantity and the Signs of the Times*, wherein he criticizes the prevailing ideologies of materialism, occultism, evolutionism, progressivism, individualism, and relativism. His major expositions of traditional symbolism are contained in *The Symbolism of the Cross* and *Fundamental Symbols: The Universal Language of Sacred Science*, while his exposition of pure metaphysics is most notably presented in *The Multiple States of the Being* and *Man and His Becoming According to the Vedanta*. René Guénon died in Cairo in 1951.

SEYYED HOSSEIN NASR was born in Tehran, Iran in 1933. He received his advanced education at M.I.T. and Harvard University in the USA, before he returned to teach at Tehran University from 1958-1979. He founded the Iranian Imperial Academy of Philosophy and served as its first president, and was also president of Aryamehr University for several years. Since 1984 he has been University Professor of Islamic Studies at the George Washington University and president of the Foundation for Traditional Studies, publisher of the journal *Sophia*. He is a world-renowned scholar on Islam and the Perennial Philosophy and is the author of over fifty books and five hundred articles on topics ranging from comparative religion to traditional Islamic philosophy, cosmology, art, ecology, politics, and mysticism. Among his most notable works are *Ideals and Realities of Islam, Knowledge and the Sacred* (the 1981 Gifford Lectures), *Traditional Islam in the Modern World, Sufi Essays, Religion and the Order of Nature* (the 1994 Cadbury Lectures), and *The Heart of Islam*. His *The Philosophy of Seyyed Hossein Nasr* recently appeared as a volume in the prestigious Library of Living Philosophers series. World Wisdom recently published *The Essential Seyyed Hossein Nasr*, edited by William C. Chittick.

FRITHJOF SCHUON was born in Basle, Switzerland in 1907, and was the twentieth century's preeminent spokesman for the perennialist school of comparative religious thought. Until his later years Schuon traveled widely, from India and the Middle East to America, experiencing traditional cultures and establishing lifelong friendships with Hindu, Buddhist, Christian, Muslim, and American Indian spiritual leaders. A philosopher in the tradition of Plato, Shankara, and Eckhart, Schuon was a gifted artist and poet as well as the author of over twenty books on religion, metaphysics, sacred art, and the spiritual path. Of his first book, *The Transcendent Unity of Religions*, T. S. Eliot wrote, "I have met with no more impressive work in the comparative study of Oriental and Occidental religion," and world-renowned religion scholar Huston Smith has said of Schuon that "the man is a . . . wonder; intellectually apropos religion, equally in depth and breadth, the paragon of our time." Schuon's books have been translated into over a dozen languages and are respected by academic and religious authorities alike. More than a scholar and writer, Schuon was a spiritual guide for seekers from a wide variety of religions and backgrounds throughout the world. He died in 1998.

GHAZI BIN MUHAMMAD is a practicing Muslim and a scholar with an interest in religious philosophy. Prince Ghazi was educated at Harrow School, received his B.A. from Princeton University *summa cum laude*, and his Ph.D. from Trinity College, Cambridge University. He has served both as Cultural Secretary and as Advisor for Tribal Affairs to the late H.M. King Hussein of Jordan, and Personal Envoy and Special Advisor to H.M. King Abdullah II. He has also served Jordan in a number of other important capacities including Chairman of the Aal al-Bayt Foundation for Islamic Thought; Founder and Chairman of the Board of Trustees of the Belqa University; and Chairman of the National Park of the Site of the Baptism of Jesus Christ. In addition, he has served on the Jordanian National Higher Education, Lower Education, and Religious Affairs Boards for over ten years. He is Associate Professor in Islamic Philosophy at Aal al-Bayt University, and the author of a number of works, including *The Crisis of the Islamic World*, *The Sacred Origin of Sports and Culture*, and *The Tribes of Jordan at the Beginning of the Twenty-First Century*. Prince Ghazi's contribution to this volume is written in his private capacity and is strictly an expression of his personal views.

ANANDA K. COOMARASWAMY was born in 1877, of Anglo-Ceylonese parents. After completing studies in Geology he soon became interested in the arts and crafts of his native Ceylon and India. In 1917 he relocated to the USA where he became Keeper of Indian and Islamic Art at the Boston Museum of Fine Arts, establishing a large collection of Oriental artifacts and presenting lectures on their symbolic and metaphysical meaning. An encounter with the seminal writings of perennialist author René Guénon served to confirm and strengthen his view of the Perennial Philosophy. From this period onwards

Dr. Coomaraswamy began to compose his mature—and undoubtedly most profound—works, adeptly expounding the *philosophia perennis* by drawing on his unparalleled knowledge of the arts, crafts, mythologies, cultures, folklores, symbolisms, and religions of the Orient and the Occident. In 1947 his plans to retire to India and take on *sannyasa* (renunciation of the world) were cut short by his sudden and untimely death. A representative collection of his extensive writings, entitled *The Essential Ananda K. Coomaraswamy*, was recently edited by his son Rama P. Coomaraswamy for World Wisdom.

WILLIAM STODDART was born in Carstairs, Scotland, lived most of his life in London, England, and now lives in Windsor, Ontario. He studied modern languages, and later medicine, at the universities of Glasgow, Edinburgh, and Dublin. He was a close associate of both Frithjof Schuon and Titus Burckhardt during the lives of these leading perennialists and translated several of their works into English. His books include *Outline of Hinduism, Outline of Buddhism*, and *Sufism: The Mystical Doctrines and Methods of Islam*. For many years Dr. Stoddart was assistant editor of the British journal *Studies in Comparative Religion*. Pursuing his interests in comparative religion, he has traveled widely in Europe (including a visit to Mount Athos), North Africa, India, Ceylon, and Japan. He recently edited *The Essential Titus Burckhardt: Reflections on Sacred Art, Faiths, and Civilizations* for World Wisdom, who are also preparing a volume of his writings for publication, entitled *Remembering in a World of Forgetting: Thoughts on Tradition and Postmodernism*.

MARCO PALLIS was born in Liverpool, England in 1895, and received his education at the universities of Harrow and Liverpool. He was widely respected as a teacher and writer of religious and metaphysical works, and was also a gifted musician and composer, as well as a mountaineer, traveler, and translator of perennialist works. For many years he corresponded with the eminent perennialist writers Ananda K. Coomaraswamy, René Guénon, and Frithjof Schuon. His writings include the best-selling *Peaks and Lamas*, an engaging account of his mountain experiences in Tibet before its invasion by Chinese communist troops, and *The Way and the Mountain*, a collection of articles on Tibetan Buddhist themes informed by a universalist perspective. He also wrote many articles for the British journal *Studies in Comparative Religion*, the most important of which formed the basis of his work *A Buddhist Spectrum: Contributions to Buddhist-Christian Dialogue*, recently published by World Wisdom. Marco Pallis died in 1990.

TAGE LINDBOM was born in Sweden in 1909. After completing a doctorate in history at the University of Stockholm in 1938, he was for many years director of the Labor Movement Archives and Library and became one of the intellectual architects of the Swedish Welfare State. After World War II, however, he began to have serious doubts about the cause he was promoting and underwent a slow but profound intellectual and spiritual change. In 1962 he published *Sancho Panzas väderkvernar* (*Sancho Panza's Windmills*), a book that rejects the assumptions behind Social Democracy and related movements. Lindbom subsequently published many books in Swedish, most of which explore the tension between religion and modern secular ideologies. Two of these have appeared in English: *The Tares and the Good Grain* and *The Myth of Democracy.* Tage Lindbom died in 2001.

REZA SHAH-KAZEMI is a Research Associate at the Institute of Ismaili Studies in London. His areas of research are Comparative Religion, Islamic Studies, Shi'i Studies, and Sufism. He has edited, translated, and written numerous books and articles, including *Paths to Transcendence: According to Shankara, Ibn Arabi, and Meister Eckhart* (recently published by World Wisdom), *Doctrines of Shi'i Islam, Avicenna, Prince of Physicians, The Other in the Light of the One: The Universality of the Qur'an and Interfaith Dialogue,* and *Justice and Remembrance: An Introduction to the Spirituality of Imam Ali.* At present he is engaged on a new, annotated English translation of Imam Ali's *Nahj al-balagha.*

WHITALL N. PERRY was born in 1920 of a prominent Boston Quaker family. Travels in his youth through Europe, the Near, Middle, and Far East sparked an interest in Platonism and Vedanta, which brought him under the personal influence of Ananda K. Coomaraswamy. He spent five years in Egypt in close contact with René Guénon, after whose death he moved to Switzerland with his family, where he became a close associate of Frithjof Schuon for many years. In addition to his monumental *A Treasury of Traditional Wisdom,* he contributed articles on metaphysics, cosmology, and modern counterfeits of spirituality to various journals, several of which were collected together to form his book *Challenges to a Secular Society.* More recently he published a traditional cosmological critique of Darwinist evolution entitled, *The Widening Breach.* He has been referred to as "the most authoritative traditionalist of American background," and "a latter-day transcendentalist in the tradition of Emerson and Thoreau." Whitall Perry died in 2005.

BIOGRAPHICAL NOTES

MARTIN LINGS was born in Burnage, Lancashire, in 1909. After a classical education he read English at Oxford where he was a pupil and later a close friend of C. S. Lewis. In 1935 he went to Lithuania where he lectured on Anglo-Saxon and Middle English at the University of Kaunus. After four years he went to Egypt and was given a lectureship in English Literature at Cairo University where he lectured mainly on Shakespeare. He later returned to England and took a degree in Arabic at London University and subsequently joined the staff of the British Museum where he was Keeper of Oriental Manuscripts until his retirement in 1973. He is the author of *The Sacred Art of Shakespeare: To Take Upon Us the Mystery of Things* (with a Foreword by H.R.H the Prince of Wales), *Ancient Beliefs and Modern Superstitions*, *The Eleventh Hour: The Spiritual Crisis of the Modern World in the Light of Tradition and Prophecy*, and *Symbol & Archetype: A Study of the Meaning of Existence*. Among his works on Islamic mysticism are: *The Book of Certainty: The Sufi Doctrine of Faith, Vision, and Gnosis*, *A Sufi Saint of the Twentieth Century*, *What is Sufism?*, and *Sufi Poems: A Mediaeval Anthology*. His acclaimed biography of the Prophet, entitled *Muhammad: His Life Based on the Earliest Sources*, has been translated into a dozen languages and is internationally recognized as a masterpiece. His most recent publications are *Mecca: From Before Genesis Until Now*, *Splendors of Islamic Calligraphy and Illumination*, and *A Return to the Spirit: Questions and Answers*. Martin Lings died in May 2005, less than two days after completing work on the present anthology. World Wisdom is preparing an anthology of his writings, to be entitled *The Essential Martin Lings* (edited by Reza Shah-Kazemi and Emma Clark, forthcoming 2008).

CLINTON MINNAAR was born in South Africa in 1972. An early interest in world religions and contemplative spirituality saw him complete an undergraduate degree at the University of Cape Town, majoring in Comparative Religion, Philosophy, and English. After finishing a teaching degree, he pursued his interest in the "traditionalist" or "perennialist" school of thought, writing an MA on the mystical experience debate. He has traveled widely in North Africa, the Middle East, Europe, and North and South America in order to visit religious and cultural sites and contact noted spiritual authorities. He lives with his wife in Buenos Aires, Argentina.

INDEX

For a glossary of all key foreign words used in books published by
World Wisdom, including metaphysical terms in English, consult:
www.DictionaryofSpiritualTerms.org.
This on-line Dictionary of Spiritual Terms provides extensive
definitions, examples and related terms in other languages.

Titles in the Perennial Philosophy Series by World Wisdom